Boston

Kim Grant

LONELY PLANET PUBLICATIONS
Melbourne • Oakland • London • Paris

Boston
1st edition – August 2000

Published by
Lonely Planet Publications Pty Ltd A.C.N. 005 607 983
192 Burwood Rd, Hawthorn, Victoria 3122, Australia

Lonely Planet Offices
Australia PO Box 617, Hawthorn, Victoria 3122
USA 150 Linden St, Oakland, CA 94607
UK 10a Spring Place, London NW5 3BH
France 1 rue du Dahomey, 75011 Paris

Photographs
Most of the images in this guide are available for licensing from
Lonely Planet Images.
email: lpi@lonelyplanet.com.au

John Singer Sargent, *Isabella Stewart Gardner*, 1888,
photograph courtesy of Isabella Stewart Gardner Museum, Boston

Front cover photograph
Baseball fans at Fenway Park (David Madison/Tony Stone)

ISBN 0 86442 642 9

text & maps © Lonely Planet 2000
photos © photographers as indicated 2000

Printed by The Bookmaker Pty Ltd
Printed in China

Contents

PLACES TO STAY   146

PLACES TO EAT   156

ENTERTAINMENT   177

SHOPPING   193

EXCURSIONS   207

ARCHITECTURAL GLOSSARY   234

INDEX   243

BOSTON MAP SECTION   251

The Author

Kim Grant

Kim Grant grew up near Boston and began taking the commuter train into the city on weekends as soon as she could board trains alone. After graduating from Mt Holyoke College in 1984, landing her first guidebook gig and traveling for a couple of years in Europe on $10 a day, she 'settled' in Boston's North End. In need of permanent parking and photographic studio space, she then moved to a circa-1900 Victorian in Dorchester, Boston's largest, oldest and most diverse neighborhood.

She alternates guidebook authoring with fine-art photography and is currently working on a series of large format, black-and-white abstractions, *Shifting Perspectives: Sand and Land*. She is the author of *Cape Cod, Martha's Vineyard & Nantucket: An Explorer's Guide* and *Best Places to Stay in Hawaii*; coauthor of Lonely Planet *New England* and of *Best Places to Stay in New England*; and contributing editor of Insight *New England*.

Her photographs appear in many Lonely Planet, Insight and Explorer's guides, as well as in regional and national travel magazines.

FROM THE AUTHOR

Thanks, thanks and more thanks to Lisa Otero, whose tireless efforts and support know no bounds. Although I have made Boston my home since 1986, I would have found it impossible to write a book like this without the help of many fearless friends, chief among them Julia Regan. After Julia and I researched one of her favorite neighborhoods under the pressure of a deadline, she declared, 'I thought this would be fun. I was wrong. You're my friend. Do me a favor. Get a new job.'

Thanks to Bob Taylor, my 7th-grade history teacher, whose knowledge and passion about post-Blackstone Boston are legendary. Thanks to Wendy Zazik for walking my walking tours and for knowing where to find Boston's best noodle kugel. Thanks to David Lawless, who knows that single boys have more fun than married girls. Thanks to Beth Anderson for her appreciation of fine South End food. And thanks to Martha Grant for her help and support. With friends like these, who needs paid assistants? Thanks to the Greater Boston Convention & Visitors Bureau for many leads. Thanks to the fine columnists and reporters at the *Boston Globe*, who provide daily accompaniment to my morning cappuccino.

And finally, kudos go to fellow planeteer Tom Brosnahan, who pitched this job to me, and to Edwin Bacon, who penned the charming *Boston: A Guide Book*, published by Ginn & Co in 1903. And, oh, did I thank Lisa?

At Lonely Planet, hats off to the incredibly diligent and eminently reasonable Rachel Bernstein, who coaxed me with encouragement rather than a big stick. Cartos Darin Jensen and Bart Wright worked wonders with Boston's messy, antiquated streets.

This Book

From the Publisher

This 1st edition of *Boston* was edited in Oakland by Rachel Bernstein, with the vigilant guidance of senior editors Michele Posner and Jacqueline Volin. Proofreading and more was done by Susan Charles Bush. Many thanks to Brigitte Barta for jumping in at the last minute and to Kate Hoffman for her invaluable support throughout. Cartographers Bart Wright and Darin Jensen drew the maps, and Bart adroitly wrangled them to glory with help from Chris Gillis, Monica Lepe, Amy Dennis and the oversight of Alex Guilbert.

Henia Miedzinski designed the book with assistance from Susan Rimerman. Illustrations were the brainchild of Hayden Foell and were created by Hayden, Hannah Reineck, Hugh D'Andrade, Trudi Canavan and John Fadeff, all of whom were coordinated by Beca Lafore. Ken DellaPenta created the index. Simon Bracken designed the cover.

Stanley J Forman, the Isabella Stewart Gardner Museum and Bell Atlantic all generously agreed to have artwork reproduced here. Thanks are due author Kim Grant for her delightful anecdotes and positive outlook and to all the Boston natives transplanted to the Bay Area who tossed in their two cents.

Save Fenway Park! Go Sox!

Foreword

ABOUT LONELY PLANET GUIDEBOOKS

The story begins with a classic travel adventure: Tony and Maureen Wheeler's 1972 journey across Europe and Asia to Australia. Useful information about the overland trail did not exist at that time, so Tony and Maureen published the first Lonely Planet guidebook to meet a growing need.

From a kitchen table, then from a tiny office in Melbourne (Australia), Lonely Planet has become the largest independent travel publisher in the world, an international company with offices in Melbourne, Oakland (USA), London (UK) and Paris (France).

Today Lonely Planet guidebooks cover the globe. There is an ever-growing list of books and there's information in a variety of forms and media. Some things haven't changed. The main aim is still to help make it possible for adventurous travelers to get out there – to explore and better understand the world.

At Lonely Planet we believe travelers can make a positive contribution to the countries they visit – if they respect their host communities and spend their money wisely. Since 1986 a percentage of the income from each book has been donated to aid projects and human rights campaigns.

Updates Lonely Planet thoroughly updates each guidebook as often as possible. This usually means there are around two years between editions, although for more unusual or more stable destinations the gap can be longer. Check the imprint page (following the color map at the beginning of the book) for publication dates.

Between editions up-to-date information is available in two free newsletters – the paper *Planet Talk* and email *Comet* (to subscribe, contact any Lonely Planet office) – and on our website at www.lonelyplanet.com. The *Upgrades* section of the website covers a number of important and volatile destinations and is regularly updated by Lonely Planet authors. *Scoop* covers news and current affairs relevant to travelers. And, lastly, the *Thorn Tree* bulletin board and *Postcards* section of the site carry unverified, but fascinating, reports from travelers.

Correspondence The process of creating new editions begins with the letters, postcards and emails received from travelers. This correspondence often includes suggestions, criticisms and comments about the current editions. Interesting excerpts are immediately passed on via newsletters and the website, and everything goes to our authors to be verified when they're researching on the road. We're keen to get more feedback from organizations or individuals who represent communities visited by travelers.

Lonely Planet gathers information for everyone who's curious about the planet – and especially for those who explore it firsthand. Through guidebooks, phrasebooks, activity guides, maps, literature, newsletters, image library, TV series and website we act as an information exchange for a worldwide community of travelers.

Research Authors aim to gather sufficient practical information to enable travelers to make informed choices and to make the mechanics of a journey run smoothly. They also research historical and cultural background to help enrich the travel experience and allow travelers to understand and respond appropriately to cultural and environmental issues.

Authors don't stay in every hotel because that would mean spending a couple of months in each medium-sized city and, no, they don't eat at every restaurant because that would mean stretching belts beyond capacity. They do visit hotels and restaurants to check standards and prices, but feedback based on readers' direct experiences can be very helpful.

Many of our authors work undercover, others aren't so secretive. None of them accept freebies in exchange for positive write-ups. And none of our guidebooks contain any advertising.

Production Authors submit their raw manuscripts and maps to offices in Australia, USA, UK or France. Editors and cartographers – all experienced travelers themselves – then begin the process of assembling the pieces. When the book finally hits the shops, some things are already out of date, we start getting feedback from readers and the process begins again…

WARNING & REQUEST

Things change – prices go up, schedules change, good places go bad and bad places go bankrupt – nothing stays the same. So, if you find things better or worse, recently opened or long since closed, please tell us and help make the next edition even more accurate and useful. We genuinely value all the feedback we receive. Julie Young coordinates a well-traveled team that reads and acknowledges every letter, postcard and email and ensures that every morsel of information finds its way to the appropriate authors, editors and cartographers for verification.

Everyone who writes to us will find their name in the next edition of the appropriate guidebook. They will also receive the latest issue of *Planet Talk*, our quarterly printed newsletter, or *Comet*, our monthly email newsletter. Subscriptions to both newsletters are free. The very best contributions will be rewarded with a free guidebook.

Excerpts from your correspondence may appear in new editions of Lonely Planet guidebooks, the Lonely Planet website, *Planet Talk* or *Comet*, so please let us know if you *don't* want your letter published or your name acknowledged.

Send all correspondence to the Lonely Planet office closest to you:

Australia: PO Box 617, Hawthorn, Victoria 3122
USA: 150 Linden St, Oakland, CA 94607
UK: 10A Spring Place, London NW5 3BH
France: 1 rue du Dahomey, 75011 Paris

Or email us at: talk2us@lonelyplanet.com.au

For news, views and updates see our website: www.lonelyplanet.com

HOW TO USE A LONELY PLANET GUIDEBOOK

The best way to use a Lonely Planet guidebook is any way you choose. At Lonely Planet we believe the most memorable travel experiences are often those that are unexpected, and the finest discoveries are those you make yourself. Guidebooks are not intended to be used as if they provide a detailed set of infallible instructions!

Contents All Lonely Planet guidebooks follow the same format. The Facts about the Country chapters or sections give background information ranging from history to weather. Facts for the Visitor gives practical information on issues like visas and health. Getting There & Away gives a brief starting point for researching travel to and from the destination. Getting Around gives an overview of the transport options when you arrive.

The peculiar demands of each destination determine how subsequent chapters are broken up, but some things remain constant. We always start with background, then proceed to sights, places to stay, places to eat, entertainment, getting there and away, and getting around information – in that order.

Heading Hierarchy Lonely Planet headings are used in a strict hierarchical structure that can be visualized as a set of Russian dolls. Each heading (and its following text) is encompassed by any preceding heading that is higher on the hierarchical ladder.

Entry Points We do not assume guidebooks will be read from beginning to end, but that people will dip into them. The traditional entry points are the list of contents and the index. In addition, however, some books have a complete list of maps and an index map illustrating map coverage.

There may also be a color map that shows highlights. These highlights are dealt with in greater detail later in the book, along with planning questions. Each chapter covering a geographical region usually begins with a locator map and another list of highlights. Once you find something of interest in a list of highlights, turn to the index.

Maps Maps play a crucial role in Lonely Planet guidebooks and include a huge amount of information. A legend is printed on the back page. We seek to have complete consistency between maps and text, and to have every important place in the text captured on a map. Map key numbers usually start in the top left corner.

Although inclusion in a guidebook usually implies a recommendation, we cannot list every good place. Exclusion does not necessarily imply criticism. In fact, there are a number of reasons why we might exclude a place – sometimes it is simply inappropriate to encourage an influx of travelers.

Introduction

It's hard to pinpoint the lure of Boston, and that's exactly what attracts visitors, retains college graduates and draws back the temporarily sidetracked. Boston is more than the sum of her historic buildings, cultural attractions, academic institutions and fine restaurants. In the end, most Boston visitors come to the same opinion: The city is spirited, lovely, historic, a jumble of contemporary paradoxes and, perhaps most important, it's manageable.

There is a monumental sense of permanence in Boston; the past, after all, is always just a shadow or a building away. Boston clings to old traditions but is also quick to adopt new ones. It's a city with a future, stubbornly journeying forward. How else can you account for the fact that the center of the city is (and will continue to be for years) a giant construction site?

Boston is an amalgam of vibrant neighborhoods, from working-class Charlestown to elegant Beacon Hill, from the hip South End to the Italian North End. Despite the ethnic diversity of its residents old and new, Boston doesn't seem to change. In a curious way, something deeply embedded in the city's character eventually converts newcomers into Bostonians as if by osmosis.

Boston's magnetism comes in part from its long history, by North American standards anyway, as a busy and prosperous port and the regional center of commerce. Thinking of this quaint and charming city as the 'Hub of the Universe' and the 'Athens of America' might seem a bit of braggadocio now, but in the 19th century these were not empty boasts. The city's numerous beautiful buildings, its large population of literati, artists and educators, its varied cultural institutions and its world-renowned academic institutions retain and radiate the city's glory. Regardless of the inevitable changes, Boston's soul somehow remains both grand and familiar.

Bostonians see themselves as civilized and their city as mature. Bostonians aren't

Boston celebrities grace the Cafe Du Barry mural on Newbury St.

trendsetters. They're in it for the long haul, which helps explain the city's conservative character. Contrary to their reputation, however, Bostonians are neither crusty, musty nor genteel, but down-to-earth folks who value loyalty. Of course, loyalty taken to its extreme seems to define Boston's parochial and provincial political system. Some characterize it as cutthroat, others relish it as a good friendly brawl. Either way it's intriguing, as liberals and libertarians battle it out on issues that affect the present and future livability of Boston.

And Boston is nothing if not 'livable.' It's got more than its share of culture and distractions without the pace or intimidation of its southern neighbor, New York City, the great American metropolis. It's cleaner, safer, friendlier and easier to negotiate. And yet, Boston does suffer from being within a four-hour drive of the Big Apple. When Boston's top professionals and artists reach the pinnacle of success, many of them take that final step up the career ladder to New York City. But Boston, for professionals and nonprofessionals alike, is just the right size. It's really a small town with big city amenities.

The city's numerous universities and colleges attract students from all over the world. From September through May, the city overflows with their exuberance. This renewable source of cultural energy supports numerous sporting events, foreign cinema, theater, art galleries, literary cafés, hip bars, musical performances, shopping and nightlife.

Despite impetuous drivers and insane traffic, Boston is one of the easiest cities to explore on foot. You can walk everywhere. And at this leisurely pace, it's easier to register the city's pulse. Thanks to low-rise buildings that allow the city to retain a human scale and an urban core that is home to people of all classes, Boston has a thriving street life. Its brick sidewalks and sidewalk cafés have more in common with London or Paris than with Chicago or Los Angeles.

The Atlantic Ocean, Boston Harbor and the Charles and Mystic Rivers vary the cityscape and provide light and a sense of openness. Urban planning, including a long 'emerald necklace' of parks, gardens and verdant thoroughfares designed by the great American landscape architect Frederick Law Olmsted, brings a bit of the country right into the city. Having said that, you must remember that Boston is the hub of New England. And part of its lure is that it serves as a great jumping-off point for nearby mountains and beaches. Just 30 minutes outside of town, you'll find yourself among cornfields, gardens, beautiful colonial towns, scenic rivers and country roads ideal for cycling.

Even if you have a sense of Boston due to her pivotal role in American history, keep an open mind; she may surprise you. The country's founding fathers – many of whom walked these same streets – would expect nothing less. Just when you've written off residents as dour and preoccupied, someone will probably offer you assistance. Just when you've decided Boston is full of stuffed shirts and bow ties, you'll encounter a band of pierced, orange-haired, skateboarding teens. Just when you've equated Boston to a tightly wound parent, the curfew will be lifted and she'll spin like a top. Then again, the bars still close at 2 am, and the T shuts down well before that. The Grand Dame can let her hair down only so far.

Facts about Boston

HISTORY
17th-Century Origins

Prior to 1600 AD, there were plenty of Native American tribes throughout New England, but none on the centrally located Shawmut Peninsula (the original extents of Boston proper). This 800-acre hilly, tree-covered peninsula was connected to the mainland by a narrow causeway or 'neck.' To the east was an excellent harbor; to the west a great back bay, an estuary of the Charles River; to the north was another hilly but smaller peninsula, known today as Charlestown.

In 1614, English explorer Captain John Smith toured the New England coastline for King James I. Though the coast had many natural ports such as Essex, Plymouth, Providence and Salem, Boston was blessed with the best geography. Captain Smith liked what he saw, calling it 'the paradise of all those parts.' Back home, his published reports were so glowing that merchants and adventurers took great interest in New England. In 1620, an English separatist group (the Pilgrims) – simple farmers and tradesmen who wanted to worship separately from the Church of England – built the first permanent English settlement in New England at Plymouth Harbor, some 50 miles south of Boston.

In 1624, 27-year-old Reverend William Blackstone (or Blaxton), an ordained Anglican minister from the Church of England and a Cambridge University graduate, became the first European to settle on the Shawmut Peninsula. Blackstone was a man of means whose servants built a cottage on the south side of Beacon Hill, near present-day Spruce and Beacon Sts. Soon after, Scotsman David Thompson settled on a Boston Harbor island. Now there were two settlers in the environs of Boston Harbor. Within a mere 70 years it was well on its way to being what it remains today, New England's largest and most important city.

In England, King Charles I decreed that all Englishmen follow the dictates of his Anglican Church. But the self-proclaimed Puritans – among them wealthy, educated and powerful lawyers and merchants – wanted to reform and purify the Church. Their dream was to settle far enough away that they would be able to worship freely. With influential friends at the highest levels of government, in 1629 they managed to get King Charles to charter the Massachusetts Bay Colony in New England.

The Puritans planned their exit from England carefully. Elder John Winthrop, a deeply religious member of the landed English gentry, was named the official representative of the Massachusetts Bay Colony. On the voyage from Southampton, England, in March 1630, he penned his vision of their Puritan mission: 'We shall establish a city upon a hill – a Beacon Light for all mankind.' The city would be built by Puritan saints (led by himself) and it would be home to a holy society, founded on the Bible, to serve as a model of godliness to decadent Europe. It would become an inspiration for all. Ah, such modest, humble beginnings . . . is it any wonder Bostonians cannot imagine a city to rival theirs?

Winthrop's flagship *Arbella* arrived in Salem three months later but found the harbor too small. An advance party of some 100 Puritans, under the leadership of the Reverend Francis Bright, was sent to claim the peninsula just north of Shawmut (then known as Mishawum) and build settlements there. Streets were laid out on the south side of Bunker Hill, where Winthrop settled. Almost immediately, though, the community faced illness and lack of food and water. The small spring they found was not capable of serving the 700 residents.

The Charlestown settlers dubbed Shawmut Peninsula 'Trimountaine' because of the three clearly visible hills. Blackstone, although somewhat of a hermit, invited the new settlers over to his side of the river to show them sources of spring water, pasture for animals and a fine, deep harbor for ships. Winthrop liked what he saw, and on September 7 they named it Boston after a town in Lincolnshire, England. Soon after, Blackstone sold his house and his orchards to find a more secluded place. The center of Puritan culture and life in the New World was established. And in October, Governor Winthrop wrote home to his wife, 'We are here in paradise' – a boast you might hear on the streets today.

Reading, Writing & Religion

Puritanism was intellectual and theocratic, and so the leading men and women of early Boston society were those who understood and followed biblical law – and could explain the dogma in powerful rhetoric. The 'Three Rs' were very important to the Puritan leaders; knowledge of the word of God, as expressed in the Bible, would keep Satan away. It comes as no surprise that they established the Boston Public Latin School in 1635 (today it remains an elite public high school) and Harvard College in 1636. In 1647, they passed the first public school law, insuring that communities of 50 or more households would hire instructors to teach the Three Rs, their wages to 'be paid by the inhabitants in general.' A mere five years later, Boston had a public library, and by 1704 produced the 13 original colonies' first newspaper, the *News-Letter*. With this foundation, it is no wonder that excellence in education remains central to the city.

Puritan churches were organized as independent congregations. Elected leaders (called Selectmen) ran community affairs between annual town meetings, when citizens would decide by a show of hands which local projects to undertake and how to fund them. Local self-government was born in Boston.

In spite of these democratic leanings, the Puritans were not tolerant folks. People who disagreed with the leaders were expelled from the colony. Those who dared return, as did Quaker Mary Dyer, were hanged.

Back in England in 1688, monarchs William and Mary insisted on appointing a royal governor for the colony and allowing the governor's council to be elected by members of the Great and General Court (the name of the Massachusetts legislature to this day). The legislature would be elected by property owners, thus concentrating political power in a land-owning elite.

For the colonists, material success and property acquisition became more and more important. Prosperity came by using your imagination, making shrewd business decisions, working hard and evading England's navigation laws. Bostonians were successful with cod fishing, coastal trading, shipbuilding and the production of rum from molasses. By 1692, a large segment of the 7000-strong population had built fine homes and climbed the social ladder. Boston was the wealthiest town in the American colonies.

In the early 18th century, as England warred with France, the colonies operated with greater independence. But in 1760 there was a major setback – a terrible fire around Dock Square leveled 300 buildings. Ships, docks and stores were destroyed; more than 1000 people were homeless. In the hard times that followed, unemployment was high and taxes were raised to pay for reconstruction.

Cradle of Liberty

Late-18th-century Boston is often called the 'Cradle of American Liberty.' Certainly, Boston took center stage as a hotbed of revolutionary ideas and the breeding ground for protests against the authority of George III of England. Patriot leaders, incensed by the king's efforts to control the freewheeling economies and political liberties that had developed in the colonies, began concerted efforts to assert their independence.

As far back as 1753, King George III and Parliament instituted a program (the Townshend Acts) to raise money in America, reduce colonial self-government and assert more royal authority. Americans reacted strongly against the taxes. Boston's leaders, well informed and politically mature, often led the way.

In 1761, when the British customs collector in Boston asked for a hearing on the use of new writs of assistance (search warrants, signed by the king, but with no targets, times or individuals specified), James Otis, Jr, stood up and objected to the arbitrary power of the new writs. John Adams, one of the most intelligent leaders of the American Revolution, took notes. Otis, during a four-hour speech, declared that the writs were:

...[I]nstruments of slavery...A man's house is his castle...This writ, if it is given, would totally destroy the right of privacy. Customs agents could enter our houses whenever they pleased. We would have to let them in. Each search would bring on another until our whole country is torn up in hate and blood!

Britain needed cash to retire her debts and to station a standing army of 10,000 troops in America. In 1765, the British Parliament passed the Stamp Act to raise the funds. Colonists would now be required to buy special stamps to execute a will, sell a house, get an inn license, buy a newspaper, dice or playing cards.

Bostonians, led by Samuel Adams, an older cousin of John Adams, objected violently. 'Sons of Liberty,' self-avowed supporters of American liberty and rights, attacked officials and supporters of the new

'Son of Liberty' Sam Adams

act. Adams described the new law as a bold attempt to remove people's right to tax themselves. He helped ignite the anger of colonists throughout America. Parliament repealed the act one year later, realizing it was more trouble than it was worth. Boston rejoiced.

In 1767, British customs agents triggered more problems than they solved. They were arbitrary; they antagonized people; they engaged in 'customs racketeering.' If they seized a ship for violations, the ship and its cargo were sold and the proceeds divided between the English treasury, the governor of the colony and the customs officers. All they had to do was show 'probable cause.'

The customs agents took particular aim at John Hancock, probably Boston's richest merchant. When they seized his ship, *Liberty*, for failing to post bond, fellow Boston merchants united in his defense. The English Parliament sent British regiments to protect their officials in September 1768.

In 1769, Charles Townshend (of the Townshend Acts fame and now the treasurer of the British government) was back. This time he proposed taxes on glass, lead, paper, paint and tea. The money raised was to pay the salaries of English officials in America. The tax collectors would be quartered in Boston – of course, as the chief American city, Boston always drew London's attention. The next year, protest escalated and erupted in what soon became known as the Boston Massacre (see 'Boston Massacre').

Tempest in a Teapot

More trouble came in 1773. The British Parliament passed a Tea Act, granting a monopoly to the huge and financially troubled British East India Co. American patriots objected strongly and colonial coastal merchants refused tea shipments. In 1774, the standoff between the governor and the merchants reached the point of no return. The royal governor refused to allow three tea ships to return full to London. The Sons of Liberty refused to allow the tea to be off-loaded and taxed. When the owner of the *Dartmouth* was denied a pass to leave port

Boston Massacre

The Boston Massacre site, in front of the Old State House balcony, is marked by a circle of cobblestones. It was here that, on March 5, 1770, Sons of Liberty Sam Adams, John Hancock and about 40 other protesters provoked the British soldiers with snowballs, curses and trash. Panicked British soldiers fired on the angry mob. Five townspeople were killed, sparking anti-British sentiment. The troops were moved quickly to Castle Island (in present-day South Boston). A propagandist and jack-of-all-trades, Paul Revere helped fan the flames by widely disseminating an engraving that depicted the scene as an unmitigated slaughter. Interestingly, John Adams and Josiah Quincy, both of whom opposed the heavy-handed authoritarian British rule, represented the accused soldiers in court. The lawyers firmly believed that all accused were entitled to a fair trial. (Seven of the nine soldiers were acquitted, and the remaining two had their hands branded as a sign they were guilty of manslaughter.)

on December 16, Sam Adams rose at a special town meeting and said, 'This meeting can do nothing more to save the country!' This was a signal to patriot supporters to meet on Griffin's Wharf. According to plan, a band of men disguised as Indians moved quickly and silently in the dark chill of the evening. More than 100 of them boarded the tea ships with hatchets ready. A large crowd gathered.

The mate of the *Dartmouth* wrote in his ship's logs:

They came on board the ship, and after warning myself and the Custom's House Officer to get out of the way, they unlaid the hatchets and went down in the hold, where there was 80 whole and 34 half chests of tea, which they hoisted upon deck, and cut the chests to pieces, and hove the tea overboard, where it was damaged and lost.

When all of the tea had been destroyed, the anonymous 'Indians' disappeared into the night. Later, Paul Revere and others carried

Commemorative stamps, issued July 4, 1973

the news of the Boston Tea Party to other colonies.

Although Boston had long been a flash point for patriotic fervor, when all of England read about the destruction of tea in Boston Harbor, angry members of Parliament passed four bills to single out and punish Boston for its wicked deeds. To the British Prime Minister, Boston was 'the center of rebellious commotion in America, the ring leader in every riot.' Parliament closed the port of Boston to all trade until England was compensated for the ruined tea. There would be no jury trials for indictments against British officials. And finally, British troops would be housed in private homes in Boston. General Thomas Gage was sent to rule Boston by martial law.

Up and down the coast, colonists talked about this 'horrid attack upon the town of Boston.' Sam Adams sent letter upon letter to every colony, making the case for Boston and Massachusetts Bay against the British. Anger bubbled higher. Adams and John Hancock set up an extralegal colonial Provincial Congress. Minutemen, local citizens who would defend their rights against British tyranny with military force at a minute's notice, began training on town commons.

Shot Heard 'Round the World

Along with General Gage came 4000 British troops and a fleet of warships. In the spring of 1775, when Gage learned that minutemen were storing military supplies in Concord (18 miles west of Boston), he sent 700 troops to destroy the stockpile. At dawn on April 19, 1775, these British forces were confronted on the Lexington town green by about 70 minutemen. The British charged and fired into the assembly, killing eight and wounding 10. Paul Revere, Sam Adams and John Hancock escaped into the countryside.

Later that morning in Concord, the British captured some supplies, but were soon attacked at North Bridge. There were casualties on both sides. This so-called shot heard 'round the world was the opening volley of the War for Independence. British troops were attacked throughout the day as they retreated to Boston. At the day's end, far more British lives had been lost than American.

These events, commemorated as Patriots' Day in Massachusetts and Maine (then a part of the Bay State), united the 13 colonies. Paul Revere rode to tell New York and other colonies what happened. John Hancock, Sam Adams and John Adams went off to the Continental Congress in Philadelphia to lobby for a unified declaration of independence. George Washington, of Virginia, was chosen to command the newly formed American Army, which was keeping General Gage and his troops bottled up in Boston.

In early 1776, General Washington dispatched Colonel Henry Knox (born in the South End) to Fort Ticonderoga on Lake George, where he collected cannons and ammunition to be dragged back to Cambridge by sleigh and oxen. Washington seized Dorchester Heights, and his army installed the cannon facing Boston. British general William Howe was trapped. After much plundering (especially of two of Hancock's ships), the British sailed out of Boston Harbor on March 17, 1776 (celebrated today as Evacuation Day). Washington and the

Continental Army had won; Boston was now liberated.

Rebuilding & Federalism

The British left behind a town in terrible disrepair. Trees were gone; fences, barns, warehouses and wharves were used for firewood; meeting houses stabled animals; private homes were turned into hospitals; public buildings were defaced. Only 6000 people lived in Boston now, down from 16,000 prior to the British invasion.

Boston was slowly rebuilt, but even after independence was won in 1783, times were tough. Money was scarce, prices were high, skilled workers were hard to find and the wharves were in rubble or obsolete. Politically, the US government under the Articles of Confederation was weak.

When a Federal Constitution was submitted to the states for approval in 1787, Boston supported it but western Massachusetts farmers did not. A standoff ensued between Federalists and anti-Federalists at the Massachusetts Constitutional Convention in 1788. Sam Adams and John Hancock suggested the Constitution be approved with a provision: The first Congress elected under it would write amendments to create a Bill of Rights. Massachusetts then supported the new Constitution by a narrow margin.

Boston celebrated, and its political leaders became vocal supporters of the new Federalism. John Hancock served as governor until his death in 1793, followed by Sam Adams until his death in 1803.

Ocean trade slowly regained its importance. Commerce with the West Indies, South America and China revived fortunes, bringing prosperity and wealth to Boston. Yankee merchants built great mansions and rose politically and socially. By 1810, the town had a population of about 30,000.

The War of 1812 with Great Britain was very unpopular in Boston. From the start, it was called 'Madison's

Colonel Henry Knox

War,' after Republican President James Madison. Boston, a Federalist town, refused to support the war with men or money. When the war ended successfully for America, those who had opposed it were disgraced. The Federalist Party, formed during the war, died as a political entity.

Brahmins Are Born & the City Incorporates

When commerce and shipping suffered during the War of 1812 and the preceding Jeffersonian embargoes, Boston's maritime merchants looked for new ways to invest their money. Factories and the burgeoning industrial revolution were primed. In particular, cotton thread and textile manufacturing were very successful. Frances Lowell, Nathan Appleton, Patrick T Jackson and Abbot and Amos Lawrence were among dozens of Boston Yankees to make substantial fortunes in textile manufacturing.

The upper classes, the Yankee blue-blooded merchant-manufacturers, now dominated the town's spiritual, social and political life. Though typically conservative and traditionalist in their outlook, Bostonians were firm believers in American ideals of freedom. They began to accept a new liberal Unitarian religion and possessed a sense of responsibility for the welfare of the town and its citizens. As an untitled aristocratic class (called Brahmins, in reference to the highest caste in the Hindu social system in India), they considered it their birthright 'to keep Boston a model of excellence...a latter day concept of a city upon a hill.'

On January 7, 1822, the city of Boston was incorporated with a population of 43,000. The first two mayors, John Phillips and Josiah Quincy, were Harvard graduates and Boston Brahmins. Quincy, elected to six straight terms, did much to modernize Boston. Dubbed the 'Great Mayor,' he saw his job as making Boston into a 'Great City.'

Reform Movements & Abolitionism

Between the 1830s and the 1840s there were many reform movements in Boston. Mayor Quincy himself started a welfare reform movement. He sold the old almshouse and replaced it with the House of Industry. People in need of public assistance would be required to work until they could get off the dole. A temperance society was formed to attack alcoholism, educational reform was led by Horace Mann and a movement to improve conditions in mental hospitals and prisons was encouraged by Dorothea Dix.

Boston became a breeding ground for writers and publishers, arts and letters, intellectual clubs and magazines, medicine and technology. Beacon Hill was the nexus for this cultural growth and development.

It was a radical reform movement, however, that gripped conservative Boston for 30 years. The Abolition Movement, which advocated nothing short of the eradication of slavery in the US, was born in Boston. Newspaper writer and editor William Lloyd Garrison, operating out of a small office on Washington St, began publishing a monthly paper called the *Liberator* in 1831. Garrison was an agitator. Loathed in the South and considered a meddlesome fanatic in the North, he even accused leading Brahmin families of silently agreeing with organized slavery. Local churches, he went on, were allies of the institution of slavery.

By 1835, Garrison was a force to be reckoned with. In October, when he was attending an anti-slavery meeting, a mob broke in and dragged him to Boston Common to be hanged. He was rescued but told to leave Boston. Garrison charged that the attack was planned 'by gentlemen of property and standing from all parts of the city.' A local editor confirmed that the mob included wealthy and influential men. Nothing was proved, but it was clear that business leaders wanted Garrison out of Boston.

As the years went by, more and more Brahmin leaders joined the anti-slavery movement. John Brown, the militant abolitionist who led the fight to rid Kansas of slaveholders and help free slaves in Virginia, was a case in point. Brown came to Boston to get money, weapons and supplies for his activities in Kansas and Virginia. He was assisted by the influential 'Secret Six,' Bostonians including Franklin Sanborn,

Thomas Higginson, Samuel Howe and Theodore Parker.

When the Civil War broke out in 1861, President Lincoln called for volunteers. Massachusetts called up four regiments, two of which were among the first units to defend the capital. Once Lincoln issued the Emancipation Proclamation in 1863, the 54th Massachusetts Regiment became the first African-American regiment raised in any state. The 54th saw action in South Carolina under Brahmin General Robert Gould Shaw's leadership (also see Beacon Hill in Things to See & Do).

Expansion & Immigration

After the war, Boston became wealthier through industry, business, finance and railroads. The city grew in size, too. Bays and estuaries were filled in the Back Bay and the South End. The surrounding districts of Dorchester, Roxbury, West Roxbury, Charlestown and Brighton were annexed. By 1875, Boston's population was 340,000. But for many, the city was growing too fast and had attracted too many immigrants.

Along with the early Puritans, Boston had a small and culturally rich community of African-Americans. Until 1780 this community was made up of slaves and freemen. In 1806, they built the country's first black church, the African Meeting House, an influential center for the African-American community, which numbered over 2000 people by the 1840s.

French and Irish people immigrated to Boston in small numbers in the 18th century, bringing with them their Roman Catholic faith. From 1800 to 1803, they built Boston's first Catholic church, the Cathedral of the Holy Cross, designed by the great architect Charles Bulfinch.

German Jews, emigrating from an unstable Europe, opened shops in the South End and built the city's first synagogue, Ohabei Shalom, in 1852.

In the 1840s, great waves of Irish fled domestic economic and political crisis and the devastating potato famine. Earlier Irish arrivals hadn't caused a big stir in Boston. They were poor but worked hard, building

bridges, railroad beds, buildings, wharves and reclaiming landfill areas. In 1847, almost 40,000 new arrivals flooded the city. The numbers were even greater in the years that followed. Many of the new wave of Irish immigrants were not only poor, but also in poor health. These Irish immigrants were not welcomed or easily accepted into the city's economic and social framework. In stores across the city, signs went up: 'Wanted: workers. Irish need not apply.' Religious bigotry intensified. Popularly referred to as the 'Catholic Menace,' this generation faced a very difficult assimilation into American culture and society.

But the Irish grew in strength and numbers and they were determined to succeed. They moved into Charlestown, South Boston, East Boston, Dorchester, Roxbury and West Roxbury, building cohesive neighborhood communities, which in turn formed the bases for political power. They worked hard, moving into better jobs and then into politics.

The 20th century also saw waves of immigrants from Italy, Portugal, Greece, Poland, Lithuania, Russia and China. Recently, Vietnamese, Koreans and Brazilians have been making their mark on the city, too, settling and establishing themselves in the city's older neighborhoods as earlier generations did.

Cultural Institutions Flourish

During this period of population growth, some Boston Brahmins fled town for suburbs such as Dover and Manchester-by-the-Sea. Others remained, however, to found and endow cultural institutions for the benefit of all who live in Boston.

The Museum of Fine Arts was incorporated in 1870, and six years later the holdings were moved to a new location in Copley Square. Colonel Henry Lee Higginson established the Boston Symphony Orchestra in 1881, the same year that Frederick Law Olmsted, who designed Central Park in New York City, created what came to be known as the 'Emerald Necklace,' a string of ponds and parks stretching from the Public Garden to Franklin Park. The Boston Public Library was enlarged and housed in a beautiful Renaissance-style structure in 1895.

Mayors Move the City

The first mayor of Irish descent was the popular and efficient Hugh O'Brien, elected four times beginning in 1884. His wins were the result of successful 'ward boss' politics, a system whereby Democratic district (or ward) leaders got out the vote for their candidates. In exchange for their votes, bosses provided their voters with safety, basic necessities of life and opportunities for economic advancement. Mayoral ward politics was employed again in 1902 with the election of Irish-born Patrick A Collins, an educated, dignified and conservative fellow.

In 1905, a former ward boss and the first second-generation Irish mayor was elected, John F 'Honey Fitz' Fitzgerald. Graft and patronage weakened his administration. Honey Fitz, whose theme song was 'Sweet Adeline,' was defeated in 1907 by a Republican who promised to clean up the mess at City Hall. Other leaders, through the newly formed Good Government Association, changed the city charter to reform the mayor's office. In 1909, they created a city council whose members were elected, but somehow Honey Fitz was elected again.

In 1913, and then on and off through the 1920s, '30s and '40s, James Michael Curley was elected mayor. Curley rejected ward boss politics and Boston Brahmins, carving out his own style of leadership. He was vibrant, energetic and boastful; he spoke directly to neighborhood residents. And the people responded to his cult of personality, electing him time and time again. Curley handed out favors and jobs all year long, enlarging the city hospital, building beaches and bathhouses, playgrounds, stadiums, recreation facilities and a tunnel to East Boston. While ignoring the center of the city, he raised taxes and mired the city with enormous debt.

By the 1940s, corruption was taken for granted as a part of public life in Boston. Although under indictment for mail fraud in 1945, Curley ran for office again and won. He was convicted and served time in a federal penitentiary. By 1949, the center of Boston was seedy and rundown. Businesses and people were moving out.

But a new mayor, John B Hynes, was elected that year. Mild mannered and soft-spoken (some called him 'Whispering Johnny'), Hynes was an efficient administrator, and in the next 10 years he transformed and modernized the city. He established an auditorium commission, a government center commission and a Boston Redevelopment Authority. The Old West End neighborhood was raised in the name of 'urban renewal.' The effects of that decision are still debated today.

In 1967, John F Collins, nonpartisan, honest and clean-cut, moved the city forward. The city received billions of dollars from the federal government to transform and modernize the waterfront, Quincy Market, City Hall and Government Center. Many university projects were begun. Business leaders banded together to promote growth and development. Led by Ralph Lowell of the Boston Co, they began discussing local issues in a room adjacent to the vault in the basement of the Boston Safe Deposit & Trust Co. This group of men, known unofficially as 'the Vault,' developed a vision for a 'New Boston,' and had the clout, influence and power to implement it. Boston was a city on the rebound, and the Vault would play an important role in supporting mayors, downtown development, skyline development and urban redevelopment. At times they bailed out the city financially, and they always supported leading cultural institutions with money, publicity and leadership. After Martin Luther King, Jr's, assassination in 1968, the Vault put $100,000 toward new inner-city programs.

Mayor Kevin White faced the problems of conflicting neighborhood needs throughout the city, for a while weathering the storms and promoting Boston as a truly 'livable' city. But in the mid-1970s, racism exploded. Court-ordered school busing caused extensive racial conflicts and polarized the city for years. (See 'School Busing & Segregation,' later in this chapter.)

In the 1980s, the Vault helped push Boston toward the ranks of a 'World Class City,' a destination, a hub of culture, learning and economic growth. But in 1997, the Vault ceased to operate. Through business mergers, consolidations and acquisitions, the corporate leadership in Boston had dropped to an unsustainable level; in the 1980s, there were 19 Massachusetts corporations in the Fortune 500, only six in the 1990s. In today's world economy, Boston is now a satellite, not a hub.

At the Millennium

For all its ties to the past, Boston has always looked forward. With ground recently broken on a $700 million convention center; with the country's largest public works project (see 'The Big Dig' in the Getting Around chapter); with the largest redevelopment

Boston Firms

1634	Boston Common is the first public park.
1635	Boston Public Latin School, the first public secondary school, is founded.
1716	Boston Harbor gets the first lighthouse.
1795	Paul Revere organizes the first labor union.
1800	Bostonians are first given the nickname 'Bean eaters,' since baked beans, made from a recipe of beans richly mixed with sugar, molasses and salt port, was a staple Sunday meal in colonial and Federalist Boston. Baked beans were prepared on Saturday night because on Sunday, a day of rest, no cooking was to be done.
1806	The first church built by free blacks opens on Joy St, Beacon Hill.
1831	The first abolitionist newspaper, the *Liberator*, is published.
1836	Elizabeth Peabody opens the first kindergarten.
1845	The sewing machine is invented by Elias Howe.
1861	Oliver Wendell Holmes, a 19th-century 'Proper Bostonian' doctor and poet, coins the term 'Brahmin' in his novel *Elsie Venner*. He wrote that a Bostonian 'comes of the Brahmin caste of New England, this is the harmless, inoffensive untitled aristocracy.'
1875	The first American Christmas card is printed by Lois Prang.
1876	The first telephone is demonstrated by Alexander Graham Bell.
1880	Frances Perkins, born in Boston, becomes the first woman to serve in an American President's cabinet. As Secretary of Labor under Franklin D Roosevelt, she served 12 years and helped create a minimum federal wage, child labor laws, the Social Security Act and the Fair Labor Standards Act.
1893	Arthur Shurtleff lights a candle in the window of his parents' home, beginning the tradition of Christmas lights.
1897	The first American subway system opens.
1910	Dr John Collins Bossidy of Holy Cross College refines a 1905 Harvard alumni dinner toast:

'And this is good old Boston,
the home of the ocean and the cod,
where the Lowells talk only to Cabots
and the Cabots talk only to God.

1924	Mutual funds are invented by Massachusetts Investors Trust.

Frances Perkins

project since the filling of Back Bay underway in the new Seaport District, there is no reason to think Boston is resting on the past. In fact, she is betting her future on quality-of-life issues for her citizens, on sustained pre-eminence in the technology and financial services sectors. It's a safe bet.

Boston is in the middle of an economic renaissance, although the wealth isn't trickling down evenly. Folks in Massachusetts are among the wealthiest and the stingiest in the country. The blue-blood cultural institutions receive plenty of funding, but the less established go begging (witness the conservative Boston Ballet versus the riskier Dance Umbrella, or the Museum of Fine Arts versus the Institute for Contemporary Art). New buildings are shooting up overnight, but construction cranes are still slow to move in Roxbury and Dorchester. Affluent empty-nesters, encouraged by a low crime rate, are moving back in droves. (For the first time since the 1970s, the population is expected to top 600,000 in the year 2000.) Still, young professionals with high salaries are the only ones who can reasonably afford housing in the city since the demise of rent control in the mid-1990s.

Despite the chip Boston has on its shoulder in regard to New York City, it's solidly poised to be one of the most 'livable' cities in the country. Can New York say that?

GEOGRAPHY & CLIMATE

Boston is 48.4 sq miles, smaller even than tiny San Francisco. Its topography is determined by the Charles River, which empties into Boston Harbor and separates the twin cities of Boston and Cambridge. With the exception of Beacon Hill, the city is compact and flat, not surprising since much sits atop landfill.

The city is situated on the cusp of competing weather patterns: Air masses from the Great Lakes and Canada collide with moderate Gulf Stream currents. Thus, the old saw – if you don't like the weather, wait a minute – is only a slight exaggeration.

Most September and October days are splendid, with clear blue skies, cool morn-

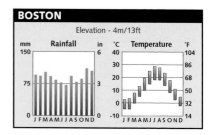

ings and evenings, and warm afternoons. November always has a few warm days known as 'Indian summer.' Winter can be bitterly cold, although snowfall accumulation is measured in inches rather than feet. During and immediately after a snowstorm the city is a romantic winter wonderland. The day after, though, is often more like the 'morning after.' Spring is fleeting, perhaps lasting only a week before humid 90° weather sets in. Blink and the leaves have turned from pods to full-blown shadow puppets. Dress in layers and be ready for anything.

Surprisingly, Boston is windier than Chicago and gets more rain than Seattle.

The short-range forecast is broadcast on the top column of the John Hancock building: steady blue, clear views; flashing blue, clouds are due; steady red, rain ahead; flashing red, snow instead. In summer, lights flash red to indicate a canceled Red Sox game.

ECOLOGY & ENVIRONMENT

Until recently, Boston Harbor served as the city's unregulated septic system and was considered the foulest body of water in the Northern Hemisphere. But in the mid-1980s, the Massachusetts Water Resources Authority (MWRA) installed state-of-the-art sewage treatment facilities. Although Boston residents now shoulder the country's highest water and sewer bills, the effort has been successful. Every New Year's Day for almost a hundred years, a group of hardy souls from South Boston, the 'L St Brownies,' dive into the harbor for a brisk swim. Although they continue to risk hypothermia, they no longer have to fear mutant bacterial infections.

The Kennedys

Ancestors of this Irish-Catholic clan immigrated to Boston during the famine in the mid-19th century, made their fortunes over a few generations and laid the foundation for an enduring American dynasty. For Kennedys, the family business is politics.

John F Kennedy, second son of Rose and Joe, was born in Brookline on May 29, 1917, and named for his maternal grandfather, Boston mayor John 'Honey Fitz' Fitzgerald. One of nine children, John Kennedy graduated from Harvard in 1940 and served in the US Navy during WWII. By 1946, he was a charismatic US Congressman from the 11th District, which included Charlestown. In 1954, Kennedy defeated incumbent US Senator Henry Cabot Lodge, Jr, a son of Boston Brahmins.

When Kennedy was elected the 35th US President in 1960, narrowly defeating Republican Vice President Richard Nixon, his youth, eloquence and good looks crowned him torchbearer for a new generation. His vigor and staunch idealism were short-lived, though. He was assassinated by Lee Harvey Oswald in 1963 in Dallas, Texas.

Rose and Joe's third son, Robert F Kennedy, served as his brother's Attorney General and most trusted advisor. Bobby Kennedy, too, was assassinated, while seeking the Democratic Party nomination for the presidency in 1968.

Youngest son Edward 'Ted' Kennedy, also a Harvard graduate, cut a controversial figure in his early years. Young Teddy had well-publicized marital and alcohol difficulties and a particularly tragic car accident in Chappaquidick off a Martha's Vineyard bridge, where he left the scene and his young female passenger drowned. In spite of his personal problems, he has served as the highly respected senior US Senator from Massachusetts since 1962. The Senate's liberal lion has a booming voice on health care issues, minimum wage laws, women's rights and the rights of the underprivileged. He considered running for president himself, but concluded that they 'have a thing about killing Kennedys.'

Ever since RFK was killed (and especially since matriarch Rose died in 1995 at the age of 104), Ted has presided over a multigenerational household that includes many young elected officials. Rose and Joe, Sr, had pushed their children to reach for greatness, instilling an unwavering sense of public service in all their progeny. Perhaps it was this same weight of responsibility that led to a tragic recklessness in some family members. The Kennedys have suffered far greater losses than any other public US family: There have been fatal plane crashes, skiing accidents and drug overdoses.

The John F Kennedy Library was opened at Columbia Point in Boston in 1979 (see Outlying Neighborhoods in Things to See & Do). Kennedy family members, friends and political associates often come to Boston to participate in special events at the library. The annual 'Profiles in Courage Award' is one of the brightest.

GOVERNMENT & POLITICS

Careers have been made observing Boston politics. Whether you're a serious scholar, investigative reporter or a comedian in need of a juicy repertoire, there is plenty of fodder. Boston has had more than its share of colorful characters and patronage-wielding leaders. It's also had fine ones with vision.

The city government consists of a mayor, who is elected to a four-year term, and a 13-member city council, each of whom is elected to two-year terms. Most city councillors represent districts that include several wards, but four are 'at-large,' meaning they represent all neighborhood interests. Councillors, who oversee the budget and operation of city agencies, meet at City Hall at noon on Wednesday. Meetings are open to the public, but the dissected minutiae can be equally excruciating and fascinating. The Boston School Committee is elected separately in nonpartisan elections.

Milestones in Medicine

Boston has always been a prominent center for medical education, treatment and research.

1781	America's first medical school is established at Harvard.
1846	General anesthesia is first used during an operation at Mass General Hospital (MGH).
1866	The surgical treatment for appendicitis is implemented at MGH.
1929	The iron lung, a machine used to save polio patients, is first used at Peter Bent Brigham Hospital (PBBH).
1954	The world's first successful kidney transplant takes place at PBBH.
1967	Open-heart surgery is first performed at Boston Children's Hospital.
1987	A gene responsible for one form of Alzheimer's disease is discovered at MGH. In 1995, research teams went on to discover the second and third genes, too.

Voters are heavily Democratic and Independent, but citywide elections are generally nonpartisan. Despite the fact that politics is a blood sport, voter turnout is low. (Wards in South Boston and Dorchester are the most active.) The next citywide mayoral election is in November 2001.

Nowhere in the US is politics more provincial and ethnicity-driven than in Boston. The late Thomas P 'Tip' O'Neill, respected Speaker of the House of Representatives, coined the phrase 'All politics is local.' If the mayor can keep the garbage picked up, streets cleared quickly after a snowstorm and the parks green, he's 'in like Flynn.' (The long-serving Irish-Catholic Mayor Ray Flynn left office in July 1993 to become Ambassador to the Vatican.) Mayor Tom Menino, Boston's first Italian-American mayor, was elected by winning 18 of 22 wards and 64% of the vote. While he's made micromanaging a priority (the streets are visibly cleaner), Menino is also interested in education, jobs, economic development and public safety.

ECONOMY
Financial Services
Mutual funds, an enormously popular investment tool for individual retirement plans, originated in Massachusetts. The largest company, by far, is Fidelity Investments, a privately held company controlled by Ned Johnson and his daughter Abigail. Massachusetts Financial Services (MFS) and Putnam Investments are also based in Boston. Fleet Financial Group and Bank-Boston merged in 1999 (as Fleet Boston), creating a banking juggernaut.

Science & Technology
Boston has long been considered the premiere university center in the USA. For technology, though, it all began back in 1865 when the Massachusetts Institute of Technology (MIT) opened its doors on Berkeley St in Back Bay. By 1928, MIT researchers developed the first computer. Wang Computers, Digital Computers, Prime and Data General all began in the Boston area.

Many graduates, having enjoyed the city in their youth, chose to stay in the area, helping fuel local booming commerce in computer research, Internet and software development, and computer and telecom hardware and manufacturing.

Among the area's many high-tech companies, EMC leads the pack with a market capitalization that outpaced practically every other American company in the late 1990s. (In 1999, Gillette, the Mach3 razor powerhouse based in South Boston, was valued at about the same amount, $65 billion.) As of 1998, the Boston area was second only to California's Silicon Valley in the amount of venture capital dispersed to high-tech companies.

Cambridge, particularly Central and Kendall Squares, has become a mecca for the genome industry, intent on developing new drugs and therapies based on the mapping of 100,000 human genes. Small biotech companies, pharmaceutical giants and academic bastions, such as the Whitehead Institute/MIT Center for Genome Research, constantly vie for advantages and collaborations.

Raytheon, with huge air defense department contracts (for the 'smart' Patriot missiles that rained down in the Gulf War, for instance), is also based in the Boston area.

POPULATION & PEOPLE

At the end of WWII, nearly 800,000 people lived in Boston, the majority of whom were Irish. Urban renewal and suburban flight reduced those numbers, but the core of the city was never abandoned like it was in some cities. Today, Boston is home to about 575,000, making it the 20th-largest US city. About 600,000 people work in Boston, just one of three cities that has more jobs than residents. (DC and San Francisco are the other two.) About 40% are registered voters and about 23% are full- or part-time students. There are about 62,000 youth enrolled in public schools.

More than 3 million souls inhabit Greater Boston, and the breakdown goes like this: 58% are Caucasian (or white); 26% are African-American; 11% are Latino; 5% are Asian and less than 1% trace their ancestry to Native American peoples. The largest ethnic group is Irish, but there are also blocks of Italians, Greeks, Russians, Americans, Lithuanians, Jews, Poles, Yankees of English ancestry and many of other European origins. Into the 21st century, Boston is also attracting immigrants from Brazil, Haiti and Southeast Asia.

ARTS

Boston is synonymous, in many minds, with culture. The place isn't known as the 'Athens of America' for naught. Although high culture is mainly what comes to mind, what with Boston's great universities and rich literary, philosophical and political traditions, rest assured that Boston is home to a number of decidedly lowbrow artistic pursuits, too. Also see the Entertainment chapter.

Literature

The city's traditional reverence for the written word was brought by the Puritans and nurtured over the centuries by the area's great universities and literary societies.

Phillis Wheatley (1753–84), an African-American poet, was encouraged to get an education by her slave master. She began writing poetry at the age of 14, and her later work was celebrated in both North America and Europe.

Ralph Waldo Emerson (1803–82) and Henry David Thoreau (1817–62) wrote compelling essays about their beliefs and attempts to live in accordance with the mystical unity of all creation, a religious philosophy Emerson named Transcendentalism. Thoreau's writings, notably *Walden, or Life in the Woods* (1854), which advocated a life of simplicity and living in harmony with nature, and *Civil Disobedience* (1849), a treatise well before its time, qualified him as America's first hippie.

Concordian Nathaniel Hawthorne (1804–64) was America's first great short-story writer and author of *The Scarlet Letter* (1850) and *The House of the Seven Gables* (1851).

Henry Wadsworth Longfellow's (1807–82) poems, 'Song of Hiawatha' and 'Paul Revere's Ride,' are memorized by school children as cherished accounts (though more myth than history) of American lore.

Louisa May Alcott (1832–88) lived much of her life in Concord, too. Her largely autobiographical novel *Little Women* (1868) is a classic, beloved by generations of young women.

In 1903, Harvard graduate and sociologist Dr WEB Du Bois (1868–1963) wrote his seminal tract *The Souls of Black Folk*, in which he sought to influence the way blacks dealt with segregation, urging pride in African heritage.

Louisa May Alcott

Dr WEB DuBois

FACTS ABOUT BOSTON

School Busing & Segregation

In 1954, the US Supreme Court (in *Brown v Board of Education of Topeka*) held that racial segregation in public schools was illegal. Shortly thereafter, the NAACP (National Association for the Advancement of Colored People) declared that, since Boston neighborhoods were racially segregated, school assignment based on neighborhood residence amounted to de facto school segregation. When the School Committee ignored the *Brown* decision and plenty of requests for action by the NAACP, the NAACP brought a class-action suit against the School Committee.

Federal Judge W Arthur Garrity, Jr, presiding over the *Morgan v Hennigan* case in 1972, took two years to

STANLEY J FORMAN

The Soiling of Old Glory, Pulitzer Prize, 1977

study the arguments and hand down a courageous 152-page decision. He found that the school system was in fact deliberately segregated. Black youngsters had been given indefensibly inferior educations. Garrity was compelled to do what no elected officials had the backbone to do: upend the underpinnings of systemic discrimination in Boston. He ordered that students be bused to other neighborhoods in order to create racial balance in schools. Beginning in September 1974, about 15,000 African-American students were bused into white neighborhoods daily, pitting the most adversarial communities of South Boston and Roxbury against each other. (The number rose to 25,000 students the following year.)

Storms of protest exploded in South Boston, East Boston and Charlestown. There were strikes, boycotts and violence in the streets. Even though opposition in white neighborhoods was strong (to say the least), busing continued. City Councillor Louise Day Hicks (who would later run against and lose to Ray Flynn for mayor) led the vitriolic diatribes. Judge Garrity received threats almost daily; federal marshals were posted outside his home. But there was no turning back the truth that public institutions could not benefit one constituency to the exclusion of another. It took years for tempers to cool, but by about 1983, bitter racial tensions had calmed considerably.

When Ray Flynn took office in 1984 in a racially divided city, the new 'people's mayor' declared harmony his priority. This blunt desire to eradicate racial tension was a radical departure. Until then, it had been easier to ignore the flames of division. The following year, Judge Garrity returned control of the Boston schools to the elected city School Committee. By this time, the school population – after suburban 'white flight' and an influx of Latino and Asian students – was almost 75% students of color. But by this time, too, thanks to Garrity's courage and some forward-looking political leaders, the city knew it had to face its demons. The reckoning continues to this day. Garrity reviewed court challenges to official efforts to achieve access to school parity until his death in 1999, and the issues, though less contentious than they were in the '70s, are still not resolved.

Pulitzer Prize-winning novelist Edith Wharton (1862–1937) was born in New York, but gained entry into Boston society when she married a local banker. Her novels offer keen observations of the social mores of Boston Brahmins.

Henry James' *Bostonians* (1886) and John P Marquand's *Late George Apley* (1937) are piercing novels of Boston parlor society.

The Last Puritan (1935), by George Santayana (1863–1952), explores what it might be like for someone with 17th-century Puritan ideals to attend Harvard in the 20th century.

Robert McCloskey's *Make Way for Ducklings* (1941), a children's book that has become a Boston classic, describes the story of a mother duck and her ducklings lost in Back Bay and the colorful characters and sights they encounter.

Johnny Tremain (1943), by Esther Forbes, describes the Revolutionary War as seen by a fictional boy.

The Friends of Eddie Coyle (1972), by George Higgins, narrates life in one of Boston's less heralded neighborhoods; it provides a crash course in the Boston dialect.

Music

Plenty of nationally known alternative and rock bands (Aerosmith, Boston, Pixies and the Cars, for example) got their start in Boston clubs.

Boston is also home to a thriving folk tradition. Tracy Chapman sang in Harvard Square while a student at Tufts University. Patty Larkin got her start here as well. Club Passim is the most venerated folk venue.

Jazz thrives (but not like in New York City), inspired in part by the influential presence of Berklee College of Music, but the blues scene is a bit less developed. Cambridge has a few respected venues that attract well-known performers like GE Smith, Cesar Rosas, Duke Robillard, Big Jack Johnson and Abbey Lincoln. There are also plenty of smaller clubs where you'll find talented acts.

Classical music has a long-celebrated tradition in Boston. The Boston Symphony Orchestra, founded in 1881 by Henry Lee Higginson, and currently under the direction of maestro Seiji Ozawa, is finely woven into the cultural fabric of the city. There is no better place than the grand and acoustically perfect Symphony Hall to observe Boston's old guard during the winter season. The city's favorite 'pop' icon, the Boston Pops, plays popular classics, rousing marches and Broadway show tunes in Symphony Hall throughout the spring and fall.

Theater

Boston's strong Puritan roots have always exercised a stranglehold over her desire to become a world-class city, and this clash is most apparent in the city's stunted theater tradition. It was not until the mid-1800s that Boston even attempted to host performances like those routinely staged in Europe or New York.

In 1860, Edwin Booth was Boston's featured thespian. (His career was derailed when his brother, John Wilkes Booth, assassinated President Lincoln in 1865.) Throughout the late 1800s,

Dude looks like a lady

Film & Television

Boston, with its diverse architecture, scenic coastline and college campuses, is a hot film location. Many films and TV shows that take place in Boston (like *Ally McBeal, the Practice* and the dearly departed *Cheers*) are actually shot elsewhere, and scenic clips are spliced in for local flavor.

The original *Thomas Crown Affair* (1968), starring Steve McQueen and Faye Dunaway, depicts the city as the perfect place to stage the perfect crime.

Love Story (1970), with Ryan O'Neal and Ali MacGraw as Harvard and Radcliffe undergraduates, told us that 'love means never having to say you're sorry.'

The Paper Chase (1973) stars John Houseman as the classically stern, Socratic Harvard law professor.

Director William Friedkin of *The Brink's Job* (1978) insisted on authentic North End locations, and hired local ex-cons to play toughs.

The Bostonians (1984) stars Vanessa Redgrave and Christopher Reeve in a period piece based on the Henry James novel of Boston politics and manners circa 1876.

The Good Mother (1988), a divorce drama directed by Boston native Leonard Nimoy, was shot in Cambridge and Somerville.

Glory (1989), starring Denzel Washington and Matthew Broderick, tells the true story of the first Civil War black volunteer infantry unit.

The Firm (1994), starring Tom Cruise as a wide-eyed Harvard law graduate, includes shots of Boston and Cambridge.

With Honors (1994) stars Joe Pesci as a homeless man adopted by Harvard student Brendan Fraser and his pals.

Good Will Hunting (1997) put Southie on the Hollywood map and started the careers of Cambridge boys Matt Damon and Ben Affleck (who wrote the screenplay and starred along with Robin Williams).

Amistad (1997), with an all-star cast directed by Stephen Spielberg, tells the true story of an 1839 mutiny aboard a slave ship and the ensuing legal battle to vindicate and free the mutineers.

The art-house hit, *Next Stop Wonderland* (1997), a heartwarming independent film about a young woman's dating travails, refers to the final outbound stop on the T Blue Line.

A Civil Action (1998), based on Jonathan Harr's gripping chronicle of the decade-long lawsuit over industrial chemical pollution in the suburb of Woburn, stars John Travolta.

various societies formed and clamored for censorship and decorum. Vaudeville and burlesque, said to have originated in Boston, merely served to keep the censors working overtime.

Boston's high-handed morality made it the butt of many jokes, as savvy marketing moguls designated their productions 'banned in Boston' and were therefore guaranteed a full house elsewhere. In 1929, Eugene O'Neill's *Strange Interlude* was banned and moved to nearby Quincy, where it was enthusiastically received. Boston loosened up a bit in the 1940s and '50s and became a try-out venue for Broadway-bound shows like Tennessee Williams' *A Streetcar Named Desire*, and the musical extravaganza *Oklahoma!*

In 1965, the American Civil Liberties Union (ACLU), stalwart guardian of free expression, took the city to court, finally exposing the tacit censorship agreement that

Boston English

The Boston dialect is famous for broad-vowel English. 'Pahk the cah in Hahvahd Yahd' (translation: Park the car in Harvard Yard) is the common illustration of the peculiar 'r.' During JFK's presidency, his speech was satirized for its disappearing r's ('chowdah' for chowder) and for r's that mysteriously replaced 'a' at the end of words ('Cuber' for Cuba). Then there is the adverb 'wicked' (pronounced 'wikkid' and meaning 'very') and the adjective 'bizarre' (pronounced 'bzah'). All together now: 'The weathah heah is wikkid bzah.'

Bostonians are also known for abbreviating names. Massachusetts Avenue becomes 'Mass Ave'; Commonwealth Avenue is always 'Comm Ave'; Harvard Business School becomes 'the B-School'; Cape Cod is 'the Cape'; the subway system is always 'the T.'

Some place names just don't follow standard American English usage and pronunciation:

It's **Boston Common**, not 'commons.'

Copley is 'kop-lee,' not 'kope-lee.'

Faneuil: Nobody agrees on pronunciation, but it's most common to say 'fannel' or 'fan-yul.'

The **Public Garden** is singular, not plural, and never called the Boston Garden.

Tremont St is pronounced 'treh-mont,' not 'tree-mont.'

Worcester is an hour west of Boston, but to save grave embarrassment, it's 'wooster.' (Locals say 'woostuh.')

Bostonians have also reinvented food and place names. Some tips:

Tonic is a carbonated soft drink or soda pop.

Grinders are hot or cold meat sandwiches, known elsewhere as a submarine sandwich or 'sub.'

A **frappe** is a milkshake (blended ice cream and milk drink).

Jimmies are tiny, waxy chocolate bits sprinkled on ice cream treats.

Southie is South Boston, the neighborhood.

Boston cream pie bears no relation to pie; it's yellow cake with a custard filling, covered in chocolate icing.

existed between City Hall and theater managers. Still, the Puritans' posthumous reach was not entirely severed. The musical *Hair* was closed prematurely in 1970, allegedly because it depicted the desecration of the American flag.

Censorship is no longer a problem in Boston, but its legacy casts a long shadow. Unfortunately, the city is thus seen as a less than desirable venue for interesting alternative or cutting edge theatrical productions, whether homegrown or from afar.

Dance

The Puritans' tenacious reach probably also had something to do with Boston's failure to develop much of a reputation for dance. The city's premier company, the Boston Ballet, performs classics as well as ambitious new work. Its annual performances of the *Nutcracker* are a holiday tradition. Otherwise, Dance Umbrella at the Emerson Majestic Theatre features a push-the-envelope roster of internationally acclaimed performers such as Bill T Jones, Mark Morris and the Alvin Ailey Dance Co.

Painting

John Singleton Copley (1738–1815) is considered the first great American portrait painter. Many of his best-known works, though painted after he relocated to London in 1774, are at the Museum of Fine Arts. Winslow Homer (1836–1910), famous for realistic Maine coast scenes, began as a popular press illustrator before dedicating himself to painting. By the 20th century, Boston supported world-class artists like John Singer Sargent (1856–1925), who painted telling portraits of Boston's upper class, and Childe Hassam (1859–1935), who used Boston Common landscapes for his impressionist works. After Hassam, Boston lost pace with the rest of the western world. Today, Newbury St galleries specialize in fairly conservative fare (see Newbury St in the Shopping chapter). For more cutting edge work, look for artists' open studios, especially in the Fort Point Channel area.

Public Art

City Hall doesn't have a great tradition of commissioning public art. Certainly there is an ample statuary along the Comm Ave mall and in the Public Garden, but you might find the 75 installations in T stations just as interesting. Notable creations are detailed in the Things to See & Do chapter.

SOCIETY & CONDUCT

Some cautions are in order: Don't call Boston 'Beantown.' Don't wear a NY Yankees cap in the vicinity of Fenway Park. Don't park in a tow zone – you'll be towed. Don't jaywalk or ignore traffic signals. Don't expect to get an authoritative answer if you ask for directions. Don't swim in the Charles River. Don't wear orange in Southie on St Patrick's Day. Don't call the North End 'Little Italy.' Don't wear your Harvard sweatshirt until you get home.

RELIGION

Boston is home to large numbers of Christian Protestants (including Unitarians, Anglicans, Quakers, Baptists, Christian Scientists and Mormons), Roman Catholics and smaller numbers of Jews, Muslims, Hindus and Buddhists, agnostics and atheists. A few religious traditions began in Boston, among them Christian Science (founded in 1866 by Mary Baker Eddy), which now has churches in 70 countries throughout the world, and Transcendentalism.

Facts for the Visitor

PLANNING
When to Go

Boston draws crowds throughout the year, but you can count on a lull, with due cause, in November and from January through March. Spring is ephemeral, but it's that much more sweet. If you time your visit right – late April to early June – you'll long remember the magnolias in Back Bay and early strains of cheering from Red Sox Nation. June through August, though at times uncomfortably steamy, is high tourist season, so accommodations are more expensive and difficult to secure. The influx of tourists is somewhat balanced by the outflow of students on summer hiatus. September and October are the most predictably pleasant times to visit. Though there isn't much foliage in the city, New England leaf peepers fly in and out (so rooms are still expensive and hard to obtain). The city puts on festive finery between Thanksgiving and New Year's Day. January and February winds and temps are downright harsh, but rooms are available and less expensive. A freak April Fool's snowstorm, burying the poor little daffodils, isn't an impossibility.

What to Bring

Boston is a fairly casual city; only a few restaurants require jacket and tie and their counterparts. Nor are Bostonians particularly fashion-conscious. If someone looks really cool, or is wearing only black, chances are they're European, Asian or Middle Eastern students.

Often in the spring and fall, the best times to visit, you need a jacket in the morning and evening, but only a t-shirt by day. Bring the warmest coat, scarf and gloves you own for

Mayor Curley, beloved by Bostonians great and small.

FACTS FOR THE VISITOR

Bird's-Eye View

KIM GRANT

The Prudential Center

For a bird's-eye view of Boston, head to the 60th-floor **John Hancock Observatory** of New England's tallest building (☎ 617-247-1977, 572-6429), 200 Clarendon St. The ticket booth is at Trinity Place and St James Ave. In addition to providing a good overview of the neighborhood walking tours, elucidating bonuses include a 1775 topographical map of Boston and an audio presentation about the Revolutionary War battles that took place in and around Boston. It's open 9 am to 11 pm daily; until 6 pm Sunday November through March. Admission is $5 adults, $3 seniors and children age 5 to 7. The last tickets are sold one hour before closing.

The 50th-floor **Prudential Center Skywalk** (☎ 617-859-0648), 800 Boylston St, offers a spectacular 360° view of metro Boston and Cambridge. (The John Hancock Observatory has views on three sides only.) It's open 10 am to 10 pm daily, and the last tickets are sold 30 minutes prior to closing. Tickets are $4 adults, $3 seniors and children age 2 to 10.

wintertime visits. You might not need them every day, but if you do, you're less likely to catch pneumonia. In the summer, you could actually take a dip in Boston Harbor, so bring your suit.

Maps

Although you'll be hard-pressed to beat this guide's maps, the Arrow map of Boston is excellent. Also look for the smaller, laminated 'Streetwise' maps of the city, useful for longer stays, at about $6. 'Professor Pathfinder' (☎ 800-933-6277) produces a detailed map of Harvard Square, the university and other parts of Cambridge.

If you plan on bicycling beyond the banks of the Charles River, get hold of the fantastic *Boston's Bike Map*, produced by Rubel BikeMaps (☎ 617-776-6567, www.bikemaps .com), PO Box 1035, Cambridge, MA 02140. It costs $4.25 and is available from the Globe Corner Bookstore (see 'Bookstores' in the Shopping chapter) or directly from Rubel. They also produce 30 little laminated 'Pocket Rides' ($1.95 each) for trips within Greater Boston and from area commuter rail stations. The rides are worth every penny.

ORIENTATION

For a city of its stature, Boston is quite small. The sights and activities of principal interest to travelers are contained within an area that's only about 1 mile wide by 3 miles long. Boston's neighborhoods are quite distinct and compact, and best explored on foot. There's no right or wrong order or way to explore; most of the neighborhoods abut one another.

Brahmin Beacon Hill, its brick streets lit by gas lanterns and lined with patrician townhouses, is one of the loveliest areas for strolling. Downtown boasts many of the important colonial Freedom Trail sites. Architecture buffs will delight in the contrast between 20th-century skyscrapers and 18th-century mercantile structures in the Financial District. The aromas and accents of the North End rival any Little Italy in America. The rejuvenated waterfront and newly burgeoning Seaport District renew Boston's historic maritime ties. Back Bay, created as a mid-19th-century landfill project, is more orderly, with streets laid out east to west in alphabetical order. The South End, a newly gentrified area, is thick with restaurants, artsy shops and renovated Victorian brownstones. Kenmore Square is home to a vibrant nightclub scene and lots of students, while Fenway includes a 4-mile-long grassy byway that leads to two important museums and an arboretum.

The Charles River, with a popular grassy esplanade along both banks, separates Boston from Cambridge, home to Harvard University and the Massachusetts Institute of Technology (MIT). Cambridge's 'other' squares (besides Harvard) are often more vibrant and happening than their famous relative.

TOURIST OFFICES
Local Tourist Offices
For city and statewide information, contact the Massachusetts Office of Travel & Tourism (MOTT; ☎ 617-973-8500, 800-447-6277 for a getaway guide, ☎ 800-227-6277 for recorded events line, vacationinfo@state.ma.us, www.massvacation.com), Transportation Building, 10 Park Plaza, suite 4510, Boston, MA 02116. It's open 9 am to 5 pm weekdays.

Drop in on the Greater Boston Convention & Visitors Bureau's (GBCVB) year-round Boston Common Visitors Information Center (☎ 617-426-3115), Tremont and West Sts, to pick up subway and bus maps and miscellaneous information. The center (with public restrooms) is open 8:30 am to 5 pm daily (except from 9 am Sunday).

Their booth in the center court of the Prudential Center mall, 800 Boylston St (Back Bay), is open 9 am to 5 pm daily.

The National Park Service Visitors Center (NPS; ☎ 617-242-5642, www.nps.gov/bost/), 15 State St, has plenty of historical literature, a short slide show and free walking tours of the Freedom Trail. The center is open 9 am to 5 pm daily (until 6 pm in summer).

In Harvard Square, the visitors information booth (☎ 617-441-2884, 800-862-5678) has information on local events and self-guided walking tours. The kiosk is staffed by volunteers 9 am to 5 pm daily.

Pre-Departure Tourist Information
In advance of your visit, request an information packet from the GBCVB (☎ 617-536-4100, 800-888-5515, visitus@bostonusa.com, www.bostonusa.com), 2 Copley Place, suite 105, Boston, MA 02116.

TRAVEL AGENCIES
Budget travel specialists include the Council on International Educational Exchange's Council Travel (CIEE, or Council Travel; Map 8; ☎ 617-266-1926, 800-226-8624, www.ciee.org), 273 Newbury St. They can satisfy just about every travel-related need. They're open 9 am to 7 pm daily except Sunday.

Other Council Travel offices include Harvard Square (Map 11; ☎ 617-497-1497), 12 Eliot St, 2nd floor, which is open 9:30 am to 5:30 pm weekdays, except 10:30 am Wednesday, and 10 am to 2 pm Saturday; and on the MIT campus at Stratton Student Center (Map 12; ☎ 617-225-2555), 84 Mass Ave, with the same weekday hours as the one in Harvard Square.

DOCUMENTS
Passports & Visas
To enter the US, Canadians must have proof of citizenship, such as a citizenship card with photo ID or a passport. Visitors from other countries must have a valid passport, and many visitors are required to have a US visa.

However, there is a reciprocal visa-waiver program in which citizens of certain countries may enter the USA for stays of 90 days or less with a passport but without first obtaining a US visa. Currently these countries are Andorra, Argentina, Australia, Austria, Belgium, Brunei, Denmark, Finland, France, Germany, Iceland, Ireland, Italy, Japan, Liechtenstein, Luxembourg, Monaco, the Netherlands, New Zealand, Norway, San Marino, Slovenia, Spain, Sweden, Switzerland and the UK. Under this program you must have a roundtrip ticket that is nonrefundable in the USA, and you will not be allowed to extend your stay beyond 90 days.

Other travelers will need to obtain a visa from a US consulate or embassy. In most countries, the process can be done by mail.

FACTS FOR THE VISITOR

Your passport should be valid for at least six months longer than your intended stay in the USA, and you'll need to submit a recent photo 1^{1}/$_{2}$ inches square (37mm x 37mm) with the application. Documents of financial stability and/or guarantees from a US resident are sometimes required, particularly for those from Third World countries.

Visa applicants may be required to 'demonstrate binding obligations' that will ensure their return to their countries. Because of this requirement, those planning to travel through other countries before arriving in the USA are generally better off applying for their US visa while they are still in their home country – rather than while on the road.

The most common visa is a Non-Immigrant Visitor's Visa, B1 for business purposes, B2 for tourism or visiting friends and relatives. A visitor's visa is good for one or five years with multiple entries, and it specifically prohibits the visitor from taking paid employment in the USA. The validity period for US visitor's visas depends on what country you're from. The length of time you'll be allowed to stay in the US is ultimately determined by US immigration authorities at the port of entry. If you're coming to the USA to work or study, you will probably need a different type of visa, and the company or institution that you're going to should make the arrangements. Allow six months in advance for processing the application. For information on work visas and employment in the US, see the Work section, later in this chapter.

Visa Extensions & Reentry

If you want, need or hope to stay in the USA longer than the date stamped on your passport, go to the local INS office (or call ☎ 800-755-0777, or look in the local white pages telephone directory under 'US Government') *before* the stamped date to apply for an extension. Anytime after that will usually lead to an unamusing conversation with an INS official who will assume you want to work illegally. If you find yourself in that situation, it's a good idea to bring a US citizen

HIV & Entering the USA

Everyone entering the USA who isn't a US citizen is subject to the authority of the Immigration & Naturalization Service (INS). The INS can keep people from entering or staying in the USA by excluding or deporting them. This is especially relevant to travelers with HIV (human immunodeficiency virus). Though being HIV-positive is not grounds for deportation, it is 'grounds for exclusion,' and the INS can invoke it to refuse admission.

Although the INS doesn't test people for HIV at customs, it may try to exclude anyone who answers 'yes' to this question on the nonimmigrant visa application form: 'Have you ever been afflicted with a communicable disease of public health significance?' INS officials may also stop people if they seem sick, are carrying AIDS/HIV medicine or, sadly, if the officer happens to think the person 'looks gay,' though sexual orientation is not legally grounds for exclusion.

It's imperative that visitors know and assert their rights. Immigrants and visitors who may face exclusion should discuss their rights and options with a trained immigration advocate before applying for a visa. For legal immigration information and referrals to immigration advocates, contact the National Immigration Project of the National Lawyers Guild (☎ 617-227-9727, fax 227-5495), 14 Beacon St, suite 602, Boston, MA 02108; or the Immigrant HIV Assistance Project, Bar Association of San Francisco (☎ 415-782-8995), 465 California St, suite 1100, San Francisco, CA 94104.

with you to vouch for your character. It's also a good idea to have some verification that you have enough money to support yourself.

In Boston, call the INS at ☎ 617-565-3879 for information or ☎ 800-870-3676 for forms. The Boston office is in the John F Kennedy Federal Office building, 5th floor, Government Center, Boston, MA 02203.

Travel Insurance

A travel insurance policy to cover medical expenses, luggage theft or loss, and cancellations or delays in your travel arrangements is a good idea. At the very least, you want catastrophic coverage for the worst case scenario. Coverage depends on your insurance and type of ticket, so ask both your insurer and your ticket-issuing agency to explain the finer points. STA Travel and Council Travel offer travel insurance options at reasonable prices. Ticket loss is also covered by travel insurance.

Other Documents

An International Driving Permit is useful for foreign visitors. Local traffic police are more likely to accept it as valid identification than an unfamiliar document from another country. Your national automobile association can provide one for a small fee. If you plan on doing a lot of driving, join your national automobile association or the American Automobile Association (AAA). Hotels often offer AAA discounts.

Most hostels in the USA are members of Hostelling International/American Youth Hostel (HI/AYH), which is affiliated with the International Youth Hostel Federation (IYHF). You can purchase membership on the spot when checking in. Most hostels allow nonmembers to stay but charge them a few dollars more.

Students should obtain an International Student Identification Card (ISIC) to take advantage of student discounts. Students will also need a picture ID to show they're over 21 to buy alcohol and gain admission to clubs and bars.

If you're over age 65, bring along proof of age to take advantage of senior discounts. Organizations such as American Association of Retired Persons (AARP) offer membership cards for further discounts and extend coverage to foreign citizens (see Senior Travelers, later in this chapter).

Photocopies

All important documents (passport data page and visa page, credit cards, travel insurance policy, air/bus/train tickets, driver's license, etc) should be photocopied before you leave home. Leave one copy with someone at home and keep another with you, separate from the originals.

US EMBASSIES & CONSULATES

US diplomatic offices abroad include the following:

Australia
(☎ 2-6270-5000)
21 Moonah Place, Yarralumla ACT 2600
(☎ 2-9373-9200)
Level 59 MLC Center 19–29 Martin Place, Sydney NSW 2000
(☎ 3-9526-5900)
553 St Kilda Rd, Melbourne, Victoria

Canada
(☎ 613-238-5335)
100 Wellington St, Ottawa, Ontario K1P 5T1
(☎ 604-685-4311)
1095 W Pender St, Vancouver, BC V6E 2M6
(☎ 514-398-9695)
1155 rue St-Alexandre, Montreal, Quebec

France
(☎ 01 42 96 12 02)
2 rue Saint Florentin, 75001 Paris

Germany
(☎ 228-33-91)
Deichmanns Aue 29, 53170 Bonn

Ireland
(☎ 668 8777)
42 Elgin Rd, Ballsbridge, Dublin

Israel
(☎ 3-519-7575)
71 Hayarkon St, Tel Aviv

Japan
(☎ 3-224-5000)
1-10-5 Akasaka Chome, Minato-ku, Tokyo

Netherlands
(☎ 70-310-9209)
Lange Voorhout 102, 2514 EJ The Hague
(☎ 20-310-9209)
Museumplein 19, 1071 DJ Amsterdam

New Zealand
(☎ 4-722-068)
29 Fitzherbert Terrace, Thorndon, Wellington

Norway
(☎ 22-44-85-50)
Drammensvein 18, Oslo

Sweden
(☎ 8-783-5300)
Strandvagen 101, S-115 89 Stockholm

FACTS FOR THE VISITOR

Switzerland
(☎ 31-357-70-11)
Jubilaumsstrasse 93, 3005 Bern

UK
(☎ 0171-499-9000)
24 Grosvenor St, London W1
(☎ 31-556-8315)
3 Regent Terrace, Edinburgh EH7 5BW
(☎ 232-328-239)
Queens House, 14 Queen St, Belfast BT1 6EQ

Consulates in Boston Most foreign embassies in the US are in Washington, DC, but a lot of countries, including the following, have consular offices in Boston. If your country's embassy or consulate is not listed below, call ☎ 617-555-1212 in Boston; ☎ 202-555-1212 in Washington, DC or look in the yellow pages telephone directory under 'Consulates.'

Your Own Embassy

As a tourist, it's important to realize what your own embassy – the embassy of the country of which you are a citizen – can and can't do.

Generally speaking, it won't be much help in emergencies if the trouble you're in is remotely your own fault. Remember that you are bound by the laws of the country you are in. Your embassy will not be sympathetic if you end up in jail after committing a crime locally, even if such actions are legal in your own country.

In genuine emergencies, you might get some assistance, but only if other channels have been exhausted. For example, if you need to get home urgently, a free ticket home is exceedingly unlikely – the embassy would expect you to have insurance. If you have all your money and documents stolen, it might assist in getting a new passport, but a loan for onward travel is out of the question.

Embassies used to keep letters for travelers or have a small reading room with home newspapers, but these days the mail holding service has been stopped and even most newspapers are out of date.

Australia
(☎ 617-542-8655)
20 Park Plaza, 4th floor, Boston, MA 02116
Canada
(☎ 617-262-3760)
3 Copley Place, suite 400, Boston, MA 02116
France
(☎ 617-542-7374)
31 St James Ave, suite 750, Boston, MA 02116
Germany
(☎ 617-536-4414)
3 Copley Place, suite 500, Boston, MA 02116
Ireland
(☎ 617-267-9330)
535 Boylston St, Boston, MA 02116
Italy
(☎ 617-542-0483)
100 Boylston St, suite 900, Boston, MA 02116
Netherlands
(☎ 617-542-8452)
6 St James Ave, Boston, MA 02116
UK
(☎ 617-248-9555)
Federal Reserve Plaza, 25th floor, 600 Atlantic Ave, Boston, MA 02210

CUSTOMS

US Customs allows each person over the age of 21 to bring 1 liter of liquor and 200 cigarettes duty-free into the USA. US citizens are allowed to import, duty-free, $400 worth of gifts from abroad, and non-US citizens are allowed to bring in $100 worth. Should you be carrying more than $10,000 in US and foreign cash, traveler's checks, money orders or the like, you need to declare the excess amount. There is no legal restriction on the amount that may be imported, but undeclared sums in excess of $10,000 may be subject to confiscation.

MONEY
Currency

US dollars are the only currency accepted in Boston. The US dollar is divided into 100 cents (¢). Coins come in denominations of 1¢ (penny), 5¢ (nickel), 10¢ (dime), 25¢ (quarter) and the seldom seen 50¢ (half dollar). Quarters are the most commonly used coins in vending machines and parking meters, so it's handy to have a stash of them. Bills, all the same size and color, come in $1,

$2, $5, $10, $20, $50 and $100 denominations – bills with a new design are in circulation, but are the same value as the old. There is also a $1 coin that the government has tried unsuccessfully to bring into mass circulation; they look similar to quarters.

Exchanging Money

To exchange foreign currency, call Fleet Boston (☎ 617-434-4275, 788-5000) for the nearest location, or head to their International Personal Banking Office in Harvard Square (☎ 617-556-6050), 1414 Mass Ave, Cambridge. At Logan Airport, there are Fleet Foreign Currency Exchanges at Terminal C (☎ 617-569-1172, 2nd level), open 8:30 am to 10 pm daily, and Terminal E (☎ 617-567-2313, 1st level), open 8:30 am to 10 pm weekdays, 11:30 am to 10 pm weekends. At press time, exchange rates were:

country	unit		dollars
Australia	$1	=	US$0.68
Canada	C$1	=	US$0.69
euro	€1	=	US$1.1
France	FF1	=	US$0.17
Germany	DM1	=	US$0.56
Hong Kong	HK$10	=	US$0.13
Japan	¥92	=	US$0.01
Netherlands	f1	=	US$0.50
New Zealand	NZ$1	=	US$0.53
UK	UK£1	=	US$1.69

Cash & Traveler's Checks

Traveler's checks, which can be replaced if lost or stolen, are as good as cash in the US – but only if they are in US dollars. Keep a record of the check numbers separate from the checks themselves. Buy checks in denominations of $100, with one packet of $20, so that at the end of your stay you aren't left with too many dollars.

ATMs

ATMs, found at most banks and in most shopping areas, are convenient for obtaining cash from a bank account back home. They're open 24 hours a day. There are various ATM networks, and most banks are affiliated with several. Exchange, Star, Plus and Cirrus are the predominant networks. For a nominal service charge, you can withdraw cash from an ATM using a credit card or a charge card. Credit cards usually have a 2% fee with a $2 minimum, and you are charged interest on the withdrawal until you pay it back. Using bank cards linked to your personal checking account is usually far cheaper. Check with your bank or credit card company for particulars.

Credit & Debit Cards

Major credit cards are accepted at hotels, restaurants, gas stations, shops and car-rental agencies. In fact, you'll find it hard to perform certain transactions such as renting a car or purchasing tickets to performances without one. Even if you loathe credit cards, they're a good idea for emergencies. Visa and MasterCard are the most widely accepted.

Places that accept Visa and MasterCard are also likely to accept debit cards. A debit card deducts payment directly from the user's checking account. Instead of an interest rate, users are charged a minimal transaction fee. Confirm with your bank that your debit card will be accepted in other states or countries.

Carry copies of your credit card numbers separately from the cards. If you lose your credit cards or they get stolen, contact the company immediately. Following are toll-free numbers for the main credit card companies. Contact your bank if you lose your ATM card.

American Express	☎ 800-528-4800
Diners Club	☎ 800-234-6377
Discover	☎ 800-347-2683
MasterCard	☎ 800-826-2181
Visa	☎ 800-336-8472

Security

Be cautious – but not paranoid – about carrying money. If your hotel or hostel has a safe, keep your valuables and excess cash in it. It's best not to display large amounts of cash in public. A money belt worn under your clothes is a good place to carry excess currency when you're on the move or otherwise unable to stash it in a safe. The back pocket of your pants is a prime target for pickpockets, as are handbags and the outside pockets of day packs and fanny packs (bum bags).

Costs

The cost of living in Boston is among the highest in the nation. With advance planning you can secure a hostel bed, but if that's not your bag, expect to spend at least $75 nightly (probably more like $125). There are plenty of places to spend more.

Food can be very reasonable. The occasional splurge at a first-rate restaurant will cost anywhere between $25 and $50 depending on where you are, but good restaurant meals can be found for $10 – or even half that for some lunch specials.

Getting around the city is cheap on the T, and although most excursions are within reach of public transportation, a car will save you time and energy.

Tipping

Tipping is expected in restaurants and better hotels, and by taxi drivers, hairdressers and baggage carriers. Tip 15% unless the service is terrible (in which case a complaint to the manager is warranted), or up to 20% if the service is great. In bars, the unspoken minimum is $1 for one or two beers; otherwise, it's 15%. For cabbies, the minimum on a $6 fare is $1; from there it's 10%. Hairdressers get 15% for satisfactory service. Baggage carriers (skycaps in airports, hotel attendants) get $1 per bag and 50¢ for each additional bag. Valet parking warrants $2, paid on receipt of your car.

Taxes

There is no national sales tax (such as VAT), but there are state and local taxes. In Boston, lodging sales tax is 12.45%, unless it's a three-room B&B, in which case it's nil. There is no sales tax on clothing, unless it's a pricey luxury item. Otherwise, restaurant meals, drinks, car rentals and most other purchases are taxed at 5%. The prices in this book do not include taxes.

POST & COMMUNICATIONS
Post

Boston's main post office (Map 6; ☎ 617-654-5326), 25 Dorchester Ave, is just one block southeast of South Station. It never closes. Mail can be sent to you here marked c/o General Delivery, Boston, MA 02205, USA.

Post offices are generally open from 8 am to 5 pm weekdays and 9 am to 3 pm on Saturday, but it all depends on the branch. Neighborhood branches are indicated on each map, but you can check the phone numbers in the 'Government Listings' section of the white pages.

Postal Rates Postage rates are fairly cheap and stable, increasing every few years. At press time, rates for 1st-class mail within the USA are 33¢ for letters up to 1oz (22¢ for each additional ounce) and 20¢ for postcards.

International airmail rates (except to Canada and Mexico) are 60¢ for a half-ounce letter, and 50¢ for a postcard. Letters to Canada are 46¢ for a half-ounce letter, and 40¢ for a postcard. Letters to Mexico are 40¢ for a half-ounce letter, and 35¢ for a postcard. Aerograms are 50¢.

The cost for parcels airmailed anywhere within the USA is $3.20 for 2lb or less, increasing by $1 per pound up to $6 for 5lb. For heavier items, check at the post office.

Telephone

Taken together, the Bell Atlantic Boston Area Yellow Pages and separate White Pages, which include Brookline, Cambridge and Somerville, are comprehensive telephone directories.

All phone numbers within the USA consist of a three-digit area code followed by a seven-digit local number. The area code for Boston proper is 617. In the Excursions chapter, listings have area codes of 508, 781 and 978. If you are calling locally, just dial the seven-digit number. If you are calling long distance, dial ☎ 1 + area code + seven-digit number.

Pay phones are usually 35¢; hotels often charge astronomical access charges. Toll-free

FACTS FOR THE VISITOR

phone numbers begin with 1-800 or 1-888. Numbers beginning with 900 usually incur high fees.

For local directory assistance, dial ☎ 411. For directory assistance outside your area code, dial 1 + three-digit area code of the place you want to call + 555-1212. For toll-free directory assistance, dial ☎ 1-800-555-1212. Dial ☎ 0 for the operator.

International Calls

If you're calling from abroad, the international country code for the USA is 1. To make a direct international call from Boston, dial ☎ 011 + country code + area code + number. You may need to wait as long as 45 seconds for the ringing to start. International rates depend on the time of day and the destination. Call the operator (☎ 0) for rates.

Phone Debit Cards

A long-distance alternative is phone debit cards, which allow purchasers to pay for calls in advance, with access through a toll-free 800 number. In amounts of $5, $10, $20 and $50, these are available from some supermarkets and convenience stores.

There's a wide range of local and international phonecards. Lonely Planet's eKno Communication Card (see the insert at the back of this book) is aimed specifically at independent travelers and provides budget international calls, a range of messaging services, free email and travel information – for local calls, you're usually better off with a local card. You can join online at www.ekno.lonelyplanet.com or by phone from Boston by dialing ☎ 800-707-0031. To use eKno from the US once you have joined, dial ☎ 800-706-1333.

Check the eKno website for joining and access numbers from other countries and updates on super budget local access numbers and new features.

Fax & Telegram

Fax machines are common and easy to find in the USA, at shipping companies such as Mail Boxes Etc, photocopy stores and hotel business service centers, but be prepared to pay high prices (over $1 a page). Telegrams

can be sent through Western Union (☎ 800-325-6000).

Email & Internet Access

Most hotels that cater to business travelers make Internet and email access easy. Or you may head to a public library to log on (but not receive email). For a worldwide list of cybercafés, browse www.traveltales.com or www.netcafeguide.com. Copy centers, such as Kinko's, often charge high hourly rates for computer usage. At press time, there was only one cybercafé left in Boston: Designs for Living (Map 10; ☎ 617-536-6150), 52 Queensberry St.

INTERNET RESOURCES

The World Wide Web is a rich resource for travelers. You can research your trip, find bargain airfares, book hotels, check weather conditions or chat with locals and other travelers about the best places to visit (or avoid!).

There's no better place to start your Web explorations than the Lonely Planet website (www.lonelyplanet.com). Here you'll find succinct summaries on traveling to most places on earth, postcards from other travelers and the Thorn Tree bulletin board, where you can ask questions before you go or dispense advice when you get back. You can also find travel news and updates to many of our most popular guidebooks, and the sub-WWWay section links you to the most useful travel resources elsewhere on the Web.

Websites are listed throughout this text. They are particularly useful in checking up-to-the-minute entertainment offerings.

BOOKS

Most books are published in different editions by different publishers in different countries. As a result, a book might be a hardcover rarity in one country while it's readily available in paperback in another. Fortunately, bookstores and libraries can search by title or author, so your local bookstore or library is the best place to find out about the availability of the following recommended titles.

Boston does not have a shortage of truly exceptional general- and special-interest bookstores. Whether looking for used or new titles, they'll do well by you. (See 'Bookstores' in the Shopping chapter.)

Guidebooks

Lonely Planet's *New England* covers the spectacular, diverse region that surrounds Boston. Susan Wilson's *Boston Sites & Insights* provides in-depth historical anecdotes on 50 major landmarks. Architecture buffs will appreciate the *AIA Guide to Boston*, by Susan and Michael Southworth, which criticizes and praises historic and modern buildings. *Blue Laws, Brahmins & Breakdown Lanes*, by Karen Cord Taylor, is an opinion-ated and insightful A–Z guide with 'dead-on observations' of life in this quirky, conservative city.

History & Politics

J Anthony Lukas's *On Common Ground: A Turbulent Decade in the Lives of Three American Families* is the definitive account of the 1970s turbulent busing trauma. Jack Beatty's *Rascal King: The Life and Times of James Michael Curley, 1874–1958* follows the trajectory of the state's most 'colorful' politician. Edwin O'Connor's *Last Hurrah*, a fictional novel about Curley, weaves fact and fiction in an entirely credible narrative.

The Pulitzer-prize winning *Paul Revere and the World He Lived In*, by Esther Forbes, focuses on precolonial, colonial and postcolonial Boston.

Furthering the architecture discussions are Jane Holtz Kay's *Lost Boston*, and *Cityscapes of Boston*, by Peter Vanderwarker and Robert Campbell. *Boston: A Topographical History*, by Walter Muir Whitehill, is a fascinating and lively history of Boston from the 1600s to the 1960s. Alex Krieger and David Cobb's *Mapping Boston* is a wonderful new book (1999) that chronicles Boston's development and history through maps, photos and essays.

Also see Literature in Facts about Boston.

NEWSPAPERS & MAGAZINES

Boston is one of the few remaining cities to have two major dailies: the highly regarded *Boston Globe* (www.boston.com), owned by the *New York Times*, and the plucky tabloid *Boston Herald* (www.bostonherald.com). The *Globe* publishes a useful Thursday 'Calendar' section and a daily feature 'Go!', while the *Herald* has a Friday 'Scene' section. *Boston Magazine* (www.bostonmagazine .com), the city's glossy monthly, has a humorous 'Thank God We're a Two Newspaper Town...' column.

The sassy, biweekly *Improper Bostonian* is available free from blue sidewalk dispenser boxes. The *Boston Phoenix* (www .bostonphoenix.com), the 'alternative' paper that focuses on arts and entertainment, is published weekly.

KIM GRANT

Boston Bricks' sampling of local newspapers

The venerable *Atlantic Monthly*, eclectic, esoteric and cerebral, is published in Boston.

TELEVISION
There are no television surprises in Boston. WGBH (channel 2), the public television affiliate, pays more attention to national and world affairs (it produces the award-winning *Nova* and *Frontline* programs) than it does to local programming. It's strong on children's programming, having reintroduced an updated version of *Zoom*.

PHOTOGRAPHY & VIDEO
For equipment and film purchases, head to Bromfield Camera (Map 4; ☎ 617-426-5230), 10 Bromfield St; SBI (Map 11; ☎ 617-576-0969), 57 JFK St, or Ferranti-Dege (Map 11; ☎ 617-499-2750), 1300 Mass Ave, both in Harvard Square; or Calumet (Map 12; ☎ 617-576-2600), 65 Bent St, in East Cambridge.

For quality same-day processing, Color Tek (Map 6; ☎ 617-345-9080), South Station Concourse, and (Map 8; ☎ 617-267-6503), 251 Newbury St, is the best choice.

Overseas visitors thinking about purchasing videos here need to know that the USA uses a standard not compatible with some other countries.

TIME
Boston is on Eastern Standard Time, five hours earlier than GMT/UTC, and three hours later than Pacific Standard Time. Daylight saving time is observed. Clocks are set ahead one hour on the first Sunday in April and back one hour on the last Sunday in October.

ELECTRICITY
In the USA, voltage is 110V and the plugs have two (flat) or three (two flat, one round) pins. Plugs with three pins don't fit into a two-hole socket, but adapters are easy to buy at hardware stores or drugstores.

WEIGHTS & MEASURES
Distances are in feet, yards and miles; weights are in ounces, pounds and tons. Gasoline is measured in US gallons, which are about 20% less than the imperial gallon.

There is a conversion chart on the inside back cover of this book.

LAUNDRY
There are self-service, coin-operated laundry facilities in most neighborhoods. Service is reasonable – about $1.50 to wash and $1 to dry. Look under 'Laundries – Self-Service' or 'Cleaners' in the yellow pages.

TOILETS
Public toilets are so difficult to find in Boston that a website sprang up to expose them: www.boston-online.com/restrooms.html. The humorous interactive site also rates their cleanliness. In 2000, the city will finally get about 16 automatic public toilets to be placed in high-traffic tourist areas.

HEALTH
For most foreign visitors, no immunizations are required for entry, though cholera and yellow fever vaccinations may be required

of travelers from areas with a history of those diseases. There are no unexpected health dangers, excellent medical attention is readily available and the only real health concern is that a collision with the medical system can cause severe injuries to your financial state.

Medical Attention

In a city world-renowned for health care, Massachusetts General Hospital (MGH; ☎ 617-726-2000) is one of the city's biggest and best. They can often refer you to smaller clinics and crisis hotlines. In real emergencies call ☎ 911 for an ambulance. But note that ER charges in the USA are incredibly expensive. It's a very good idea to have health insurance while traveling; many travel insurance policies include medical coverage. See Travel Insurance, earlier in this chapter.

CVS (☎ 617-876-55190), Porter Square shopping mall, Mass Ave, Cambridge, is the area's only 24-hour pharmacy.

WOMEN TRAVELERS

Although women often experience less harassment in Boston than in other major American cities, it's not a bad idea to travel with a little extra awareness of your surroundings.

Check the yellow pages under 'Women's Organizations & Services.' Women's bookstores, found in the yellow pages under 'Bookstores,' are good places to find out about gatherings, readings and meetings, and often have bulletin boards where you can find or place travel and short-term housing notices. See 'Bookstores' in the Shopping chapter.

If you are the victim of a crime, call the police (☎ 911). Boston's rape crisis hotline is ☎ 617-492-7273.

The National Organization for Women (NOW; ☎ 617-232-4764, www.now.org), 214 Harvard Ave, Brighton, is a good resource for any women-related information.

Planned Parenthood (☎ 617-616-1600, 616-1616 hotline, www.plannedparenthood .org), 1055 Comm Ave, offers medical advice and counseling.

GAY & LESBIAN TRAVELERS

Gay men are most visible in the South End, lesbians in the outlying neighborhood of Jamaica Plain. Although many companies doing business in Boston have adopted gay-friendly policies, Mayor Menino's administration has tried but been thwarted by the City Council and state. Nothing changes quickly in Boston, especially conservative religious attitudes. Incidents of gay-bashing are reported with consistency in the Fenway area, just south of the community gardens.

Some good numbers to know are the Fenway Community Health Center (Map 10; ☎ 617-267-0900), 7 Haviland St; AIDS Action Hotline (☎ 800-235-2331); and the Bisexual Resource Center (Map 9; ☎ 617-424-9595), 29 Stanhope St. Check the yellow pages under 'Social & Human Services' for extensive listings of community resources.

Glad Day Gay Liberation Bookshop (Map 8; ☎ 617-267-3010), 673 Boylston St, is the No 1 gay bookstore in Boston; see 'Bookstores' in the Shopping chapter. Pick up a copy of the weekly *Bay Windows* and monthly *Sojourner* here.

DISABLED TRAVELERS

Boston makes attempts to be wheelchair accessible (curb cuts, ramps on public buildings, special T van service), but it falls short for such a so-called world-class city. For resources, check out www.geocities.com/Paris/ 1502/index.htm.

A number of organizations specialize in the needs of disabled travelers:

Access-Able Travel Source
(☎ 303-232-2979, fax 239-8486, PO Box 1796, Wheat Ridge, CO 80034, www.access-able.com) Has an excellent website with many links.

Society for the Advancement of Travel for the Handicapped (SATH)
(☎ 212-447-7284, 347 Fifth Ave No 610, New York, NY 10016, sathtravel@aol.com)

Travelin' Talk
(☎ 931-552-6670, fax 552-1182, PO Box 3534, Clarksville, TN 37047, trvlntlk@aol.com) An international network of people providing assistance to disabled travelers.

Twin Peaks Press
(☎ 360-694-2462, 800-637-2256, PO Box 129, Vancouver, WA 98666) A quarterly newsletter; also publishes directories and access guides.

SENIOR TRAVELERS

Boston is a popular destination for the retired set. Though the age when the benefits begin varies, travelers from 50 years and up can expect to receive cut rates and benefits at hotels and museums.

Some national advocacy groups that can help in planning your travels include the following:

American Association of Retired Persons
AARP (☎ 800-424-3410, www.aarp.org) 601 E St NW, Washington, DC 20049, is an advocacy group for Americans 50 years and older and is a good resource for travel bargains. US residents can get one-year/three-year memberships for $8/20. Citizens of other countries can get same memberships for $10/24.

Elderhostel
This organization (☎ 877-426-8056), 75 Federal St, Boston, MA 02110-1941, is a nonprofit organization that offers seniors the opportunity to attend academic college courses throughout the USA and Canada. The programs last one to three weeks and include meals and accommodations, and are open to people 55 years and older and their companions.

Grand Circle Travel
This group (☎ 617-350-7500, 800-597-3644, www.gct.com), 347 Congress St, Boston, MA 02210, offers escorted tours and travel information in a variety of formats and distributes a free useful booklet, *Going Abroad: 101 Tips for Mature Travelers*.

BOSTON FOR CHILDREN

Boston is one giant living history museum, the setting for many educational and lively field trips. The Museum of Science on the Charles River in East Cambridge is serious hands-on fun and the Children's Museum at Fort Point Channel is first rate. Also on the waterfront, children enjoy the reenactment of dumping bales of tea into the harbor at the Tea Party Ship before heading over to the New England Aquarium. In the Public

Garden, the *Make Way for Ducklings* statues are a perennial hit with small ones; the swan boats are a bit slow for antsy kids raised on computer games. The Franklin Park Zoo is a prime afternoon's outing.

Simply getting around the city on the subway is the least expensive and possibly most adventurous thing to do in Boston.

Kidding Around Boston, by Helen Byers, and *Kids Explore Boston*, by Susan D Moffat, are both good. If you're unaccustomed to traveling with children, you might find some encouragement in Lonely Planet's *Travel with Children* (1995), by Maureen Wheeler.

CULTURAL CENTERS

The French Library (Map 8; ☎ 617-266-4351, www.frenchlib.org), 53 Marlborough St, founded in 1946, sponsors a Bastille Day celebration (July 14) and regular lectures on travel, cooking and all things French; receptions often follow. The library is open 10 am to 8 pm Tuesday through Thursday, until 5 pm on Friday and Saturday. See International Film in the Entertainment chapter.

The Goethe Institute (Map 8; ☎ 617-262-6050, www.goethe.de/uk/bos), 170 Beacon St, sponsors a cultural program of German events and evening classes, and has a well-stocked library. It's open 9 am to 5 or 5:30 pm weekdays.

DANGERS & ANNOYANCES

The crime rates in Boston have dropped in recent years, but that doesn't mean you should be lax with regard to pickpockets, muggers and carjackers. And while Boston doesn't have quite the same problem with scams, gangs, drugs, and prostitution that other US cities have, that doesn't mean you won't see it. This book does not cover areas frequented by gangs.

A few specifics, though: Avoid the Fenway after dark. The mayor and City Council have just about eradicated the last vestiges of the Combat Zone, one block in either direction from the Chinatown subway station along Washington and Essex Sts. It's the singular seedy area still in Boston proper. One or two

Colleges & Universities

Greater Boston has over 35 campuses, too many to mention here. This brief listing should help you get further information.

Harvard University (Map 11; ☎ 617-495-1000), founded in 1636, radiates along Mass Ave from Harvard Square. Free hourlong tours are given at 10 am and 2 pm weekdays (at 2 pm on Saturday) from the information office (☎ 617-495-1573, www.harvard.edu), Holyoke Center, 1350 Mass Ave. There are additional tours in summer.

The Massachusetts Institute of Technology (Map 12; MIT; ☎ 617-253-4795, www.mit.edu), a scientific mecca founded in 1861, is also spread along Mass Ave east of Central Square. There are free tours at 10 am and 2 pm weekdays from 77 Mass Ave, Building 7 lobby.

Northeastern University (Map 10; ☎ 617-373-2000, www.neu.edu), Huntington Ave, boasts one of the country's largest work-study cooperative programs.

Boston University (Map 10; BU; ☎ 617-353-2000, 353-2169, www.bu.edu), west of Kenmore Square, enrolls about 30,000 graduates and undergraduates, and has a huge campus and popular sports teams.

University of Massachusetts, Boston (UMass; ☎ 617-287-5000, www.umb.edu), Morrissey Blvd, is on Columbia Point, surrounded by Dorchester Bay on three sides.

Massachusetts College of Art (Map 10; ☎ 617-232-1555, www.massart.edu), Huntington Ave, hosts regular gallery exhibits at 621 Huntington Ave.

Other well-established universities in the outlying neighborhoods include:

Boston College (☎ 617-552-8000, www.bc.edu) is on Comm Ave (MA 30) in Chestnut Hill. The nation's largest Jesuit community boasts Gothic towers, a good art museum and excellent Irish and Catholic ephemera collections.

Wellesley College (☎ 781-282-1000, www.wellesley.edu), a Seven Sisters women's college in Wellesley, sports a lovely green campus and the excellent Davis Museum & Cultural Center. Take the MBTA Commuter Rail, plus a 10-minute walk, or drive MA 16 to MA 135.

Tufts University (☎ 617-628-5000, www.tufts.edu), in Medford, has about 8500 students and a good basketball team. From the Davis Square T station, board the No 94 or No 96 bus to campus.

KIM GRANT

One of Massachusetts College of Art's galleries

Brandeis University (☎ 781-736-2000, www.brandeis.edu), a heavily Jewish school on South St in Waltham, features the Rose Art Museum specializing in New England art. Take the MBTA Commuter Rail from North Station to the Brandeis/Roberts stop on the Fitchburg line.

X-rated businesses whose leases have not expired are still hanging on by a thread.

In general, always lock cars and put valuables out of sight. Be aware of your surroundings and who may be watching you. Avoid walking on dimly lit streets at night, particularly when alone. Walk purposefully. Use ATM machines in well-trafficked areas only. Lock valuables in your suitcase or in a hotel safe.

EMERGENCIES

Dial ☎ 911 for police, ambulances and fires; this is a free call from any phone. In Boston, call the Good Samaritans (☎ 617-247-0220) for suicide prevention; for the rape crisis center call ☎ 617-492-7273; and call ☎ 617-371-3030 for the Bay Cove Substance Abuse Center.

Traveler's Aid Society (Map 6; ☎ 617-542-7286, 737-2880), 17 East St (just off Atlantic Ave, across from South Station), is a non-profit agency that helps stranded travelers in despair. From stolen wallets to practical information to transportation assistance to 'bedless in Boston,' Traveler's Aid is there to help from 9 am to 5 pm weekends. The Logan Airport 'Terminal E' Traveler's Aid (☎ 617-567-5385) is staffed noon to 9 pm daily.

LEGAL MATTERS

If you are stopped by the police, bear in mind that there is no system of paying fines on the spot. For traffic offenses, the police officer will explain your options to you.

If you are arrested for more serious offenses, you are allowed to remain silent. There is no legal reason to speak to a police officer if you don't wish, but never walk away from an officer until given permission. All persons who are arrested are legally allowed (and given) the right to make one phone call. If you don't have a lawyer or family member to help you, call your embassy. The police will give you the number upon request.

The drinking age is 21 and you need photo ID to prove your age. You could incur stiff fines, jail time and penalties if caught driving under the influence of alcohol.

Drinking outdoors, in public, is illegal. During festive holidays and special events, road blocks are sometimes set up to deter drunk drivers.

BUSINESS HOURS & PUBLIC HOLIDAYS

Businesses generally are open 9 am to 5 pm weekdays. Most shops stay open longer and through the weekends, and many big supermarkets are open 24 hours. Banks are generally open 8 am to 4 pm weekdays; some are open for a few hours on Saturday morning.

National public holidays are celebrated throughout the USA. Banks, schools and government offices (including post offices) are closed and transportation and other services are on a Sunday schedule. Holidays falling on a weekend are usually observed the following Monday.

New Year's Day January 1
Martin Luther King Jr's Birthday January – 3rd Monday
Presidents' Day February – 3rd Monday
Memorial Day May – last Monday
Independence Day July 4
Labor Day September – 1st Monday
Columbus Day October – 2nd Monday
Veterans Day November 11
Thanksgiving Day November – 4th Thursday
Christmas Day December 25

SPECIAL EVENTS

These are just the highlights, a few events and festivals it may be worth planning your trip around. Call the GBCVB (☎ 617-536-4100, 800-888-5515, www.bostonusa.com) for details on the following:

January & February
 Chinese New Year Late January or early February. The first day is celebrated with a colorful parade, firecrackers, fireworks and lots of food.

March
 St Patrick's Day the 17th. Ireland's patron saint is honored by all those who feel the Irish in their blood and by those who want to feel Irish beer in their blood. Everyone wears green (or you might get pinched). The large and vocal South Boston Irish community hosts a parade on West

Harvard and the Head of the Charles Regatta

Broadway St, but since the mid-1990s, it's been marred by the decision to exclude gay and lesbian Irish groups from marching. Officially, the day off is for celebrating Evacuation Day, the day the British pulled out of Boston Harbor in 1775.

April
Patriots' Day 3rd Monday. Paul Revere's historic ride from the North End to Lexington and battles in Concord and Lexington are reenacted. See Shot Heard 'Round the World in Facts about Boston.

Boston Marathon 3rd Monday. Later in the morning, thousands of runners compete in a 26.2-mile run (www.bostonmarathon.org) that has been an annual event for more than a century. The race finishes on Boylston St in front of the Boston Public Library.

May
Lilac Sunday 3rd Sunday. Arnold Arboretum celebrates the arrival of spring, when more than 400 varieties of fragrant lilacs are in bloom. It is the only day of the year that visitors can picnic on the grass at the venerable arboretum.

Magnolia trees Mother Nature decides the date. Trees bloom all along Newbury St and Comm Ave.

June
Bunker Hill Day The 17th. A parade and battle reenactment at Charlestown's Bunker Hill Monument.

Gay Pride Mid-month. Tens of thousands of participants and spectators line the parade route, which culminates in a big party on Boston Common.

July
Independence Day The 4th. The Boston Pops give a free evening performance of Tchaikovsky's *1812 Overture*, complete with brass cannon and synchronized fireworks for a half million people. It's broadcast nationally.

Harborfest 2nd week. During this weeklong maritime celebration, you can sample dozens of chowders at the Chowderfest on City Hall Plaza.

July & August
Italian festivals Weekends throughout the summer. North End patron saints are honored with food and music.

September
Boston Film Festival Two weeks mid-month. Indies are screened at venues citywide.

October
Head of the Charles Regatta 3rd weekend. The

KIM GRANT

Gay Pride brings thousands out to the streets.

world's largest rowing event (www.boston.com/head_of_the_charles) draws more than 3000 collegiate rowers, while cheering fans line the banks of the river, lounging on blankets and drinking beer (technically illegal).

Halloween The 31st. Kids and adults dress in costumes.

December
Boston Ballet Late November to early January. The *Nutcracker* at the Wang Center is staged until early January

Tree lighting 1st week. Boston Common trees and the Prudential Center Christmas tree are lit and remain lit throughout December.

Boston Tea Party reenactment Sunday prior to the 16th. Costumed actors march from Old South Meeting House to the waterfront and dump bales of tea into the harbor.

First Night The 31st. New Year's celebrations begin early and continue past midnight, culminating in fireworks over the harbor. Purchase a special button that permits entrance into events citywide.

WORK
The easiest work to get is for high-tech know-it-alls. If you're not a US citizen, you need to apply for a work visa from the US embassy in your home country before you leave. If you are caught working illegally, you'll be deported and barred from the US for at least five years.

The type of visa varies depending on how long you're staying and the work you plan to do. It can be difficult to get proper documentation unless you already have a job offer from an employer who considers your qualifications to be unique and not readily available in the US. See Visa Extensions & Reentry in the Documents section for warnings on longer stays.

Getting There & Away

AIR

Boston has one major airport and two minor ones within an hour's drive. Depending on where you are coming from, it may be cheaper (but certainly less convenient) to fly into New York City and take the train or bus to Boston. It's about four hours on the ground from New York to Boston.

Airports

Logan International Airport On MA 1A in East Boston, Logan (☎ 800-235-6426, www.massport.com) is served by most major national and international carriers. Its five separate terminals are connected by a frequent shuttle bus (No 11).

The nonprofit Traveler's Aid Society (☎ 617-567-5385), an agency that assists travelers in need, maintains a booth at Terminal E, where all international flights arrive and depart; the booth is usually open noon to 9 pm daily.

Manchester Airport A quiet alternative to Logan, the Manchester Airport (☎ 603-624-6556, www.flymanchester.com) is just 55 miles north of Boston in New Hampshire. Larger carriers such as Continental, Northwest, Southwest, United and US Airways fly here.

TF Green Airport Just outside Providence, Rhode Island, in Warwick, TF Green (☎ 401-737-8222, www.pvd-ri.com) is also serviced by all major carriers except TWA. Southwest Airlines, in particular, offers very competitively priced tickets. The airport is about 45 minutes (and 45 miles) south of Boston.

Major Airlines

The following airlines serve the Boston area.

US-Based Airlines
Air Tran ☎ 800-247-8726

America West ☎ 800-235-9292

American Airlines ☎ 800-433-7300
Website: www.americanair.com

Continental Airlines ☎ 800-525-0280
Website: www.continental.com

Delta Air Lines ☎ 800-241-4141
Website: www.delta-air.com

Frontier ☎ 800-432-1359

Midway Airlines ☎ 800-446-4392

Midwest Express ☎ 800-452-2022

Northwest Airlines ☎ 800-447-4747
Website: www.nwa.com

Southwest Airlines ☎ 800-435-9792
Website: www.iflyswa.com

TWA ☎ 800-892-4141

United Airlines ☎ 800-538-2929
Website: www.ual.com

US Airways ☎ 800-428-4322
Website: www.usairways.com

Virgin Atlantic ☎ 800-862-8621
Website: www.virgin.com

International Airlines
Aer Lingus ☎ 800-223-6537

Air Canada ☎ 800-776-3000

Air France ☎ 800-237-2747

Air New Zealand ☎ 800-262-1234
Alitalia ☎ 800-223-5730
British Airways ☎ 800-247-9297
Canadian Airlines ☎ 800-426-7000
Iceland Air ☎ 800-223-5500
KLM ☎ 800-374-7747
Korean Air ☎ 800-438-5000
Lufthansa ☎ 800-645-3880
Olympic Airways ☎ 800-223-1226
Qantas Airways ☎ 800-227-4500
Sabina ☎ 800-955-2000
Swissair ☎ 800-221-4750
TAP, Air Portugal ☎ 800-221-7370

Buying Tickets

The plane ticket will probably be the single most expensive item in your budget. It is always worth putting aside a few hours to research. Start shopping for a ticket early – some of the cheapest tickets must be bought months in advance, and some popular flights sell out early. If you're buying tickets within the US, check the weekly travel sections of newspapers like the *New York Times*, *Los Angeles Times*, *Chicago Tribune* and *San Francisco Examiner*. Council Travel (☎ 800-226-8624, cts@ciee.org) and STA (☎ 800-777-0112) have offices in major cities nationwide.

For those coming from outside the US, peruse travel sections of *Time Out* and *TNT* in the UK, or the Saturday edition of newspapers like the *Sydney Morning Herald* and the *Age* in Australia.

Note that high season in Boston is mid-April to mid-October (summer) and the week before and after Christmas.

Cheap tickets are available in two distinct categories: official and unofficial. Official ones have a variety of names including advance-purchase fares, budget fares, Apex and super-Apex. Unofficial tickets are simply discount tickets that the airlines release through selected travel agents (not through airline offices). The cheapest tickets are often nonrefundable and require an extra fee for changing your flight. Many insurance policies will cover this loss if you have to change your flight for emergency reasons.

Use the fares quoted in this book as a guide only. Quoted airfares do not necessarily constitute a recommendation for the carrier.

If traveling from the UK, you will probably find that the cheapest flights are advertised by obscure bucket shops. Many are honest and solvent, but there are a few rogues who will take your money and disappear. If you feel suspicious about a firm, don't give them all the money at once – leave a deposit of 20% or so and pay the balance on receiving the ticket. If they insist on cash in advance, go elsewhere. And once you have the ticket, call the airline to confirm that you are booked on the flight.

Instead of going to the airport, head to the Boston Airline Center (Map 4; no phone), 155 Federal St, Monday to Friday to pick up tickets for major carriers.

Regardless of how you buy your ticket, once you have it, write down its number, together with the flight number and other details, and keep the information somewhere separate. If the ticket is lost or stolen, this will help you get a replacement.

Buy travel insurance early (see Travel Insurance in Facts for the Visitor).

You can also take advantage of online reservations services that search multiple airlines for a good fare:

Atevo Travel
www.atevo.com
Biztravel.com, Inc
www.biztravel.com
CNN Interactive's Travel Guide
www.cnn.com/TRAVEL
Excite Travel by City.Net
excite.com/travel
Internet Travel Network
www.itn.net
Microsoft Expedia
www.expedia.com
Preview.Travel
www.previewtravel.com
Travelocity
www.travelocity.com

Visit USA Passes Almost all domestic carriers offer Visit USA passes to non-US

Air Travel Glossary

Baggage Allowance This will be written on your ticket and usually includes one 20kg (40lb) checked item, plus two carry-ons.

Bucket Shops These are unbonded travel agencies specializing in discount airline tickets.

Cancellation Penalties If you have to cancel or change a ticket, there are often heavy penalties involved; insurance can sometimes be taken out against these penalties.

Check-In Airlines ask you to check in a certain time ahead of the flight departure (usually one to two hours). If you fail to check in on time and the flight is overbooked, the airline can cancel your booking and give your seat to somebody else.

Confirmation Having a ticket doesn't mean you have a seat until the agent has checked with the airline that your status is 'OK' or confirmed. Meanwhile, you could just be 'on request.'

Courier Fares Businesses often need to send urgent documents or freight securely and quickly. Courier companies hire people to accompany the package through customs and, in return, offer a discount ticket that is sometimes a phenomenal bargain. This is legitimate, but there are two short-comings – the short turnaround time of the ticket (usually not longer than a month) and the limitation on your luggage allowance. You may have to surrender all your allowance and take only carry-on luggage.

Lost Tickets If you lose your airline ticket, an airline will usually treat it like a traveler's check and, after inquiries, issue you another one. Legally, however, an airline is entitled to treat it like cash; and if you lose it, then it's gone forever.

No-Shows No-shows are passengers who fail to show up for their flight. Full-fare passengers who fail to turn up are sometimes entitled to travel on a later flight. The rest are penalized.

citizens. The passes are actually a book of coupons – each coupon equals a flight. Typically, the minimum number of coupons is three or four and the maximum is eight or ten, and they must be purchased in conjunction with an international airline ticket anywhere outside the USA except Canada and Mexico. Coupons cost anywhere from $100 to $160, depending on how many you buy. Most airlines require that you plan your itinerary in advance and complete your flights within 60 days of arrival, but rules can vary between individual airlines. A few airlines may allow you to use coupons on standby, in which case call the airline a day or two before the flight and make a 'standby reservation.' Such a reservation gives you priority over all other travelers who just appear and hope to get on the flight the same day.

Round-the-World Tickets These have become very popular in the last few years. Airline RTW tickets are often real bargains and can work out to be no more expensive or even cheaper than an ordinary return ticket. The official airline RTW tickets are usually put together by a combination of two airlines, and they permit you to fly anywhere you want on their route systems as long as you do not backtrack. Read the small print; other restrictions and time limits often apply. Your best bet is to find a travel agent that advertises or specializes in round-the-world tickets.

Within the USA
Getting a flight into Boston should present no problems. To secure the cheapest fare, purchase tickets 14 to 21 days in advance. Ask about 'companion fares,' letting two people travel for the price of one. Given the competitive nature of the airline industry, generally when one carrier offers a deal, others quickly follow suit.

Roundtrip fares from the West Coast can often be found for $400, but don't be surprised if it's $500 during the summer. Flights from Miami average about $300; with a bit

Air Travel Glossary

Onward Tickets An entry requirement for many countries is that you have a ticket out of the country. If you're unsure of your next move, the easiest solution is to buy the cheapest onward ticket to a neighboring country or a ticket from a reliable airline that can later be refunded if you do not use it.

Open Jaw Tickets These are return tickets on which you fly out to one place but return from another. If available, these can save you backtracking to your arrival point.

Overbooking Airlines hate to fly with empty seats, and since every flight has some passengers who fail to show up, airlines often book more passengers than they have seats. Usually excess passengers make up for the no-shows, but occasionally passengers (usually those who check in late) get bumped.

Point-to-Point Tickets These are discount tickets that can be bought on some routes in return for passengers waiving their rights to a stopover.

Reconfirmation At least 72 hours prior to departure time of an onward or return flight, you must contact the airline and 'reconfirm' that you intend to be on the flight. If you don't do this, the airline can delete your name from the passenger list and you could lose your seat.

Restrictions Discount tickets often have various restrictions on them – such as advance payment, minimum and maximum periods you must be away (for example, a minimum of two weeks or a maximum of one year) and penalties for changing the tickets.

Travel Periods Ticket prices vary with the time of year. There is a low (off-peak) season and a high (peak) season, and often a shoulder season as well. Usually the fare depends on your outward flight – if you depart in the high season and return in the low season, you pay the high-season fare.

of flexibility, you'll find fares from Chicago for about $250, a bit more from Denver.

The DC-to-Boston and New York-to-Boston corridor, frequented by business travelers, is often overpriced at $250. It might behoove you to fly from Baltimore to Providence on Southwest for $160 roundtrip and take a bus.

Canada

Travel CUTS (☎ 416-966-2887 in Toronto) has offices in all major cities. The *Toronto Globe & Mail* and *Vancouver Sun* carry travel agents' ads. From Vancouver, expect to spend about CA$625 to CA$725; from Toronto, it's more like CA$300. Canadian Air (www.cdnair.ca) and Air Canada (www.aircanada.ca) have great last-minute Web deals.

UK & Ireland

Check the ads in magazines like *Time Out*, plus the *Evening Standard* and *TNT*. Also check the free magazines widely available in London – start by looking outside the main railway stations.

Most British travel agents are registered with the ABTA (Association of British Travel Agents). If you have paid for your flight to an ABTA-registered agent who then goes out of business, ABTA will guarantee a refund or an alternative.

London is arguably the world's headquarters for bucket shops, which are well advertised and can usually beat published airline fares. Good, reliable agents for cheap tickets in the UK are Trailfinders (☎ 020-7937-5400), 194 Kensington High St, London, W8 7RG; Council Travel (☎ 020-7437-7767), 28a Poland St, London, W1, and STA Travel (☎ 020-7581-4132), 86 Old Brompton Rd, London SW7 3LQ. The Globetrotters Club, BCM Roving, London WC1N 3XX, publishes a newsletter, *Globe*, that covers obscure destinations and can help you find traveling companions. In winter, you can probably find flights for $300 roundtrip, but during the summer it may be as much as $700.

GETTING THERE & AWAY

Continental Europe

In Amsterdam, NBBS is a popular travel agent. In Germany, try STA (☎ 4969-43-01-91), Bergerstrasse 118, 60316 Frankfurt 1. Council Travel (☎ 01 44 41 89 80) is at 1 Place de l'Odeon, 75006 Paris. For great student fares, contact USIT Voyages (☎ 01 42 34 56 90), at 6 rue de Vaugirard, 75006 Paris.

Other Council Travel offices include (☎ 211-36-30-30), Graf Adolph Strasse 18, 40212 Düsseldorf and (☎ 089-39-50-22), Adalbertstrasse 32, 80799 Münich 40.

Australia & New Zealand

STA Travel has offices in the major cities of Australia and New Zealand. They sell tickets to everyone but have special deals for students and travelers under 30. Head offices are STA Travel (☎ 1300-360-960, 9347-6911), 224 Faraday St, PO Box 75, Carlton South, Melbourne, VIC 3053, Australia, and (☎ 0800-100-677, 309-0458), 10 High St, Auckland, New Zealand. Both in New Zealand and in Australia, STA Travel and Flight Centres International are major dealers in cheap airfares; check local travel agents' ads in the yellow pages and call around. Qantas Airways flies to Los Angeles from Sydney, Melbourne (via Sydney or Auckland) and Cairns. United flies to San Francisco from Sydney and Melbourne (via Sydney) and also flies to Los Angeles.

The cheapest tickets will have a 21-day advance-purchase requirement, a minimum stay of seven days and a maximum stay of 60 days. Flying with Air New Zealand is slightly cheaper, and both Qantas and Air New Zealand offer tickets with longer stays or stopovers, but you pay more.

On Air New Zealand, from Auckland to Los Angeles, you'll spend NZ$2150 (US$1125) in high season, but it'll cost an additional US$400 or so to fly from Los Angeles to Boston. It's only about US$100 less expensive in low season. From Sydney to Boston on Qantas it costs about A$2350 (US$1550) in low season, about A$400 (US$250) more in high season.

Asia

Bangkok and Singapore are the discount ticket capitals of the region, but their bucket shops can be unreliable. Ask advice of other travelers before buying a ticket. STA Travel, which is dependable, has branches in Hong Kong, Tokyo, Singapore, Bangkok and Kuala Lumpur. Many flights to the West Coast go via Honolulu, Hawaii. Others, to the East Coast, go through Anchorage, Alaska.

Japan Air Lines, United and Northwest have daily flights from Tokyo to the West Coast, from where you can continue to Boston.

Central & South America

Most flights from Central and South America go via Miami, Houston or Los Angeles, though some fly via New York. Most countries' international flag carriers (some of them, such as Aerolíneas Argentinas and LANChile), as well as US airlines, including United and American, serve these destinations, with onward connections. Continental has flights from about 20 cities in Mexico and Central America, most of which arrive at Dallas-Fort Worth airport.

BUS

Boston has a streamlined bus station (no phone), at 700 Atlantic Ave at Summer St, adjacent to the South Station train station and above the Red Line.

Regional Transit

Bonanza Bus Lines (☎ 617-720-4110, 800-556-3815, www.bonanzabus.com) provides service between Boston and Cape Cod, Providence, Hartford, Albany and New York City. Plymouth & Brockton (☎ 508-746-0378, 778-9767, www.p-b.com) provides frequent service to most towns on Cape Cod, including Hyannis and Provincetown. Also see To/From the Airport in the Getting Around chapter.

Greyhound

Greyhound (☎ 617-526-1800, 800-231-2222 for reservations, www.greyhound.com), the only nationwide bus company, has reduced local services, but still runs cross-country. Buses depart for New York City throughout the day. Express buses take about 4¹/₂ hours and cost $34 one way, $60 roundtrip (children are half-price). Very long-distance bus trips are often available at bargain prices by purchasing or reserving tickets three days in advance.

TRAIN
Amtrak
Amtrak (☎ 617-482-3660, 800-872-7245, www.amtrak.com), the national railway system that connects cities all over the continental US and Canada, stops at South Station and at Back Bay Station on Dartmouth St (on the Orange Line).

Express service (four hours) to New York City costs $45 to $66 one way, depending on the day and time. Service to Manhattan on a new 'Acela' high-speed train (under three hours) should be running by the time you read this.

Rail travel is generally cheaper by purchasing special fares in advance. Roundtrips are the best bargain, but even these can be as expensive as airfares. The best value overall is their Explore America fare, enabling you to travel anywhere within 45 days, with up to three stopovers. Additional stopovers can be arranged at extra cost. Your entire trip must be reserved in advance and seats are limited, so book as far ahead as possible.

For non-US citizens, Amtrak offers a variety of USA Rail Passes that must be purchased outside the US (check with a travel agent). Prices vary from high to low season and sleeping accommodations cost extra. Advanced booking is recommended.

Commuter Rail
North Station (Map 3; ☎ 617-222-3200, 800-392-6100, www.mbta.com), 150 Causeway St, is accessible via eponymous Green and Orange Line T stations. This is the departure station for excursions to Salem, Gloucester and Rockport on the Rockport line, and for Concord on the Fitchburg line.

Take the Red Line to South Station (Map 6; ☎ same as North Station, above), on Atlantic Ave at Summer St, for excursions to Plymouth, Providence and Wellesley (on the Worcester line). Amtrak trains also depart from South Station. See Excursions for information on getting to other nearby areas.

CAR & MOTORCYCLE
From western Massachusetts, the Massachusetts Turnpike ('Mass Pike,' or I-90, a toll road) takes you right into downtown. After paying a toll in Newton, drive east 10 more minutes on the pike and pay another 50¢; then the fun begins.

There are three exits for the Boston area: Cambridge, Copley Square (Prudential Center) and Kneeland St (Chinatown). Then the turnpike ends abruptly. At that point, you can head north or south of the city on the I-93 Expressway (the Central Artery; see Getting Around) or directly past South Station, into downtown.

From New York and other southerly points, take I-95 north to MA 128 to I-93 north, which cuts through the heart of the city. From northerly points, take I-93 south across the Tobin Bridge, which merges into the Central Artery.

Approaching the city from the south, you'll feel the Central Artery construction's greatest impact.

HITCHHIKING
Hitchhiking is never entirely safe, and we don't recommend it. Travelers who decide to hitch should understand that they are taking a small but potentially serious risk. People who do choose to hitch will be safer if they travel in pairs and let someone know where they are planning to go.

In Massachusetts, hitchhiking is illegal on state highways and the Mass Pike, including rest stops and anywhere on or near exit ramps.

ng Around

KIM GRANT

The T turns into a pumpkin at 12:30 am (pending legislation).

Boston is a small city and your feet will often prove faster than the subway, especially if you have to change subway lines. If you're thinking about driving around the city, think some more; in fact, keep thinking until you change your mind.

TO/FROM THE AIRPORT
Logan International Airport
Downtown Boston is just a few miles from Logan International Airport, and is accessible by subway (the T), bus, water shuttle, van shuttle, limo, rental car and taxi.

Subway (The T) The T, or the MBTA subway (☎ 617-222-3200, 800-392-6100, www.mbta.com), is the fastest and cheapest way to reach the city from the airport. From any terminal, take a free, well-marked shuttle bus (No 22 from Terminal A and B, or No 33 from Terminal C, D and E) to the Airport T station on the Blue Line, purchase an 85¢

token and you'll be downtown within 30 minutes. The subway operates from about 5:30 am to about 12:30 am daily.

Bus There is a direct bus (☎ 617-439-3131, 800-235-6426) between Logan and the South Station Transportation Center, bay No 25. Participating carriers include Bonanza, Concord Trailways and Plymouth & Brockton. Buses depart from the lower level of all Logan terminals from 7:45 am to 10:15 pm. From South Station, buses operate from 5:55 am to 9:15 pm. Buy tickets onboard at Logan or at the South Station counter. Buses depart every 15 to 30 minutes and cost $6 adults, free for children under 12.

Water & Van Shuttle Accessible via free shuttle buses from each terminal, the Airport Water Shuttle (☎ 617-439-3131, 800-235-6426) whisks passengers to Rowes Wharf (Map 6), Atlantic Ave, in seven minutes.

Once downtown, though, you'll probably still have to take the subway. (The closest T station to Rowes Wharf is Aquarium on the Blue Line, a five-minute walk.) However, the water shuttle across Boston Harbor provides a great view of Boston's skyline.

Purchase tickets onboard; one way is $10 adults, $5 seniors, free for children under 12. (Roundtrip is $17 adults.) The shuttle runs every 15 minutes from 6 am to 8 pm weekdays; every 30 minutes from 8 pm to 11 pm on Friday; every 30 minutes from 10 am to 11 pm on Saturday; and from 10 am to 8 pm on Sunday. There are no boats on Thanksgiving, Christmas, New Year's Day or July 4th. Buy tickets onboard. Also see 'Boston by Boat.'

Check with your individual hotel for specific airport van shuttles that come to your hostelry. Rates range from $6 to $10.

Car & Taxi If you are driving downtown from the airport, the Sumner Tunnel ($2 toll) will dump you into the North End and Government Center, where there are immediate on-ramps for the I-93 Expressway (the Central Artery) north and south. When you're going from Boston to the airport, take the Callahan Tunnel (no toll). The new Ted Williams Tunnel ($2 outbound toll), a mile south of the city off I-93, is open to buses, taxis and limos every day, but to noncommercial vehicles (that's you) only on weekends.

Plentiful but pricey, taxis line up at every terminal on demand; traffic snarls can translate into a $20 fare (plus tip) to downtown.

Manchester Airport

Vermont Transit (☎ 800-231-2222) offers three buses daily (12:20 pm, 2:35 pm and 6:35 pm) from the airport to Boston's South Station. Fares are $14 adults, $7 children; doubled for a return trip.

Flightline Airport Express (☎ 800-245-2525), a reservation-only company that requires 24-hour notice, has service into Boston for $85 for one or two people, $97 for three. Depending on how much you save on your airline ticket by flying into Manchester, this option may still make sense.

TF Green Airport

Bonanza Bus Lines (☎ 888-751-8800) departs from this Rhode Island airport for Boston's South Station hourly from 9 am to 9 pm, with one early bus at 7:50 am and a late one at 10:30 pm; tickets are $16 adults, $8 children age 2 to 11.

In order to catch an Amtrak train from Providence to Boston, you have to take a bus from the airport to Providence. So it makes much more sense just to take the direct Bonanza bus to Boston.

SUBWAY (THE T)

The MBTA (Map 15; ☎ 617-222-3200) operates the USA's oldest subway, built in 1897, known locally as 'the T.' There are four color-coded lines – Red, Blue, Green and Orange – that radiate from the principal downtown stations. These central stations are Park St, which has an information booth, Downtown Crossing, Government Center and State. When traveling away from any of these stations, you are heading outbound.

The T operates from about 5:30 am to 12:30 am. But in response to a legislative request, a pilot program was introduced in early 2000 to extend T service on Friday and Saturday nights to about 2:30 am. This 'radical' idea may or may not be retained.

On the Green Line, the 'B' line heads along Commonwealth Ave (Comm Ave) through

T Visitor Passes

Visitor passes for unlimited travel are available for one week ($18), three days ($9) and one day ($5). Purchase passes at the Boston Common Visitors Information Center and the following T stations: Park St, Government Center, Back Bay, Alewife, North Station, South Station, Hynes and Airport. Bostix (Faneuil Hall Marketplace and Copley Square) also sells passes.

For longer stays, monthly unlimited-travel passes are available from the first of the month to the 15th; subway-only passes are $27.

GETTING AROUND

Boston University on its way to the Boston College terminus. The 'C' line follows Beacon St and ends at Cleveland Circle after passing through Coolidge Corner in Brookline. The 'D' line skirts Fenway and the Riverway for a stretch before stopping at Brookline Village and ending at Riverside. On Huntington Ave, the 'E' train is useful for Northeastern University and the Museum of Fine Arts.

Purchase tokens at all stations (85¢ adults, 40¢ children) except those west of Symphony ('E' branch) and Kenmore ('B,' 'C' and 'D' branches) on the Green Line, which are aboveground stops. No additional fare is collected when heading outbound from an aboveground Green Line station. When you head inbound, though, you must have exact change to board these trains. Some fares heading inbound are higher than 85¢.

If you are exiting the Red Line at Braintree, you must deposit an additional token. When boarding at the Braintree station, the fare is $1.70.

BUS

The MBTA also operates bus routes within the city, but these can be difficult to figure out for short-term visitors. Besides, the subway goes to 95% of the places you'll want to go. Most bus fare is 60¢.

CAR & MOTORCYCLE

A car is the last thing you want or need in Boston. But, for convenience and to save time, you may want to rent one for a Cape Cod or Cape Ann excursion.

Driving

Not only are streets a maze of confusion, choked with construction and legendary traffic jams, but Boston drivers have their own rules. (For instance, at a yellow traffic light they hit the accelerator rather than the brakes. When attempting to merge into another lane, they don't make eye contact with the driver in the other lane.) Yes, driving is often considered a sport – in a town that takes its sports very seriously.

Parking

Since on-street parking is limited, you could end up paying as much as $25 (for three to eight hours) to park in a lot. Rates average $8 for the first hour.

There are a few tricks to avoiding hefty parking fees. The First Federal Parking

Boston by Boat

As the harbor has become cleaner and more integral to Boston's renewed sense of self, the number of boats has proliferated. In fact, if you let your imagination roam a bit, the harbor might feel like the Grand Canal in Venice.

MBTA Water Shuttle This boat (☎ 617-222-3200) plies the waters between Lovejoy Wharf (Map 5), Charlestown Navy Yard (Map 5) and Long Wharf (Map 6). Another route circulates between Lovejoy Wharf, the federal courthouse (Map 6) and the World Trade Center (Map 6). Boats run year-round and one-way tickets cost $1; buy tickets onboard.

To/From Charlestown Boston Harbor Cruises (Map 6; ☎ 617-227-4320, www.bostonharbor-cruises.com), 1 Long Wharf, operates year-round boats to the USS *Constitution* in Charlestown for $1. For more information on Boston Harbor Cruises, see Activities in Things to See & Do.

City Water Taxi This service (☎ 617-422-0392) makes on-demand taxi stops at about 15 waterfront points. Since it costs $10 no matter where you're going, it really makes sense only for the airport. Having said that, though, more useful stops (due to their proximity to lodging places) include Lovejoy Wharf, Charlestown Navy Yard, Sargents Wharf and the southern end of Christopher Columbus Park (all on Map 5). Service operates between April and October.

garage on Devonshire and Federal Sts has low rates of $9 daily, thanks to a city lease. At the garage on Congress St across from the Haymarket T stop, customers of participating North End establishments get a great break. Some lots have 'early bird' specials if you arrive by 8 am or so.

Cheap lots include the following:

Dock Square Parking near Faneuil Hall
in by 9 am, out by 7 pm
Government Center Garage Congress St
in by 10 am, out by 7 pm
Harbor Garage near the New England Aquarium
in by 9 am, out by 7 pm
North Station/Fleet Center Garage Causeway St
out by 6 pm

The Radisson Hotel garage and 75 State St garage have the cheapest evening weekday rates (about $6). For all-day Sunday parking, head to the Downtown Crossing garage, Franklin St; on Saturday, to the Bedford St garage, one block from Lafayette Place; First Federal Parking garage, Devonshire and Federal Sts, on either day. Lastly, check Fan Pier lots, across Fort Point Channel, for day rates of $6 or so.

If you need a space, any space, the parking lot beneath Boston Common (access via Charles St South) is rarely full. Other than that, look for the blue 'P' sign around town and cross your fingers.

The best time to keep an eye out for an on-street meter is 8 or 9 am. But be sure to have lots of quarters on hand. Tickets for parking violations begin at $25.

Expressways

Two highways skirt the Charles River: Storrow Drive runs along the Boston side and Memorial Drive (more scenic) parallels Storrow on the Cambridge side of the Charles. There are exits off Storrow Drive for Kenmore Square, Back Bay and Government Center.

Both Storrow Drive and Memorial Drive are accessible from the Mass Pike and the I-93 Expressway. A turnpike extension that connects the Ted Williams Tunnel to the airport is expected to open mid-2002.

KIM GRANT

Boston: a city resigned to its lawless drivers

Rental

To rent a car, you must have a valid driver's license, be at least 25 years of age and present a major credit card such as MasterCard or Visa.

Many rental agencies have bargain rates for weekend or weeklong rentals with unlimited mileage, often in conjunction with airline tickets. You'll find the cheapest rates with advance bookings. Rates fluctuate from $175 to $275 weekly for a compact car, not including a 5% sales tax, a $10 convention center surcharge and a $10 airport surcharge, all of which means that Boston has the nation's highest one-day rental fees.

Basic liability coverage is required by law and is included in the rental cost. Collision insurance (about $15 daily), also called the Liability Damage Waiver, is optional; it covers the full value of the vehicle in case of an accident. Some credit cards cover collision insurance if you charge the rental to your card. Seat belts are mandatory for the driver and all passengers in Massachusetts.

All major rental-car agencies are represented at the airport; free shuttle vans take you to their nearby pick-up counters. Rental car companies with offices downtown include:

Avis (Map 3; ☎ 617-534-1420, 800-331-1212)
3 Center Plaza at Government Center

Budget (Map 7; ☎ 617-497-1800, 800-527-0700)
24 Park Plaza

Enterprise (Map 8; ☎ 617-262-9215, 800-736-8222)
Prudential Center, 800 Boylston St, ground floor

Hertz (Map 7; ☎ 617-338-1500, 800-654-3131)
24 Park Plaza

National (Map 13; ☎ 617-661-8747, 800-227-7368)
1663 Mass Ave, between Harvard and Porter Squares

Rent a Wreck (Map 12; ☎ 617-576-3700, 800-535-1391) McGrath-O'Brien Hwy, Cambridge

Thrifty (Map 4; ☎ 617-330-5011, 800-367-2277)
125 Summer St at High St, near South Station

TAXI

Taxis do not cruise Boston streets in droves like they do in New York. But they are usually plentiful enough (you may have to walk to a major hotel to be assured one). If you miss the last T, expect to spend about $10 from Harvard Square to Copley Square in Back Bay. From the North End or Faneuil Hall to Kenmore Square, it'll cost you about $7 without much traffic.

Expect trouble hailing a cab during bad weather and between 3:30 and 6:30 pm weekdays. Recommended taxi companies include Checker Cab (☎ 617-536-7000), Independent (☎ 617-268-1379) and Metro Cab (☎ 617-242-8000).

BICYCLE

Daredevil Bostonians cycle around town, but for the most part there are no bike lanes, so use caution if you take to the city streets on two wheels. For information on biking and renting bicycles in Boston, see Activities in Things to See & Do. Also see Maps in Facts for the Visitor.

Bicycles on the T You can take your bike on any MBTA subway line, except the Green Line, during off-peak hours (transla-

tion: Bikes are OK from 10 am to 2 pm and after 7:30 pm weekdays, anytime on the weekend). Be sure to get on the last train car only. Bike permits are required ($5 for 3 years) and available from the Back Bay Orange Line T station at Dartmouth and Columbus Sts. Bicycles are never permitted on MBTA buses, except from the airport terminal to the MBTA Water Shuttle (as long as the shuttle's not too full).

ORGANIZED TOURS

You can get a good sense of this city by taking advantage of a tour by foot, trolley or boat. Also see Things to See & Do and America's Walking City for a close look at neighborhoods and historic sites.

Walking Tours

MyTown If you've had your fill of Paul Revere and John Hancock, it might be time for some talk-story about immigrants, the working class and people of color.

The two-hour tours of the South End (Map 9; ☎ 617-536-8696), led by teens, are $10 adults, sliding scale for youth and students; call for times and days. Meet at the A Phillip Randolph statue inside the Back Bay T station, near the Amtrak ticket window.

Boston Park Rangers Free naturalist-led and historical walks around the Emerald Necklace, Boston Common and the Public Garden are offered by the Boston Park Rangers (Map 4; ☎ 617-635-7383), at Tremont St on Boston Common. Also see 'Emerald Necklace' in Things to See & Do. The schedule varies, so it's best to call ahead.

Historic Neighborhoods From June through August, there are regular architecture tours (5:30 pm Wednesday); tours of the new Seaport District (5:30 pm Thursday); and a 'Make Way for Ducklings' tour for children (11 am Saturday).

Call for non-summer schedules and departure points (☎ 617-426-1885), 99 Bedford St. Tours usually last 90 minutes. Reservations are required; $12 adults, $5 age 15 and under.

Harbor Walk 'Boston by Sea: A Maritime Trail,' a new land-and-water trail (☎ 617-574-5950, www.bostonbysea.org), theoretically spans 43 miles from Milton to Revere, but the most accessible portion is the inner harbor walk from the Charlestown Navy Yard to Fan Pier in South Boston. Many miles of boardwalk run along historic piers and provide great views of the harbor.

Look for the self-guided maps at the NPS and the Boston Common Visitors Information Center. Or call for information on new tours, which weave maritime-related tales of clipper ships, sacred codfish, opium, the Orient and secret underground tunnels for fugitive slaves.

Ben Franklin Alive Take a 1-mile colonial walk with an Emmy Award-winning Franklin as he ponders the colonial era and events that shaped his youth from 1706 to 1723. Meet at 1 Milk St, the site of Franklin's birthplace (Map 4). Tickets cost $35, including lunch at the acclaimed Maison Robert. Tours are given at 9:30 am Wednesday in July and August. Inquire about a new Abigail Adams Revolutionary Boston tour.

Michele Topor's North End Devoted foodies will drool over this culinary adventure (☎ 617-523-6032). Chef Topor's two- to three-hour tour includes olive oil and balsamic vinegar tastings and a family-style lunch or dinner at an authentic trattoria. Reservations are required.

WalkBoston The Shawmut Peninsula Walk map ($4.95 at bookstores; ☎ 617-451-1570) traces Boston's original shoreline through the North End, Beacon Hill and Chinatown. Through this five- or six-hour self-guided walk, you'll be amazed at how much of present-day Boston used to be under water.

Ghosts & Gravestones Billed as a 'frightseeing' tour (Map 7; ☎ 617-269-3626), Charles St South and Boylston St, you'll stroll through two historic graveyards (with flashlights) and hop onto a trolley for commentary on not-so-proper Bostonian antics.

The two-hour tour, which departs at 7 pm Wednesday through Sunday from June through October, costs $28 adults, $15 children age 4 to 12; reservations are necessary.

Trolley Tours

JFK's Boston With the help of audio-taped stories by Senator Ted Kennedy and words by JFK himself, you'll pick up quite a bit of information as you head out to Brookline, where John was born in 1917. Tours (Map 7; ☎ 617-269-7150), depart from Charles St South and Boylston St at 9 am Sunday from late May to mid-October. Tickets ($27 adults, $15 children age 4 to 12) include entrance to the JFK Library.

Literary Trail This refreshing tour elucidates Boston's moniker as 'Athens of America.' Developed by the Boston History Collaborative, the four-hour trolley tour (☎ 617-574-5950, www.lit-trail.org) includes storied literary sites and narrated tales of great authors, poets and social activists in Boston, Cambridge and Concord. While the narrative covers four centuries, it concentrates on mid-19th-century writings and gathering places.

The 20-mile, five-hour tour begins at the Omni Parker House (Map 4) at 12:30 pm Saturday, year-round. Tickets cost $35 adults, $31 college students; reservations required. For those who prefer to wander the trail on their own, look for the $9.95 booklet in local bookstores.

'Transportainment' If you're going to be in town only a couple of days, trolley tours offer great ease and flexibility because you can hop on and off as you like at about 18 sites, catching the next trolley that comes along (if it has room).

The narration is a strange mix of the arcane, an endless list of Boston firsts, bad jokes, substantive information, drivel, more entertainment than scholarly erudition and a lot of tidbits that elicit a quizzically uplifting 'huh.'

Except for the color of their trolleys (red, ☎ 617-236-2148; orange-and-green,

The Big Dig

The depression of the Central Artery and creation of a Third Harbor Tunnel (CA/T) from Boston to the airport is quite simply the largest public works project ever undertaken in the history of the US. But nothing else about the massive project is simple, except perhaps the moniker 'the Big Dig' (☎ 617-951-6400, www.bigdig.com).

It's been compared to the digging of the Panama Canal, the English Channel Chunnel and the Alaskan Pipeline. Its goal: nothing short of building an 8- to 10-lane highway below the current six-lane one without disrupting the nearly 200,000 cars that use the highway daily, and without disrupting 29 miles of underground utility lines (owned by 31 different companies) that handle upwards of 17 million phone calls per day. The CA/T project has been likened to performing open heart surgery on someone while she is running a marathon.

When the Central Artery opened in 1959, physically and psychologically dividing the city, it carried 75,000 vehicles daily. Today, the highway is crumbling and has an accident rate four times the national urban interstate average. Boston has been severed from the waterfront. 'Rush hour' is ten hours long. Somewhere in between then and now, city and state planners conceived of and agreed on a solution. But they agreed for different reasons.

Everybody likes the sensible idea of widening the artery and depressing it. But while some praise a modern road's ability to draw cars, prosperity and suburbanites into the city, another camp is motivated more by its promise to rejoin the city and enhance the urban environment with a swath of

All aboard the gravy train!

GETTING AROUND

☎ 617-269-7150; blue, ☎ 617-269-3626; and white, ☎ 617-742-1440), all four trolley operators offer essentially the same services for the same price. But as one trolley driver said, 'The quality of the tour depends entirely on who's behind the wheel.' Tickets cost $20 to $23 adults, $16 seniors and students, $6 to $9 children. White trolleys offer multilingual narration.

All trolleys originate across from the New England Aquarium (Map 6), but you can also purchase tickets next to the Boston

Common Visitors Information Center. Purchase a ticket before boarding.

Boat Tours

Boston Harbor Ninety-minute narrated historical sightseeing trips are operated by Boston Harbor Cruises (Map 6; ☎ 617-227-4320, www.bostonharborcruises.com), at 1 Long Wharf, from May through October for $15 adults, $12 seniors, $10 children. There are additional sunset cruises (7 pm, May through September).

The Big Dig

downtown parkland. (In either case, the consequences of doing nothing were ugly: During every waking hour, traffic would be practically at a standstill by 2010.)

By the time the current plan was approved, funding secured and construction begun, some thought it was already a boondoggle. Yes, the new highway will accommodate traffic flows of about 245,000 daily, but many predict it will be just as clogged when it opens in mid-2005 as the old Central Artery was when construction began in earnest in 1991 – thanks to the truthful adage, if we build it, they will come. Critics point out that perhaps more should have been done to lessen dependence on automobiles instead of encouraging people to continue to drive to and through Boston. They implore that a 'world-class' city should have a rail or bus link between North and South Stations, but to no avail.

There's one thing that naysayers and their counterparts can probably agree on: The Big Dig may very well be one of the principal forces driving the Boston economy. It's a veritable feeding frenzy, a gravy train for contractors and service providers. Government watchdog agencies rigorously review the big construction contracts that will top $12 billion, but hundreds of millions more are spent unmonitored.

The project is perhaps best described by a list of firsts, superlatives, money spent and engineering feats accomplished:

- Enough concrete – 3.8 million cubic yards – will be poured to build a sidewalk from Boston to San Francisco and back three times.

- With only a 1-inch margin of error, 12 33,000-ton tubes were connected on the bottom of Boston Harbor; the tubes are now called the Ted Williams Tunnel.

- The world's most powerful ventilation fans will keep tunnel air cleaner than surface air.

- Moving all the displaced dirt requires 541,000 truckloads, which would span from Boston to central Brazil if they were lined taillight to headlight. Trucks, by the way, go through on-site 'showers' to lessen their tracking of dirt around the city.

- The cable-stayed bridge across the Charles River will be the world's widest, and the first with an asymmetrical design.

- About 150 cranes tower over the project, more than any single project anywhere in the world.

- Between the peak construction years of 1998 and 2000, the project cost about $3 million daily. About 4000 construction workers will toil away during the year 2000.

If you just want to photograph the skyline, take Boston Harbor Cruises' pleasant, inexpensive ($2) 30-minute weekday lunchtime cruise at 12:15 pm from late May to early September. Mass Bay Lines (Map 6; ☎ 617-542-8000) has sunset and harbor tours departing from Rowes Wharf, May through October. Constitution Cruises (Map 5; ☎ 617-242-8900), between the Charlestown Bridge and Bunker Hill Pavilion in Charlestown, has 40-minute sightseeing tours for $5 adults, $4 seniors, $3 children.

Science at Sea During July and August, the New England Aquarium has 90-minute educational harbor tours (Map 6; ☎ 617-973-5281) for $12.50 adults, $9.50 seniors, $8.50 children. The hands-on marine life investigation really gets kids involved.

Charles River Cruises An hourlong narrated trip of the Charles River Basin is offered by the Charles River Boat Co (Map 12; ☎ 617-621-3001), at the Cambridgeside Galleria in East Cambridge, for $8 adults,

$7 seniors, $6 children. The boat cruises upstream to Harvard and downstream to the Boston Harbor locks. Trips depart weekends in May and September, and noon to 5 pm daily late May to early September. The ticket booth is located in Canal Park (the park area with a fountain and food stalls in back of the mall).

Land & Sea Boston Duck Tours (Map 8; ☎ 617-723-3825) offers unusual land-and-water tours using modified WWII amphibious vehicles. Though odd, they're one of

Boston's most popular 'attractions.' Rain or shine, the narrated tour splashes around the Charles River for about 25 minutes, and then assaults city streets for another hour. The ticket booth within the Prudential Center opens at 8:30 am, but people line up before then in the summer. Tickets sell out by noon on weekends. Boats depart (on the Boylston St side of the Pru) every 30 minutes from 9 am until one hour prior to sunset daily April through November. Tickets cost $21 adults, $18 seniors and students, $11 children.

Things to See & Do

Boston's 18th-century historic sites are perched side-by-side with 19th-century architectural gems, 20th-century museums and other postmodern cultural diversions. They are all woven into this chapter by neighborhood and are accessible by subway. With the exception of Kenmore Square & Fenway and the South End, Boston's neighborhoods are small enough to walk in a few hours without straining yourself. In this book, Cambridge, though a separate city, is treated as a Boston neighborhood. Outlying neighborhoods are all accessible via the subway. Recreational activities are discussed at the end of the chapter.

BEACON HILL (MAP 2)

There are two faces to Beacon Hill: Pinckney and Myrtle Sts, which run east-west along the crest of the hill, act as the dividing line. On the south slope, below Pinckney St to Boston Common, houses are grand and distinguished. On the north slope, above Myrtle St to Cambridge St, row houses are more modest. Charles St, which divides 'the flats' from the hill, is lined with antique shops, neighborhood haunts and fancy restaurants.

Boston's anti-slavery activity is documented along the neighborhood's Black Heritage Trail, and the city's Freedom Trail meanders through Beacon Hill as well (see 'Historical Tours' in America's Walking City). Freedom Trail sites include Park St Church, the Old Granary Burying Ground, State House and Boston Common.

Black Heritage Trail sites include the Middleton-Glapion House, Phillips School, Abiel Smith School, Smith Court, William Nell House, Shaw Memorial, African Meeting House, Holmes Alley, Lewis Hayden House and the Charles St Meeting House.

Both the Park St and the Charles/MGH T stops bring you right into Beacon Hill.

Park St Church

This noble 1810 church (☎ 617-523-3383), with its elegant 217-foot steeple at Tremont and Park Sts, is both a stunning visual landmark and an important historic site. From this church's pulpit in 1829, William Lloyd Garrison railed against slavery, and on Independence Day in 1831, Katherine Lee Bates' hymn, 'America' (the unofficial national anthem), was first sung. The congregation's influence spread far from Boston; it sent early-19th-century Congregationalist missionaries to establish a Hawaiian church, which in turn proselytized throughout the Pacific.

The church is open 9:30 am to 3:30 pm Tuesday through Saturday from mid-June through August and by appointment the rest of the year.

Old Granary Burying Ground

The graveyard dates to 1660 (two others in Boston are even older) and is graced by exceptional headstone carvings and the remains of numerous revolutionary leaders, including Paul Revere, Samuel Adams, James Otis and John Hancock. Also buried here are Crispus Attucks (the freed slave who died in the Boston Massacre when British soldiers fired into a group of protesting colonists in 1770), Benjamin Franklin's parents (he's buried in Philadelphia), Peter Faneuil (of Faneuil Hall fame) and Judge Sewell, the only magistrate to denounce the

Old Granary Burying Ground

KIM GRANT

hanging of the so-called Salem witches. The graveyard was so crowded with Revere's compatriots that when Revere died at the ripe old age of 83, there was barely room for him.

Shaw Memorial

The magnificent bas-relief Robert Gould Shaw Memorial, across Beacon St from the State House, was sculpted by Augustus St Gaudens after nearly 13 years of work. It honors the 54th Massachusetts Regiment of the Union Army, the nation's first all-black Civil War regiment, depicted in the 1989 film *Glory*. The soldiers, led by 26-year-old Shaw (the son of a wealthy Brahmin family), steadfastly refused their $10 monthly stipend for two years until Congress upped it to $13, the amount white regiments were paid. Shaw and half his men were killed in a battle at Fort Wagner, South Carolina.

A highly recommended, free National Park Service (NPS) tour of the Black Heritage Trail departs from here.

State House

Within the golden-domed Massachusetts State House at Beacon and Bowdoin Sts, the idiosyncrasies of governance and politics are played like a sporting match. The commanding capitol building, designed by Boston's beloved Charles Bulfinch and completed in 1798, is the country's oldest extant capitol. (The state's constitution is the world's oldest existing constitution.) The capitol was built upon the highest peak in Boston, on grazing land owned by John Hancock, who stipulated that his house on the western side of the new capitol not be torn down after he died. (It was 'removed' in 1863 – so much for posthumously honoring the former governor's wishes.) The corner stones were laid by Samuel Adams and Paul Revere; Revere returned four years later to cover the leaking dome with copper. Today, it's weatherproofed with 23-carat gold leaf.

A free 40-minute tour, offered between 10 am and 3:30 pm daily except Sunday (reservations recommended; ☎ 617-727-3676), includes anecdotes about the history, art collection, architecture and local political per-

Abolitionist Frederick Douglass

sonalities, as well as a visit to the legislative chambers when congress is in session. A carving of the 'Sacred Cod' hangs in the House chambers as testimony to the importance of this now-dwindling species to the economy of Massachusetts. Self-guided tours are possible 9 am to 5 pm daily except Sunday.

On the front lawn, a number of statues honor important Massachusetts figures, among them politician Daniel Webster; Civil War general Joe Hooker (while the general did 'encourage' women to 'entertain' his soldiers, the term 'hooker' did not originate with him); religious martyr Anne Hutchinson; Quaker Mary Dyer, who was hanged on Boston Common in 1660; President John F Kennedy; educator Horace Mann and Senator Henry Cabot Lodge.

African Meeting House & Abiel Smith School

The African Meeting House was built in 1806 by African-American tradesmen and is now the country's oldest standing black church (☎ 617-723-8863), 8 Smith Court.

Abolitionists William Lloyd Garrison (who began the New England Antislavery Society here) and Frederick Douglass delivered stirring calls to action within this hall. The plain interior belies the passions roused within, but on a quiet day you can almost hear the fiery orations reverberating off the hallowed walls. When African-Americans migrated from Beacon Hill to the South End and Roxbury in the late 19th century, the Irish and Jews, in turn, relocated here from the North End. For a while, the meeting house served an Orthodox Jewish congregation.

The building is closed until mid-2001 for a much-needed refurbishing of the original wood floors and pews. The Museum of Afro-American History (☎ 617-739-1200, www .afroammuseum.org), located within the adjacent Abiel Smith School, is an excellent place to learn about Beacon Hill's African-American roots. The resource center has an extensive library, interactive computer programs and permanent exhibits, including a replica classroom. It's open 10 am to 4 pm daily except Sunday; admission is free.

Boston Common

Established in 1634, the 50-acre green is the country's oldest public park. The Common has long been a place of amusements and protests, military trainings and concerts. While the park is certainly full of life, it's also full of monuments to more than 350 years of activity. The **Park St T Station**, a national landmark, is one of the subway's four original stations. **Flagstaff Hill**, great for sledding in winter, is crowned by a Civil War **Soldiers & Sailors Monument**. During the Revolutionary War, British troops camped here; until 1830, the land was used for cattle grazing. The bronze **Boston Massacre Monument** memorializes the 18th-century colonists' quest for freedom from economic tyranny (see the Cradle of Liberty and 'Boston Massacre' in the Facts about Boston chapter). The 18th century also saw many public hangings at the **Great Elm Site**. Near Tremont and Boylston Sts, artist Gilbert Stuart is buried in the 1756 **Central Burying Ground**.

Although there is still a grazing ordinance on the books, today the Common serves picnickers, sunbathers, people-watchers and squirrel-feeders. The **Frog Pond** (see Activities, later in this chapter), site of the city's first public water system in 1848, hosts winter skating and summertime splashing. Shakespearean drama is performed each August at the **Parkman Bandstand** (see 'Free Outdoor Fun' in the Entertainment chapter). Colorful characters are often heard spouting off from atop a soapbox, real or imagined, near the Park St T station.

KIM GRANT
Parkman Bandstand on Boston Common

The **Boston Park Rangers**, who offer free tours of the Common and Public Garden, are based at the **Visitors Information Center** (☎ 617-426-3115), on Tremont St near West St. The center (with public restrooms) is open 8:30 am to 5 pm daily (from 9 am Sunday).

Public Garden

The Public Garden is a 24-acre botanical oasis of cultivated flower beds, clipped grass, ancient trees, ornamental flowering species and a tranquil lagoon ringed by weeping willows. Until it was filled in the early 19th century, it was (like the rest of Back Bay) a tidal salt marsh. You can't picnic on the lawn like you can on the Common, but this formal French-style park has plenty of benches. Pick one in front of the **Swan Boats**, pedal-powered vessels that ferry children and adults around the pond while ducks swim alongside squawking for bread crumbs. Boat rides, from mid-April to late September, cost $1.75 for adults and just under $1 for children. (Children accustomed to animated computer games will likely get antsy after about 30 seconds; some adults might too.)

Hidden among notable specimen trees you'll find the **Ether Fountain** (it's a curious thing to memorialize an intangible substance), the **George Washington Statue**

(whose replica sword is stolen every year by enthusiastic fraternity freshmen), the **George Robert White Memorial** in honor of a generous Boston benefactor, and the *Make Way for Ducklings* statues, commemorating the children's book.

KIM GRANT

GOVERNMENT CENTER & FANEUIL HALL (MAP 3)

This 'neighborhood' might be more accurately called 'odds and ends.' Its disparate elements include Boston's most touristed destination (Faneuil Hall and its adjacent marketplace) and its least visited (the Old West End). You'll find the oldest block in Boston (the charming Blackstone Block) and one of the newest areas (Government Center was built from the ground up in the 1960s). In between, the North Station area has lively bars, a hostel, a transportation center and a sports arena.

Government Center occupies Scollay Square of yore. Before it was razed in the early 1960s, the bustling area was home to bawdy clubs and seedy nightlife. Prior to its decline and pave-over, it had been the site of several important historic events. The first Quaker meeting was held here (remember,

KIM GRANT

Enough boiling water for 3,632 cups of tea – if only they hadn't dumped it into the harbor.

in Boston they hanged Quakers such as Mary Dyer then); the *Liberator*, an antislavery newspaper, was published from this site; John and Abigail Adams lived here with their son John (both men were later US presidents), as did Zabdiel Boylston, the inventor of the smallpox vaccine; Alexander Graham Bell invented the telephone in his office here; and Thomas Edison invented the stock ticker from the very same office.

The only site on the Freedom Trail is Faneuil Hall, but it's an important one.

Many T stations are convenient to Faneuil Hall: Government Center (Green and Blue Lines), State (Orange and Blue Lines) and Aquarium (Blue Line). Haymarket (Orange and Green Lines) is closest to the Blackstone Block. North Station is on the Green and Orange Lines. From any of these T stations, you can also walk to the North End or south along the waterfront.

Boston City Hall & Plaza

Erected in the 1960s, Government Center is a cold 56-acre concrete plaza surrounded by federal and state office buildings. Designed by IM Pei (who did the Kennedy Library and John Hancock Tower), it's home to the fortresslike Boston City Hall, a top-heavy mass of concrete, brick and glass. There have been plans afoot for years to create a more inviting City Hall Plaza, but city planning, mired as it is in local politics, creeps at a snail's pace. The high-rise **John F Kennedy**

Federal Building anchors the northern edge of the plaza. The plaza is, though, well suited to large public gatherings and summertime performances (see 'Free Outdoor Fun' in the Entertainment chapter).

The plaza's high points are the gracefully curved brick **Sears Crescent**, at Court and Tremont Sts, with its 227-gallon **steaming kettle** on the western tip of the building. The sweeping curve of the modern **Center Plaza**, on Cambridge St, mirrors the Sears Crescent nicely. There is a tiny opening through the building that peers onto Pemberton Square and the grand French Second Empire Suffolk County Courthouse. The courthouse makes at least one cameo appearance in every episode of *Ally McBeal*.

Faneuil Hall Marketplace

Between North and Congress Sts, **Faneuil Hall**, pronounced 'fannel' or 'fan-yul,' was first constructed as a market and public meeting place in 1740 by Boston benefactor and merchant Peter Faneuil and was enlarged by Bulfinch in 1899. Over the years,

numerous orators have held forth here; the 2nd floor is still used for public meetings. On the 4th floor, the **Ancient & Honorable Artillery Co of Massachusetts** (☎ 617-227-1638), which was chartered in 1638, maintains a strangely interesting collection of antique firearms, political mementos and curious artifacts. The hall (☎ 617-242-5675) is open 9 am to 5 pm daily.

Dock Square, between the hall and Congress St, is graced with a statue of Sam Adams. Also, note the outlines of Boston's 1630 shoreline, sandblasted in the pavement.

East of Faneuil Hall, four granite buildings comprise the Faneuil Hall Marketplace (☎ 617-338-2323). The central Greek Revival **Quincy Market** was the heart of Boston's produce and meat industry for almost 150 years, while the **North Market** and **South Market** buildings flanking it were commercial warehouses. All were redeveloped in the 1970s into today's colorful, festive shopping and eating mecca. Behind them, **Marketplace Center**, built in 1985, insulates the area from the noisy expressway.

KIM GRANT

Faneuil Hall and Quincy Market offer dozens of shops, quick eateries and unending people-watching.

Blackstone Block

Named after Boston's first settler, there's no other place in Boston where you can step back in time so easily. This tiny warren of streets, bounded by Union, Blackstone, Hanover and North Sts, dates back to the 17th and 18th centuries. Established in 1826, **Ye Olde Union Oyster House**, 41 Union St, is Boston's oldest restaurant. Around the corner in Creek Square, the circa 1767 **Ebenezer Hancock House**, 10 Marshall St, is a gem (it now houses offices). Ebenezer, a mason and bricklayer, was John Hancock's brother. At the base of a souvenir shop next-door, the 1737 **Boston Stone** served as the terminus for measuring distances to and from 'the Hub.' The addition of the 1982 **Bostonian Hotel**, on North St, could have been disastrous to this historic block, but its intimate scale fits perfectly and the architects preserved all the old streets, including the adjacent Scott Alley, a narrow covered passageway. The open air **Haymarket** (see 'Farmers' Markets' in the Shopping chapter) takes place on Blackstone St.

KIM GRANT

The dramatic Holocaust Memorial

Check out the two lifelike bronze **James Michael Curley statues**, on North St, between Union and Congress Sts. One likeness wasn't enough to capture the controversial mayor's irrepressible spirit. Just beyond, between Union and Congress Sts, is the 1995 **New England Holocaust Memorial**, comprised of six glass columns etched with 6 million numbers in memory of those who perished during the Holocaust. Inside each tower is a pit, representing a major Nazi death camp, with smoldering coals sending plumes of steam up through the glass towers. While the presentation is particularly dramatic at night, its placement across from boisterous bars is quite disconcerting.

Old West End

Once a teeming maze of row houses and narrow streets, the neighborhood was razed in the 1950s and replaced with wider roads, massive concrete government buildings and clusters of high-rise apartment buildings. Consequently, there's nothing much here to recommend. (The area's two remaining historic sites, Old West Church and First Harrison Gray Otis House, are discussed in Beacon Hill: Bastion of Brahmins & Black History, in America's Walking City.)

The **Ether Dome** (☎ 617-726-2281), off North Grove St, is located in Mass General's 1823 Bulfinch building, the oldest hospital building in the complex. You can visit the 4th-floor domed operating room (usually open 8 am to 6 pm) where ether was first used as an anesthetic in 1846. Mass General remains one of the world's finest teaching and research hospitals.

North Station Area

This little grid of narrow streets and brick commercial buildings is noteworthy primarily because it comes as such a surprise, wedged between the expressway, the grand **New Chardon St Courthouse**, at New Chardon and Merrimac Sts, and the **Fleet Center** sports arena and **North Station** on Causeway St. Between the car traffic and the elevated Green Line, it's noisy and lively with pubs, sports bars and a funky charity thrift shop. The **Sports Museum of New England**

(☎ 617-624-1234) is located on the 5th and 6th floors of the Fleet Center on Causeway St. It houses interactive hockey and basketball exhibits that feature sports legends such as Bobby Orr and Larry Bird. Admission is $5 adults, $4 seniors and children.

DOWNTOWN & FINANCIAL DISTRICT (MAP 4)

The Financial District has a long history: Family trust funds have been managed on State St since the 17th century, and the area has been a bustling commercial center ever since. Plenty of historic buildings still illustrate the history, and most of the streets were laid out in the 17th and 18th centuries, so getting around can be confusing.

There are five Freedom Trail sites downtown: the King's Chapel and its Burying Ground, Old Corner Bookstore, Old South Meeting House, Old State House and the Boston Massacre site. Also see America's Walking City for a route that will introduce you to many of the buildings and interesting stories of downtown.

Use the State T stop on the Blue and Orange Lines for points northern, and Park St on the Green or Red Lines or Boylston on the Green Line for western and southern sights.

King's Chapel & King's Chapel Burying Ground

The compact granite church you see today (☎ 617-227-2155), 58 Tremont St, was designed by Peter Harrison and built in 1754 around the original 1688 wooden structure to avoid disrupting services. When the external building was complete, the wooden church was taken apart and tossed out the windows. After the revolution, it became the country's first Unitarian church. If the church seems to be missing something, it is: Building funds ran out before a spire could be added. The church houses the largest bell ever cast by Paul Revere as well as a lovely sounding organ.

Free classical recitals are given at 12:15 pm Tuesday year-round. The church is open 10 am to 4 pm Saturday, September through April; 9 am to 4 pm Monday and

KIM GRANT

King's Chapel Burying Ground with Old City Hall

Thursday through Saturday and from 1 to 3 pm Sunday in summer.

The adjacent burying ground contains the graves of John Winthrop, the first governor of the fledgling Massachusetts Bay Colony; William Dawes, who rode with Revere to warn of the British march on Lexington and Concord; Elizabeth Pain, the model for Hawthorne's Hester Prynne in *The Scarlet Letter*; and Mary Chilton, the first woman to set foot in Plymouth. It's probable that for every grave marker, there are an additional 15 unmarked graves.

Just down School St is a marker for the site of the first public school.

Old Corner Bookstore

This circa 1718 building once housed Boston's most illustrious publishing company, Ticknor & Fields, publisher of books by Thoreau, Emerson, Hawthorne, Longfellow and Harriet Beecher Stowe. Between 1845 and 1865, the authors often held lively discussions and meetings here. Today, the Boston Globe Store sells front-page reprints of historic events covered in the eponymous newspaper.

Old South Meeting House

This brick meeting house (☎ 617-482-6439), 310 Washington St, with a soaring steeple, was built in 1729, but another stood here as early as 1670. (Ben Franklin was baptized in the first building.) The largest hall in pre-revolution Boston, Old South was the scene of a typically feisty town meeting where colonists decided to protest the British tea taxation (see A Tempest in a Teapot in the Facts about Boston chapter and the Waterfront & Seaport District section, later in this chapter). Phillis Wheatley, a former slave and the nation's first recognized African-American poet, worshiped here. When this congregation moved to Back Bay in 1875, Ralph Waldo Emerson and Julia Ward Howe gathered support to convert the church into a museum.

The meeting house is open 10 am to 4 pm daily from November through March, and 9:30 am to 5 pm daily the rest of the year. Admission is $3 adults, $2.50 seniors and students, $1 children.

Old South Meeting House

Old State House

The location of the 1713 Old State House (☎ 617-720-3290, www.bostonhistory.org), 206 Washington St, is significant. It once commanded a waterfront view down State St and stood at the head of Washington St, the city's only 18th-century thoroughfare.

Although the Boston Massacre took place in its shadow, the site is best known for its balcony, from where the Declaration of Independence was first read to Bostonians on July 18, 1776. Note the rooftop replica lions and unicorns, symbols of the English Crown. The originals were torn down after the Declaration of Independence was read. The first governor of Massachusetts, John Hancock, was inaugurated here. Inside, a museum operated by the Bostonian Society is definitely worth a visit. It houses revolutionary memorabilia pertinent to Boston's (and thus the nation's) history.

The building is open 9 am to 5 pm daily. Admission is $3 adults, $2 seniors and students, $1 children. The highly informative **National Park Visitors Center** (☎ 617-242-5642), 15 State St, is nearby.

In the traffic island across from the balcony of the Old State House are cobblestone markers for the **Boston Massacre site** (see 'Boston Massacre' in the Facts about Boston chapter).

State St & Custom House

State St, named King St until the revolution, was the most important thoroughfare during colonial times. Starting in 1710, crewmen and cargo docked at Long Wharf (which, prior to landfill reclamation, extended all the way to the Custom House) and traveled straight up to the Old State House and then down Washington St. What Wall St is to New York, State St was to colonial Boston.

The lower portion of the Custom House, begun in 1837, resembles a four-sided Greek temple. In 1913, the federal government, having exempted itself from local height restrictions, decided something more grand was needed and financed a 500-foot tower to crown it. Bostonians were aghast at the city's first skyscraper, a whopping 16 stories tall, but have since grown to love it, especially its

22-foot illuminated clock. Today, the most memorable building in Boston's skyline is – gasp! – a Marriott luxury time-share condo. Free 30-minute daily tours at 10 am and 4 pm are offered on the observation deck (☎ 617-310-6300). The 1st floor has a small free exhibit of maritime art and artifacts from the Peabody Essex Museum. Go inside to check out the lobby rotunda.

A maze of streets converge on North Square.

NORTH END (MAP 5)

Boston's original neighborhood is still the most tight-knit quarter of the city. Physically cut off from the city by the expressway, the enclave is a world unto itself and hopes to remain that way. Wandering through the maze of streets today, it's hard to imagine anyone living here besides ancestors of the current Italian-American residents. It has, however, been home to a number of ethnic communities.

The North End was a fashionable Tory enclave prior to the revolution. When the Loyalists decamped for Nova Scotia, free blacks settled around Copp's Hill, calling the area 'New Guinea.' After they relocated to Beacon Hill in search of better employment opportunities, successive waves of Irish, eastern European Jews, Portuguese and Italians settled here and opened small businesses in the 19th and early 20th centuries.

North End Freedom Trail sites include the Paul Revere House, Old North Church and Copp's Hill Burying Ground.

To get here, take the Green or Orange Line to the Haymarket T station, head toward the expressway and follow signs to the pedestrian path underneath it. (Because of Central Artery construction, the walkways are rerouted week by week.) You'll emerge at Cross St. Cross at the light and turn right to reach Hanover St. As you'll soon see, the narrow jumble of streets is not receptive to autos; you could crawl faster than drive in the North End.

Paul Revere House

Originally built in 1680 in the wake of the fire of 1676, this small clapboard house (☎ 617-523-1676, www.paulreverehouse.org), 19 North Square, violated building codes by not using brick. The house has survived and is worth a visit – and not just because it's the oldest house in Boston. The hourlong tour provides a great history lesson. A blacksmith (and goldsmith, silversmith, copper engraver and false teeth maker), Revere was one of two horseback messengers who carried advance warning of the British march into Concord and Lexington on the night of April 18, 1775 (see the Excursions chapter). Father of 16 children, Revere owned the house for 30 years but lived here only for 10 years during the revolutionary period. Behind the house, the family well stood next to the outhouse – you can imagine the unhealthy results!

The house is open 9:30 am to 4:15 pm daily, until 5:15 pm mid-April through October (closed Monday, January through March). Tickets cost $2.50 adults, $2 seniors and students, $1 children. For an extra $1.50, you can visit the Pierce-Hichborn House next-door, too.

Old North Church

Also called Christ Church, this 1723 place of worship (☎ 617-523-6676, www.oldnorth .com), 193 Salem St, is Boston's oldest church and a beloved national historic landmark. It's best known as the place where sexton Robert Newman hung two lanterns

Festivals

North End social clubs each have a patron saint whom they honor yearly by hoisting its life-sized likeness onto a wooden platform and carrying it through the streets. Residents toss confetti from balconies, along with dollar bills that are pinned to banners streaming off the saint.

You can count on a festival almost every weekend in July and August. Some festivals, though, are bigger than others, particularly St Anthony's in late August. Although still quite traditional, many North Enders escape these weekends, complaining that the events are too commercial. Nonetheless, don't miss a chance to attend if you're in the area. Most festivals have outdoor bands and street vendors selling greasy food.

A summertime saint's parade

from the steeple on the night of April 18, 1775, as a signal that the British would march on Lexington and Concord via the sea route. The 175-foot steeple, made in three tiers, houses the oldest bells (1744) still rung in the US. Today's steeple is a 1954 replica, since severe weather toppled two prior ones. The 1740 weather vane is original. Inside, tall box-pews, many with brass nameplates of early parishioners who had to purchase their pews, fill the graceful interior. The pews were designed to retain the warmth generated by boxes filled with heated bricks in winter. The brass chandeliers used today were first lit on Christmas in 1724. Note the candles – there is no electric lighting in the church.

Old North sponsors 'Paul Revere Tonight,' in which a costumed actor portrays Revere, from mid-June through October. Tickets are $12 adults, $8 children.

A gift shop next-door sells revolutionary memorabilia. At the back of the gift shop is a tiny 'museum' displaying such oddities as a strand of George Washington's hair and a vial of liquid purported to be tea from the Boston Tea Party. Often overlooked are several quaint courtyards located to the left of the church entrance. The church is open 9 am to 5 pm daily, until 6 pm July through October (except when there are funerals – this remains an active church); the grand organ is played at the 11 am Sunday service.

Copp's Hill Burying Ground

There are excellent views of the waterfront and Charlestown Harbor from the city's second-oldest cemetery (1660), home to an estimated 10,000 souls. The oldest graves, located just beyond the crest of the hill, belong to cobbler William Copp's children. (Copp was the original purchaser of the land.) Look around for rebel activist Daniel Malcolm's headstone, used for target practice by the British. (Take the path to the crest, turn left and walk toward Snowhill St until you reach the large tree on the left; Malcolm's grave is to the left of the tree.) During the Battle of Bunker Hill on June 17, 1775, British troops rained artillery onto Charlestown from here. There are upwards

KIM GRANT

Gravestones date back to the mid-17th century in Copp's Hill Burying Ground.

of a thousand free blacks from the late 18th and early 19th centuries buried here, along with politically powerful religious leaders Increase (father), Cotton (son) and Samuel (grandson) Mather. Their graves are located near the Charter St gate.

CHARLESTOWN

Charlestown was settled a year before Boston and then completely destroyed by the British during the revolution. Townspeople rebuilt quickly, and today most houses in the core date to the early 19th century. (Charlestown was incorporated into Boston in 1873.) Streets are lined with gas lanterns and attached brick row houses, wooden residences and stone houses, now restored and occupied by young urban professionals. This influx of new blood has caused tension between the blue-collar 'townies' and their new neighbors. The streets are great for plain old wandering, and there is plenty of history to explore here.

Freedom Trail sites include Bunker Hill Monument and the USS *Constitution*.

It's logical to combine this with a visit to the North End. It takes about 15 minutes to walk from Commercial and North Washington Sts across the Charlestown Bridge. Turn right onto Constitution Rd to reach the Navy

Yard or cross the oasis-like City Square and head into the heart of town. Or take a ferry from Long Wharf to the Navy Yard or a shuttle to Lovejoy Wharf (see the Getting Around chapter). Or take the T Green or Orange Line to North Station and head across the Charlestown Bridge. You can also take bus No 93 from Haymarket T. If you are driving (gasp), there is free parking (gasp) on both sides of Constitution Rd.

The Locks & Paul Revere Park

Immediately to the west of the Charlestown Bridge (site of a toll ferry benefiting Harvard College until 1786), the dam and locks control the water levels between the Charles River Basin and Inner Harbor. Upwards of 1000 pleasure boats and an inestimable number of fish pass through daily in the summer. No other section of the Charles River shoreline is hidden like it is here, severed from the rest of the city by industry. The locks provide a great vantage point for watching the Central Artery construction project (see 'The Big Dig' in the Getting Around chapter). It's a gritty and noisy viewing station, but it provides a dose of reality after one too many trips to Faneuil Hall. The adjacent Paul Revere Park, a welcome oasis if you don't mind a perpetual snake of cars hulking above you on a rusting elevated highway, is but one new link in a forthcoming plan for 7 miles of area recreational pathways.

Charlestown Navy Yard

The Navy Yard, where British troops landed to fight the Battle of Bunker Hill, offers more than a nice view of Boston's skyline. Its current mission is to interpret the art and history of naval shipbuilding. A mere museum on the topic might prove boring, but touring the USS *Constitution* and walking around the dry docks and impressive granite buildings makes for a fascinating history lesson. A thriving shipbuilding center from 1800 until the early 1900s, the Navy Yard was decommissioned in 1974. The area has been remarkably preserved and resurrected with shops, recreation areas and residential and office space.

Begin your introduction to both the Navy Yard and Bunker Hill Monument at the **Bunker Hill Pavilion** (☎ 617-241-7575), Constitution Rd, open 9 am to 5 pm daily April through November (until 6 pm in summer). The 18-minute multimedia **Whites of Their Eyes Exhibit** (9:30 am to 4:40 pm) elucidates the battle quite nicely. Tickets are $3 adults, $1.50 children.

Free half-hour tours of the Navy Yard are offered at 11 am daily during the summer from the pavilion. On your own, have a look at **Dry Dock No 1**, the country's oldest shipbuilding dry dock (1833); the hexagonal **Telephone Exchange**, atypically intimate and ornate for a shipyard building; and the **Commandant's House**, a brick Georgian-style mansion.

The **Ropewalk**, where all navy rope was made for 135 years, is more than 1000 feet long. Its granite walls are 2½ feet thick and have many isolated sections, all the better to snuff out frequent fires. It's the only remaining complete ropewalk in the US, but it's closed to the public. When metal workers invented 'die-lock' chain next-door in 1926, it put the ropemakers out of business.

The NPS offers free guided 45-minute tours of a refurbished WWII destroyer, the

USS *Cassin Young* (☎ 617-242-5601), at 10 and 11 am and 2 and 3 pm, with a few more times in the summer. You can always tour the main deck on your own. After all the walking around, **Shipyard Park** is a good place to relax.

USS *Constitution* Dating to 1797, the nation's oldest commissioned warship afloat is nicknamed 'Old Ironsides' for never having gone down in 33 battles. Her hull is 25 inches thick at the waterline and made of oak, not iron.

A few other notable facts: Paul Revere was paid almost $4000 to outfit her in copper hardware and sheathing; construction costs were 260% over budget (perhaps the Big Dig isn't doing so badly after all); the captain's son died on her maiden voyage; Oliver Wendell Holmes made a name for himself by penning a poem about her; for her last mission in 1853 she seized an American slave ship off the coast of Africa; in 1886, Congressman John F 'Honey Fitz' Fitzgerald introduced a bill to permanently moor her in Massachusetts.

Outfitted in period uniforms, perky Navy personnel give free and entertaining 30-minute tours of the top deck, gun deck and cramped quarters. In order to maintain the ship's commissioned status, she is taken out onto Boston Harbor every Fourth of July, turned around and brought back to the dock. Tours (☎ 617-242-5670) are offered 9:30 am to 3:50 pm, 365 days a year.

USS *Constitution* Museum Across from the ship, this free museum (☎ 617-426-1812) has colorful gallery displays for nautical buffs, interactive exhibits for kids and many informative short videos about ship life and the ship's battles (if you're into that kind of thing). The museum is open 9 am to 6 pm daily April through October, from 10 am to 5 pm the rest of the year.

From City Square to Monument Square

Recent Central Artery construction in City Square unearthed the foundation for the

'Great House,' widely believed to be John Winthrop's 1630 house. (He soon moved across the Charles to the Shawmut Peninsula.) After reading the informative dioramas, wander up Main St, detouring through **John Harvard Mall**, a gem of a walled, tree-covered brick plaza. A 1630 fort once crowned Harvard Mall, atop Town Hill; bronze plaques detail the specifics. Before the local minister – one John Harvard – died of consumption, he donated half his £800 estate and all 300 of his books to a young Cambridge college in 1638, which saw fit to name its school after him. (For that sum Harvard wouldn't name a park bench after you today!) Both **Harvard Square** and **Harvard St**, behind the mall, are enchanting, too. From here, there are two scenic ways to reach Monument Square.

Follow **Main St** and turn right onto Winthrop St to check out the now-tranquil and pacifist **Winthrop Square** (militia trained here for 250 years) before following it around to the left. Or take Harvard St to **Monument Ave** or Pleasant St. At the corner of Main and Pleasant Sts, the circa 1780 **Warren Tavern** (☎ 617-241-8142) was one of the first buildings constructed after the town was burned. It's still a fine place for a drink. The narrow streets surrounding Monument Square are picturesque, lined with restored mid-19th-century Federal and colonial houses.

Bunker Hill Monument

The area known today as Bunker Hill is actually Breed's Hill. Regardless of its name, the hill on which the memorial stands is the site of a crucial Revolutionary War battle that took place on June 17, 1775. Although won by the British, the colonists fought valiantly and British casualties were very high. According to oft-quoted legend, colonial colonel William Prescott, hoping to preserve the element of surprise, commanded his troops, 'Don't fire 'til you see the whites of their eyes.' The face-to-face combat that ensued was the bloodiest of the war. A battle reenactment takes place every June. Musket firing demonstrations are given Thursday

through Sunday (at 10:30 and 11:30 am; 2:30 and 3:30 pm) in the summer.

Bunker Hill Monument (☎ 617-242-5641), a 221-foot granite obelisk rising from atop the hill, offers a fine view of Boston for those willing to climb 294 steps. The Marquis de Lafayette laid the cornerstone in 1825, but it took another 15 years of fund-raising to finish it. (Ironically, the battlefield itself was sold to finance the monument.) NPS park rangers are on hand in summer to give talks; the obelisk is open 9 am to 4:30 pm daily (admission is free).

LEE FOSTER

Like Stairmaster, but with a view

WATERFRONT & SEAPORT DISTRICT (MAP 6)

Boston's harbor and waterfront have long played vital roles in the city's development, but not since colonial times have they felt so vibrant and full of promise. When the Big Dig concludes and the Central Artery is depressed in 2004, the waterfront and downtown will be reunited and this area will look and feel completely different. After the expressway is dismantled, the swath of new open land should be mostly parkland. There is perhaps no other modern city engaging in such a radical transformation of its core. In the meantime, construction is noisy and relentless and traffic patterns unpredictably change overnight.

The waterfront, east of Atlantic Ave, has been made more accessible with each passing year. A public path, officially designated the 'HarborWalk,' runs along the outer edge of most wharf buildings. Thus, you can skirt the water's edge from Columbus Park to the Aquarium, the Tea Party Ship and new federal courthouse.

The South Boston Seaport District, located across Fort Point Channel, is also undergoing enormous transition. There have

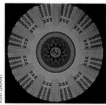

Presidential Seal, Custom House ceiling

KIM GRANT

always been spectacular views of Boston from here, but until recently the area had been neglected by city officials, ignored by developers and inaccessible to the public. For many years, it remained the well-kept secret of struggling artists who live and work in the area's dilapidated warehouses. Needless to say, the revitalization now threatens to displace the Fort Point Channel artists' community. The area's development presents the most important urban planning issues Boston has faced since the master plan for Government Center (or perhaps the filling of Back Bay).

The newly designated Seaport District stretches from Fan Pier all the way down Northern Ave and beyond the Fleet Boston Pavilion. It extends southeast to Summer St and a convention center to be completed in 2002. Explore now and then come back in five years to see how much you recognize; note that in early 2000, the Seaport District

---

Boston Harbor Islands State Park

Until recently, Boston Harbor had the unenviable distinction of being the country's dirtiest harbor. After a massive, multimillion-dollar clean-up in the mid-1990s, the harbor is gaining a healthier reputation. It's a good thing, too, since there are more than 30 large and small islands that offer plenty of history, picnic spots, nature walks and fishing. A kiosk (☎ 617-223-8666), on Long Wharf, dispenses details on all islands overseen by the National Park Service and a number of state agencies.

Georges Island, the jumping-off spot for all other islands, features a 19th-century fort. It's the only island with fresh water and food. Lovell Island is the largest, good for walking along dunes, marshes and meadows. Look for wild raspberries on Bumpkin Island and for a variety of birds on Grape Island. Gallop's has a sandy beach, while Peddock's is the most diverse, with the remains of a circa 1900 fort. Allow a half day to visit Georges, and a whole day to visit the outer islands. Boston Light, the nation's oldest staffed lighthouse (1716), guards the harbor's entrance at Little Brewster Island; it's open only for tours.

Boston Harbor Cruises (Map 6; ☎ 617-227-4320, www.bostonharborcruises.com), 1 Long Wharf off Atlantic Ave, offers regular ferry service from May through October. Purchase roundtrip tickets ($8 adults, $7 senior, $6 children) to Georges Island where you catch free water taxis (another five to 10 minutes) to smaller islands. Boats run hourly. For information on camping on the islands, see Waterfront & Seaport District in Places to Stay.

KIM GRANT

Rowes Wharf, with the Boston Harbor Hotel and ferry terminals

was renamed the 'South Boston Waterfront,' a name that may or may not stick.

Fort Point Channel, the Children's Museum, the Boston Tea Party Museum and Leather District are served by South Station on the Red Line. It's about a 15-minute walk to Fan Pier from here. Aquarium, on the Blue Line, serves Long Wharf. A myriad of boats ply the waterfront (see 'Boston by Boat' in the Getting Around chapter).

Waterfront
Columbus Park to Central Wharf To escape Faneuil Hall crowds or the cramped North End, head to Columbus Park just north of Long Wharf. Although it's in need of some rejuvenation, it's still fine for a picnic. There are plenty of benches, moored sailboats, a grassy knoll, a trellised archway draped with wisteria and a cobblestone walkway.

The 1847 **Custom House Block**, on Long Wharf, is typical of the granite warehouses that lined all these wharves. The adjacent 1763 **Chart House** is the only remaining brick warehouse. Heading south, **Central Wharf** is home to the New England Aquarium, which sponsors the **Big Dig/Central**

Artery Exhibition across the street at East India Row.

New England Aquarium Teeming with sea creatures of all sizes, shapes and colors, the aquarium (☎ 617-973-5200, www.neaq .org), on Central Wharf off Atlantic Ave, is equally popular with adults and children. Harbor seals and sea otters, frolicking in a large entrance observation tank, introduce the main indoor attraction: a three-story, cylindrical saltwater tank. It swirls with more than 600 creatures great and small, including turtles, sharks and eels. Leave time to be mesmerized by the *Echo of the Waves* sculpture, not to mention 'Coastal Rhythms,' which explores the lives of animals at water's edge and their habitats. Sea lion shows take place four or five times daily.

You can have a quick meal here and catch whale watching cruises as well (see Activities, later in this chapter). The Aquarium is open 9 am to 5 pm weekdays, until 6 pm on weekends, and until 8 pm on Wednesday and Thursday in the summer. Admission is $12 adults, $10 seniors, $6 children. Seniors are free on Monday afternoon from January to late May.

Rowes Wharf One of Boston's most beautiful and successful commercial developments anchors the southern edge of the waterfront. The Boston Harbor Hotel, with an enormous domed, arched gateway, shares its prime waterfront location with ferry boat terminals. The octagonal glass pavilion is undoubtedly the country's most elegant ferry waiting room. There are public restrooms in the ferry terminal building.

Seaport District

Separated from Boston proper by the jellyfish-laden Fort Point Channel, the new commercial zone can be reached via two gateways, each symbolizing the political battle charting the area's future. The sleek new Evelyn Moakley Bridge is named after the late wife of Boston's powerful US congressman, who rakes in millions of federal dollars for city projects. The bridge diverts auto traffic from the old Northern Ave Bridge, a creaky but beloved erector-set bridge that swings open to allow boat traffic to pass. It remains to be seen whether the old bridge will be preserved as a pedestrian link to Fan Pier and the Seaport. Will this mean an 'incremental annihilation' of the working harbor, as some suspect? Answering this question pits politicians, architects, business leaders and environmentalists against one another. As the old makes way for the new, the retail lobster establishment **James Hook & Co Lobsters**, established in the 1920s, clings to life between the two bridges. So does the Barking Crab (see Places to Eat).

The Seaport District plan calls for 5000 to 8000 units of housing, small-scale city blocks, mostly low-level buildings, condos, offices, a few parks, hotels, a $700 million convention center and a new Institute for Contemporary Art on the water's edge. Major questions are being hashed out as this is written: Is there enough land set aside for parks; will it become a 24-hour neighborhood or will it empty out after 5 pm; will any of it remain a working port or will it end up looking like Back Bay; can South Boston residents actually afford to live here; how many developers will get variances to build *really* tall buildings?

Federal Courthouse

The sweeping **federal courthouse** occupies the most prominent site on **Fan Pier**, just over the Moakley and Northern Ave Bridges. In September 1787, 500 copies of the document that would become the US Constitution were printed and distributed to the members of the Constitutional Convention in Philadelphia. Only nine copies remain and one is on display at the courthouse through 2004. Walk around the building, inside and out, to get a good sense of Boston's combination of links to the past and visions of the future. On the water side, there is a lovely park with brick and granite walkways. Downtown views are stunning from here.

The area southeast of the courthouse is not particularly welcoming to pedestrians. Nonetheless, heading east along Northern Ave and the water, **Commonwealth Pier** supports the **World Trade Center**, where conventions are held. The ferry to Provincetown departs from here (also see the Excursions chapter). Just beyond is the country's oldest continually operating **fish pier**. And on the pier beyond that, whale watching cruises depart (see Activities, later in this chapter) and the **Fleet Boston Pavilion** hosts outdoor summer music performances (see the Entertainment chapter).

Fort Point Area Beyond the Summer St or Congress St Bridges over Fort Point Channel is a district of old brick warehouses, the center of the nation's wool trade until the 1960s. The core of this enclave, referred to as the Fort Point neighborhood, stretches along and around the first few blocks of Congress and Summer Sts. Note the gracefully curving **Melcher St warehouses**. Most old buildings contain artists' lofts, design studios and warehouses with busy loading docks. But as the area becomes more developed, the artists who revitalized it are being squeezed out and put on the endangered species list.

The nucleus for the Fort Point Arts Community is their gallery-cum-café (☎ 617-423-4299), at 300 Summer St (see Art Galleries in the Shopping chapter), and the **A St Diner**, at Melcher and A Sts, a neighborhood institution with Formica tables, red benches and kitschy and avant-garde art. It serves a mix of artists, businesspeople and construction workers. You want to know what's happening to this district? Step into the microcosm.

Children's Museum The iconic giant white milk bottle on Fort Point Channel is the only sign necessary for this delightful museum (☎ 617-426-8855, www.bostonkids.org), 300 Congress St. Children of all ages can be entertained for an entire day with interactive educational exhibits. There are bubble displays, dress-up areas, a two-story climbing gym and an exhibit on what it's like to be a Tokyo teen.

The museum is open 10 am to 5 pm Tuesday through Sunday and on Monday when school is not in session. From 5 to 9 pm Friday year-round, admission is reduced to $1 for everyone. (Be forewarned, it's crowded then!) Otherwise, admission is $7 adults, $6 seniors and children (2 to 15), $2 for one year olds.

***Beaver II* & the Boston Tea Party Museum** The ship and museum (☎ 617-338-1773, www.historictours.com), Congress St Bridge, stands as testimony to spirited colonists who refused to pay the levy imposed on their beloved beverage. In 1773, after a rabble-rousing town meeting at the Old South Meeting House, the rabble donned Native American garb as disguise, boarded the *Beaver* (the *Beaver II*, which you board today, is an approximate replica)

KIM GRANT

A cold (milk) plunge at the Children's Museum

and dumped all the tea overboard in rebellion. Costumed guides tell the story, while the adjacent museum offers multilingual information and a complimentary cup of tax-free (Salada) tea.

The ship and museum are open 9 am to 5 pm daily March through November (until 6 pm late May to mid-September); admission to both sites is $8 adults, $7 students, $4 children.

South Station Area When it was built in 1900, South Station was the world's largest railroad station. Decades of heavy use took their toll, but a late-1980s renovation brought the magnificent gateway back up to par. Today, the curved five-story building is formally called the South Station Transportation Center to include the abutting bus station. The grand terminal is alive with fast-food eateries, café tables, a newsstand and, on many summer afternoons, live concerts.

Across the street, the aluminum-sheathed **Federal Reserve Bank** (☎ 617-973-3453 gallery, ☎ 617-973-3451 tours), 600 Atlantic Ave, has a ground-floor public art gallery, Thursday lunchtime concerts at 12:30 pm and Friday morning tours once a month. Connected by an outdoor passageway to the rear of South Station, the **US post office**, officially called the South Postal Annex, is open 24 hours a day, 365 days a year.

Leather District This little pocket of uniform brick buildings – along South and Lincoln Sts – was built after the great fire of 1872. Many of the five- and six-story buildings have Romanesque arches, big windows and carved ornamentation. They shelter some fine art galleries, a few funky restaurants and shops and increasingly pricey residential lofts.

THEATER DISTRICT & CHINATOWN (MAP 7)

'Midtown Cultural District' is a fancy name, used only by the mayor's office, for the Theater District. The area, home to large and smaller-scale performance venues, is roughly bordered by Tremont, Boylston and Charles St South. Its neighbor, Chinatown, doesn't rival San Francisco's, but it is a thriving, colorful and tight-knit community. It is bordered by Essex, Hudson, Tremont and Marginal Sts, but the New England Medical Center has taken over much of Chinatown south of Kneeland St. Bay Village is a quiet enclave of attached three-story brick townhouses, wedged inside Stuart, Arlington, Marginal and Charles St South.

The Chinatown T station is on the Orange Line; the Boylston T station, closer to the Theater District and Bay Village, is on the Green Line. From South Station on the Red Line, it's just a five-minute walk to get to Chinatown.

Theater District

During the 18th century, waterfront wharves and marshy shoreline made up the area around Stuart and Washington Sts, but by the mid-1800s, thanks to a landfill, it was terra firma. A thriving theater district was

KIM GRANT

The Yin Yang mural, Chinatown

born, extending north on Tremont St to the Orpheum and back down along Washington St. Actors from England and Europe performed on these stages in so many theaters so close together that underground tunnels were built between them, allowing patrons to go from one to another without getting wet during rainstorms.

Through the 1940s, Boston had over 50 theaters. The area today is tiny by New York standards, but the opulent palaces that remain have recently received long-needed face-lifts.

The **Wang Center for the Performing Arts**, 268 Tremont St, built in 1925, is opulent, baroque, gilded and cavernous. The Wang, as it's known, was modeled on the Paris Opera Comique, then became a movie palace, then fell into a state of disrepair to be bailed out by early computer innovator An Wang. The Wang is now operated by Joe Spaulding, who is both lionized as having

Piano Row

The Beaux Arts **Emerson Majestic Theatre**, 219 Tremont St, was restored to its ornate majesty and luster by Emerson College in 1983. The lavish, high rococo-style space, decked with marble and neoclassical friezes, showcases many nonprofit and multicultural performance troupes.

While the lavish **Colonial Theatre**, 106 Boylston St, is ingeniously enveloped by an office building, inside it's still resplendent with all the gilded ornamentation, mirrors and frescoes it had in 1900.

Boylston Place

Off Boylston St is Boylston Place, a pedestrian-only alley marked by Greek tragedy and comedy masks and lined with bars and nightclubs (see the Entertainment chapter). As suburban patrons spill out of nearby theaters, things start to hum here. A bit of daytime action takes place within the adjacent, massive and drearily named **State Transportation Building**, 10 Park Plaza, which takes up the entire block of Stuart St and Charles St South. Here you'll find an atrium courtyard with fast-food vendors, free lunchtime concerts and art exhibits. **Piano Row**, on Boylston St between Charles and Tremont Sts, was the American epicenter of music publishing and piano building in the 19th and early 20th centuries. There are still a few piano stores here.

Bay Village

An often overlooked but charming neighborhood, Bay Village is certainly worth a stroll. With its early-19th-century brick houses, the enclave resembles a scaled-down Beacon Hill. Today, it's home to a tight-knit gay community. Buildings of particular note include 1 Bay St (built in the 1830s), Fayette St row houses and Art Deco details on 115 Broadway. At the corner of Arlington St and Columbus Ave, the **Park Plaza Castle**, more formally known as the First Corps of Cadets Armory, was built in 1897 for an organization originally founded in 1741 to guard the governor of Mass Bay Colony. It's now used as exhibition and convention space for the Park Plaza Hotel and hosts the popular 'Crafts at the Castle' sale in early December.

single-handedly saved theater in Boston and maligned for having dumped smaller local productions in favor of more profitable commercial ones.

Across the street, the illustrious **Shubert Theatre**, 265 Tremont St, with Florentine doors, a marble entryway and Ionic columns, originally hosted *The King and I*, *Camelot* and Richard Burton's *Hamlet*. Its chandelier replicates one that's in Le Petit Trianon at Versailles.

Just next door to the Wang Center is the **Wilbur Theater**, 246 Tremont St, with a colonial revival exterior. The Wilbur premiered Thornton Wilder's *Our Town* and Tennessee Williams' *A Streetcar Named Desire*, starring a youngster named Marlon Brando. It has just 1000 seats.

The small **Charles Playhouse**, 76 Warrenton St, was originally built as a church and wasn't converted to a theater until the late 1950s.

Chinatown

This tiny area is overflowing with authentic restaurants (many open until 4 am), bakeries, markets selling live animals, import and textile shops, and phone booths topped with little pagodas. The enormous **Chinatown Gate** guards the entrance at Beach and Kingston Sts. In addition to the Chinese, who began arriving in the late 1870s, this community of 8000 also includes Cambodians, Vietnamese and Laotians. **Beach St**, **Harrison Ave** and **Tyler St** are the most colorful.

The nearly nonexistent **Combat Zone**, around the Chinatown T station, consists of a handful of unmistakably XXX-rated theaters and bookstores.

BACK BAY (MAP 8)

During the 1850s, when Boston was experiencing a population and building boom, Back Bay was an uninhabitable tidal flat. To solve the problem, urban planners embarked on an ambitious and wildly successful 30-year project: to fill in the 450-acre marsh (using the dam that had been dotted with mills running from Beacon Hill to Brookline), lay out an orderly grid of streets (including service alleys), erect magnificent Victorian brownstones and design high-minded civic plazas.

It would take one day to fill enough land for two house lots – one day, that is, of 35-car trains hauling gravel every 45 minutes between Boston and a nearby quarry. The hard labor was done by Irish immigrants.

The result, Back Bay, is one of Boston's architectural treasures. Although the neighborhood is home to successful young professionals and blue-blood Bostonians, Back Bay also has a fringe student population that tempers its tendency toward stodginess. (During the Great Depression, when many families couldn't afford to maintain these lavish single-family houses, the buildings were subdivided into apartments or converted into dormitories.) Back Bay is at its most enchanting late April to early June, when magnolia and dogwood trees are in bloom.

The area is bounded by the Public Garden and Arlington St to the northeast, Mass Ave to the southwest, the Charles River to the northwest and Stuart St and Huntington Ave to the southeast. Cross streets are laid out alphabetically from Arlington St to Hereford St.

Although this is a large neighborhood, the alphabetical grid street pattern is easy to decipher, so getting around is a breeze. Take the Green Line T to Copley for Copley Square (or the Orange Line to Back Bay), to Hynes/ICA for the hip end of Newbury St and to Prudential ('E' branch of the Green Line) for the Christian Science Center.

Comm Ave Mall

A solid link in Frederick Law Olmsted's Emerald Necklace (see 'Emerald Necklace,' later in this chapter), this grand boulevard – the Champs Élysées of Boston – connects the Public Garden with the Back Bay Fens. The grassy nine-block parkway is dotted with a diverse selection of public sculptures (almost one for every block), benches for relaxing and stately trees. A new sculpture on the only plot remaining, between Fairfield and Gloucester Sts, might be installed by early 2001. (It will be the mall's only statue representing the accomplishments of women.) Unfortunately, the trees on the mall are succumbing to the virulent Dutch elm disease. As they do, they're being replaced with more disease-proof varieties. A two- or three-block stroll down the mall is a great introduction to the neighborhood's stately brownstones.

Gibson House Museum

To appreciate how opulent Back Bay mansions were furnished in the 19th century, visit the Gibson House (☎ 617-267-6338), 137 Beacon St near Arlington St. Interestingly, the exterior of this splendid five-story Victorian brownstone barely merits a glance. Inside, though, it's filled with a charming mishmash of bric-a-brac, mementos and antiques. The house is open Wednesday through Sunday May through October; weekends from November through April. Tours are given at 1, 2 and 3 pm. Tickets are $5 for everyone older than age 12; children are free. The Victorian Society (☎ 617-789-3927) is headquartered here.

Newbury St

International boutiques and galleries get
tonier as you get closer to the Public Garden
(see Newbury St in the Shopping chapter).
The closer you get to Mass Ave, the more
nose rings, platform shoes and dyed hair
you'll see. Newbury St is fun at night when
shops are closed but the well-lit windows are
dressed to the nines, and when darkness
cloaks your less-than-Armani attire.

Institute for Contemporary Art

Although the ICA (☎ 617-266-5152), 955
Boylston St, doesn't have a permanent collection, it livens up Boston's conservative art
scene by showcasing avant-garde art by
well-known national artists and unknown
regional artists. The quirky space, within a
renovated 19th-century firehouse and police
station, isn't always conducive to highlighting art at its best. It's open noon to 5 pm
Wednesday through Sunday (until 9 pm
Thursday, until 7 pm Friday). Tickets are $6

adults, $4 seniors and students over 12, free
under 12; it's free 5 to 9 pm on Thursday.

Christian Science Church

Known to adherents as the 'Mother Church'
(☎ 617-450-3790, www.tfccs.com), 175 Huntington Ave at Mass Ave, this is the international home base for the Church of Christ,
Scientist, or Christian Science, founded by
Mary Baker Eddy in 1866. The grand 1894
classical revival basilica, which can seat 5000
worshippers, boasts the largest organ in the
western world. (The amazing 14,000-pipe
organ was made in Boston.) The expansive,
formal plaza has a 670-foot-long **reflecting
pool**.

The offices of the internationally regarded daily newspaper, the *Christian Science Monitor* (www.csmonitor.com), which
Eddy founded at age 88, are next-door.
There's also an elegant reading room and
the **Mapparium**, one of Boston's hidden
treasures. The Mapparium is a room-sized,

The Christian Science Mother Church reigns over its reflecting pool.

stained-glass globe that you can walk through on a glass bridge. Geopolitical boundaries are drawn as the world appeared in 1935. The acoustics, which were a surprise to the designer, are a wonder: No matter how softly you whisper into the ear of your companion, everyone in the room will hear you perfectly!

Hours for the Mother Church, currently undergoing extensive renovation, were not set at the time of this writing, but tours are still given at 11:30 am on Sunday (following services) and 1:15 and 2:15 pm on Wednesday. The Mapparium is closed for renovations until autumn 2000. Admission to both is free.

Copley Square

This high-minded square – set between Dartmouth, Clarendon and Boylston Sts and St James Ave – is surrounded by significant historic buildings, including Trinity

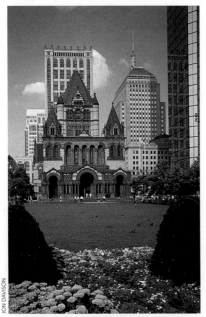

Copley Square has a blend of architecture both old and new.

Church and the Boston Public Library. The plaza itself has always been overlooked though, and even with recent renovations, there are still problems with the fountain, trees and grass.

The magnificent **New Old South Church** (☎ 617-536-1970), 645 Boylston St, is often referred to as the 'new' Old South because, up until 1875, the congregation worshiped in their original home, now called the Old South Meeting House. It's open 9 am to 5 pm daily from mid-June to early September; the rest of the year hours are variable, but if you arrive by 4:30 pm on weekdays and 2 pm on weekends, you'll probably get in.

Duck into the 1912 **Fairmont Copley Plaza Hotel**, at St James Ave and Dartmouth St, with Boston's most opulently appointed lobby. Crystal chandeliers, veined marble and other lavish touches abound in the lobby, restaurant, bar, 'oval room' and grand ballroom. This 'plaza hotel' was designed by the same architect who did New York's famed Plaza Hotel.

Next-door, the 62-story **John Hancock Tower**, 200 Clarendon St, was constructed with more than 10,000 panels of mirrored glass. Because it reflects more sky and clouds than land, the building isn't nearly as intrusive as its mass would suggest. Designed in 1976 by IM Pei, the tower suffered serious initial problems: Inferior glass panes were installed and when the wind whipped up (which it does frequently here), the panes popped out, plummeting hundreds of feet to the ground. The area was quickly cordoned off and all the panes were replaced. Luckily, no one was ever hurt (but the engineers' egos took a drubbing). A sophisticated early-detection glass monitoring system was added to warn of future stress problems. Recalling that Back Bay is one great landfill, the building's weight also caused water table problems (flooded basements) for the tower's neighbors. There are great views from the **observatory**.

The plaza has plebeian-sized, down-to-earth elements, too. Since the finish line for the Boston Marathon is in front of the Boston Public Library and runners end up in a staging area here, the plaza honors the

JON DAVISON

athletes who compete. Don't overlook the **Boston Marathon Monument**, embedded in the sidewalk on Boylston St near Dartmouth St. The *Tortoise & the Hare*, a bronze cast by sculptor Nancy Schon (who cast *Make Way for Ducklings* in the Public Garden), honors the philosophical differences between sprinters and slow-and-steady long-distance runners. There's also a refreshing fountain and a Farmers' Market from 11 am to 6 pm Tuesday and Friday, June to late October.

Trinity Church

Designed by Henry Hobson Richardson from 1872–77, the church (☎ 617-536-0944), 206 Clarendon St, is one of the nation's truly great buildings. But for all his creative work, the Harvard-educated Richardson was paid less than one percent of the final construction costs. (The project did come in at almost four times over the original estimated cost of $200,000; what's an artist to do?) The granite exterior, with a massive portico and side cloister, uses sandstone in colorful patterns. The grand but compact French and Romanesque building rests on 2000 wooden pilings, typical of massive Back Bay buildings, which must be kept submerged in water in order to maintain their strength and integrity. The church is open 8 am to 6 pm daily and for Sunday services.

Boston Public Library

The esteemed Boston Public Library (☎ 617-536-5400, www.bpl.org), 666 Boylston St, dates to 1852 and lends credence to Boston's reputation as the 'Athens of America.' True to the exterior's inscription, all of its fine lectures and programs are free.

The library contains great works of art and special collections. You'll find John Adams' presidential papers here; the BPL is the only public institution to house a presidential library. Frequent tours are given to various collections, including the rare book collection (which, for some reason, boasts a lock of John Hancock's hair). The 3rd floor features John Singer Sargent's unfinished Judaic and Christian murals, which were criticized for anti-Semitic messages. Many

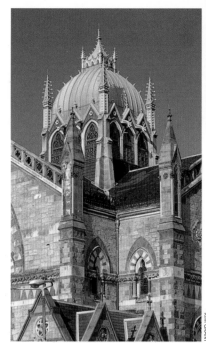

New Old South Church

KIM GRANT

wished he hadn't departed from his usual portraits.

The original McKim building, inspired by Italian Renaissance palazzi, features enormous bronze doorways by Daniel Chester French flanked by iron gates and lanterns. From there, a palatial marble staircase leads to the absolutely splendid **Bates Hall Reading Room**, restored in mid-1990 to its original glory. (The whole library is undergoing a 10-year renovation project.) Even the most mundane musings are elevated by the barrel-vaulted, 50-foot coffered ceilings. Some of the furniture dates to the library's 1895 opening.

Although more than 2 million people visit annually, most bypass the walled-in tranquil Italian-style **courtyard** garden, which has a reflecting pool and trees. It's open 9 am to 9 pm Monday through Thursday, 9 am to 5 pm Friday and Saturday, 1 to 5 pm Sunday.

THINGS TO SEE & DO

BPL by the Numbers

The Boston Public Library, which has been experiencing a renaissance akin to when it first opened its doors, is massive in its holdings and statistics. The BPL:

- was the first free municipal library in the US

- boasts more than 6.1 million books (12 for every resident of Boston) and 1.25 million rare books

- was the first library to allow patrons to borrow books

- holds more than 17,000 current magazines and 370,000 maps

- instituted the first branch system linked to a central library

- issues more than 500,000 library cards and answers 1.2 million queries annually

- is one of only two US public libraries belonging to the international Association of Research Libraries (the New York Public Library is the other)

- houses 10 million patents, one million manuscripts, 675,000 photographs and 120,000 musical scores

- has 400 online databases that take up practically no space and old-fashioned shelves that run for 65 miles

- established the first separate children's room and has 500,000 children's books – 128 of which are copies of *Make Way for Ducklings*

- suffered from a basement flood during the summer of 1998 that destroyed tens of thousands of books and maps

SOUTH END (MAP 9)

The South End is Boston's most ethnically, racially and economically diverse neighborhood. Sammy Davis, Jr, and Louis Mayer (of Metro-Goldwyn-Mayer movie mogul fame) both grew up here, as did Lebanese immigrant and poet Kahlil Gibran. Martin Luther King, Jr, and Coretta Scott King lived here while MLK was a Boston University theology student.

The South End doesn't have many sights per se, but parts of it are charming and it is home to several vibrant communities. Huge sections have been claimed by artists, gay men and young professionals (sending real estate prices soaring), but south of Washington St is less gentrified. Here, housing projects and halfway houses rub elbows with converted condos. The neighborhood has a convivial atmosphere; residents hang out on front porch stoops on warm summer evenings and bar- and restaurant-hop down Tremont St year-round.

By the mid- to late-1800s, the South End tidal flats had been filled and the area became fashionable, a spacious alternative to Beacon Hill. But by the end of the century, the middle class had fled to new suburbs like Brookline and the upper class jumped ship for Back Bay. The neighborhood slumped until the 1970s, when landlords began converting the elegant but decrepit brownstones from rooming houses to condos.

Today, the South End is finally the trendy area that early developers intended. Boasting the country's largest concentration of Victorian row houses, it's been designated a National Historic District. Side streets retain their London-style architectural flavor with side-by-side residences, steep stoops and tiny ornamental gardens.

The South End is bounded by Huntington Ave, Mass Ave, Albany St and the Mass Turnpike. Columbus Ave and Tremont St, lined with au courant restaurants, are the principal commercial streets.

This large neighborhood is not well served by public transportation. On the Orange Line, the Back Bay T station is convenient for the eastern edge, Mass Ave for the western. Prudential, on the 'E' branch of the Green Line, is best for sites in between.

Columbus Ave Area

Paved and landscaped, perfect for strolling or urban jogging, the **Southwest Corridor Park** is almost 5 miles long. It goes from behind the Copley Place mall on Dartmouth

Community Activism

The South End has a rich and deeply rooted history of community activism. As early as 1968, activists feared gentrification would bring displacement. To dramatize Boston's lack of affordable housing, community leader Mel King and nearly 100 others staged a protest on the parcel that **Tent City**, a mixed-income housing project, would eventually occupy at Dartmouth St and Columbus Ave. Built in 1988, Tent City was the first development to link high-end commercial projects with more affordable ones that benefit all community members; in order to build Copley Place, developers had to build Tent City.

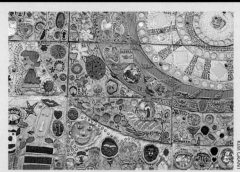

Mosaic adorns the Villa Victoria.

The primarily Puerto Rican housing project, **Villa Victoria**, between West Dedham and West Brookline Sts, was built during the 1970s in response to another community's fears of displacement. Although the buildings are not particularly aesthetic, the thriving enclave emphasizes outdoor spaces, shops and barrier-free walkways for the wheelchair-bound.

Deep in the South End, between Harrison Ave and the expressway, the **Pine St Inn** provides social services and shelter to homeless individuals. Housed in the former Fire Dept Headquarters, modeled after the Palazzo Vecchio in Florence, Italy, the organization is highly visible in more ways than one.

Renamed in honor of onetime slave and Underground Railroad organizer Harriet Tubman, the **United South End Settlements** (also known as the Harriet Tubman House), at Columbus and Mass Aves, houses an energetic social service agency.

St to the Forest Hills T station near Arnold Arboretum. Walk northeast from Mass Ave for rewarding views of the Back Bay skyline. **St Botolph St** is also pleasant for walking.

Triangular **Columbus Square**, at Columbus Ave and Warren St, has two statues honoring activism and freedom: the **Harriet Tubman Statue** (she spoke in Boston often, galvanizing abolitionists) and the **Emancipation, 1913 Statue**, erected on the 50th anniversary of the Emancipation Proclamation.

Tremont St

It might as well be called 'restaurant row' for the number of fashionable eateries that have sprung up along the South End stretch of Tremont. In addition, a number of particu-

larly quaint, tranquil streets and parks (most completed in the 1850s and 1860s) are just off Tremont, including the elliptical **Union Park** between Tremont St and Shawmut Ave. The narrow Rutland Square, just north of Tremont St, is really just a strip of grass and flowers that are surrounded by an iron gate, but the intimate scale brings the whole street together.

A contemporary arts scene also thrives in the South End, and nowhere more so than at the **Boston Center for the Arts** (☎ 617-426-5000), 539 Tremont St. The BCA houses theaters and exhibition spaces, including the **Cyclorama**, an enormous domed performance venue. Around the corner, ballerinas practice pirouettes at the spiffy **Boston**

THINGS TO SEE & DO

Ballet Center (☎ 617-695-6950), 19 Clarendon St; call about special tours. The Boston Ballet performs at the Wang (see the Entertainment chapter).

South of Washington St

Washington St was the only through road in 17th- and 18th-century Boston. For most of the 20th century, the Washington St El, one of the country's first elevated trains, followed alongside it. When the Orange Line was rerouted underground in the 1980s, the El was demolished, leaving a wide scar. While it was noisy and ugly, the El did provide a key link to economic opportunity downtown for the communities it served. The link has not been replaced. For years, blighted Washington St was ignored, but in the wake of a red-hot real estate market, developers' interest in the area has been reignited. This area is in a state of flux, as its character changes significantly from one block to another. Women may not feel safe alone here at night.

The large brick warehouses between Harrison Ave and Albany St have long housed artists in walk-up flats. South End Open Studios in mid-September provides public access to this artistic enclave.

When the 1875 **Cathedral of the Holy Cross**, on Washington St at Union Park St, was built, it was America's largest Catholic cathedral, as big as Westminster Abbey. It's definitely worth a look.

KENMORE SQUARE & FENWAY (MAP 10)

The Kenmore Square area – with rowdy bars and dance clubs, inexpensive but nondescript eateries and dormitories disguised as brownstones – is the epicenter of Boston University (BU) student life. The behemoth BU stretches along Comm Ave, and a half dozen other area colleges add to the mix. This lively, somewhat seedy area is also dominated by Fenway Park (home of the Boston Red Sox) and sports bars.

South of Kenmore Square is Fenway, a large area named for its centerpiece, the Back Bay Fens (the marshy banks of the Muddy River) or 'the Fens.' The Fens are

Gas station-cum-compass

one section of an interconnected park system (see 'Emerald Necklace,' later in this chapter).

There are many similarly named sites and landmarks here, so the nomenclature can be confusing, even to Bostonians. To keep it straight: Fenway is the neighborhood. The Fenway is a winding former carriageway, now a highway, that skirts the Fens. Fenway Park is a baseball stadium. North of the Fens is a little cluster of streets lined with low-quality student housing (with nicely maintained exteriors) and modestly priced restaurants.

A number of cultural institutions, including two renowned museums – the Museum of Fine Arts and the Isabella Stewart Gardner Museum – are in Fenway, along and just off Huntington Ave.

Beacon St and Comm Ave run through Kenmore Square; Brookline Ave originates in the square and runs past Fenway Park. The 'B,' 'C' and 'D' branches of the Green Line stop at Kenmore (the stop for Fenway Park) and then head aboveground.

Fenway Park

What's Boston's most cherished landmark? Site of Boston's greatest dramas and worst defeats? To many Bostonians, it's not Bunker Hill or the Freedom Trail, not Harvard or MIT, but tiny Fenway Park, home of baseball's Red Sox, where names like Babe Ruth, Ted Williams, Carl Yastrzemski and Jim Rice are uttered and remembered as reverently as any hero from Boston's colonial history. Pitcher Pedro Martinez and shortstop Nomar Garciaparra are the new stars in this constellation, adding to their legacies game by game.

Nestled between the Fens and the Mass Pike, Fenway Park is truly an integral part of Boston. The park is little more than a hundred yards from Kenmore Square and adjoins Lansdowne St (also known as Ted Williams Way). Fenway Park remains a baseball mecca. One of the last survivors of old-style baseball parks, the field itself has a devoted following beyond that of the team. Only Wrigley Field in Chicago rivals it in age and uniqueness.

Red Sox fans are nothing if not loyal (the Red Sox are a top draw in the major leagues), despite the team's failure to win a World Series in more than 80 years. Much of the team's ill fate is attributed to the legendary 'Curse of the Great Bambino,' the 1918 sale of their best young pitcher, Babe Ruth, to the hated rival New York Yankees. The Red Sox have not won a World Series since that season, while Babe Ruth and the Yankees went on to achieve success and fame throughout the century. In 1999, hopes were higher than they had been for years, with fans waving 'Reverse the Curse' placards. But the Yankees beat the Sox for the American League Pennant and went on to win the World Series – again. Many believe the sale of Ruth to be among the worst transactions in professional sports history.

Baseball played in Fenway is made special by the unique geometry of the park. Thanks to its downtown location, an economy of space gives fans an intimate proximity to the playing field. The Fenway Faithful claim to feel more a part of the ball game than might be possible in larger, more modern parks. Fenway also has the one and only 'Green Monster,' a towering left-field wall that compensates for the relatively short distance from home plate. The Green Monster consistently alters the regular course of play – what appears to be a lazy fly ball could actually drop over the Monster for a home run, and what appears to be a sharp double into the gap may be played off the wall to hold the runner to a single.

So fabled and important a site as Fenway Park certainly should have protection against urban development. However, that's not the case. The current plan – always subject to change and massive high hurdles – is to build a new adjacent stadium sometime in the near future. According to a current plan, only the Green Monster will survive the rehaul.

Tours (☎ 617-236-6666) of the stadium are offered from Gate D on Yawkey Way on the hour between 10 am and 2 pm weekdays (when there isn't a game) mid-April to mid-September. Tickets cost $5 adults, $4 seniors, $3 children.

For more information on attending a game, see Spectator Sports in the Entertainment chapter.

The 'B' branch runs along Comm Ave with stops at Blandford (for the Photographic Resource Center), BU East, BU Central and BU West. The 'C' branch follows Beacon St out to Coolidge Corner (see Outlying Neighborhoods, later in this chapter). The 'D' branch runs along the Riverway; it stops at 'Fenway' which, despite its name, is not the closest stop to Fenway Park or the Back Bay Fens. The 'E' branch runs along Huntington Ave, stops at Symphony and then runs aboveground to Northeastern, Museum (for the MFA and Gardner) and Longwood (for MassArt). The trolley then turns onto South Huntington Ave and Centre St for Jamaica Pond (at Pond St).

Emerald Necklace

Widely considered the father of landscape design architecture, Frederick Law Olmsted made an indelible mark on Boston's urban landscape, linking patches of green space from Boston Common to Franklin Park, some 7 miles distant. His firm spent nearly 20 years on the project, between 1878 and 1896. Olmsted was both a physical and social engineer. In addition to solving drainage and sewage problems, it was his noble contention that parks bring together people of all social and economic backgrounds.

The interconnected parks begin with Boston Common, the Public Garden and Comm Ave Mall, none of which Olmsted designed but which he intended to link to the newer parks. From there, the Back Bay Fens leads to the Riverway, Jamaica Pond, Arnold Arboretum and Franklin Park.

The **Frederick Law Olmsted National Historic Site** (☎ 617-566-1689), 99 Warren St off Brookline Ave in Brookline, which includes the house, office and grounds, is run by the NPS and is open for tours; call for times and directions. It's about a mile from the Brookline Hills stop on the 'D' branch of the Green Line.

The Boston Park Rangers (see Organized Tours in the Getting Around chapter) give weekly free guided walks and talks around the individual parks and a daylong tour of the entire Necklace two or three times per year. You can certainly walk the distance on your own, but doing the full trek all at once won't leave you much time or energy to explore the individual parks. The Riverway and the Jamaicaway are busy auto thoroughfares, less than peaceful byways. Consequently, the entire route might be best appreciated as a bicycle ride. The Riverway and Jamaica Pond have separate bicycle and running paths. Bicycling is not permitted within the Public Garden.

Back Bay Fens (Map 10) The aptly named Muddy River comes almost to a standstill here, in a wide swath of parkland bordered by Park Drive and the Fenway. The river's winding banks are choked with phragmites, a tall invasive reed that frequently serves as camouflage for sexual encounters. In recent years, there have been a number of gay-bashing incidents; it's not advisable that anyone linger in the Fens after dark.

The Fens has sites that draw visitors by day: the beloved Community Gardens, near Boylston St and Park Drive; the elegant Kelleher Rose Garden, near Jersey St and Park Drive, with over 2000 bushes; open grassy areas where college students sunbathe; ball fields; and two original Olmsted stone bridges.

You can reach the Fens from the Comm Ave Mall by walking south along Charlesgate West or East, but it might make more sense to combine a visit with the MFA or Gardner Museum ('E' branch of the Green Line).

Jamaica Pond The idyllic spring-fed pond, on the west side of the Jamaicaway, is more than 50-feet deep and great for boating (☎ 617-522-6258) and fishing. Joggers circle the mile loop around the pond. In summer, picnickers converge near the bandstand for concerts. Take the 'E' branch of the Green Line to the corner of Centre and Pond Sts and walk down Pond.

Arnold Arboretum The 265-acre arboretum (☎ 617-524-1717, www.arboretum.harvard.edu), 125 The Arborway, is a gem – particularly in spring. Under a public/private partnership between Boston and Harvard University, it's planted with more than 14,000 botanical specimens, including exotic trees and flowering shrubs. Dog walking, Frisbee throwing, bicycling and general contemplation are encouraged, but picnicking is not allowed. It's free and open daily from dawn to dusk. A visitors center is located at the main gate, just south of the traffic circle/rotary at MA 1 and MA 203.

Emerald Necklace

Take the Orange Line to Forest Hills and walk a quarter-mile northwest to the Forest Hills gate (follow signs). The aboveground 'E' branch of the Green Line is much slower than the Orange Line.

Franklin Park & Franklin Park Zoo Back in the late 1800s, in an effort to solicit Ben Franklin to contribute some of his trust fund toward the expensive park, the city named it in his honor. It didn't work; the city had to borrow $2 million to build the park, but nevertheless retained the name.

At 500-plus acres, the park is an underutilized resource. That's partly because of its location – bordering an iffy (by night) neighborhood – and partly because it's large, the layout is confusing and parts are disconcertingly deserted. Still, on weekend afternoons the park is full of families from the nearby multiethnic neighborhoods of Jamaica Plain, Dorchester and Roxbury. The park provides a slice of city life most tourists never experience. In addition to ball fields, there's a popular public golf course (☎ 617-265-4084) here. The park is bordered by Seaver St, Blue Hill Ave, Morton St (MA 203) and Forest Hills St. Take the Orange Line to Stony Brook, Green St or Forest Hills and head east for a few blocks until you reach the park's western edge. Keep your wits about you and don't linger longer than the sun.

The 70-acre zoo (☎ 617-541-5466, www.zoonewengland.com), on Blue Hill Ave at Columbia Rd, boasts a Tropical Forest pavilion, complete with lush vegetation, waterfalls, lowland gorillas, a leopard and warthogs. It's a well-designed ecosystem with nearly invisible barriers between you and the animals. The mixed-species Bongo Congo features zebras, ostriches and ibex. There's also an Australian Outback Trail, with wallabies, emus and kangaroos.

The zoo is open 10 am to 5 pm April through September (until 6 pm on weekends) and until 4 pm October through March. Tickets costs $6 adults, $5 seniors, $3 children. The zoo is perfectly safe and worth a visit, though don't expect it to compare with those in New York or San Diego. Take the Orange Line to Forest Hills, then ride the No 16 bus, which departs every 15 minutes and takes about five minutes to reach the zoo.

KIM GRANT

Community Gardens, Back Bay Fens

Museum Visitor Passes

If you're planning a blitz on Boston museums, City Pass (www.citypass.net) can save you some cash. The pass is valid for nine days and admits you to the John F Kennedy Library, John Hancock Observatory, New England Aquarium, Isabella Stewart Gardner Museum, Museum of Fine Arts and the Museum of Science. Priced at $27.50 adults, $20.50 seniors, $14 age 12 to 17, the pass saves you 50% off the total cost of admission.

Kenmore Square

Over the years, Kenmore Square has been a transient home for '60s hippies, '70s and '80s punk rockers, students and panhandlers. These days it's a bit worn and tattered around the edges, though renovations are in the works. There's not much to do in the square itself, but it's easy to find: Look for the mammoth 60-sq-foot **Citgo sign** that has marked the spot since 1965. Two blocks away, **Lansdowne St** is Boston's 'club central,' since the strip is lined with boisterous bars and nightclubs.

Boston University

From Kenmore Square to the BU Bridge and beyond (for another three or four blocks anyway), the overwhelming presence on Comm Ave is BU. The country's third-largest independent university is nothing much to look at. It's mostly concrete, with the exception of some fine houses it has converted on **Bay State Rd**, north of Comm Ave. Since the campus is squeezed between two major roads, it can't expand anywhere but up. Loaded with dining areas, game rooms, TVs and lounges, the **George Sherman Student Union**, 775 Comm Ave, is just east of University Rd.

Photographic Resource Center One block west of Kenmore Square, the experimental PRC (☎ 617-353-0700), 602 Comm Ave, in BU's Morse Auditorium, is one of the few centers in the country devoted ex-clusively to this art form. It's open noon to 5 pm Tuesday through Sunday, until 8 pm on Thursday. Admission is $3 adults, $2 seniors and students; free on Thursday. The well-stocked library is open Tuesday, Thursday and Saturday.

BU Beach This grassy strip between Storrow Drive and Bay State Rd is hardly tranquil, but it does receive afternoon sun. Consequently, on warm days BU students come here to 'study' between classes, avec beach towels and sans shirts. It also has some nice sculpture.

Mugar Memorial Library BU's main research library (☎ 617-353-3696), 771 Comm Ave, has outstanding Special Collections and 20th Century Archives that balance pop culture and scholarly appeal. There are several rotating exhibits on the 1st, 3rd and 5th floors; you may see Bette Davis' Oscar statue for the 1935 *Dangerous* (Davis grew up in nearby Somerville and Newton), works by President Teddy Roosevelt and by the poet Robert Frost, as well as letters by BU alumnus Dr Martin Luther King, Jr. It's quite a remarkable assemblage.

BU's Special Collections are open 9 am to 5 pm weekdays. Special requests require 48 hours notice.

Isabella Stewart Gardner Museum

The Gardner (☎ 617-566-1401, www.boston .com/gardner), 280 the Fenway, is a magnificent Venetian-style palazzo built to house 'Mrs Jack' Gardner's collection, but was also her home until her death in 1924. A monument to one woman's exquisite taste for acquiring unequaled art, the Gardner is filled with almost 2000 priceless objects, primarily European, including outstanding tapestries and Italian Renaissance and 17th-century Dutch paintings.

Mrs Jack's will stipulated that the collection not change one iota after her death. That helps explain a few notably empty spaces on the walls: In 1990, the museum was robbed of nearly $200 million worth of paintings, including a beloved Vermeer. The walls on which they were mounted will remain bare until the paintings are recovered (highly unlikely). It doesn't look like much more than a stately home from the outside, but the palazzo itself, with a four-story greenhouse courtyard, is a masterpiece, a tranquil oasis, alone worth the price of admission. The Gardner has a lovely café that's open for lunch. The museum is open 11 am to 5 pm Tuesday through Sunday. Admission is $11 adults, $7 seniors, $5 students ($3 on Wednesday for students), under 17 free.

Huntington Ave

Dubbed 'Avenue of the Arts,' a concentrated area of major and minor artistic and cultural venues (also see the Entertainment chapter), Huntington Ave extends from Horticultural Hall and Symphony Hall at Mass Ave to the Massachusetts College of Art, or MassArt. Beyond MassArt is **Longwood Medical Area**, northwest of Huntington Ave and southeast of Brookline Ave. It's home to the Mass College of Pharmacy, prestigious Harvard Medical School and renowned Children's Hospital, Brigham & Women's Hospital and Beth Israel Hospital.

Horticultural Hall This grand 1901 English baroque building, 300 Mass Ave, houses the world's largest independent library devoted to gardening. It's home to the venerable Massachusetts Horticultural Society (MHS; ☎ 617-536-9280), founded in 1829. Although the MHS is in financial trouble (it had to sell parts of its 'priceless' library in 1980 and it lost the title to its hall in 1992), it intends to build an ambitious botanical garden on downtown land created by the Big Dig. Stay tuned. In the meantime, head to the 2nd floor for a peek; it's open 9 am to 4:30 pm weekdays.

Symphony Hall Across the street, at 301 Mass Ave at Huntington Ave, the preeminent Boston Symphony Orchestra (☎ 617-266-1492, www.bso.org) performs at this National Historic Landmark. Designed by McKim, Mead & White in 1900, it was the world's first concert hall designed according to acoustic principles; it's still one of the top

ISABELLA STEWART GARDNER MUSEUM, BOSTON

Isabella Stewart Gardner's plunging neckline in this 1888 portrait by Sargent caused quite a stir.

The MFA in Half a Day

The Museum of Fine Arts' encyclopedic collections (☎ 617-267-9300, www.mfa.org), 465 Huntington Ave, are second in this country only to New York's Metropolitan Museum of Art. The main museum is tricky to navigate, but the West Wing, designed by IM Pei in 1981, is a breeze.

Particularly noteworthy are the MFA's holdings of American art, which include more than 60 portraits by John Singleton Copley, 50 by Gilbert Stuart and many by Winslow Homer, John Singer Sargent, Edward Hopper and the Hudson River School. American decorative arts, including furniture, are also well represented. Hunt for the American silver collection, which includes Paul Revere's *Liberty Bowl*. For a real adventure, head to the dusty, musty basement galleries of colonial American art and artifacts. You'll feel like you've stumbled into a 17th-century flea market.

The museum has one of the world's most comprehensive collections of Japanese art, from porcelain to woodblock prints to painted silk screens and samurai regalia. Don't miss the dimly lit temple-like room displaying six massive and awesome Buddhas.

When the museum joined forces with Harvard for a 1905 archaeological expedition at the Great Pyramids at Giza, they hauled back a world-famous collection of mummies and related objects. The recently refurbished galleries provide the royal treatment these treasures deserve. You'll also find one of the most significant collections of Nubian art outside the Sudan.

The collection of European paintings dating from the 11th to the 20th centuries is outdone by only a handful of museums around the globe. Check out the huge stash of French impressionist paintings, including 36 by Claude Monet. It's the largest Monet collection outside France. Look for Donatello's relief, *Madonna of the Clouds*, one of the few rare, authentic works of his displayed in this country.

When it's time to rest, head to Tenshin-En, 'Garden of the Heart of Heaven,' a tranquil Japanese garden. There is also an early-20th-century European garden, the Fraser Garden Court. In warm weather, the outdoor Calderwood Courtyard café serves light meals. A pleasant ground-floor café is nice for tea and cake. There is also an inexpensive and unassuming basement-level cafeteria. Lectures are given and films screened in the Remis Auditorium. Concerts, from jazz to chamber, are held in the courtyard.

The museum is open 10 am to 4:45 pm weekdays (until 9:45 pm Wednesday), 10 am to 5:45 pm weekends; the West Wing stays open until 9:45 pm Thursday and Friday. Admission is $12 adults, $10 seniors, students under 17 are free (except during regular school hours – they wouldn't want kids skipping school to come to the museum!).

three. Every aspect was designed to not trap or muffle music: Seats are upholstered in leather; floors are hardwood oak; balconies are shallow; and the stage angles in so that the music is projected forward. Group tours are offered by appointment, but individuals can latch onto them.

Boston University Theater Home to the highly regarded **Huntington Theatre Co**, 264 Huntington Ave, this theater was a relatively late arrival to the cultural scene, having been built in 1925. The Greek Re-

vival facade fronts an intimate venue with only 850 seats.

The New England Conservatory of Music Founded in 1867, the NEC is the country's oldest music school. The majority of the performances are held at **Jordan Hall** (☎ 617-262-1120 for concert information), on Gainsborough St at Huntington Ave. Eben Jordan, of Jordan Marsh department store fame, contributed his money in 1904 to help build the acoustically superior, intimate hall.

Northeastern University Founded in 1898, the Northeastern campus stretches out along Huntington Ave between Gainsborough and Ruggles Sts. With 20,000 undergrads and 5000 graduate and law students, the Curry Student Center is always busy.

Museum of Fine Arts, Boston This prominent cultural institution houses a world-renowned collection (see 'MFA in Half a Day'). But since Malcolm Rogers took over in 1994, the grand dame's been shaken up. Blockbuster shows (such as *Monet in the 20th Century* and *Herb Ritts: Work*) are denounced as pandering to pop culture. And in a move dubbed the 'Boston Massacre' by art world wags, Rogers consolidated many departments and abruptly fired curatorial staff. Yet, Rogers has 'opened things up,' attendance has doubled, children's programs have blossomed and the long-closed Huntington Ave entrance has reopened.

Massachusetts College of Art MassArt (☎ 617-232-1555, www.massart.edu) was the country's first and remains its only four-year independent public art college. In 1873, state leaders decided the new textile mills in Lowell and Lawrence needed a steady stream of designers, so they figured they'd better educate some. From the beginning, women have comprised more than half the student body.

MassArt fosters 'a holistic notion that art is at the core of an ability to envision a future.' It turns out 'fine art' artists as well as urban planners, high-tech designers and fashion entrepreneurs. Contemporary photographer William Wegman, whose poses weimaraner dogs in various costumes, is one of the most visible alumni. There are two professional galleries (the main one is at 621 Huntington Ave) and more than seven other informal on-campus galleries. It's open 10 am to 6 pm weekdays, 11 am to 5 pm Saturday; free.

CAMBRIDGE

Cambridge, a city of 100,000, is known around the globe as the home of intellectual

KIM GRANT

Intellectualism runs rampant in Harvard Square.

heavyweights Harvard University and MIT. With upwards of 25,000 students, it's a diverse and youthful place, to say the least. Shabby-chic charm predominates, but there are still enclaves of fabulously expensive residences belonging to the politically connected and well-heeled, and immigrant and working-class neighborhoods.

Founded in 1638, Cambridge was home to the country's first college (Harvard) and first printing press, putting an early lock on the city's reputation as a hotbed of ideas and intellectualism.

Cambridge has long been a bastion of progressive politics. Cantabrigians, as residents are called, vehemently opposed the Vietnam War early on; they produced a booklet on how to survive a nuclear war before anyone else did; they embraced the environmental movement before recycling became profitable; and they were one of the first communities to ban smoking in public buildings.

One April Fool's Day not long ago, pranksters put up an official-looking sign that read: 'People's Republic of Cambridge. Passports Please.'

Harvard Square Area (Map 11)

Although the Square has lost its grungy edge – independently owned shops continue to be gobbled up by national chains – it's still worth your while to check out the overflowing cafés, shops, bookstores, restaurants and street musicians. The 'pit,' the brick plaza above the T station, is a mecca for skateboarders with baggy pants and homeless teenagers. The surrounding streets abound with students and teachers, protesters and tourists.

When people refer to 'the Square,' they mean the four- or five-block area radiating from the intersection of Mass Ave and JFK St. In fact, the Square isn't a square at all, but rather a triangle of brick pavement above the Harvard T station, where you'll find the 1928 national landmark **Out of Town News**, with a worldwide selection of magazines and newspapers. The adjacent **information kiosk** has lots of good resources. Note the 21-foot sculpture *Omphalos*, Greek for 'navel' – an apt metaphor for a community that thinks of itself as the center of the universe. Across Mass Ave, chess players hang out all day at the outdoor **Au Bon Pain** café.

Across from the T station, **the Coop** is the country's oldest college cooperative. It was founded in 1882 in response to students' perception that local merchants were price fixing and gouging. (There are highly sought after public restrooms here.)

Find the curved building at Brattle and JFK Sts, and then look for the 2nd-floor sign, **Dewey, Cheetam & Howe**. This is the epicenter of *Car Talk*'s Click and Clack, the two wisecracking brothers Tom and Ray Magliozzi (☎ 617-876-6632, www.cartalk.com). They host a hilarious National Public Radio talk show about car repairs (and life repairs) that broadcasts from 'our fair city.'

KIM GRANT

All the news that's fit to sell

The Harvard T stop on the Red Line is directly below the Square.

More Harvard Sights Between Brattle and Garden Sts, and Appian Way and Mason St, the modest but lovely **Radcliffe Yard** is home to the principal buildings of Radcliffe College, founded in 1879 as the sister school to the then all-male Harvard. The two colleges merged in 1977, and in 1999 Radcliffe ceased to exist except as a network of research institutions (including one for the study of women, gender and society). Within Radcliffe Yard, the **Schlesinger Library** (☎ 617-495-8647) houses the country's preeminent collection of books, photos and oral histories pertaining to women. It's open 9 am to 5 pm weekdays, until 8 pm Wednesday when school is in session.

The distinguished **Harvard Graduate School of Business** (the B-School) is located across the Charles River. Head south on JFK St, cross the Larz Anderson Bridge and head left onto the campus. The B-School has a particularly noteworthy cylindrical chapel with an adjacent pyramid and tiered garden. Students tend to gather at Kresge Hall, where the dining room is located. Aldrich Hall has amphitheater-like classrooms that facilitate 'case method' teaching; note Yousuf Karsh's black-and-white portraits of faculty members in the front hallway. Graduate Jim Koch, founder of Boston Beer Co (makers of Sam Adams), is credited with hatching the American craft brewing industry.

The **JFK School of Government** (☎ 617-495-8290), at Eliot and JFK Sts, was founded in 1936 and changed its name to honor the slain president in 1966. The Kennedy School, extolling bipartisan principles, has faculty members as diverse as conservative former senator Alan Simpson and liberal former Massachusetts governor Michael Dukakis. The C-SPAN broadcast, *Forum*, which deals with weighty matters and looks so darn serious on TV, is actually produced in the cafeteria. The only portrait of JFK painted when he was alive hangs in the entrance.

The **Loeb Drama Center** (☎ 617-547-8300), 64 Brattle St, is home to the professional, prestigious and nonprofit American

Carpenter Center for the Visual Arts, Harvard University

KIM GRANT

Repertory Theater (see Theater in the Entertainment chapter), which presents unconventional adaptations of classics as well as new American plays. There isn't a single bad seat in the small auditorium and the productions are always entertaining and thought-provoking.

The **Harvard College Observatory** (Map 13; ☎ 617-495-9059), 60 Garden St, is open to the public at 7:30 pm the third Thursday of each month for a free 60-minute film and lecture. If the sky is clear, you can peer through the telescopes. Astronomy buffs can call ☎ 617-496-7827 for short recorded lectures about current star conditions.

Harvard Museums The **Carpenter Center for the Visual Arts** houses studios, the excellent Harvard Film Archive (see Cinema in the Entertainment chapter) and two galleries devoted to modern art and photography. Its photography collection is worth seeking out. The center (☎ 617-495-3251), 24 Quincy St, is open 9 am to 11 pm daily.

The **Fogg Art Museum** (☎ 617-495-9400, www.artmuseums.harvard.edu), 32 Quincy St, concerns itself with no less than the history of western art from the medieval to the

present. There is also a selection of decorative arts. It is open 10 am to 5 pm Monday through Saturday, 1 to 5 pm Sunday. Free tours are given at 11 am weekdays (except during summer when they are given only on Wednesday). Tickets, which include admission to the Busch-Reisinger and Arthur Sackler Museums, cost $5 adults, $4 seniors, $3 students, free to those under 18. The Fogg, Busch-Reisinger and Sackler are free 10 am to noon on Saturday and all day Wednesday.

Entered through the Fogg, the **Busch-Reisinger Museum** specializes in Northern European art. Free tours are given at 1 pm weekdays.

The **Arthur Sackler Museum** (☎ 617-495-9400), 485 Broadway, is devoted to ancient, Asian, Islamic and later Indian art. It boasts the world's most impressive collection of Chinese jade as well as fine Japanese woodblock prints. Free tours are given at 2 pm weekdays.

The university operates four distinct museums in the **Harvard Museums of Natural History** (including the Peabody Museum, below), 24 Oxford St, devoted to archaeology, botany, minerals and zoology. Although it seems to be more geared to teaching than to visitors, the eclectic collection might pique your interest. The Museum of Comparative Zoology has impressive fossils. The Botanical Museum, perhaps the most well known of the museums, houses more than 800 handblown-glass reproductions of flowers and plants. The Mineralogical & Geological Museum boasts a 1642lb amethyst geode from Brazil and a gallery devoted to rough and cut gemstones of New England. The museums (☎ 617-495-3045, www.hmnh.harvard.edu) are open 9 am to 5 pm Monday through Saturday, 1 to 5 pm Sunday. Tickets, good for all four museums, cost $5 adults, $4 seniors and students, $3 children. Admission is free 9 am to noon Saturday. (Better yet, hit their museum shop, Harvard Collections; see Arts & Crafts in the Shopping chapter.)

Adjacent to the Museums of Natural History, the multicultural **Peabody Museum of Archaeology & Ethnology** (☎ 617-496-1027, www.peabody.harvard.edu) boasts a strong collection of North American Indian artifacts. The Hall of the North American Indian traces how native peoples responded to the arrival of Europeans. The museum has the same hours and prices as the Museums of Natural History.

The small **Semitic Museum** (☎ 617-495-4631), 6 Divinity Ave, has changing exhibits from its Near East archaeological and photographic collections. The free museum is open 10 am to 4 pm weekdays, 1 to 4 pm Sunday.

Widener Library Behind this mass of Corinthian columns and steep stairs are 4.9 million books, 10 floors of stacks (shelves) and 5 miles of books. Widener was built in memory of rare book collector Harry Elkins Widener, who had the misfortune of returning from England aboard the *Titanic*. Apparently Harry gave up his seat in a lifeboat to retrieve his favorite book from his stateroom. When he returned, all the lifeboats were full. The Widener family made two stipulations to their $2 million library grant: that the building's exterior mortar or bricks not be altered (Harvard circumvented this

by connecting the library to another with a glass breezeway) and that a reading room like Harry's be built and fresh flowers placed in it daily. Legend states that the bequest also required that students pass a swimming test. (The myth asserts that the Wideners were convinced young Harry would have lived had he known how to swim.) The library has some great art but, unfortunately, is not open to the public.

Colonial Cambridge The phrase 'George Washington slept here' is well worn in Cambridge. There's lots of colonial history in and around the **Cambridge Common**, a public park since 1631. The general pitched camp here from 1775 to 1776 and is said to have gathered a Continental Army under a giant elm. To this day, it still looks as if a few too many horses have been trampling on the grass. On the little traffic island south of the common, where Mass Ave and Garden St intersect, look for bronze hoofprints embedded in the sidewalk. **Dawes Island** memorializes the 'other rider,' William Dawes, who rode through Cambridge to Lexington on April 18, 1775, to warn that the British were coming.

Across Garden St just south of Appian Way, **Christ Church** was designed in 1761 by America's first formally trained architect, Peter Harrison (who also did Boston's King's Chapel). Although Washington's troops used it as a barracks after its Tory congregation fled, he ordered services be held here on New Year's Eve, 1775. The interior is simple, but elegant. When he was a Harvard student, President Teddy Roosevelt taught Sunday school here.

Heading toward the Square on Garden St, the **Old Burying Ground** is on the right. Harvard's first eight presidents are buried in the revolutionary-era cemetery. Around the corner at Church St is the wooden **First Parish Church**, home to the Nameless Coffeehouse (see the Entertainment chapter).

Brattle St One of the area's most prestigious residential addresses, Brattle St is lined with magnificent (and mostly private)

18th- and 19th-century mansions. Dubbed Tory Row in the early 1770s, it was generally home to wealthy British loyalists. But in 1775, Washington got his revenge by appropriating most of these houses for his patriot cohorts.

Head west out of the Square along Brattle St. The beloved 1890 **Brattle St Theatre** (☎ 617-876-6837), No 40, is one of the country's oldest movie houses.

Next-door at No 42, the **Cambridge Center for Adult Ed** (historically known as the Brattle House) is an 18th-century colonial clapboard gem. Margaret Fuller, feminist editor of *The Dial*, once lived here. At No 54, the former **Blacksmith House** is an apropos site to honor the blacksmith in Longfellow's poem. The sculpted steel Chestnut Tree Memorial is complete with an anvil and set of blacksmith tools.

Designed in 1882 by HH Richardson, the private **Stoughton House**, No 90, has been called 'perhaps the best suburban wooden house in America.' Parts of the adjacent and notable private **Henry Vassal House**, No 94, may date to 1636; the chimney is a whopping 8 sq feet. The **Hooper-Lee-Nichols House**

(☎ 617-547-4252), No 159, is home to the Cambridge Historical Society and open for tours 2 to 5 pm Tuesday and Thursday. The circa-1690 home is decorated in various periods and there's an informative model that depicts Brattle St prior to the revolution. Admission is $5. Inquire about the CHS' excellent Brattle St walking tours offered June through October.

The **Longfellow National Historic Site**, a stately and immense home (☎ 617-876-4491, www.nps.gov/long), 105 Brattle St, is another of Washington's appropriations: The general liked it so much that he moved his headquarters here during the siege of Boston. Henry Wadsworth Longfellow lived here for 45 years from 1837 (when he first rented a room here) until 1882. (He received the house as a gift from his new father-in-law after marrying Frances Appleton in 1843.) During that time, he wrote *Evangeline* and *Hiawatha*. Now under the auspices of the NPS, the Georgian mansion, which contains many of Longfellow's books and other belongings, is being elegantly restored to Longfellow's period. Its reopening date is currently unknown.

THESE CANNON WERE ABANDONED AT FORT INDEPENDENCE (CASTLE WILLIAM) BY THE BRITISH FORCES WHEN THEY EVACUATED THE CITY OF BOSTON MARCH 17, 1776

KIM GRANT

Cannons mark the area where George Washington camped on Cambridge Common.

East Cambridge & Kendall, Inman & Central Squares (Map 12)

East Cambridge Before there was the lively **Cambridgeside Galleria** mall (see Cambridge in the Shopping chapter) and the **Lechmere Canal Park**, an attractive man-made lagoon connecting to the Charles River, there was Cambridge's first settler, Thomas Graves, who lived here in 1628. Time passed; Tories and Yankees came and went, immigrants came and stayed, factories churned out goods and then turned idle. Then came the techies. By the late 1980s, the empty lots and blight had been erased. Today, it's impossible to ignore the blocks and blocks of red brick buildings housing Internet, biotech and high-tech start-ups. Blue-collar East Cambridge is slowly being microchipped away, but what's left lies along Cambridge St as it heads into Inman Square.

Take the Green Line to Lechmere for East Cambridge.

Museum of Science This museum (☎ 617-723-2500, www.mos.org), Science Park at the Charles River Dam, is an educational fun house, especially for children. With more than 600 interactive exhibits, daily live presentations and three 'discovery rooms,' you could spend an entire day here. Favorite exhibits include the world's largest lightning bolt generator, a full-scale space capsule, a World Population Meter (a baby is born every second or so), a 'virtual reality fishtank' of the undersea world and a 20-foot model of a *Tyrannosaurus rex* dinosaur.

The museum also houses the **Hayden Planetarium** and **Mugar Omni Theater**. The planetarium boasts a state-of-the-art projection system that casts a heavenly star show, programs about black holes and other astronomical mysteries, and evening laser light shows with rock music. The Omni, a five-story wraparound theater, makes you feel as if you're actually experiencing whatever is projected around you: the Grand Canyon, Antarctica or even the inside of a human body. Also see Cinema in the Entertainment chapter.

The main museum is open 9 am to 5 pm daily, until 9 pm Friday, and until 7 pm daily in July and August. Tickets to the museum cost $10 adults, $7 seniors and children. Individual tickets to Omni or planetarium shows cost $7.50 adults, $5.50 seniors and children; combination tickets save about $3.

The Skyline Room Cafeteria offers good food and views. To get here, use the Science Park stop on the Green Line.

Kendall Square As small as a microchip, Kendall Square is alive and well thanks to the high-tech and biotech industries that have moved into renovated brick warehouses. The 20- and 30-something employees work too hard to make this area cyberglitzy, though. Still, the One Kendall Square complex, at Hampshire and Broadway Sts, is its social nucleus – with restaurants, bars, coffeehouses and a nearby cinema.

The **Kendall/MIT T Station** has enchanting, interactive sonic sculptures you can activate by pulling levers mounted on the station platform walls. The musical instruments hang between the tracks while platform panels tell the history of Cambridge and the technological innovations of MIT.

Aboveground, in a traffic island where Broadway and Main St intersect, techies

JON DAVISON

Van de Graf generator at the Museum of Science

hang with skateboarders around the sculpture *the Galaxy*, a stainless-steel globe with puffs of steam rising from beneath it.

Inman Square Northwest of Kendall Square and east of Harvard Square, this residential neighborhood is just far enough off-the-beaten tourist path that its character should remain intact, in the short term at least. Home to a thriving immigrant community, primarily Portuguese, Inman has a diverse selection of restaurants.

Inman Square is a 15-minute walk from either Harvard or Central Square.

Central Square When Starbucks descended on Mass Ave at Prospect St and was resolutely picketed and boycotted by residents, many proclaimed it was the beginning of the end for this gritty and funky square. Although change is coming, Central Square has retained enough cool music clubs, ethnic eateries and shops to keep it interesting. It's still the nexus for Cambridge's punk scene.

The square has had an economically checkered history. It was developed in the late 1700s after the West Boston Bridge (now the Longfellow Bridge) connected Cambridge with Boston. As more bridges were built, funneling traffic into the square, it earned its name as a 'central' crossroads.

Dude, got any NECCO wafers?

In the late 1800s, City Hall was sited here, but after the T was extended to Harvard Square, people bypassed Central. Buildings were torn down or reduced to low-rises during the Great Depression, and when suburban malls went up in the '70s and '80s, Central Square stores suffered. But as all things old become new again, this is, again, Central Square's time.

Indestructible Wafers

Do other kids around the country still grow up snarfing rolls of little pastel-colored, chalky wafer candies made by **NECCO Candy Co** (☎ 617-876-4700), 254 Mass Ave? In a bind, they're great for practicing first communion or as poker chips or checkers. Did you know that enough NECCO wafers are sold each year to go around the world once; that it takes 40 minutes to work your way through a roll of them, on average; that Martha Stewart is a fan (it makes sense – they match her paint chip palette); that 120 wafers are consumed around the world every second of every day of the year; that Admiral Byrd took 2^1/$_2$ tons of them to the South Pole in the 1930s for a two-year stay; that they have an indefinite shelf life (under dry conditions)? And what about those little candies that show up only around Valentine's Day imprinted with 'Love Ya' or 'Cutie Pie' or, in a nod to changing times, 'Fax me'? They're made here, too. The factory isn't open for tours, but if you walk from Central Square to the MIT Museum (see MIT, later in this chapter), you can't help notice the sweet aroma. The candy store is open 11 am to 2 pm Wednesday through Friday, but you can always find the sweet treats in a convenience store. Perhaps it's not just a New England thing, even though NECCO is short for New England Confection Co.

Charles River Esplanade

The Charles River, once lined with sawmills and leather manufacturers, was a smelly, marshy tidal estuary until the early 1900s, when the Charles River Dam was built. While there's been progress cleaning up the pollution caused by years of river-side dumping, you shouldn't swim or fish here yet – despite Governor Bill Weld's publicity stunt in the mid-1990s. He dove in, fully clothed, to show how safe it was.

Today, both sides of the curvaceous Charles River are graced with grassy banks and paved byways, perfect for bicycling, in-line skating, jogging, walking and festivals. Sailing, rowing and sculling are popular pastimes. Sightseeing boats ply the river as well. (See Activities, later in this chapter.) It's about 2 miles from the Museum of Science (on the Cambridge side) and the Charles River Dam (where the river opens into Boston Harbor) to the Larz Anderson Bridge. Storrow Drive snakes along the Boston side of the river, Memorial Drive along the Cambridge side.

Bridges The **Longfellow Bridge**, nicknamed the 'Salt & Pepper Bridge' because its towers resemble shakers, affords one of Boston's best skyline views. To prolong the view glimpsed on the Red Line between Charles/MGH and Kendall, walk across the bridge, preferably just prior to sunset.

Despite its name, the **Harvard Bridge**, Mass Ave, leads to MIT, not to its academic neighbor. The bridge is known for a bit of recent lore. While Oliver Reed Smoot was an MIT undergraduate between 1958 and 1962, he devised a new unit of measurement, the **'smoot'**. Smoot and his fraternity pals decided to measure the bridge, using the young man as a yardstick (or a 'smootstick'). They purportedly lay Smoot on the ground, end over end, and marked their progress until they got from one side to the other. Turns out that the bridge measures 364.4 Smoots and the markings are so popular that they have been preserved.

According to www.uselessfacts.net, the **BU Bridge** is the only place in the world where 'a boat can sail under a train driving under a car driving under an airplane.' What you do with that information is up to you.

Neither the **River St Bridge** nor the **Western Ave Bridge** is particularly notable, although it's useful to know that they lead to Central Square.

The charming **Weeks Memorial Bridge** offers the best vantage point during the Head of the Charles Regatta in late October. The course runs from the BU Bridge to a half mile beyond the Eliot Bridge (which is just beyond the Anderson Bridge). The bridge connects the Harvard B-School to the main Cambridge-side campus. The **Larz Anderson Bridge** leads to Harvard Square.

Boston Shore The most popular and picturesque portion extends from Mass Ave to Arlington St. On warm days, Bostonians migrate here to sunbathe, picnic, sail and feed water fowl gliding along the tranquil riverbank. See Map 2 for sites along the Boston Shore. This stretch includes Storrow Lagoon and the **Hatch Memorial Shell**, a 1940 Art Deco semicovered stage where free outdoor movies and concerts are held throughout the summer (see 'Free Outdoor Fun' in the Entertainment

MIT The MIT campus extends southwest of Kendall Square and east of Central Square, along the Charles River. Join one of the excellent guided campus tours to best appreciate MIT's scientific contributions. Also see 'Colleges & Universities' in the Facts for the Visitor chapter.

Perhaps surprising for such a renowned scientific institution, the East Campus (on the east side of Mass Ave) is bejeweled with public art. One takes the form of a dormitory, the sinuous S-shaped Baker House, designed by Alvar Aalto. Some other, non-architectural notable pieces include Henry

Charles River Esplanade

chapter). Just west of the Arthur Fiedler Footbridge is the aluminum **Arthur Fiedler bust**, a mod 1984 sculpture of the maestro who led the Boston Pops for 50 years until 1979. Most of the little white sailboats tacking back and forth on the Charles originate from the **Community Boating** boathouse, just south of the Longfellow Bridge.

Cambridge Shore Graceful brick buildings topped with various colored spires line the banks just east of the Larz Anderson Bridge; these are Harvard houses or dormitories. The best views of downtown Boston are from anywhere between the Longfellow and Harvard Bridges. Memorial Drive is closed to cars on Sunday in the summer so rollerbladers have more room.

The most picturesque boathouse is Harvard's **Weld Boathouse** (Map 11), just east of the Anderson Bridge, which the school leases from the state for an 'extravagant' $500 annually. The world's richest academic institution finagled an even better deal for the **Newell Boathouse** (Map 11), on the opposite shore. That costs $1 a year, and the lease on Newell extends through the year 2900. The **BU Boathouse** (Map 10), just east of the BU Bridge, and the **MIT Boathouse** (Map 12), just west of the Harvard Bridge, are both on the Cambridge side. The MIT boathouse contains one of the nation's best rowing simulators, complete with honest-to-goodness water currents of 10mph.

Getting There & Away There are a number of T stations within easy reach of the river. From east to west they include: Charles/MGH on the Red Line; Kendall/MIT, also on the Red Line (in Cambridge, then it's a five-minute walk to the Longfellow Bridge); Hynes/ICA on the Green Line in Back Bay (walk north on Mass Ave for the Harvard Bridge); Mt Fort station on the 'B' branch of the Green Line (for the BU Bridge); and Harvard Square station on the Red Line (for the Larz Anderson Bridge). From the corner of Beacon and Arlington Sts, you can walk across Storrow Drive via the Arthur Fiedler Footbridge.

There is street parking along parts of Memorial Drive (near MIT) but not Storrow Drive.

KIM GRANT

View of Beacon Hill from Longfellow Bridge

Moore's *Three-Piece Reclining Figure*, in Killian Court on Memorial Drive; Alexander Calder's *Big Sail*, between the Green Building and Memorial Drive; Louise Nevelson's *Transparent Horizon*, between the Landau Chemical Engineering Building and the East Campus Alumni Houses near Ames St; Beverly Pepper's *Dunes 1*, in front of the Compton Laboratory; and Picasso's *Figure découpé*, in front of the Hermann Building at the far eastern edge of campus near Wadsworth St and Memorial Drive.

The **List Visual Arts Center** (☎ 617-253-4680), Weisner Building, 20 Ames St, mounts

THINGS TO SEE & DO

KIM GRANT

Community boating on the Charles River

rewarding and sophisticated shows that push the contemporary art envelope in painting, sculpture, photography, video, architecture and design, as well as other works that defy general categorization. The free galleries are open noon to 6 pm daily (except Monday), until 8 pm Friday.

The **MIT Museum** (☎ 617-253-4444) has exhibition spaces all across campus but the main one is located at 265 Mass Ave. It boasts the world's largest collection of holographic images and an 'MIT Hall of Hacks.' An extensive nautical collection and photographs by and about stroboscopic legend Harold 'Doc' Edgerton are elsewhere; inquire at the main exhibition space, open 10 am to 5 pm Tuesday through Friday, noon to 5 pm weekends.

There are great Boston skyline views across the Charles River from Memorial Drive along the East Campus.

Davis Square, Mass Ave to Porter Square & Huron Village (Map 13)

Davis Square Although Davis is in Somerville, it's just north of Cambridge and accessible via the T, so it's included here. Please forgive us, City of Somerville. Having said that, Davis Square is way more hip than any square in Cambridge. The working-class city of Somerville, where statues of the Virgin Mary overlook new BMWs, is changing, and nowhere is it changing more than in Davis Square. Davis has been transformed with trendy bars, cappuccino counters, gourmet restaurants and art. Somerville has a huge contingent of artists who are encouraged by City Hall, and Davis Square is the recipient of much of it. (Perhaps there was a kernel of truth in the catch phrase 'Somerville, the Paris of the '90s.') Somerville, and Davis Square in particular, are no longer the butt of jokes; it's hip to be *this* square.

Davis Square is directly above its eponymous Red Line T stop.

Mass Ave to Porter Square So what happened to all those funky, quirky shops that were in Harvard Square before it was inundated with national chains? They fled north, north of the Law School that is. The stretch of Mass Ave up to Porter Square has some hip shops and more than a few restaurants and cafés. It takes about 25 minutes to walk from Harvard to Porter Square without stopping, but of course, the main reason to walk it is to stop all along the way. You also can take the Red Line T to Porter.

Huron Village There's barely a 'there' here, but that's the point. This little mite of a village is lovely precisely because it's Cambridge without the hip-hop hype, Cambridge without the airs, Cambridge without the crowds. It's best on a sunny Sunday morning (or the equivalent) when you have time for a leisurely walk from Harvard Square, past Cambridge Common on Garden St, and left on Huron Ave. Beyond the village, really just a strip of little shops and eateries, turn left on Lexington Ave and right on Brattle St where you will eventually see Mt Auburn Cemetery. After wandering around the beautifully landscaped graveyard, head back to Harvard Square via Brattle St, which would be a tour of about 1¹/₄ hours without stopping. Pick up some lunch supplies at Formaggio Kitchen (see Food & Drink in the Shopping chapter) and turn the jaunt into an excuse for a three-hour picnic.

It takes about 20 minutes to walk up Mass Ave from the Harvard Red Line T stop to Huron Village.

Mt Auburn Cemetery On a sunny day, this delightful spot (☎ 617-547-7105), 580 Mt Auburn St at Coolidge and Brattle Sts, is worth the 30-minute walk west out of Harvard Square. Developed in 1831, its 170 acres were the first 'garden cemetery' in the US. Until then, the colonial notion of moving a body and rearranging grave markers around a cemetery was commonplace. Pick up a self-guided tour map of the rare botanical specimens and of the notable burial plots, including those for Mary Baker Eddy (founder of the Christian Science Church), Isabella Stewart Gardner (socialite and art collector), Winslow Homer (19th-century American painter) and Oliver Wendell Holmes (US Supreme Court Justice). The cemetery is open 8 am to 5 pm daily (until 7 pm during daylight saving time). Bus No 71 out of Harvard Square station (adjacent to the Red Line) runs past the cemetery.

OUTLYING NEIGHBORHOODS
There are a number of other communities – some within the city of Boston and some adjacent – that exemplify the Boston area's contemporary diversity. All are within easy reach by subway.

South Boston
This tight-knit, predominately white, working-class, Irish-Catholic community has lots of great harbor views and a number of Irish pubs along West and East Broadway. While this main thoroughfare is experiencing some gentrification, it remains the real thing. For a study in contrasts, stop into **Amrhein's** (☎ 617-268-6189), 80 West Broadway, which has been here more than 100 years and serves hearty fare, onion rings and

beer. **Boston Beer Garden** (☎ 617-269-0990), 734 East Broadway, complete with café-style accordion doors that open onto the street, serves crab cakes and portobello mushrooms. Take the Red Line to Broadway.

From the Broadway T station, hop on Bus No 11 or walk 45 minutes along West Broadway (about halfway through it becomes East Broadway) to **Castle Island**, at Marine Park. Although no longer an island, it is the site of five-pointed **Fort Independence** (☎ 617-727-5290), which you can tour for free in the summer. A fort has stood here, at the entrance to the Inner Harbor, since 1634; this one dates to 1801. A walking path circles the fort, and an adjacent causeway, popular with residents of all ages, circles the harbor. Head southwest from here along Day Blvd as it hugs the shore to Carson Beach (see Activities, later in this chapter). From the nearby JFK/UMass T station, you can take the Red Line back into Boston or continue along the harbor path to the JFK Museum and U Mass Boston (see below).

During the 1776 siege of Boston, from high atop a hill between G and Old Harbor Sts, George Washington and his troops set up cannons that ultimately convinced the British to go home. To reach the **Dorchester Heights Monument**, walk east along West Broadway from the Broadway T station, turn right onto Dorchester St and head up any of the little streets to the hill. (Or take Bus No 11 and get off near Dorchester St.)

Dorchester
Harbor Point, on Mt Vernon St off Day Blvd and directly east of the JFK/UMass Red Line T station, exemplifies the best of Dorchester, Boston's largest and most economically and racially diverse neighborhood. This formerly failed housing project, with a dramatic location on the water's edge, was transformed in the late 1980s into a successful development with a mix of affordable and market-rate housing. There is a scenic shoreline boardwalk and path that extends from Carson Beach to the JFK Library (see below) on **Columbia Point** and beyond to the **U Mass Boston** campus. The university recently made a commitment to

public art, acquiring some outdoor sculpture. The Puritans, by the way, landed here in 1630 and quickly built homesteads near Savin Hill, due west.

Adjacent is the **Commonwealth Museum & Massachusetts Archives** (☎ 617-727-9268, www.state.ma.us/sec/mus), which displays documents dating to the first days of colonization. This is the storehouse for all the archeological relics unearthed by the Big Dig. The museum is open 9 am to 5 pm weekdays, 9 am to 3 pm Saturday. Admission is free.

John F Kennedy

John Fitzgerald Kennedy Library & Museum Herein lies assorted memorabilia related to the 35th US president: papers, videotape, speeches and photographs. Check out the introductory film about JFK. The building was designed by architect IM Pei, also responsible for the dramatic John Hancock Tower in Back Bay. The monumental white and black structure successfully blends cylindrical elements with strong pyramid-like lines.

Interestingly, the library also serves as an archive for writer Ernest Hemingway's manuscripts and papers. About 95% of his works can be accessed if you're interested in research, but there is no exhibit space. What's the connection? Kennedy helped Mary Hemingway, Ernest's fourth wife and widow, get the manuscripts and papers out of Cuba during the first and most intense days of the embargo. When she died, she willed them here, because the library offers the public better access than most libraries.

The museum (☎ 617-929-4500) is open 9 am to 5 pm daily. Admission is $8 adults, $6 seniors and students, $4 over age 12. From the JFK/UMass Red Line station, catch a free shuttle to the museum or to campus.

Revere Beach

Also known as the 'North Shore Riviera,' Revere Beach lives. Yeah, yeah…it's the country's first public beach, but who cares. Just like in its heyday, Revere Beach is classic urban Boston. It's *Baywatch*, Boston-style. It's people-watching extraordinaire. Thanks to a colossal reclamation project, the formerly trashy wide beach now boasts fine white sand. But for some reason (go 'figga'), a whole lot of people prefer setting up lawn chairs on the concrete walkway and seawall.

Take the Blue Line to Revere Beach or Wonderland and walk east for one or two blocks. (Just follow the boom boxes.) One added bonus: You can sunbathe while watching the jets take off from Logan Airport – no wonder everyone has boom boxes! Head to nearby **Kelly's Roast Beef** (☎ 781-284-9129), 410 Revere Beach Blvd, for clams after getting fried yourself; it's the ultimate Ra-vee-ah dining experience.

Roxbury

In the mid-1950s, the Nation of Islam founded **Muhammad's Mosque No 11** (☎ 617-442-6082), at 10 Washington St. Malcolm X (then Malcolm Little) lived with his sister and two aunts from 1941 to 1946 in a little house about a mile away from the mosque. In 1998, the decrepit structure was saved from demolition and designated a historic landmark. The house, at 72 Dale St, is not open to the public.

Coolidge Corner & Brookline Village (Map 14)

Although it seems to be part of Boston proper, Brookline is a distinct entity, with a separate city government. Off-the-beaten tourist path, it combines lovely, tranquil residential areas with a few lively commercial zones: **Coolidge Corner** ('C' branch of the Green Line) and **Brookline Village** ('D' branch of the Green Line). Each features cafés, eclectic shops and a number of fine restaurants in all price ranges. In addition, both areas have deeply rooted Jewish and Russian populations. There are more synagogues and kosher eateries here than anywhere in Boston.

Brookline is a 'streetcar suburb,' a historical term describing its development after electric trolleys were introduced in the late 1800s. Its main historic attraction is the **John F Kennedy National Historic Site** (☎ 617-566-7937), 83 Beals St. JFK spent the first three years of his life in this modest three-story house, until 1920. Matriarch Rose Kennedy oversaw its restoration and furnishing in the late '60s. From the Coolidge Corner T station, walk north on Harvard St for several blocks to Beals St. The house is open 10 am to 4:30 pm Wednesday through Sunday mid-March through November; mandatory guided tours are offered hourly; admission is $2.

ACTIVITIES
Beaches

This isn't southern California, but you can swim off South Boston's Day Blvd. Take the Red Line T to JFK/UMass, exit downstairs near the buses and then head left (north). Carson Beach, complete with a snack bar and changing rooms, is on the right, where sunburned brick masons share sand with elderly Vietnamese immigrants and elementary school kids from the Dominican. Forget about swimming after a day of heavy rains; the water sewage treatment plant can't handle the runoff. If red flags are up, don't swim. Also see Revere Beach, above.

Bicycling

Although you have to be a kamikaze to ride on inner-city streets, people do. Ride defensively since autos drive offensively. Both sides of the Charles River are popular, but you can also ride along the Emerald Necklace (see 'Emerald Necklace,' earlier in this chapter) or out to nearby Watertown and back. The more adventurous can invest in a Rubel BikeMap (see Maps in Facts for the Visitor).

As for renting, Community Bicycle Supply (Map 9; ☎ 617-542-8623), 496 Tremont St, is open April through September for rentals; Back Bay Bicycles (Map 8; ☎ 617-247-2336), 336 Newbury St at Mass Ave, has year-round rentals. Located between Harvard and Porter Squares in Cambridge, Ata Cycle (Map 13; ☎ 617-354-0907), 1700 Mass Ave, and the Bicycle Exchange (Map 13; ☎ 617-864-1300), 2067 Mass Ave, rent year-round, too.

Also see Bicycle in the Getting Around chapter.

Boating & Kayaking

The Charles River Canoe & Kayak Center has two locations: (☎ 617-965-5110), 2401 Comm Ave in Newton, MA 30 near I-95, and (☎ 617-462-2513) on Soldier's Field Rd just a bit upstream from the Eliot Bridge. You can rent a boat from April to mid-October (through October in Newton). Canoes cost $10 per hour, rowboats $11, double kayaks $13, kids' kayaks $5. Rowing shells are available for $25 per session, if you can demonstrate proficiency. The Newton center is across from a tranquil stretch of the Charles River. Take the T Green Line, 'D' branch to Riverside and then it's a 20-minute walk; call for directions. The Soldier's Field Rd location is a 20-minute walk from the Harvard Red Line T station, on the opposite side of the river.

Community Boating (Map 2; ☎ 617-523-1038), at the Charles River Esplanade near the Charles St Footbridge, offers experienced sailors unlimited use of sailboats, kayaks and windsurfers for $50 for two days, April through October. You'll have to take a little test to demonstrate your ability. Locals can get a 45-day unlimited membership for $75, 75 days for $120 and a full season for $190, including all the free lessons you need to gain confidence. It's a bargain.

Also see Boat Tours in the Getting Around chapter.

Bowling

This retro sport is making a comeback. And candlepin bowling, with straight pins and little two pound balls, is as New England as lobsters. Sacco's Bowl-Haven (Map 11; ☎ 617-776-0552), 45 Day St in Davis Square, is traditional with funky two-tone bowling shoes and 1930s ball returns. Lanes &

Games (Map 13; ☎ 617-876-5533), 195 MA 2 east near the Alewife Red Line stop in North Cambridge, is pretty traditional, too. At Boston Bowl (☎ 617-825-3800), 820 Morrissey Blvd, Dorchester, 'cosmic' bowling – with fog machines, black lights and a throbbing beat – is reserved for weekends. It's open 24 hours and best reached by car.

Cruises

Music Cruises Mass Bay Lines (Map 6; ☎ 617-542-8000), Rowes Wharf, and Bay State Cruise Co (Map 6; ☎ 617-748-1428), 164 Northern Ave, have entertainment cruises with DJs or bands for $16 to $20, from about mid-June to mid-September.

Schooners The *Liberty Clipper* and the *Schooner Liberty* (Map 6; ☎ 617-742-0333), Long Wharf, make a two-hour, 12-mile sail around the harbor three times daily from June through September. Tickets are $25 adults, half-price for children.

In-Line & Ice Skating

Beacon Hill Skate (Map 7; ☎ 617-482-7400), 135 Charles St S, rents in-line skates hourly ($8) and daily ($20). Glide to the Esplanade,

KIM GRANT

A picture-perfect day for sailing

or better yet, to Memorial Drive on the Cambridge side of the Charles River, which is closed to auto traffic from 11 am to 7 pm on Sunday in warm weather.

Ice skating on the Boston Common Frog Pond Rink (Map 2) is an extremely popular activity – even for restrained Bostonians – from mid-November to mid-March. (It's less crowded during the week.) Skate rentals ($5), lockers ($1) and restrooms are available at the pondside kiosk (☎ 617-635-2120), which has a limited menu of hot food. Skating costs $3 if you're 14 or older. There's also skating on the Public Garden lagoon, but the ice is rougher and it's subject to natural freezing conditions (or a lack thereof).

Alternate Activities

The cinderblock **sauna** at Dillon's Russian Steam Bath (☎ 617-884-9434), 75 Chestnut St near City Hall, a legendary bath in Chelsea since the late 1880s, sets you back only $15 for an all-day session – if you can take the heat. For an extra $9, let them whack you with a soapy oak-leaf broom (a 'platza,' pronounced 'plate-zah'). Thirty-minute massages cost $20. Monday is re-served for women, otherwise it's men only. Call for directions.

For an easier-to-reach and moderately priced **massage** (20 minutes for $30) or other **spa treatment** (seaweed wraps for $70), head to the excellent, low-key Michele International (Map 4; ☎ 617-423-0123), 125 Pearl St.

The Folk Arts Center of New England (☎ 617-491-6084), 1950 Mass Ave, Cambridge, sponsors free Copley Square **folk dances** at 7:30 pm Tuesday in July and August.

Whale Watching Cruises

Whale sightings are practically guaranteed at Stellwagen Bank, a fertile feeding ground 25 miles out to sea. The big humpback whales are awesome, breaching and frolicking, and in the spring and fall, huge pods of dolphins make their way to and from their summers in the Arctic. Trips take about 4½ to 5 hours, with onboard commentary provided by naturalists. Dress warmly even on summer days.

The AC Cruise Line (Map 6; ☎ 617-261-6633), 290 Northern Ave, offers family-friendly trips: Up to four children are free

Get face-to-face with sealife at the New England Aquarium.

KIM GRANT

when accompanied by two paying adults ($22 adults, $16 seniors). Trips depart at 10 am on weekends from mid-April to mid-October, and daily (except Monday) from late June to early September.

Tickets for the New England Aquarium Whale Watching tour (Map 6; ☎ 617-973-5281), Central Wharf, cost $26 adults, $21 seniors and students, $16.50 to $19 children (no children under age 3 permitted). Call for departure times from April to early November. Their catamaran cuts the travel time (but not viewing time) by an hour.

Boston Harbor Cruises (Map 6; ☎ 617-227-4320) also has daily whale watching tours departing from Rowes Wharf and Long Wharf May through October. Tickets are $28 adults, $24 seniors, $22 children.

America's Walking City

Boston's intimate neighborhoods are a tapestry of historical anecdotes, politics, personalities and architectural styles. They are bursting at the seams with their jumble of beautiful buildings and lively little museums. The best way to unravel their spirit is by feeling the uneven brick sidewalks beneath your feet. In between visiting revolutionary hangouts and Victorian gems, though, don't forget to check out the Bostonians all around you. It's really the intersection of the past with the present that makes the trajectory so interesting.

HISTORICAL TOURS

Boston could very well be the country's preeminent walking city. Perhaps that explains the proliferation of special-interest walking trails.

Freedom Trail

The 2¹/₂-mile Freedom Trail (www.thefreedomtrail.org), devised in 1951, is the granddaddy of walks. Sixteen historically important sites, including colonial and revolutionary-era buildings, are connected by a double row of red sidewalk bricks (or a painted red line) that begins near the Park St T station. Three million people are drawn to the route yearly.

It takes one hour to walk it nonstop, a few hours to take in some of the sites and a full day to revel thoroughly at each. A bronze medallion in the sidewalk marks each site, and there are plenty of directional signposts, maps and informational kiosks along the route. Only three sites along the trail charge admission.

At press time, the International Institute of Boston, headquartered at 1 Milk St on the site of Ben Franklin's birthplace, planned to open a new museum honoring immigrants in mid-2000.

During the high season of June through August, the National Park Service (Map 4; ☎ 617-242-5642), 15 State St, offers six free ranger-led walking tours daily (on the hour from 10 am to 3 pm). Between mid-April and November, tours are offered at 10 am and 2 pm weekdays; 10 and 11 am, 1 and 2 pm weekends. It's limited to 30 people on fall

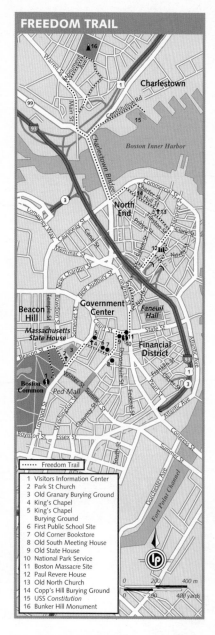

FREEDOM TRAIL

...... Freedom Trail

1 Visitors Information Center
2 Park St Church
3 Old Granary Burying Ground
4 King's Chapel
5 King's Chapel
   Burying Ground
6 First Public School Site
7 Old Corner Bookstore
8 Old South Meeting House
9 Old State House
10 National Park Service
11 Boston Massacre Site
12 Paul Revere House
13 Old North Church
14 Copp's Hill Burying Ground
15 USS Constitution
16 Bunker Hill Monument

weekends, so stop in beforehand to reserve your place on a tour. There are no tours from December to mid-April.

Black Heritage Trail

Africans arrived in Boston as slaves in 1638, a mere eight years after the city was founded, but by the 1776 revolution there were far more free blacks in Boston than there were slaves. Furthermore, when the first federal census was taken in 1790, Massachusetts was the only state without slaves.

KIM GRANT

Boston was the country's center of anti-slavery activity for 30 years prior to the Civil War. It was a haven for escaped slaves, with abolitionists openly defying the 1850 Fugitive Slave Law.

The histories of Boston and the free black community on Beacon Hill, most of which settled between Joy and Charles Sts on the north slope, are woven together through a dozen stories and 19th-century sites on the 1½-mile Black Heritage Trail. The best way to take it all in is by an excellent free tour given by National Park Service rangers (NPS; ☎ 617-742-5415) from late May to early September, daily at 10 am, noon and 2 pm. In the off-season, call to request a tour, which departs from the Shaw Memorial on Beacon St and takes about two hours.

BLACK HERITAGE TRAIL

Women's Heritage Trail

Five separate trails (☎ 617-522-2872) mark Boston women's contributions to various causes. The trails are not marked, so to explore, purchase a $9.95 booklet from the NPS (☎ 617-242-5642), 15 State St, or at many Freedom Trail sites. It's well worth the investment of time and money.

Each self-guided neighborhood walk tells a different story: 'A Search for Equal Rights' downtown; 'A Diversity of Cultures' in the North End; 'Writers, Artists & Activists' of Beacon Hill; 'Women's Action for Economic & Social Justice' in Chinatown; and 'Educators, Artists & Social Reformers' of Back Bay. Each trail takes about 90 minutes, more if you want to linger at any of the sites.

BEACON HILL: BASTION OF BRAHMINS & BLACK HISTORY

Stately 19th-century brick townhouses, lavender windowpanes, gas lanterns, precious courtyards, colorful window boxes, rooftop gardens and picturesque narrow alleyways – this is the stuff of Beacon Hill, Boston's most handsome and affluent residential neighborhood. Although seemingly exclusive, Beacon Hill has never been the domain solely of blue-blood Brahmins. Free African-Americans settled here in the early 19th century; they were followed by Jewish and Irish immigrants. More recently, a number of the grand residences have been subdivided into small condos for young professionals and students. The Black Heritage Trail and the Freedom Trail both make their way along the streets of Beacon Hill; see Things to See & Do for descriptions of these memorable sites. This tour (Map 2) will take between one and a half and three hours, depending on how long you linger at individual sites.

Begin at the corner of Tremont and Park Sts, formerly called 'Brimstone Corner'; one theory about this name has to do with fiery preaching that occurred inside the **Park St Church**. The other involves a stash of gunpowder stored in the church's basement during the War of 1812. Beyond the church on Tremont St is the **Old Granary Burying Ground**. Just a bit down Tremont St is the Green and Red Lines' **Park St T station**, one of four original stations for the country's oldest subway system. When it was inaugurated in 1897, the T was a whopping six-tenths of a mile long.

Head up Park St toward the golden-domed **Massachusetts State House**, completed in 1798. Behind the east wing of the State House, **Ashburton Park** contains a memorial column to the revolution. (You can conveniently visit the park later in the tour, too.) Just down Beacon St to the right, at No 10¹/₂, is the genteel and classy **Boston**

Title page: Financial District from Northern Ave Bridge (photo by Kim Grant)

Left: Golden-domed Massachusetts State House

Athenæum (☎ 617-227-0270, www
.bostonathenaeum.org), closed until
mid-2001 for restoration. When it
reopens, visitors can tour the neoclassical reading rooms of this
impressive private library and art
gallery, owned by 1049 sharehold-
ers whose shares trace back to
1807. George Washington's personal library is here, as is an extensive
collection of detective fiction.

At the corner of Park and Beacon
Sts, facing the State House, is the
noble **Shaw Memorial**. Elegant **Beacon St**, with its lovely views of
Boston Common, was the former
home of distinguished **Little, Brown
& Co**, No 34, publishers of *Bartlett's
Familiar Quotations* and Fanny
Farmer's *1896 Boston Cooking-School Cook Book*. Turn right up Joy St
to the **Appalachian Mountain Club** (☎ 617-523-0636), No 5. The
revered outdoor club, founded here in 1876, dispenses information
about outdoor activities in Boston and throughout New England. The
office is open 8:30 am to 5:30 pm weekdays.

Turn left on **Mt Vernon St**, one of the Hill's loveliest streets. A word
of caution: Watch your step while looking at architectural delights. The
brick sidewalks, torn asunder by errant tree roots, are a serious hazard.
The private **32 Mt Vernon St** was the residence of suffragist and
reformer Julia Ward Howe, composer of the stirring 'Battle Hymn of the
Republic,' and her husband Dr Samuel Howe, who founded the Perkins
School for the Blind and organized the Committee of Vigilance, dedicated to assisting fugitive slaves. Across the street at No 55, the **Nichols
House Museum** (☎ 617-227-6993) is Beacon Hill's only former residence open to the public. The 30-minute tour is particularly engaging,
and costs $5 per person. It's offered noon to 4:15 pm Tuesday through
Saturday mid-April through October, and Thursday through Saturday
the rest of the year except January. The Beacon Hill Garden Club (☎ 617-
227-4392), which sponsors an annual spring garden tour, is based here.

Just down the street, the 1805 **Swan Stables**, No 50, have been converted from horse and buggy stalls to coveted condos. The original
owners deemed that the property should never exceed 13 feet – so as
not to obscure the view of the main **Swan Houses** at Nos 13, 15 and 17
Chestnut St. To reach them, backtrack to Walnut St, hang a right and
then another one onto lovely **Chestnut St**. Also dubbed the 'Daughter
Houses,' these identical brick row houses were built by Charles Bulfinch
for Hepsibah Swan's daughters. They are unremarkable but for a restrained use of ornamentation: boot scrapers, door knockers, hitching
posts, iron balconies and fences. Just down the street, **29A Chestnut St**,
with rare and authentic purple windowpanes, is perpendicular to the
street and overlooks a pretty side garden. Actor Edwin Booth resided
here when his brother assassinated President Lincoln.

Right: Townhouse
on Beacon St

KIM GRANT

Head up Willow St for a glimpse of Boston's narrowest and most photographed street, the charming cobblestone **Acorn St**, once home to coachmen who worked for the adjacent mansion dwellers.

Continue up Willow and turn right onto Mt Vernon St, where the private **Second Harrison Gray Otis House**, No 85, typified Bulfinch's grand plan for this prestigious street in 1802. On land bought from painter John Singleton Copley for a mere $1000 per acre, Bulfinch envisioned a series of freestanding mansions set back from the road, but alas, this was the only one to materialize. (A population boom and economic slump quashed the plan.) Note the bumpy cobblestone driveway. Writer Henry James called this showy stretch of **Mt Vernon St** the 'most respectable street in America.' Indeed.

Head back to the cobblestone **Louisburg Square** (pronounced 'Lewisburg'), an elegant cluster of multimillion-dollar brick row houses that face a private elongated park owned by the square's residents. There is not a single more prestigious address in Boston. Louisa May Alcott moved to No 10 after gaining literary success. (She lived nearby at 20 Pinckney St as a child.) Senator John Kerry and his wife Teresa Heinz live at the northern corner of the square at Pinckney St.

Turn right up **Pinckney St**, particularly lovely when bathed in late afternoon light and anytime in the spring when the trees are blossoming. During a 1920s renovation of **62 Pinckney St**, a secret closet door was discovered that led to a tiny attic space where two spoons and

tin plates were found. It is assumed that the original owner's wife, Susan Hilliard, a resolute abolitionist, provided a stopping point for runaway slaves on the Underground Railroad during the 1850s. (The house is private.) Across the street, the **Phillips School** (formerly known as Boston English High School) was the first public grammar school in Boston to be racially integrated. Unfortunately, it was not integrated by gender as well. It's now condominiums. Head uphill past the **Pie-Shaped House**, No 56, which looks quite unremarkable from the front. Since the rear of the house is narrowed to a point by its neighbors, it would more accurately be called 'piece of pie-shaped house.' Continuing with anomalies, the 1884 **House of Odd Windows**, No 24,

Top left: Narrow Acorn St

Bottom left: Even the statues are elegant on Louisburg Square has no less than seven windows, none of which are identical. The former carriage house was built by Ralph Waldo Emerson's nephew, William Ralph Emerson. At **9¹/2 Pinckney St**, a gated tunnel leads to a courtyard where three hidden houses are located. An 1830s ordinance decreed that this passageway be built to accommodate a boy with a basket on his head and one fat cow. Next-door, the small, circa 1795 clapboard **Middleton-Glapion House**, No 5, is one of Boston's best-preserved colonial structures. It was built by an African-American coachman and his mulatto barber friend, whom you half expect to walk out the front door.

As you'll soon see, Pinckney St and parallel Myrtle St act as a dividing line between the stately south slope (where you've been walking) and the less conforming north slope. Take a left onto **Joy St**, the only through street connecting Beacon and Cambridge Sts. Joy St demarcated 19th-century white and black communities; whites lived on the south slope, blacks on the north. If you'd like to rest for a moment, head right on Derne St to Ashburton Park.

Otherwise, walk downhill to **Cambridge St**, a busy commercial street that comes as something of a shock after rarefied Beacon Hill. Across the street lies what's left of the Old West End; it's almost nothing but concrete buildings. The **Old West Church**, 131 Cambridge St, is an early-19th-century Federal-style brick edifice designed by Asher Benjamin and similar to his Charles St Meeting House. The church has an extraordinary pipe organ. Next-door, the magnificent **First Harrison Gray Otis House**, No 141, was the first of three houses designed at the turn of the 18th century for Mr Otis, a real estate developer, US senator and Boston mayor. The Federal brick house is wonderfully symmetrical, if perhaps a bit severe. Note the squat 3rd floor, which is a hair's breadth higher than 6 feet. The Society for the Preservation of New England Antiquities (SPNEA; ☎ 617-227-3956) rescued the house after it had become a women's bath and rooming house. Guided tours are given on the hour 11 am to 4 pm Wednesday through Sunday; tickets cost $4 adults, $3.50 seniors, $2 children.

KIM GRANT

Retrace your steps back up Joy St to the **Abiel Smith School**, No 46, at the corner of **Smith Court**; the school served local families in the 1830s. At the time, there were 2000 African-Americans on Beacon Hill, with more children than the school could accommodate. The school building now includes the Museum of Afro-American History. Around the corner, the wooden **William Nell House**, 3 Smith Court, dating to 1800, was a black rooming house and hiding place for escaping slaves. Across the narrow street is the **African Meeting House** (closed for renovations until mid-2001).

At the end of the street, pass through the narrow and winding **Holmes Alley** to South Russell St. Now turn around and come through it again, this time imagining yourself a slave fleeing a 'slavecatcher'

Right: Part of downtown's *Boston Bricks*

KIM GRANT

(bounty hunters who pursued run-away slaves across state borders and returned them to their own-ers). The alley was well known to slaves but not to traders; from South Russell St it looked like a dead end. In the mid-18th century, the doors fronting the alley were left unlocked so fleeing slaves could hide at any time. If no doors were open, slaves would run to the end to blend into groups of free blacks congregating at the meeting house. But slavecatchers were so unsuccessful that they rarely returned to Boston after an initial visit; a few were even tarred and feathered.

Turn up South Russell St, take a right on narrow **Myrtle St**, a byway where ropemaking factories were located. These buildings effectively separated north and south slope development until 1803. There is still a historic insularity between the two slopes, as evidenced by the corner markets and everyday service shops on the north slope. No commercial 'blemishes' of this sort appear on the south slope. Take an immediate right on Irving St, then an imme-diate left on Revere St and peek down **Rollins Place**, noting the two-story wooden portico at the end. It's a false front!

Take a right down Anderson St and another on Phillips St. The Lithuanian **Vilna Shul**, No 16, was founded in 1919 when the Jewish community on Beacon Hill was at its apex. Former Star Trek star Leonard Nimoy (who grew up in the Old West End) attended services here and is said to have conceived of his TV character's Vulcan hand signal ('live long and prosper') from a religious symbol in the synagogue. Although many synagogues are converted African-American meeting houses, this one was built as a synagogue.

Phillips St was a hotbed of abolitionist activity in the 19th century, and its proximity to the Charles River proved key. The river, after all, could carry escapees faster than land-based routes could, and it didn't leave a trace of anyone's passage. The private **Lewis Hayden House** is Boston's most important abolitionist site, having served as refuge to many runaway slaves. In fact, an underground tunnel ran from the Charles River to Hayden's house. It's said that his house was never searched for fugitives because Hayden kept a stash of gunpowder in the basement and threatened to blow up the house if its threshold was crossed. When slavecatchers came to his doorway, the militant Hayden, who himself had been born a slave (of Senator Henry Clay), would sim-ply proclaim 'leave in peace or leave in pieces.'

Continuing along, radical abolitionist John Sweat Rock resided at **83 Phillips St** during the 1860s. He was a self-taught dentist, doctor and lawyer who went on to become the first African-American to argue before the Supreme Court. He's credited with coining the phrase 'Black

Left: Charles St Meeting House

Is Beautiful.' Just ahead is **Lindell Court**, also known as 'flower lane,' and across the street is **Primus Ave**, a terraced alley of apartments. Turn left on West Cedar St and left on Revere St, where you'll find more quaint cul-de-sacs at **Bellingham Place**, **Sentry Hill Place** and **Goodwin Place**. Head back to West Cedar St, turn left, head downhill on Pinckney St and take a left onto **Cedar Lane Way**, another remarkably narrow byway with proportionally tiny houses and gardens.

Turn right on Mt Vernon St to **Charles St** and the 'flats,' filled in by Otis and Bulfinch in the early 1800s after leveling peaks on the Hill. Charles St, by the way, was named after the Charles River, which in turn was named after King Charles I. There are plenty of places here to shop or take a break before finishing this tour. Otherwise, the Asher Benjamin-designed **Charles St Meeting House**, across the street at No 70, is a classic example of Federal-style brick architecture, although it's been converted to commercial use. During the 19th century, the meeting house provided a pulpit for abolitionist leaders William Lloyd Garrison, Frederick Douglass, Harriet Tubman and Sojourner Truth. At the corner of River and Mt Vernon Sts, the old firehouse was the site for

Right: Purple windowpanes in the Appleton-Parker Houses

KIM GRANT

KIM GRANT

MTV's 1997 *Real World*. On the opposite corner, the **Sunflower Castle**, 130 Mt Vernon St, is *the* most amusing house in this very sober neighborhood. The 1840 house was transformed in 1878 into a timber and stucco Tudor, complete with a bright yellow exterior and an ornamental sunflower. The Gothic-Revival **Church of the Advent** (entrance on Brimmer St), which dates to the late 1880s, boasts a jewel-like interior as well as a fanciful facade. The high altar and screen above it were donated by congregation member Isabella Stewart Gardner. Lore suggests that Gardner once washed the church steps during Lent to atone for her sins.

Turn left on Brimmer St through the flats until you arrive at Beacon St, which fronts the **Public Garden**, the country's first botanical garden. (You can visit the garden now or return at the end of this tour.) As you head uphill on **Beacon St**, it's almost impossible to envision a time when it was called 'Poor House Lane,' due to its proximity to an almshouse on Park St. Near the corner of Charles and Beacon Sts, Boston's first settler, Reverend William Blackstone, set up residence, tended apple orchards and rode his trained bull. His property would eventually become Boston Common.

Along the way you may have noticed a number of houses with **purple windowpanes**. Most are reproductions, but at 63–64 Beacon St, they're the real thing. Between 1818 and 1824, glass shipments from England to America were defective, resulting in the glass' manganese oxide turning purple. Over time the panes have become a status symbol. Keep heading uphill to the **Prescott House**, No 54–55, two brick row houses with iron balconies, columns and typical fanlight doorways. No 55 houses the National Society of Colonial Dames in the commonwealth of Massachusetts (just a little reminder that Beacon Hill was, and remains, Brahmin central).

Mr Otis moved around a bit, and his **Third Harrison Gray Otis House**, No 45, completed in 1806, was his last and perhaps his most grand residence. As a condition of ownership, the current occupants, the

Left: Cool off in Boston Common's Frog Pond

American Meteorological Society (☎ 617-227-2425), must keep the house open free to the public. Just go in and ask for a tour. Next-door is the exclusive **Somerset Club**, No 42–43, a monumental granite edifice that stands out among its neighbors. Just uphill, the **Appleton-Parker Houses**, No 39–40, where poet Longfellow wooed Fanny Appleton, are a typically handsome Greek Revival duo with more authentic purple windowpanes. From here, head into the **Boston Common**, the country's first public park, or to the Public Garden.

DOWNTOWN & FINANCIAL DISTRICT: IF THESE BUILDINGS COULD TALK

If you prefer concentrating on building cornices to sidestepping harried workers and commercial vehicles making deliveries, take this walking tour (Map 4) on Sunday, although many Financial District eateries will be closed. On weekends, it's easier to appreciate the charming and odd 'squares' – usually just the intersection of three or four streets. Serendipity happens. It's particularly delightful to round a corner and be confronted with the juxtaposition of soaring glass skyscrapers, fanciful Art Deco towers and squat granite structures.

The Financial District, bounded by State St, the expressway and Devonshire St, has Boston's prettiest little park, Post Office Square. Although this is a dense area, you're rarely more than a 10-minute walk from the waterfront.

The bustling Downtown Crossing pedestrian zone, at the intersection of Washington, Winter and Summer Sts, is packed with weekday workers, weekend shoppers, and pushcart vendors and outdoor performers every day. Recently, the neighborhood has started to come alive in the evening, too, as more Suffolk and Emerson students have moved into the area. Note that Washington St serves as a real dividing line: All streets change names as they cross it.

The Great Fire of 1872

On November 9, 1872, a fire broke out at 7:10 pm on Summer St. Within 20 hours it destroyed the heart of the commercial district, bounded by Washington, Milk, Summer and Broad Sts. Seventy-five million dollars worth of real estate on 65 acres was lost. It's been recorded as the most costly fire per acre in US history (in today's dollars, the amount would top $500 million). Eleven firemen died; the number of civilian casualties is unknown, but it's certainly true that fewer died because the blaze started on a Saturday night when weekday workers were not around. The fire had plenty of fuel: Factories and warehouses were filled with wool and other dry goods, leather products, boots and shoes. Several wharves and docks were destroyed, as well as much of the publishing district on Milk and Congress Sts. Thousands of factory workers, most of whom were women, were abruptly thrown out of work. The city's economy was devastated for years.

KIM GRANT

This walk involves a bit of backtracking since the streets were not laid out with walking tours in mind, and will take between two and four hours, depending on how long you linger at individual sites.

Begin diagonally across the street from the Park St T station on the Red and Green Lines. Note the **Cathedral Church of St Paul**, 138 Tremont St, Boston's first Greek Revival church, now sandwiched between two modern buildings. The austere facade never received the planned bas-relief figures. Head north on Tremont St, past the Park St Church, and look down Hamilton Place to the **Orpheum Theater**, where the New England Conservatory began and the Boston Symphony Orchestra first played in 1881. One theory for the origination of 'Brahmin' began here, too: Many proper Bostonians stormed out during one Brahms premier and those who stayed to hear the wild new symphony were dubbed 'Brahmins.' Continue to the 1828 **Tremont Temple**, with decorous Venetian-style windows and balconies. This is the site of the Tremont Theater, which hosted famous orators, actors and politicians (among them Abraham Lincoln, Jenny Lind, Daniel Webster and Charles Dickens). Now a Baptist church, the popular *Black Nativity* pageant is performed here each Christmas season.

At the corner of Tremont St, the **Omni Parker House**, 60 School St, is the grand dame of Boston hotels. Back in the mid-19th century, literary luminaries like Hawthorne, Whittier, Emerson and Longfellow gathered here to exchange ideas at their 'Saturday Club.' The list of notable guests doesn't stop: Charles Dickens slept here, Ho Chi Minh worked in the kitchen, JFK announced his presidency here and John Wilkes Booth stayed here 10 days before assassinating President Lincoln. (Booth

KIM GRANT

Top left: Tremont Temple

Bottom left: Site of the country's first public school

was visiting his thespian brother who was performing nearby; his visit also included some practice at a local rifle range.) Across School St is **King's Chapel** and, adjacent, **King's Chapel Burying Ground**.

Head down School St, named for the country's **first public school** (1635), Boston Public Latin School. A hopscotch sidewalk mosaic, *City Carpet*, commemorating the site of the school where Franklin, Emerson and Charles Bulfinch were educated, is just before the entrance to the **Old City Hall**, at No 45. It's no wonder that power went to flamboyant Mayor Curley's head as he wandered through the opulent French Second Empire landmark. The courtyard is flanked by a statue of Franklin and one of Boston's second mayor, Josiah Quincy, who directed the building of Quincy Market. Today the building houses offices, Ben's Café (see Places to Eat) and the famed (and pricey) Maison Robert.

Continue along School St to the **Old Corner Bookstore**. Across the street, wedged between the intimate **Spring Lane** and Water St, stands the graceful **Winthrop Building**. For the best view, head to the corner of Water and Devonshire Sts and look back. As for Spring Lane (where the Pilgrims fetched water), Mary Chilton, the only *Mayflower* passenger to re-locate from Plymouth to Boston, lived here with husband John Winslow until her death in 1679. At the corner of School and Washington Sts, the **Irish Famine Memorial** is an unfortunately cartoonish depiction that contrasts the devastating effects of the famine with the prosperity of life in America.

If you'd prefer to end this tour near the waterfront rather than near Faneuil Hall, visit the **Old State House** now (head left on Washington St for one block). Otherwise, diagonally across Washington St to the right is the **Old South Meeting House**. Turn left on Milk St and look up to see the faux-stone bust marking **Benjamin Franklin's birthplace**, at No 17. (The facade is really cast iron.) Continue down Milk St to Arch St to check out Max Bachmans' Beaux Arts *Commerce* and *Industry* figures on the **International Trust Co**, 45 Milk St. Go around to Devonshire St to see *Security* and *Fidelity*. The Great Fire of 1872 stopped here, but not before destroying part of the iron structure. Retrace your steps to

Top right: Detail, Old State House

Bottom right: Old State House

KIM GRANT

Washington St, head left, then right on Bromfield St and right on Province St. Leading up to little Bosworth St, the 17th-century **Province House Steps** are all that remain of the former 1679 residential mansion of the royal governor of Massachusetts Bay. (The steps actually led to gardens.) From here, General Gage ordered that Redcoats head to Lexington and Concord (see Shot Heard 'Round the World in Facts about Boston).

Head back to Washington St and turn right to enter the bustling pedestrian-only zone known as **Downtown Crossing**, centered at Summer and Winter Sts. Thanks to a large contingent of nearby office workers, there are plenty of places here for an inexpensive, quick lunch. **Washington St**, named after a visit by the general himself in October 1789, has been a center of commercial activity since colonial

Where Time Stands Still

Walk through the front doors of **Jacob Wirth's** (Map 7), **Locke-Ober** (Map 4) and **Ye Olde Union Oyster House** (Map 3) and you might feel like you're in a time warp. Jacob Wirth's, built in 1845 with globe lanterns and loads of brass, probably offers the same German sausage, sauerkraut and ale that it served in 1868. Coincidentally, the original part of Locke-Ober opened the same year. The grand 1st floor, complete with leather chairs, mahogany and German silver, looks exactly as it did after a renovation in 1886 and steadfastly retains the feel of a

'gentlemen's club.' Women were not admitted until 1974 and even today, slacks are frowned upon. As for the Union Oyster House, it's been serving seafood since 1826, though the building predates that by about 100 years. You can dine at the same mahogany bar where Daniel Webster slurped oysters and sipped brandy. In fact, the interior and menu changes at all three restaurants have been so inconsequential that Ralph Waldo Emerson would probably feel more comfortable than you dining in any of these establishments.

KIM GRANT

Top left: Old South Meeting House

Bottom left: Sausages and sauerkraut since 1845

times. Facing the intersection of Washington and Summer Sts, the elegant 1912 Beaux Arts facade of **Filene's** department store dismisses modern mall-bound retailers as crass capitalists who care nothing for aesthetics. **Filene's Basement** is renowned for its bargain basement sales. Turn left on Summer St and head to the corner of Chauncy St to best appreciate the three-story cylindrical window over the corner entrance to **Macy's**. The New York-based retailer bought out the venerable Jordan Marsh in 1996, much to the dismay of many Bostonians. Head back up Summer St, which turns into Winter St, and turn left onto Winter Place for a peek in the windows of **Locke-Ober**, one of the few remaining bastions of 19th-century Brahmin society.

Backtrack and turn right onto Washington St; walk two blocks and turn right on West St. Currently a restaurant, **No 15** was once the residence of the Peabody family: Hawthorne wed Sophia Peabody here, her sister Mary married Horace Mann ('Mr Public Education,' a fervent proponent of educational reform), and Sophia's other sister, Elizabeth, sold Boston's first foreign books and published *The Dial*, an early Transcendentalist journal.

Back at Washington St, turn right. Three decrepit theaters mark the passing of an era. **Modern Theatre**, a cinema plunked inside a 1913 Victorian Gothic edifice, once housed a furniture warehouse. *The Jazz Singer*, the first motion picture with sound, premiered here in the late 1920s. Next-door, the opulent 1928 Savoy Theatre, or **Opera House**, was used until 1991 by the Opera Company of Boston, but it began as a vaudeville venue with family-friendly entertainment. Since it, too, is closed, use your imagination to leap from the showy Spanish Baroque terra-cotta exterior to the Opera House's equally flamboyant interior.

Next-door, the 1928 movie palace, the **Paramount Theatre**, boasts Boston's finest Art Deco sign, now in a state of disrepair. Lower Washington, as this stretch is called, has been a thorn in every mayor's side for the last 40 years. But in 1999, developers finally broke ground on a $600 million project at the corner of Washington and Essex Sts. **Millennium Place**, with condos, apartments, retail space, a modern movie palace and the city's second Ritz-Carlton Hotel, will bring much-needed life to this formerly blighted corner.

Top right: The aged Modern Theatre

Bottom right: Opera House, also aged

KIM GRANT

If this is your only chance to dip into Chinatown, resume the tour after you've savored a few sites and smells.

Otherwise, head east on Ave de Lafayette, turn left on Chauncy St and right on Bedford St to approach the southern edge of the Financial District. Across the street, diagonally to the left, the rounded **Proctor Building**, 100–106 Bedford St, has more ornamentation than any commercial building in the city. Despite the whimsy (cornices, arches, friezes), it's easy to miss. Continue along Bedford St to the corner to view the 1876 **Bedford Building**, No 99, which has an impressive stained-glass clock several floors up. The multicolored Ruskin Gothic marble building sits across Lincoln St from **125 Summer St**. Walk to the corner of High and Summer Sts to best appreciate how this high-rise incorporated a modest 19th-century facade. Once preservationists and architects agree to wed, divorce isn't an option and the citizenry must live with the union. (This marriage worked; others don't.) Both of these buildings sit opposite the intersection known as **Church Green**, which has neither an ounce of verdant growth nor any religious fervor. For the first half of the 19th-century, though, it did boast one lovely Bulfinch-designed church and many resplendent front yards.

KIM GRANT

Head up Summer St (away from the expressway) and turn right on Devonshire St to reach **Winthrop Square**. Henry Cabot Lodge was born here in 1850, during which

KIM GRANT

Top left: Proctor Building

Middle left: Bedford Building

Bottom left: The New England Press Building

time the square was Boston's dry-goods center. After the Great Fire leveled the area (it began around the corner), William Ralph Emerson was hired to design the **New England Press Building**, 1 Winthrop Square. True to his playful form, it's both grand and a bit eccentric. A lifelike bronze of Scottish poet Robert Burns striding with his staff and collie grace the park.

Cross Kingston St and look for a narrow brick passageway, Winthrop Lane, on the left, which contains a delightful dose of public art, *Boston Bricks*. Each brick depicts themes, events and sites unique to Boston: the Underground Railroad, molasses flood, graveyards, rowers, Boston Latin, smoots, Scolly Square, fish, swan boats and the Boston stone. Return at the end of your time in Boston and see how many you recognize.

From one whimsy to another: Gaze across Devonshire St to **75–101 Federal St**, an Art Deco jewel. Although the top is best appreciated from the John Hancock Observatory or Prudential Skywalk, from street level you can see the exterior brushed and burnished aluminum bands and low-relief floral ornamentation on the Devonshire, Franklin and Federal St sides. Across the way, **100 Federal St** has been dubbed 'the Pregnant Building' because of its bulging belly. Turn right on Federal St and head to High St, where 'the Landmark,' or **United Shoe Machinery Building**, resides. Boston's first Art Deco skyscraper (1930) set the standard and tone for the building frenzy that followed here and in New York City. Its pyramid-shaped crown of tiles glistens in the sun. Turn left on High St to fully appreciate the street-level commercial signage, the interior lobby and the doorways, which retain elaborate metal ornamental framing and accents. Continue on High St and turn left on Congress St. On your right, the **Bell Atlantic Building**, complete with Art Deco phone booths

Top right: Art Deco relief on 75–101 Federal St

Bottom right: Dean Cornwell's 1951 *Telephone Men and Women at Work* marks the Bell Atlantic Building.

on the street, really shines indoors. Off the main lobby, at 185 Franklin St, is a re-creation of telephone inventor **Alexander Graham Bell's laboratory** (he worked in old Scolly Square) as well as a wonderful life-sized mural that pays homage to an entire lineage of telephone employees. The mural and exhibit are free and open to the public, even on weekends.

Across Franklin St is the city's sweetest vest-pocket park, **Post Office Square**, a delightful green space with specimen trees and plenty of benches. Stroll through the park's pergola; to the right is **Hotel Meridien**, 250 Franklin St, a former Federal Reserve Bank (1922) built in the grand Renaissance Revival style. At the northern edge of the park is **Angell Memorial Park**, a red brick triangle with a fountain that served as a watering spot for horses. Its pond sculpture (complete with bronze water lilies and pond life) is dedicated to George Angell, a founder of the Society for the Prevention of Cruelty to Animals (SPCA). Across Congress St is the circa 1929 **post office**, considered one of the city's finest Art Deco edifices. The former federal courthouse now serves as a temporary home for the state trial court.

Cross over Pearl St heading away from the park, and turn right on Water St for **Liberty Square**, where the British tax office was destroyed by an angry mob of colonists in 1765. Its name commemorates that act as well as the French Revolution, and a sculpture honors the 1956 Hungarian Revolution. Six narrow streets converge here. (On weekends it's an intimate little spot, but on weekdays it's hectic.) The rounded 1924 **Appleton Building**, 1 Liberty Square, has a simple but delightful classical Greek Revival facade. The ornate doorway is particularly noteworthy, as is the interior gilded ceiling.

Head down Batterymarch St for the 1928 **Batterymarch Building**, No 60. This Art Deco's claim to fame is the subtle change of hue as the three

Top left: Batterymarch Building

Left: Details, Board of Trade Building

KIM GRANT

narrow brick towers (connected on the Broad St side) reach higher and higher. Continue to High St for the neoclassical **Chadwick Lead Works**, No 184. Lead pellets were formed by pouring a thin stream of molten lead from the rear tower. As the stream cooled on the way down, it broke into little pellets. Sitting in the shadow of its characterless neighbor across the street, **International Place**, the Lead Works building looks downright intimate. By the way, International Place occupies the site of a hilltop fort that guarded the city from sea attacks.

Retrace your steps to the Batterymarch Building and turn right on Franklin St, then left on Broad St, an important commercial street laid out in 1805. Many early 4½-story Federal-style buildings remain, including the granite 1853 **Architects Building**, at No 50–52. Home to the Boston Society of Architects, this is one of the few structures that survived the devastating 1872 fire, and the only one with a mansard roof. Turn right on Milk St and right on India St, where you can't miss the rounded granite **Flour & Grain Exchange**, 177 Milk St, built in 1892. Complete with crownlike finials and hundreds of arched windows, the Richardsonesque building once housed the chamber of commerce.

Head up India St away from the expressway, where you finally confront the landmark you've glimpsed all day: the **Custom House**, at India and State Sts. Between the Custom House and the expressway, the **State St Block** is a massive 1858 granite warehouse that originally reached to the wharves. Head up State St, noting the allegorical maritime figures and carvings on the 1901 **Board of Trade Building**, No 131. On the right the **Richards Building**, No 114, is one of few downtown buildings with a fanciful, cast-iron facade. (Much of Boston was already built with granite when cast iron made its debut in the US.) The Italianate windows were made in Italy and put together here.

The **Fleet Center**, 75 State St, a massive granite tower strikingly accented with gold leaf, is either opulent or decadent, depending on your disposition. When it catches the afternoon sun, it demands attention and competes with the elegant Custom House Tower. Take a peek at the six-story, gleaming marble lobby inside the Great Hall.

Right: Cast-iron Richards Building

This approach on State St affords the best views of the **Old State House**, in front of which cobblestones mark the site of the **Boston Massacre**.

Before ending the tour here, decide the success of the preservationist-developer marriage that resulted in the **Stock Exchange Building**, 53 State St. Originally the site of the Bunch of Grapes Tavern, a favorite patriot meeting place reputed to have served a wicked punch, the main floor of the 1889 building replicated an old counting house. In 1984, developers wanted to demolish the entire building, but preservationists 'succeeded' in forcing them to retain the granite sheath fronting State and Kilby Sts. Was it at the expense of a new glass tower or was an important part of history saved?

NORTH END:
PATRIOTS, PASTA & PAISANI

T his warren of streets and alleys retains the Old World flavor brought by European immigrants. Notice the 'storefront social clubs' and listen for passionate discussions in Italian by old-timers. Ritual Saturday morning shopping is done at specialty stores selling handmade pasta, cannoli and biscotti, fresh cheeses and cuts of meat, flowers, a little of this or that – all within a quarter-mile radius of Boston's oldest colonial buildings.

When you get tired or hungry, there are dozens of cafés and more ristoranti per block than anywhere else in the city. Hanover St eateries, especially, are the new domain of the 20- and 30-something crowd toting cell phones and fat portfolios. The North End is convenient for young Financial District professionals who like walking to work and require a safe neighborhood. Some fear the area is losing its authentic Italian charm with this new wave of 'immigrants,' but the cultural roots are firmly established here. Gentrification isn't moving nearly as fast as the molasses flood did.

The North End today is a blend of Italian-American culture and colonial history. This circuitous tour (Map 5) begins at the corner of Hanover and Cross Sts, on the other side of the expressway from downtown. From the Government Center and Faneuil Hall areas, make your way across the Big Dig construction site from near the corner of Congress and New Sudbury Sts. Depending on how long you linger at individual sites and cafés, this tour will take you one to three hours.

Hanover St is the main commercial thoroughfare, lined with tiny shops, cafés, restaurants and double-parked cars. Two businessmen – Eben Jordan of Jordan Marsh fame and Rowland Macy of Macy's department store glory – got their starts here with small dry-goods shops. On the left is **Trio's**, No 222, a pasta shop in business for almost 40 years. Tony and Genevieve's exceptional gnocchi, tortellini, fettucine and sauces will make you wish your hotel room had a stove. Across the way at **Modern Pastry**, No 257, sample the colorful, fruit-shaped marzipan. Modern has plenty of tempting sweets, but other places do too, so pace yourself. Just across Parmenter St on the left is **Salumeria Toscana**, No 272, a gourmet Italian deli with a spellbinding array of olives. Pop into the **North End Branch Library**, 25 Parmenter St, to check out the impressive plaster model of Venice's Doge's Palace. Then retrace your steps to Hanover St and head down Richmond St to **Salumeria Italiana**, No 151, an old-fashioned deli and grocery shop. Here you'll find fixings for an Italian-style picnic: salami and *prosciutto di Parma*, cheese, classic white bean spread, fresh bread and olives.

At Richmond and North Sts, **V Cirace & Sons** has upwards of 750 different Italian wines, some gathering dust since the early 1900s. Turn left on North St and duck down the private **Baker's Alley**, leading to one of the North End's numerous hidden courtyards.

The 1710 English Renaissance brick **Pierce-Hichborn House**, at No 29, was the home of Paul Revere's boatbuilder cousin. The three-story house has a central staircase, unusual for its time. (The house is open only for guided tours, usually at 12:30 pm or 2:30 pm. Call the morning of your visit.) Next-door is the 1680 **Paul Revere House**, No 19, which has been changed on numerous occasions over the last 300 years. The 1838 **Mariner's House**, No 11, still houses homesick seamen on shore leave. In ye olden days, mariners kept an eye on the sea from atop the cupola. (The shoreline was much closer in the mid-18th century.) Now that the recently refurbished boarding house has Internet access, sailors log onto www.weather.com.

Top right: Mariner's House facade

Bottom right: Paul Revere House

Cross **North Square**, one of Boston's quintessential little triangular paved 'squares' and turn right onto Sun Court at Moon St. Turn left on North St, right on Lewis St, then right on Fulton St, for the ornate circa

Great Molasses Flood

At about noon on January 15, 1919, a 90-foot-tall tank of molasses exploded at the Purity Distilling Co, a munitions manufacturer. A 50-foot-high wave of the sticky liquid – over 2 million gallons of it – flowed down Foster and Commercial Sts at 35mph, swallowing warehouses, smashing houses and smothering 21 people and 100 horses. It was impossible to stop the 14,000 tons of gooey stuff. Various rumors circulated: The Germans did it; political anarchists did it; there was alcohol in the tank (the disaster happened during Prohibition). In the end, a structural problem with the tank was determined to be the cause. Trying to clean it up was nightmarish; even with the aid of high-pressure fire hoses and saltwater (to 'cut' the molasses), traces of molasses remained for years. Old-timers say that on certain days, the breeze still resurrects the smell.

1864 **McLauthlin Building**, at No 120, fancifully adorned with New England's first cast-iron facade. The building was converted into condos in 1979.

Former mayor John F 'Honey Fitz' Fitzgerald (JFK's grandfather), whose family emigrated from Ireland during the potato famine, was born down the way on little Ferry St in 1863. His father owned small grocery stores on North and Hanover Sts. Honey Fitz referred to his days in the 'dear old North End' so affectionately and repeatedly that residents were known as 'Dearos' during his years of political prominence. Honey Fitz's daughter Rose (JFK's mother) was born near North Square at 4 Garden Court St in 1890.

Returning to Lewis St, head to and cross Commercial St, where you'll see the back of the **Prince Building**, 45–69 Atlantic Ave. The original factory for Prince Macaroni Co is one of the earliest examples of a successful conversion from industrial space to housing and office space.

From here you could dip into the Christopher Columbus Park or walk along the sturdy granite wharf buildings that have been converted to expensive condominiums. In the mid-19th century, the famed clipper ship trade revolved around **Lewis Wharf**, where an 18th-century incident inspired Edgar Allan Poe's *Fall of the House of Usher*. Supposedly, when the Usher house was demolished in 1800, two skeletons were found clutched to one another behind a locked gate leading to a tunnel. Legend has it that an elderly husband had discovered his young wife in the arms of a sailor and he locked them in.

Retrace your steps back through North Square and follow Prince St (yes, again, of pasta fame) to Hanover St. Across the street to the left, **Mike's Pastry**, No 300, has fantastico cannoli, if you know how to order; see 'Dessert' in Places to Eat. The lobster tail, filled with sweet, whipped marscapone cheese, is another decadent option. For the best cup of cappuccino, go next-door to **Caffè Vittoria**, at No 296. Fortified with caffeine and sugar, head back across Prince St to the Roman Catholic **St Leonard's Church & Peace Garden**, built by Italian immigrants in 1873.

The garden is always lovely, but is particularly worth visiting in the spring and at Christmastime.

Continue on Hanover St to the 1804 **St Stephen's Church**, Boston's only remaining church designed by the renowned Charles Bulfinch. The elaborate facade is made of stone, brick and wood; Revere cast the belfry bell in 1805. Originally a Unitarian church, it was sold to the Catholic diocese in 1862 to serve the North End's Irish-Catholic community. Rose Kennedy was baptized here.

Across the street, the shady **Paul Revere Mall** (called 'the prado' by locals) could very well have been snatched brick for brick from Italy. It not only serves as a perfect frame for the Old North Church, but also is a lively local meeting place for all generations. And it's also a rare outdoor place to rest, while contemplating the imposing equestrian statue of Revere. Pass through the promenade to the 1712 **Ebenezer Clough House**, at 21 Unity St, one of Boston's few remaining early-18th-century houses. Clough, a member of the 'Sons of Liberty' who participated in the Boston Tea Party, was a mason who worked on the adjacent **Old North Church**. Note the little refurbished courtyards, terraces and memorial gardens between the Clough House and the church.

Head up Hull St to **Copp's Hill Burial Ground**. Across from the entrance to the graveyard, the **Narrowest House**, 44 Hull St, measures a whopping 9^1/$_2$ feet wide. The circa 1800 house reportedly was built, out of spite, to block light from the neighbor's house and to obliterate the view of the house behind it. If the northern cemetery gate is locked, peer over **Copp's Hill Terrace** for a view of Charlestown and the last two Freedom Trail sites – Charlestown Bridge and the USS *Constitution*. The Great Molasses Flood occurred near here; see 'Great Molasses Flood,' earlier.

If you intend to visit Charlestown by foot, this might be a good time to do it. Otherwise, return to Salem St and head downhill. The **North Bennet St School**, 39 N Bennet St, was founded in 1881 to help immigrants develop practical industrial skills. The illustrious school still transforms students into artisans, master carpenters, cabinet makers, violin restorers, book binders and the like.

Salem St has long been the domain of shopkeepers, and it remains the North End's most interesting commercial street. Stop in at the **Bova Bakery**, No 134, open 24 hours a day, and the aromatic **Polcari's Coffee**, at No 105, purveyor of coffee, nuts, grains and spices, all self-serve from bins, baskets and tubs. **Il Bongustaio**, No 64, is a secondhand furniture store that's bursting at the seams. Signs warn there is no room inside for browsers. If you spy through the window, look for the eccentric owner hovering around. The tiny **Dairy Fresh Candies**, No 57, specializes in domestic and imported nuts, chocolates, candies and dried fruit.

Right: Paul Revere statue, Old North Church

Around the corner to the right is the colorful fruit and vegetable market **A LaFauci & Sons**, No 46. The adjacent **Maria's Pastry** is considered the neighborhood's most authentic pastry shop. Sample the *biscotti regina*, *ossa di morti* and *torrone*, a nouggaty-chocolatey-almondy treat. **J Pace & Son**, 42 Cross St, is a friendly neighborhood Italian deli-grocer.

BACK BAY: FROM LOWLY LANDFILL TO HIGH-MINDED AESTHETIC

You could easily spend a day strolling down shady Comm Ave, window-shopping and sipping a latte on chic Newbury St, visiting grand churches or taking in remarkable *and* unified French-influenced Victorian architecture. This dense tour (Map 8) is an amalgam of residential and commercial sites, and does not include the

dozens of specialty shops you'll find on Newbury St; see Newbury St in the Shopping chapter for those. And it's a long walk that could take an entire afternoon; without stopping too much, expect to spend about two hours. Break it up with a coffee on Newbury St or a quick bite in any number of places. At least Back Bay, laid out in a grid pattern, is a breeze to navigate compared to other neighborhoods. To begin the walking tour, take the Green Line to Arlington and walk north along the Public Garden to Comm Ave.

The backbone of Back Bay is the Parisian-style boulevard, the **Commonwealth Avenue Mall**, planted with great elm trees. Head west on Comm Ave. On the right, the Italianate **Baylies Mansion**, No 5, is a relative newcomer, having been built in 1912. Occupied by the Boston Center for Adult

Left: Baylies Mansion

Bottom left: Commonwealth Avenue

Education, its grand ballroom evokes images of Le Petite Trianon at Versailles. BCAE course offerings, while quite laudable, are the hottest singles ticket in town.

At the corner of Berkeley St, the Hooper mansion at **25–27 Comm Ave** is the only house in the neighborhood with a corner yard – and what a yard it is! On the opposite side of Berkeley St, the 11-story **Haddon Hall** caused all sorts of problems for its neighbors when it was built. Its weight affected the underground water tables (remember, this is landfill) and caused adjacent basements to flood. After it was built, strict height restrictions were imposed (and occasionally violated).

Turn right on Berkeley St. On the left is **First & Second Church**, which serves one of the country's oldest congregations (founded in 1630). It utilizes nicely what remains of a medieval-style facade (the church burned in

Mary Baker Eddy

Mary Baker Eddy (1821–1910) grew up in New Hampshire a sickly, pious, stubborn child with a great love of study. Her first husband died before she gave birth to their first child. Alone, penniless and in poor health, she was forced to marry again. During that time, she began studying homeopathy and other alternative methods for wellness. As she lay alone one day in 1866, bedridden, she began to read a biblical account of how Jesus had healed the sick. By the time she put down the book, she was healed. For three years, she retreated to formulate Christian Science principles, a belief system based on a rational understanding that the mind is an inalienable part of the greater goodness that is God.

Mary Baker Eddy taught that by consciously working to gain 'the mind of Christ,' humans can enter into a state in which spirit is more powerful than – and in command of – material things, including the human body. Gaining this spiritual state involves patience, humility, repentance and tribulation, and includes among its tasks the cure of human illness through prayer.

Science & Health, which details her philosophy, was published in 1875 to mixed reviews. 'Critics took pleasure in saying that the book was wholly original, but would never be read,' Eddy noted wryly. To date, the book has sold more than 9 million copies.

In 1879, Eddy and a small group of adherents founded the Church of Christ, Scientist, which, unusual among sects at the time, encouraged the full equality of men and women. In 1881, Eddy founded the Massachusetts Metaphysical College in Boston to train practitioners in Christian Science healing arts. Men and women were equally welcome, and the training provided hundreds of women with careers, allowing them a measure of financial self-sufficiency – something Eddy prized.

1968). Across the street, the **First Lutheran Church** is plain on the inside but has a tranquil courtyard. On the northwest corner of Berkeley and Marlborough Sts, the **French Library** holds a festive annual Bastille Day celebration (see Cultural Centers in Facts for the Visitor) and is graced by blooming magnolia trees in May. Turn right on Beacon St for the over-the-top Victorian **Gibson House Museum**, No 137, which appears just as its last owner left it in 1957 (plus some dust).

Retrace your steps to Marlborough St, Back Bay's quietest, most civilized street, turn right and then left on Clarendon St. On the far corner of Comm Ave and Clarendon St, the 1872 **First Baptist Church**, an early Romanesque HH Richardson design, has an Italian campanile and a striking frieze depicting the sacraments. The church's nickname, 'the Church of the Holy Bean Blowers,' comes from the angels blowing their trumpets from on high. On the corner of Clarendon and Newbury Sts, the **Trinity Church Rectory** has a trademark Richardson arch, very similar to Harvard's Sever Hall. Think you might be related to Frederick Douglass or Mary Dyer? At 101 Newbury St, the private **New England**

Historic Genealogical Society (☎ 617-536-5740) contains millions of manuscripts and documents, dating back to the Puritans, that help people from all over the world trace their family tree. For $15, you are granted access for a day to everything but manuscripts.

Head back to the Comm Ave Mall and turn left down the middle of it. The somber **Firefighter's Monument** honors the nine men who died in **the Vendome** fire of 1972. The former 1871 French Second Empire hotel, 160 Comm Ave, was the most luxurious in Boston in its time, the first public building to have electricity. Although the interior is gutted (it's now condos), the ornamental facade remains intact – except for the rear addition that has been hideously grafted onto it.

On the opposite corner of Comm Ave and Dartmouth St, the massive 1872 **Ames-Webster Mansion** has Back Bay's most grand interior. (Alas, subdivided into offices, it's not open to the public.) You'll have to imagine guests arriving under the porte cochere, making an entrance down a grand staircase, the likes of which are not often seen this side of the Atlantic, and dancing beneath richly paneled 18-foot-high ceilings in a breathtaking hall some 60 feet long.

Continuing down the center of the mall, the **William Lloyd Garrison Statue** pays tribute to the extraordinary abolitionist. One block farther, between Exeter and Fairfield Sts, the **Admiral Samuel Eliot Morison Statue** is perhaps the most beloved on the strip. The seaman and historian is perched atop a boulder, as if on sea's edge. On the right, you can't

Top left: Firefighter's Monument

Left: Admiral Samuel Eliot Morison

miss the palatial Italian Renaissance Revival facade of the **Algonquin Club**, No 217, home to the same exclusive private club for which it was built in 1887.

Continue west for 2¹/₂ blocks to Hereford St. To the left, the French Gothic and Early Renaissance **Burrage Mansion**, 314 Comm Ave, is a wild chateau-like creature out of its element, although it's been here since 1889. The interior (now a pricey 'old-age home') is just as over-the-top; take a quick glance inside. There's a greenhouse attached to the back. Across the way at 40 Hereford St, **Fanny Farmer's School of Cookery** was founded in 1902. What would Boston's original celebrity chef think of the current disposition toward 'vertical presentation' – dishes that are lovely to look at but impossible to dig into.

Continue one block west on Comm Ave. At the corner of Mass Ave, the **Ames Mansion**, 355 Comm Ave, is Back Bay's largest mansion, built in 1882 for a railroad tycoon and soon-to-be governor of Mass-achusetts. It's now an office building. Two blocks ahead on the right, architect Graham Gund successfully incorporated the exterior of a fire-ravaged church into condos in 1983. Many units at **Church Court**, 490 Beacon St, best viewed from a distance, overlook a courtyard where the church's sanctuary was located.

Retrace your steps along Mass Ave (away from the river) and turn left on **Newbury St**. Epitomized by café hounds and haute couture crowds, Newbury St is to Boston what Fifth Ave is to New York City, on a more intimate scale. On the corner of Mass Ave, **360 Newbury St** is one of Back Bay's most talked about renovations. Built as a boxy warehouse in 1918, Los Angeles architect Frank Gehry dressed up the concrete facade with slate-colored copper and added struts on the top floors and near street level. It's a showy home for Tower Records today. Next-door, run-ning almost the length of the block, the **Newbury St Stables** once accommodated horses and carriages for those residents who didn't have their own stables. The low-rise buildings have been converted into

Right: Ames Mansion

KIM GRANT

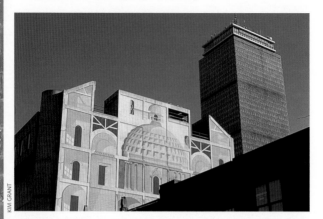

commercial spaces. Note the stable's 1981 surrealist **Tramount Mural**, a real stylistic departure for Boston. At the corner of Hereford St, the **Boston Architectural Center** (☎ 617-536-3170) is adorned with a trompe l'oeil mural by Richard Haas. It's best viewed from Boylston St or Newbury St near Mass Ave. The BAC, whose students work full time and whose faculty are volunteers, has frequently changing ground-floor exhibits on urban architecture and design.

Turn right on Hereford St and right again on Boylston St for the **Institute for Contemporary Art**, No 955. Across the street, the mammoth **Hynes Convention Center** was redesigned and expanded in the late 1980s. It's small by modern US standards, which is why the city is building a new convention center in South Boston. Head down Dalton St, keeping the Hynes on your left. Turn left on Belvidere St and then right at the **reflecting pool** of the expansive and monumental **Christian Science Church** and world headquarters complex (now undergoing renovations). Next-door, at the corner of Mass and Huntington Aves, are two grand buildings, **Horticultural Hall** and **Symphony Hall**.

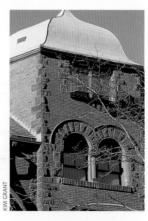

Retrace your steps back toward the convention center, keeping it on your left. Head up the stairs to cut through the **Prudential Center** plaza and mall. This controversial 1959 development complex, over a former railroad yard, was plagued by poor planning. The interior plaza and shops functioned as a wind tunnel, the mall was one floor above street level and it introduced a new and unwelcome scale of building to Back Bay. The mid- to late-1980s renovation mitigated most of those

Top left: Boston Architectural Center mural

Left: Boston Art Club

problems, making it a much more vital place. Annually in early December, a giant tree is donated by the city of Halifax (Boston aided the maritime Canadian city during a series of tragic December 1917 events) and ceremoniously lit with holiday lights. The 50th-floor **Prudential Center Skywalk** offers panoramic views.

Take a right on Boylston St, a quick left on Fairfield St and a right on Newbury St. At the corner of Exeter St, the HH Richardson Romanesque **Exeter St Theater Building** was built as a church in 1884, but the 2nd floor was converted into a movie theater in 1914. For years, the cult classic *Rocky Horror Picture Show* was screened at midnight. Despite a strong neighborhood outcry, its exceptional interior was gutted for office and retail space in 1985. Continuing on Newbury St, the party scene of Josh Winer's 1991 **Cafe Du Barry mural** depicts life-sized Boston celebrities and historical figures. Across the street, the **Copley Society of Boston** (☎ 617-536-5049), No 158, the oldest nonprofit art association in the country, has newly renovated 1st-floor galleries. Next-door, the imaginative and enigmatic 1881 **Boston Art Club**, No 270, designed by Ralph Waldo Emerson's nephew, exhibits his trademark hodgepodge of architectural forms.

Turn right on Dartmouth St where you'll quickly encounter the late-19th-century **New Old South Church**. Somehow, it fits perfectly on the corner of **Copley Square**, itself surrounded by four monumental buildings. The venerable **Boston Public Library** consists of two distinct structures: the original 1895 McKim, Mead & White building fronting Dartmouth St, and the dignified, skylit 1971 Philip Johnson wing facing Boylston St. (Both buildings are named for their architects rather than a wealthy patron.) The extravagant **Fairmont Copley Plaza Hotel** anchors the corner of St James St, where the original Museum of Fine Arts was located from 1872 to 1909. HH Richardson's Romanesque masterpiece **Trinity Church**, often called 'one of the great monuments of American architecture,' takes center stage. The **John Hancock Tower**, a reflective 62-story glass skyscraper, has an observatory from which you can take it all in.

The enormous and modern **Copley Place** shopping mall, just south of Dartmouth and Stuart Sts, is the largest privately funded development in Boston's history. The benign retail and hotel complex exemplifies the sports metaphor: No

Right: 500 Boylston St reflected in the new John Hancock Tower

KIM GRANT

FIVE HUNDRED BOYLSTON

KIM GRANT

harm, no foul. Across from the eastern side of Copley Place, fronting Dartmouth St, **Back Bay Station** is one of many handsome, light and airy MBTA subway stations (this one also serves Amtrak) built in the late 1980s when the Orange Line was depressed and extended along the Southwest Corridor. The Clarendon St entrance recalls an Italian piazza.

Head down St James Ave, keeping the Hancock Tower on your right, and turn left onto Clarendon St. At the corner of Boylston St, **500 Boylston St** is an overly grand 1988 neoclassical revival building that destroys the view of Trinity Church from the opposite approach. It overwhelms pedestrian traffic and minimizes the amount of sunlight reaching the sidewalk. Directly across from it, the monolithic **New England** provides a conservative sheath for the Mutual Life Insurance Company. MIT's first building stood on this site in 1865 and looked rather like **Louis, Boston** (just next-door at 234 Berkeley St). The stately French Academic-style building was erected in 1830 and originally housed the Museum of Natural History. On the right corner of Boylston and Berkeley Sts, the **Houghton Mifflin Building**, 222 Berkeley St, built in 1991, houses the Boston-based publishing company. Head through the Boylston St entrance to appreciate the skylit winter garden.

Opposite Houghton Mifflin, the Beaux Arts **Berkeley Building**, 420 Boylston St, is loaded with glass and frilly white terra-cotta. Turn right on Berkeley St, then left on Stuart St for the **Salada Tea Building**. The bronze doors at 330 Stuart St are delightful, decorated with bas-relief elephants and symbols of the tea trade. Retrace your steps back up Berkeley St to Newbury St, where you'll see the 1867 English Gothic Revival **Church of the Covenant**, 67 Newbury St. Turn right on Newbury St for the **Emmanuel Church** (☎ 617-536-3355, 536-3356 for concert information), at No 15, highly regarded for its musical and cultural offerings. The small memorial chapel within is noteworthy for its ironwork and stained glass. Next-door, the **Ritz-Carlton Hotel** is neither

Left: 500 Boylston St

outwardly showy nor glamorous, true to its pedigree. Art Deco details over the 2nd-story windows are its most unrestrained ornaments.

Take a right on Arlington St for the airy **Arlington St Church** (☎ 617-536-7050), at the corner of Boylston St. Back Bay's first public building (the neighborhood was filled and constructed from east to west) features 16 commissioned Tiffany windows, a bell tower and an embellished steeple modeled after London's St Martin-in-the-Fields church. The Unitarian Universalist ministry is purely progressive. The church keeps hours that are difficult to summarize, but from May to mid-October, it's usually open from 1 to 5 pm Thursday through Sunday. When it gets cold, the 'great doors' are closed, although you can still check out the sanctuary (10 am to 6 pm Monday through Thursday).

HARVARD UNIVERSITY: BRICKS & MORTARBOARDS

F ounded in 1636 by the Massachusetts Bay Colony to educate men for the ministry, Harvard is America's oldest college. (No other college came along until 1693.) The original Ivy League school has six graduates who went on to become US president, not to mention 37 Nobel laureates and 29 Pulitzer Prize winners. It educates 6500 undergraduates and about 12,000 graduates yearly in 10 professional schools. Its seal, *Veritas*, is Latin for 'truth.' At $14.4 billion, it has the largest endowment of any university. During a recent capital campaign, it raked in a staggering $1.25 million per day.

This one- to three-hour tour (Map 11) (depending on whether you duck into a museum) starts at the public information office within the **Holyoke Center** (☎ 617-495-1573), 1350 Mass Ave, which has reams of written information (some for free and some for a fee – Harvard didn't grow that big endowment by giving it away). Ask about free events open to the public; the **Harvard Box Office** (☎ 617-496-2222) sells tickets to other events. Walk south through the arcade to Mt Auburn St and look left. It's hard to miss the **Lampoon Castle**, an island two blocks in the distance. One of Cambridge's most distinctive and jocular buildings, it houses the namesake student humor magazine, which was said to have inspired the creation of the *National Lampoon* magazine. 'Poonies,' as they're called, embrace annual practical jokes such as absconding with the State House's beloved Sacred Cod (which they did in 1933). Turn right up Holyoke St where the **Hasty Pudding Building**, No 12, houses the exuberant student theater group.

Across Mass Ave, the yellow clapboard colonial **Wadsworth House** was home to Harvard presidents until 1849. Head through the gate toward the grassy quadrangle bordered by ivy-covered brick buildings. This is the 'old yard' of **Harvard Yard** fame, bordered by freshmen dormitories. On the National Register of Historic Places, it oozes privilege

Right: One of many gates from Cambridge into Harvard

KIM GRANT

but anyone is welcome to hang out under a towering tree or on the granite steps of a hallowed hall. Midway through the yard on the left, **Johnson Gate** has been the college's primary entrance since the 17th century. It's one of nine entrances built into the wall that surrounds the yard. The gate is flanked by the college's two original buildings, **Harvard Hall** and **Massachusetts Hall**. The latter, built in 1720, contains the president's office, above which are freshmen dorms. As for Harvard Hall,

George Washington and his troops (who had to reimburse Harvard for stealing five gold doorknobs) took it over in the 17th century. In 1764, the second building on this site burned to the ground, taking all of John Harvard's original book collection with it – except for one volume. Just before the fire, a student had removed a book from the library, even though this was prohibited. In the morning, he realized he had the sole survivor of the original collection. He presented it to the president of the college, who was thrilled to have it and promptly expelled the student for the original infraction. The current hall dates to 1766.

Directly across the yard is **University Hall**, a monumental building designed by Bulfinch in 1814 as a dining hall and for classrooms. In 1969, students who were protesting the Vietnam War raided the building and dragged out the administrators. Most dissension today is expressed within the confines of the *Harvard Crimson*, the college's daily newspaper, whose editors usually trundle off to work for the *New York Times* after graduation. In front of U-Hall, the life-sized bronze **John Harvard Statue**, sculpted by Daniel Chester French (of Washington, DC, Lincoln Memorial fame), is also known as the 'statue of three lies.' The inscription reads 'John

Top left: Freshmen dorms, Harvard Yard

Left: Memorial Church

Harvard, Founder, 1638' but you'll recall that the school was founded in 1636 by the Mass Bay Colony; John was merely the benefactor in 1638. Furthermore, this is not John Harvard; there were no likenesses of him available to the sculptor.

As an aside, most of the 13 upperclassmen houses are located between Mass Ave and the Charles River, east of JFK St. Distinguished by different color towers, they're easier to spot from the river. Each house accommodates 250 to 500 people, and has a computer lab, dining hall and library. There are no fraternities or sororities at Harvard, since the house system essentially meets the same needs as the Greek system.

To reach the 'new' yard, head to the back side of University Hall, which opens onto another grassy quadrangle called **Tercentenary Theatre**, where commencement exercises take place. In this quad, you'll find the new (1931) Georgian Revival **Memorial Church**, which holds nondenominational daily services and has a wonderful Fisk organ. **Sever Hall** is an 1880 architectural Romanesque Revival masterpiece by HH Richardson (he also designed Trinity Church in Back Bay). The building is lovely at night when the lights are on. Within the arched main entrance, acoustics are such that whispers are heard distinctly from one side to the other.

Opposite the church is the imposing **Widener Library**, the hub of the world's largest library system with 13.3 million volumes. Around the corner to the left, **Houghton Library** houses Harvard's rare book collection – including John Harvard's sole surviving book – and manuscripts, as well as furniture from poet Emily Dickinson's home.

Hasty Pudding Awards

Jodie Foster, Mel Gibson, Susan Sarandon, Tom Hanks, Sigourney Weaver and Robin Williams. Could a little pudding pot, a bunch of guys parading around in drag and an evening of roasting the celeb with embarrassing outtakes really draw these A-list types?…to little old Cambridge?…in February? You betcha. The Hasty Pudding Theatrical Club has toasted and roasted a 'Woman & Man of the Year' since 1951. Heads turned in 1981 when John Travolta said he was more honored to have received a pudding pot than an Academy Award nomination.

It all began back in 1795, when 21 students gathered in secrecy to 'cultivate the social affections and cherish the feelings of friendship' and 'in alphabetical order provide a pot of hasty pudding for every meeting.' Soon after, in response to increased 'rowdiness,' the group improvised a mock criminal court to try its members for 'insolence.' Over ensuing years, these productions became more and more elaborate, with the addition of costumes and scripts. In 1844, an upperclassman secretly produced an opera instead of a trial, and thus the Hasty Pudding show was born. To this day, men play both male and female roles (women are relegated to behind-the-scenes contributions) and the professional-quality shows feature no-holds-barred drag burlesque.

Head out of the yard to Quincy St, keeping Houghton Library on your right. Across the street, the concrete and glass **Carpenter Center**, No 24, is the only structure in North America designed by the renowned Frenchman Le Corbusier. Next-door, the entryway for the dignified **Fogg Art Museum**, No 32, is a replica Tuscan loggia from Montepulciano, Italy. The Fogg's western collection is comprehensive. Behind the Fogg, in the adjacent Werner Otto Hall, is the **Busch-Reisinger Museum**. Next in line comes the **Arthur Sackler Museum**, on Quincy St at Broadway. After spying the postmodern entryway, you'd be hard-pressed to guess it contains an excellent collection of Islamic and Asian art. The British architect who designed it in 1984 described Harvard's nearby buildings as an 'architectural zoo.' Critics Susan and Michael Southworth went one step further, adding that the Sackler is 'another strange beast in the lineup.'

Continue up Quincy St to Cambridge St, where **Gund Hall**, the Graduate School of Design, looms like one massive staircase. All night

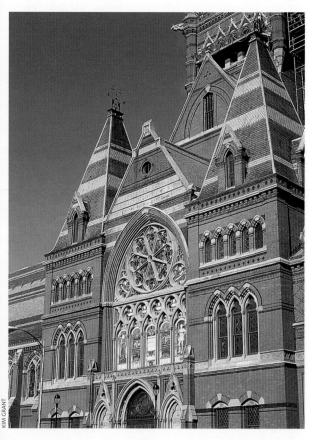

Left: Memorial Hall, Harvard University

long, students are illuminated hunched over their drafting tables. The 1st-floor gallery (☎ 617-495-4731), 48 Quincy St, has changing architecture exhibits.

Across Quincy St, the fanciful Ruskin Gothic **Memorial Hall** has a square tower, multicolored slate roof and plenty of gargoyles. It created quite a controversy in 1874 since it memorialized only Union, or northern, Civil War soldiers. Although it looks like a church, complete with glorious stained-glass windows by Tiffany and La Farge, it isn't. It contains **Sanders Theater**, Harvard's largest lecture hall, where diverse public concerts and lectures are held; both Winston Churchill and caustic social critic Camille Paglia have stood at the lectern. The handsome trusses, woodwork and chandeliers in the freshman dining room, **Annenberg Hall**, lend an air of authority inspired by the great halls of Oxford and Cambridge. It's Harvard's most impressive space. Downstairs in Memorial Hall is **Loker Commons**, the student union, a great place to hang out, perhaps even shoot some pool. The food court is open to the public and whirs up a great smoothie.

Continue west (staying atop the Cambridge St underpass) until you stumble upon a casual pile of rocks set on asphalt and grass. The **Tanner Fountain** is Harvard's very own circa 1984 Stonehenge. It's supposed to elicit the mysterious feel of ancient places, not to mention the rocky landscape the Puritans had to cultivate. The sculpture – which gives barely enough warning if you happen to be using a rock as a backrest – mists in summer and steams in winter.

The fountain guards Harvard's biggest and busiest building, the concrete **Science Center** (☎ 617-495-2779), said to resemble a Polaroid Land camera. (Polaroid is headquartered in Cambridge.) The lower level contains historic scientific instruments. To your left, note the 1876 **Holworthy Gate**. Hang a right at the Science Center and head north for the revered **Law School**. The second building on your left is **Austin Hall**, another delightfully grand Romanesque structure designed in 1883 by

KIM GRANT

HH Richardson. If the building is open, look for the 2nd-floor Ames Courtroom (the original library), where students hold an annual mock trial presided over by a US Supreme Court Justice. (Many of the distinguished jurists, including Scalia, Souter, Bryer, Kennedy and Ginsberg, were schooled here.) The Austin lecture halls easily conjure images of a crusty Socratic professor bearing down relentlessly on his students, just as in the movie *Paper Chase*. Continue in the same direction, toward the open quadrangle, keeping Langdell Hall on your left, to reach **Harkness Commons**. This student center and dining hall was designed by Bauhaus school founder Walter Gropius, who left Nazi Germany and headed the Graduate School of Design for years.

Right: Holworthy Gate with Science Center

Places to Stay

It's not cheap to sleep in Boston. Hotel rates are soaring faster than eagles on an updraft. From 1997 to 1999, Boston hotels had an astonishing 77% occupancy rate, ranking it in the top three US cities. Translation: Hotels charge what they want because they can get it. Be strategic though, and you'll be able to feed and entertain yourself once you've caught a few zzz's. Secure reservations six

Hotel Discounts

One of the best ways to gain entry into an otherwise inaccessible mid-range or top end hotel is to contact a hotel broker or reservation service. These service bureaus develop relationships with hotels during economic downturns that carry over into good times, too. These agencies have access to lower rates than you can get by calling the hotel directly.

Central Reservation Service of New England (☎ 617-569-3800, 800-332-3026, fax 561-4840, www.bostonhotels.net) offers discounts of 10% to 50% on accommodations from fancy hotels to guesthouses. It operates out of Terminal C at Logan Airport, but try not to wait until you have landed to secure a place to stay.

Hotel Reservations Network (☎ 800-964-6835, www.hoteldiscount.com) deals with upwards of 40 Boston-area economy motels and deluxe hotels. They can often find steep discounts.

Citywide Reservation Services (☎ 617-267-7424, 800-468-3593, fax 267-9408, www.cityres.com) offers similar services. During the summer, they also make reservations for Cape Cod lodging.

Accommodations Express (☎ 800-444-7666, www.accommodationsexpress.com) is worth a try if you can get through to them.

months in advance if you can. Stay on the outskirts of town. Visit off-season (November through March). Finally, if you can't find an inexpensive place, consider weekend jaunts sandwiched by weekday overnights in the surrounding areas.

Price ranges for budget, mid-range and top end accommodations are generally as follows: budget, less than $100; mid-range, $100 to $200; top end, $200 and up. Use our quoted prices as a guideline, since rates fluctuate from hour to hour – oftentimes depending on who answers the phone!

Camping

Boston is unusual in that it offers 'downtown' camping within the Boston Harbor Islands State Park. Pitching a tent on the islands takes some advance planning, but it's certainly an experience.

To get to private campgrounds, within 45 minutes of downtown, you'll need a car.

Hostels

A hostel bed costs $15 to $20 nightly. Boston has one hostel directly affiliated with Hostelling International/American Youth Hostels (HI/AYH) and two comparable, independent ones.

Motels & Hotels

Along with the groundbreaking on a new $700 million convention center (scheduled for completion in 2003) came an increase in room tax, which can add a sizable chunk onto a motel or hotel bill. The tax is currently a whopping 12.45%. Rates quoted in this text do not include this tax.

Motels Boston has its share of cookie-cutter motel chains, most of which are located in outlying neighborhoods and are simply adequate. Rates of $75 to $125 nightly (higher during special events) may seem high for what you get, with the exception of possible free parking, which would otherwise cost $20 to $25 nightly at big hotels.

Hotels Hotel prices fluctuate daily and seasonally, depending on occupancy levels, special events and the weather. Simply asking about specials can often save quite a bit of money. Prices in this guide, based on published 'rack rates,' can be an approximate guideline at best.

It's been noted when hotels permit children under 18 to stay free with their parents. Boston has a number of mid-range hotels ($100 to $200 nightly) that have stepped up to meet demand, but more Boston hotels fall in the 'top end' category.

BEACON HILL (MAP 2)
Mid-Range
The four-story *John Jeffries House* (☎ 617-367-1866, fax 742-0313, 14 David Mugar Way) has 46 rooms and suites in an early-20th-century building owned by the Mass Eye & Ear Infirmary. (You don't have to know someone having an operation to stay here.) Rooms are nicely decorated, and some still have original molding and hardwood floors; most have a kitchenette. Expect to pay $90 single, $110 to $145 for a double

or suite; off-season it drops $10 to $20 for doubles.

The *Eliot & Pickett Houses* (☎ 617-248-8707, fax 742-1364, 6 Mt Vernon Place, www.uua.org/ep), adjacent to the State House, has 20 rooms in adjoining brick townhouses. There's a great outdoor deck and comfortable living rooms. The kitchen is stocked with supplies for making breakfast or lunch. Some rooms have two four-poster beds, so families are reasonably accommodated. Doubles cost $95 with shared bath, $125 to $150 private. Few rooms are available from late September through February, when the Unitarian Universalist Association holds retreats here.

Top End
Susan Butterworth's home, *Beacon Hill Bed & Breakfast* (☎ 617-523-7376, 27 Brimmer St), really gives travelers a taste of living on the hill (even though this is the flat part of the hill). She has only three rooms, but what rooms they are! Private baths and continental breakfast are included for $220 to $250 nightly.

An elegant room at the Eliot & Pickett Houses

PLACES TO STAY

KIM GRANT

GOVERNMENT CENTER & FANEUIL HALL (MAP 3)
Budget

The *Irish Embassy Hostel* (☎ 617-973-4841, *fax 720-3998, 232 Friend St, beantownh@ aol.com*) rents 52 beds in seven rooms (with four to 10 people per room) above its lively eponymous pub. Some rooms are single sex; some are mixed. For $15, you get an extremely tidy place; sheets and bedding; admission to hear live bands in two pubs; all-you-can-eat barbecue buffet dinner Sunday through Wednesday in summer (two to three nights year-round); and $1.50 beers. It can't be beat, but don't get too comfortable; there's a six-night maximum stay. There's no lockout either. The hostel is full by the official check-in time of 9 am in summer, so make reservations as far in advance as possible. Towels can be rented for $1, but the pack room is free.

The nearby *Beantown Hostel* (☎ 617-723-0800, *fax 720-3998, 222 Friend St, beantownh@ aol.com*), operated by the Irish Embassy Hostel, has 56 beds. They supply lockers; you supply locks. Prices and information are similar to the Irish Embassy. One difference is Beantown's 1:45 am curfew.

Mid-Range

New in 1995, *Shawmut Inn* (☎ 617-720-5544, *800-350-7784, fax 723-7784, 280 Friend St, www.shawmutinn.com*), a friendly small hotel with a resident cat and many European guests, has 66 darkish rooms on five floors. All rooms have a microwave, coffeemaker and refrigerator in their kitchenette. Suites, with a foldout couch, are available for reduced weekly rentals. Rooms that face the elevated subway line are noisy, but the staff try to accommodate noise level preferences. From April to mid-November, singles and doubles cost $116 to $146; subtract $25 off-season; add $7 per additional person; continental breakfast included. Children under 12 stay free in their parent's room.

Top End

The 15-story *Holiday Inn Express – Government Center* (☎ 617-742-7630, *800-465-4329, fax 742-7804, 5 Blossom St*) has well-kept rooms with two double beds or one king for $209. Kids younger than 12 stay free with parent. Other perks: a $6.95 all-you-can-eat breakfast buffet, an adjacent supermarket and a small pool with lifeguard.

DOWNTOWN & FINANCIAL DISTRICT (MAP 4)

The seven-story top end *Harborside Inn* (☎ 617-723-7500, *888-723-7565, fax 670-2010, 185 State St, www.hagopianhotels.com*), a respectfully renovated 19th-century warehouse, has B&B-style rooms with hotel-style service. The 54 rooms have original exposed brick and granite walls, hardwood floors, area carpets and Victorian furnishings. They also have modern baths, cable TV and free local calls. Windows are well insulated from street noise. Doubles cost $170 to $210; suites sleep up to five people for $300.

The looming and luxurious Harborside Inn

The lovely 1856 *Omni Parker House* (☎ 617-227-8600, *800-843-6664, fax 227-9607, 60 School St, www.omnihotels.com*), the country's oldest continually operating hotel, recently underwent a successful face-lift. While it sits smack dab in the middle of town, you may find yourself lazily luxuriating in their deep tubs. The 552 rooms are charming but modern, too. Rack rates are $199 to $309, $169 to $259 off-season, but always ask for special promotions.

Converted into a fine hostelry in 1999, the *Wyndham Hotel* (☎ 617-556-0006, *fax 556-0053, 89 Broad St, www.wyndham.com*) hosts business travelers who pay $315 double during the week. But on weekends travelers have the place to themselves and pay 'only' $189 for state-of-the-art guest rooms and requisite top-notch amenities.

Marriott's **Custom House** (☎ 617-310-6300, 800-845-5279, 3 McKinley Square), considered a blasphemous time-share takeover by some, offers perhaps the most stunning views in Boston. The 25-story tower, one of the city's most prominent landmarks, has 80 one-bedroom suites with all the amenities and facilities you'd expect for about $300 nightly.

NORTH END & CHARLESTOWN (MAP 5)
Budget
The **Constitution Inn YMCA** (☎ 617-241-8400, 800-495-9622, fax 241-2856, 150 Second Ave), Charlestown Navy Yard, a short, scenic boat ride from downtown Boston, is an excellent choice. Although it accommodates active and retired military personnel, the Y accepts civilian guests, too. You won't see more crew cuts here than on the streets, nor will strident antiwar types be put off sleeping here. What you'll find is a good fitness center, pool, and twin bedded rooms for $69 double. For $10 more per night, you can get a room with a refrigerator.

Mid-Range
Golden Slipper (☎ 781-545-2845), Lewis Wharf, a 40-foot docked wooden boat, offers an unusual and romantic set-up. While it's sweet and cozy, with a cabin separate from the sleeping quarters, this is no yacht. The shower is funky but fully functional. As long as it's a calm night, you might enjoy cooking in the galley kitchen, too. It costs $150 for two, $220 for four, including an expanded continental breakfast delivered in a basket.

WATERFRONT & SEAPORT DISTRICT (MAP 6)
The **Boston Harbor Islands State Park** (☎ 617-223-8666) is managed by both the Dept of Environmental Management (DEM; ☎ 781-740-1605 ext 205 for information, ☎ 877-422-6762 for reservations) and the Metropolitan District Commission (MDC; ☎ 617-727-7676), 98 Taylor St,

KIM GRANT
Bring your rubber duckie to Omni Parker House.

Dorchester, MA 02122. It consists of almost 30 islands and there is camping on four: Peddock's, Lovell's, Grape and Bumpkin. Each island has about 10 to 12 individual sites and one group site that holds 50 people. Camping is allowed on Saturday from early May to mid-October and nightly from early June to early September. For more on each island, see 'Boston Harbor Islands State Park' in Things to See & Do.

Here are the important do's and don'ts: Do bring your own water and supplies; do carry in and carry out everything; do hang your food high, out of reach of animals; don't bring pets or alcohol; don't make open fires; don't expect anything more than primitive sites and composting toilets.

The MDC manages Peddock's and Lovell's Islands; call for reservations and then fax or write for free camping permits in advance. (At press time, there were docking problems at Peddock's that precluded camping.) The DEM manages the wooded Grape and Bumpkin Islands; phone for a free camping reservation.

Regular ferry service is provided by Boston Harbor Cruises (☎ 617-227-4320), 1 Long Wharf off Atlantic Ave, from early

B&Bs & Agencies

Boston B&Bs haven't exactly sprouted like weeds in city sidewalks, but visitors will find a range from budget to fancy. With the exceptions noted in the text, your best bet is to contact one of many agencies that will try to match your neighborhood desires with the thickness of your wallet. One benefit of B&Bs is that there's no room tax.

The **Bed & Breakfast Agency of Boston** (☎ 617-720-3540, 800-248-9262, 0800-895128 from the UK, fax 523-5761, bosbnb@aol.com), 47 Commercial Wharf, lists about 150 B&Bs and apartments, most of which are located downtown. Some are in historic Victorian-furnished brownstones, some are waterfront lofts; one is even in a docked wooden boat. But you must call or email them; if you show up at their door, they'll make you use the pay phone outside. Expect to pay from $70 to $100 nightly for a double with shared bath, $100 to $160 with private bath. From mid-November to mid-February, stay two nights and get the third night free, based on availability.

Bed & Breakfast Cambridge & Greater Boston (☎ 617-720-1492, 800-888-0178, fax 227-0021) has about 40 listings, mostly in Cambridge, that rent for $90 to $95 double with a shared bath, $110 to $150 private.

Bed & Breakfast Associates Bay Colony (☎ 781-449-5302, 800-347-5088, fax 449-5958, www.bnbboston.com) has over 150 listings in the Boston area, eastern Massachusetts and Cape Cod.

May to mid-October. Purchase a roundtrip ticket ($8 adults, $7 senior, $6 children) to Georges Island where you then catch a free water taxi to the smaller islands (another 15 to 60 minutes, depending on where you're going). Because of the ferry schedule, it's not practical to commute into the city for sightseeing each day: It's best to go out for a few days, island hop and come back to stay somewhere else in Boston.

THEATER DISTRICT & CHINATOWN (MAP 7)

Built in 1918, the five-story **Milner Hotel** (☎ 617-426-6220, 800-453-1731, fax 350-0360, 78 Charles St S, www.milner-hotel.com), with a tidy, tiny, tacky lobby, has a few things going for it: friendly staff, great location and even better prices. The rooms are small and drab, but you can get a quiet night's sleep for $105 to $163 double; rates drop $15 to $30 off-season. Somehow, it manages to be a charmer.

Both business travelers and tourists appreciate the **Radisson Hotel** (☎ 617-482-1800, 800-333-3333, fax 451-2750, 200 Stuart St, www.radisson.com) and its central location. This 24-story hotel has 356 rooms that rent for $199 to $300 double ($129 December to mid-March). Added bonuses include many rooms with private balconies, a fitness center and an indoor swimming pool.

BACK BAY (MAP 8)
Budget
The **463 Beacon St Guest House** (☎ 617-536-1302, fax 247-8876, 463 Beacon St), a well-situated six-story circa 1880 brownstone, has 20 guest rooms, most of which have a private bath and kitchenette. Rooms vary considerably in size; all have cable TV and phone and range from $79 to $109 double.

Mid-Range
At the **Beacon Inns & Guest Houses** (☎ 617-266-7142, fax 266-7276, 248 Newbury St), the rooms aren't anything to write home about, but the location sure is. The 20 studios cost $85 single, $99 double year-round ($490 weekly single, $575 double). Rooms have phones with free local calls, and air con.

Commonwealth Court Guest House (☎ 617-424-1230, 888-424-1230, fax 424-1510, 284 Comm Ave, www.commonwealthcourt.com) has 20 rooms with kitchenettes, cable TV and free local phone calls. Rooms aren't spiffy, but the location is great and the price is pretty darn good: $99 to $130 single or double, $75 to $105 off-season. Weekly rates are $625 double.

The **College Club** (☎ 617-536-9510, fax 247-8537, 44 Comm Ave, cclub@javanet .com), originally a private club for women college graduates in the 1940s, has 11 enormous rooms, open to both sexes, renting for $75 single with shared bath, or $120 double with private bath, and include a generous continental breakfast. Some furnishings are a bit shabby (in a worn-out Ivy League sort of way) and the bathrooms are a bit scruffy, but all-in-all it's a great value.

The **Newbury Guest House** (☎ 617-437-7666, 800-437-7668, fax 262-4243, 261 Newbury St, www.hagopianhotels.com) has 32 rooms with private bath in a four-story, circa 1882 renovated brownstone. Expect to pay $125 to $155 double ($15 less for a single), including a continental breakfast buffet. There is limited parking for $15, but you must reserve it in advance.

Top End

The **Lenox Hotel** (☎ 617-536-5300, 800-225-7676, fax 236-0351, 710 Boylston St, www.lenoxhotel.com) is another early-20th-century hotel that's undergone recent renovations. A fancy old-worldish lobby gives way to soundproof guest rooms with classical furnishings, high ceilings, big closets and

sitting areas. The 213 rooms start at $308, $189 off-season.

SOUTH END (MAP 9)
Budget

The **Berkeley Residence YWCA** (☎ 617-482-8850, fax 482-9692, 40 Berkeley St) rents over 200 small rooms to women on a nightly, weekly and long-term basis. Singles ($51), doubles ($78) and triples ($90) include breakfast. Maximum stay is 13 nights. For those on travel-study programs who want to stay three to four weeks, the weekly rate is $225 single, $300 double, $342 triple, including breakfast and dinner. Guests can use the library, TV room, laundry room and garden.

Mid-Range

A brick townhouse in a quiet residential neighborhood, the **Copley Inn** (☎ 617-236-0300, 800-232-0306, fax 536-0816, 19 Garrison St, info@copleyinn.com) offers 21 comfortable and modern guest studios for $85 to $125 nightly. Children under 12 stay free with parent.

Copley House (☎ 617-236-8300, 800-331-1318, fax 424-1815, 239 W Newton St, www.copleyhouse.com) has accommodations in seven area buildings, but everyone

A sitting room at the College Club

KIM GRANT

PLACES TO STAY

checks in at West Newton St. The studio and one-bedroom apartments are worn but serviceable with fully equipped mini-kitchens, cable TV and free local calls. It's popular with folks looking for an apartment, theater and businesspeople and tourists. Rates are $95 to $175 daily, $575 to $875 weekly.

On a quiet side street, the ***Chandler Inn*** (☎ 617-482-3450, 800-842-3450, fax 542-3428, 26 Chandler St, www.chandlerinn.com), popular with Europeans and gays, has 56 clean, albeit undistinguished rooms for $99 to $109 single, $10 more for double, about $10 less in the winter.

The brick townhouse ***Clarendon Square Inn*** (☎ 617-536-2229, 198 W Brookline St, www.clarendonsquare.com) has only three rooms (with private bath) but they're oh-so-urbane and stylish. Staying at the B&B, complete with lofty living room and roof-deck hot tub, will give you a great sense of gay, chichi South End living. Doubles are $119 to $229, depending on the season.

Top End

The two-story, 159-room ***Midtown Hotel*** (☎ 617-262-1000, 800-343-1177, fax 262-8739, 220 Huntington Ave, www.midtownhotel .com) straddles Back Bay and the South End, just two blocks from the 4½-mile Southwest Corridor Park (great for walking). Parking and use of the enclosed outdoor pool are included for $209 to $229 mid-April to mid-November, $119 to $189 off-season. Children under 18 stay free with parent.

KENMORE SQUARE & FENWAY (MAP 10)
Budget

A fantastic choice, the ***Boston International Hostel*** (☎ 617-536-9455, fax 424-6558, 12 Hemenway St, Boston, MA 02115, www .bostonhostel.com, bostonhostel@juno.com) is recently renovated and conveniently located. In addition to offering discount tickets to all kinds of activities and selling MBTA passes, the hostel offers walking tours, slide shows, free or cheap lectures, transportation to clubs and low-cost, high-speed Internet connections on its two computers. Best of all, though, the staff is as good as any concierge in a fancy hotel.

Most dorm-style bunk rooms hold six people (same sex), plus there are some doubles that can be coed. Beds cost $20 members, $23 nonmembers, nightly, with a 14-night maximum during any six-month period. US citizens can become a member for $25 on the spot ($18 for international visitors). Try to reserve at least three months ahead of time; you can make reservations with a credit card by phone, fax or email. If the hostel is full, they'll guide you elsewhere. About 10 beds are set aside for 7:30 am walk-ins; be there early. There is no lock-out period.

The ***YMCA of Greater Boston*** (☎ 617-536-7800, fax 267-4653, 316 Huntington Ave, Boston, MA 02115, www.ymcaboston.org) rents 39 rooms to men, women and families with children 16 and older from June through August. From September through May, the Y accepts men only. Shared-bath singles cost $41 ($35 with an international hosteling card), doubles $61 ($50 with card), $80 triple and $95 quad; breakfast and use of the excellent gym and pool are included. Reserve by mail two weeks prior to your visit; very few rooms are available for walk-ins. If you're going to try to get lucky, show up at 11 am.

When ***Anthony's Town House*** (☎ 617-566-3972, 1085 Beacon St) opened in 1944, nightly rates were just $6. Today, friendly management, a late noontime check-out and rates of $70 to $90 double continue to attract professors, foreigners, and students and their parents. The Victorian-era brownstone, more reminiscent of a boarding house than a boudoir from a Henry James novel, has 10 rooms with shared bath.

Mid-Range

Built in 1903, the ***Buckminster*** (☎ 617-236-7050, 800-727-2825, fax 262-0068, 645 Beacon St) has rooms from small singles to suites that can accommodate larger families or groups. As close to a pension as it gets in Boston, each floor has its own laundry and kitchen facilities, fine if you're traveling with your own pots, pans and utensils. Rooms have air con, TV and phone. Rates are $99 single, $129 double ($59 and $69 respectively, off-season).

The **Howard Johnson Fenway** (☎ 617-267-8300, 800-654-2000, fax 267-2763, 1271 Boylston St, www.hojo.com), only about 10 minutes from downtown on the T, has 94 standard rooms for about $180 (single or double), $115 to $140 off-season, including parking.

Top End
On a quiet side street, this elegant five-story brownstone, the **Gryphon House** (☎ 617-375-9003, fax 425-0716, 9 Bay State Rd, www.innboston.com), was converted into an eight-suite B&B in 1998. Along with gas fireplaces, TV and VCR, CD player and two phone lines, the rooms have retained late-19th-century period details – and there's onsite parking (free!). Each room has a different theme. It's one of the nicest places to stay in the city. Period. Rates are $179 to $234, including continental breakfast.

Kickin' back at the Gryphon House

CAMBRIDGE
Harvard Square Area (Map 11)
Staffed 24 hours a day and with a whopping 44 rooms, the **Irving House** (☎ 617-547-4600, 877-547-4600, fax 576-2814, 24 Irving St, www.irvinghouse.com) is a good value made better by its prime location. With luck and timing, you might get one of the limited free parking spaces and use of a museum pass, too. Rates, including continental breakfast

in a cozy basement room, are $149 single with private bath ($89 with shared), $164 double ($119 with shared bath), $179 triple. Children up to age 6 are free.

A Friendly Inn (☎ 617-547-7851, 1673 Cambridge St) leaves itself open to constant evaluation because of its name. ('Friendliness reviews' vary depending on who's working.) With rates of $97 single and $117 double and just a 10-minute walk to Harvard Square, no one seems to mind the curt reception. All rooms come with private bath, air con, TV, phone and continental breakfast; there's also free parking, if you're silly enough to have a car anywhere near Harvard Square.

East Cambridge (Map 12)
The 112 rooms at **Holiday Inn Express Hotel & Suites at Cambridge** (☎ 617-441-9200, 888-887-7690, fax 354-1313, 250 McGrath-O'Brien Hwy) are fully modernized and well maintained. Free local calls and a breakfast buffet are included in the rate of about $199; $139 to $159 December through March. It's a two-minute walk from Lechmere Green Line or a short, direct bus trip from Harvard Square.

Inman Square (Map 12)
A homey B&B with two guest rooms (one of which can sleep three people), **Windsor House Bed & Breakfast** (☎ 617-354-7916, 283 Windsor St) is a 10- to 15-minute walk to the T. You can borrow a coveted Cambridge on-street parking permit. Owner Heidi Lyons, who has a room on the 2nd floor, sets out a particularly generous buffet-style breakfast. Rates are $70 to $90 double April through November, less off-season.

Central Square (Map 12)
Owned by the same folks who run the Irving House (see above), the **Harding House** (☎ 617-876-2888, 877-489-2888, fax 497-0953, 288 Harvard St, www.irvinghouse.com), between Harvard and Central Squares, is a graceful 1860s Victorian B&B with 14 nicely appointed guest rooms. A couple of rooms can accommodate families; children up to age 6 are free. Hardwood floors, stained-glass

KIM GRANT

windows and oriental carpets add to the period ambiance. Continental breakfast in a sunny dining room is included; $89 to $99 single with shared bath, $165 to $210 double with private bath ($115 to $149 off-season). Limited, free off-street parking and museum passes are included.

A fusion of art, design and science, and new in 1998, *University Park Hotel at MIT* (☎ 617-577-0200, 800-222-8733, fax 494-8366, 20 Sydney St, welcome@univparkhotel.com) is the area's hippest place to stay. An atom rotates within a sculpted carpet on the elevator; computer boards are built into wood armoires; wash basins rise above marble sink tops in the bathroom. The 201 rooms and suites are awash in wood, chrome and ergonomically designed furniture. Rates are $179 to $229 for double rooms (slightly less on weekends), more for suites.

North Cambridge (Map 13)

The *Susse Chalet Cambridge* (☎ 617-661-7800, 800-524-2538, fax 868-8153, 211 Concord Turnpike/MA 2 east, www.sussechalet.com), with 78 rooms, is a five-minute walk from the Alewife T station on the Red Line. From there, it's five more minutes to Harvard Square or 30 to Boston Common. The bi-level motel, sandwiched between a bowling alley and abandoned club, is rather dismal but its rates are tempting. Ask for a room as far from the highway as possible. Parking is free; rooms are $93 to $109 March to mid-November (about $20 less off-season).

An easy 10-minute walk to the Alewife Red Line T station, the *Best Western Homestead Inn* (☎ 617-491-8000, 800-528-1234, fax 491-4932, 220 Alewife Brook Parkway, www.bestwestern.com) has 69 rooms on three floors. Friendly management, a small indoor pool and continental breakfast are included: $169 to $209 April through November ($119 to $149 off-season). Always ask about specials. A health food supermarket and movie theater are right next-door.

Mass Ave to Porter Square (Map 13)

The *Mary Prentiss Inn* (☎ 617-661-2929, fax 661-5989, 6 Prentiss St, njfandetti@aol.com),

on a quiet residential street, has 20 upscale rooms and suites within a completely renovated neoclassical Greek revival gem. The outdoor deck is particularly nice in warm weather. Rates, including full breakfast, are $149 to $229, $129 to $169 January through March.

COOLIDGE CORNER & BROOKLINE VILLAGE (MAP 14)

Brookline Manor Guest House (☎ 617-232-0003, 800-535-5325, fax 734-5815, 32 Centre St, Brookline, MA 02146) has 35 mid-range rooms with private bath and continental breakfast for $109 to $119; parking is $5 nightly.

The *Bertram Inn* (☎ 617-566-2234, 800-295-3822, fax 277-1887, 92 Sewall Ave, Brookline, MA 02146, www.bertraminn .com), an honest-to-goodness B&B that sets out homebaked cookies in the afternoon, has 14 upscale Victorian-style rooms with period antiques and private bath. Rates are complicated but boil down to about $129 to $219 in summer and fall, $99 to $144 in winter.

OUTLYING NEIGHBORHOODS
Budget

Wompatuck State Park (☎ 781-749-7160, 877-422-6762 for reservations, Union St, Hingham, MA 02043) has 275 to 400 relatively undeveloped campsites (depending on the season) on 3500 acres; it's about 30 minutes south of Boston by car, as long as it's not rush hour. There are excellent paved paths and mountain bike trails. Open early April to mid-October, sites cost $6 to $8 for two people. Take I-93 south from Boston to MA 3 south to MA 228 (exit 14). Head 7 miles north on Free St to Union St.

Normandy Farms Campground (☎ 508-543-7600, 72 West St, Foxboro, MA 02035), resembling a self-contained town more than a traditional campground, caters more to RVs than tents. It's open year-round, with a big recreation room and four pools (one indoor), and 400 open and wooded sites on more than 50 acres. A state park, great for walking, is just down the road. The campground is about 50 minutes from Boston by car; take I-93 south to I-95 south to MA 1 south for 7 miles; head east on Thurston St to West St. Rates for two in a tent are $26 to $40 nightly.

Although this ***Motel 6*** *(☎ 781-848-7890, 800-466-8356, fax 843-1929, 125 Union St, Braintree, MA 02184)* is 15 miles south of the city, you can be whisked hassle-free into Boston in 30 minutes via the T, which stops 50 feet away. Singles rent for $76, doubles $82, triples $85, quads $88; rates are about $10 less off-season. Take the T Red Line to Braintree.

The ***Newton Susse Chalet*** *(☎ 617-527-9000, 800-524-2538, fax 527-4994, 160 Boylston St/MA 9, Newton, MA 02467)*, across the street from the upscale Chestnut Hill Mall, is about 8 miles (30 minutes) west of downtown Boston on public transportation. Its 144 simple rooms rent for $90 to $117 double, $59 to $77 off-season, including free parking and cable movies. There's an outdoor pool. Ride the T Green Line, 'D' branch to Chestnut Hill, and then it's a 15-minute walk.

Mid-Range

The ***Susse Chalet Hotel*** *(☎ 617-287-9100, 800-886-0056, fax 265-9287, 800 Morrissey Blvd, Dorchester, MA 02122, www.boston-hotel.com)* and the ***Susse Chalet Inn*** *(☎ 617-287-9200, fax 282-2365, 900 Morrissey Blvd)* are both right off the I-93 Expressway, 5 miles south of the city. Between the two there are 307 standard rooms that rent for about $96 to $150 double, depending on the season. The hotel boasts a pool and an adjacent family bowling center, but the inn rooms are newer and it's closer to a grocery store. Every 30 minutes on the quarter hour a van shuttles guests from the JFK Red Line T station to the hotels.

Two miles west of Kenmore Square, the ***Best Western Terrace Inn*** *(☎ 617-566-6260, 800-528-1234, fax 731-3543, 1650 Comm Ave, Brighton, MA 02135, www.bestwestern.com)* is 20 minutes from Boston Common via public transportation. Some of the 72 rooms have kitchenettes; all have TV, refrigerator and air con. Rates are $99 to $119 single or double, including parking. Triples and quads are just $20 to $30 more. Hop on the T Green Line, 'B' branch to Mt Hood.

The ***Holiday Inn Express*** *(☎ 617-288-3030, 800-465-4329, fax 265-6543, www.hiexpress.com/bos-express)*, exit 16 off I-93 in Dorchester, is about 3 miles south of Boston. Parking is free and the Red Line is eight blocks away on a well-lit street. A 24-hour grocery store is around the corner. The 118 standard motel-style rooms with air con are $159 double April through December ($189 during foliage season), $129 the rest of the year. Take the T Red Line to Andrew.

Places to Eat

Boston has finally outgrown its reputation for stodgy, bland, overcooked food. These days, you'll have to look hard to find old standards like 'New England boiled dinner' (corned beef, potatoes and cabbage, boiled together in a pot until all three ingredients achieve the same gray color, no flavor and mushy consistency), 'seafood Newburg' (chunks of fish, scallops and shrimp in an overwhelmingly heavy cream sauce served on a pastry shell) and 'Boston baked beans' (navy beans and salt pork in molasses). Prepared by the right chef on a cold winter day, some of these dishes might be categorized as trendy 'comfort food,' but they no longer define dining in Boston, thank goodness.

Eating cheaply doesn't have to mean eating badly. Moreover, if you want to splurge, you'll find some of the country's most highly regarded restaurants. For well-heeled Bostonians, dinner is not a prelude to an evening on the town; it's the evening's entertainment. Considering the cost of a concert or theater ticket, three hours with one of Boston's celebrity chefs is a bargain.

Budget eateries are under $10 and mid-range ones are $10 to $20 per person. Top end restaurants will set you back at least $20 per person, but they're all worth a splurge; reservations are recommended.

BEACON HILL (MAP 2)
Budget
Panificio (☎ 617-227-4340, 144 Charles St) is a cozy café and bistro that serves all three meals (except it's closed Sunday dinner and all day Monday). It's particularly known for weekday breakfast and weekend brunch. Arrive early for frittatas and French toast if you intend to linger over coffee and a news-

Seafood

Seafood is king in Boston. You'll find, however, that less and less of it is from local waters. Due to stringent catch limits imposed after years of overfishing, your main dish may have logged more air miles than you have. Never fear; these days fish doesn't have to be local to be fresh.

For many, a visit to Boston is not complete without a lobster dinner. The price depends on the weight of the lobster, and the traditional preparation doesn't call for a master chef. The homely crustaceans are plucked live, yes live, from the restaurant's tank, plopped into a pot of boiling water and presented to diners with a stack of napkins, a crock of melted butter for dipping, a bib and implements to crack open the shell and claws so you can pull and pick out the succulent, chewy flesh. Elegant, it's not. Many restaurants serve baked stuffed lobster, where the meat is removed and mixed with other ingredients and the shell refilled. Most Bostonians look upon this as a tourist dish for the uninitiated.

If wrestling with your meal is not your idea of fine dining, know that any traditional seafood restaurant worth its sea salt also offers crispy fried clams, tender broiled scallops, salty-sweet Wellfleet oysters and the ever-dependable cod and scrod. (In colonial times, trade in codfish was so important that a stuffed codfish was placed in the chambers of the State House. It's still there.) No, 'scrod' is not an exotic cousin of cod; it's the generic name for local white-flesh fish (including cod) weighing under $2^{1}/_{2}$lb. Hence, your fish and chips is actually scrod and chips. Boston's Asian restaurants do marvelous things with the same catch.

The most popular soft-shell clams are 'steamers.' Steaming the clams opens the shells. Extract the meat, shuck off the wrinkled membrane from the black neck, wash off any sand by dipping the

paper. Pastas are de rigueur for dinner, lunches focus on soups and fancy sandwiches.

The ***King & I*** (☎ *617-227-3320, 145 Charles St*), with good service and ample portions, serves seafood dishes and tasty pad Thai ($7 to $10). Vegetables and tofu can be substituted for meat. Lunch specials are a value at $6. Open for lunch and dinner daily; only dinner on Sunday.

The Paramount (☎ *617-720-1152, 44 Charles St*) has seen trends come and go. Not what you'd expect on tony Charles St, it's a real neighborhood hangout, the choice of locals who don't want to cook but don't feel like dressing up. Breakfast and lunch are cafeteria-style with basic diner fare: pancakes, steak and eggs, meatloaf, lasagna. The place goes upscale at dinner without losing its down-home charm. It has the tastiest chicken piccata in town.

Istanbul Café (☎ *617-227-3434, 37 Bowdoin St*), a cozy basement dining room, offers the tastiest Turkish food this side of Izmir. (It even impressed the author of

Lonely Planet's *Turkey* guide!) Baskets of warm, crusty, Turkish-style pita bread are reason enough to dine here. So are the prices. Roasted meat sandwiches are huge, but start out with the killer appetizer sampler. Open for lunch and dinner.

Café Podima (☎ *617-227-4959, 168 Cambridge St*) is a sweet little sandwich and salad place with about 40 sandwiches and roll-ups, the most expensive being prosciutto, tomato, fresh mozzarella, roasted veggies and basil for $6.50. It's a meal. Podima is the perfect place to take a break without breaking the bank. Open until 11 pm.

Phoenicia (☎ *617-523-4606, 240 Cambridge St*), open from 11 am to 10 pm, serves generous portions of delicious, inexpensive Lebanese food in casual surroundings.

An institution, ***Buzzy's Fabulous Roast Beef*** (☎ *617-242-7722, 327 Cambridge St*) dispenses huge, juicy roast beef sandwiches and hand-cut french fries from a take-out trailer at a traffic circle (rotary) near the Charles St T station. It's open 24/7, a rarity

PLACES TO EAT

Seafood

clam in the thick 'broth' provided (not for drinking), dip in melted butter and enjoy. The most common hard-shell clams are littlenecks and cherrystones. They're best eaten raw on the half shell with a few drops of lemon juice, tomato sauce or horseradish, but they may be steamed or stuffed and baked, too. Quahogs (pronounced 'KO-hogs') are sea clams larger than your fist. They're usually cut into strips and deep-fried or used for chowder.

Ah, yes, and then there's chowder, or as locals say, 'chow-dah.' Each summer, as part of the celebrations leading up to the Fourth of July, Boston seafood restaurants vie for the title of Best Chowder at the annual Chowderfest held on City Hall Plaza. For a few dollars admission, you can sample and judge for yourself. The variations are endless, given the basic recipe: clams, clam juice, chunks of potato, milk, cream, flour, butter, onion, celery, salt and pepper.

LEE FOSTER

Ye olde oysters

Serving up roast beef 24 hours a day

for Boston. There's one in Central Square, too (☎ 617-864-2333, 647 Mass Ave).

Mid-Range

The scene of many politico power lunches, **Black Goose** (☎ 617-720-4500, 21 Beacon St) serves generous portions of delicious pasta and salads in a pretty dining room. The baked farfalle, bow-tie pasta with a creamy tomato and gorgonzola sauce, is the perfect antidote on a cold winter day. There's outdoor seating when the weather is fine. Open for lunch and dinner weekdays, dinner Saturday.

Figs (☎ 617-742-3447, 42 Charles St) excels in creative pizzas (with whisper-thin crusts) topped with goat cheese, prosciutto, portabello mushrooms and the like ($11 to $17). Although it's pricey, it will feel more like a night out than most pizza joints. Open weekdays for dinner, noon to 9 or 10 pm on weekends.

Top End

At **Lala Rokh** (☎ 617-720-5511, 97 Mt Vernon St), the sister and brother team of Azita and Babak Bina have won numerous honors for their Persian delicacies. Ask the

helpful waitstaff if you want the menu translated; many ingredients will sound familiar to Middle Eastern cuisine fans. The differences, though subtle – an aromatic spice here or savory herb there – set their cooking apart. Try *morgh*, saffron-seared chicken in a light tomato broth accompanied by basmati rice with cumin, cinnamon, rose petals and barberries ($14). The baklava, fragrant with rose water, is heavenly. Since prices are reasonable, you can order a multicourse feast for the price of one entree at other high-end restaurants. Open for dinner nightly.

GOVERNMENT CENTER & FANEUIL HALL (MAP 3)
Budget

Faneuil Hall Marketplace (☎ 617-338-2323) offers an enormous variety of mediocre take-out eateries under one roof. Within the 20 restaurants and 40 food stalls, you'll find chowder, bagels, Indian, Greek, baked goods and ice cream. The center rotunda has tables for rainy days; there are also benches outside. Open 10 am to 9 pm daily, except noon to 6 pm on Sunday. Breakfast stalls open earlier.

Bertucci's (☎ 617-227-7889, 22 Merchants Row), a popular place for a sit-down meal of brick-oven pizza ($9.25 for a large cheese, $13 for a large 'specialty') also has salads, pasta dishes and calzones. Try not to fill up on their piping hot rolls. Open 11 am to 11 pm, until midnight on weekends.

Mid-Range

Ye Olde Union Oyster House (☎ 617-227-2750, 41 Union St), circa 1826, lives up to its venerable status as Boston's most historic raw bar – you can't go wrong with the oysters and a beer. Although the intervening years have been kind to its charm and atmosphere, the menu offerings could use an update. Open for lunch and dinner.

Marshall House (☎ 617-523-9396, 15 Union St) provides a lively, less touristed but no less atmospheric alternative to its olde neighbor. It's open 11:30 am to 11 pm, bar until 2 am.

Salty Dog (☎ 617-742-2094, Quincy Market, Faneuil Hall Marketplace) serves a-cut-above seafood and pub grub. The patio is *the* place to be April through October. Say hi to Mike Kelly, the marketplace's best bartender. Open 11 am to 11 pm. The bar stays open until 2 am as long as things don't get too rowdy.

Durgin Park (☎ 617-227-2038, *North Market, Faneuil Hall Marketplace)* is known for no-nonsense service, sawdust underfoot on the old floorboards and family-style dining at large tables. The bill of fare hasn't changed much since the restaurant was built in 1827: huge slabs of prime rib, fish chowder, chicken potpie, Boston baked beans, and strawberry shortcake and Indian pudding for dessert. Open 11:30 am to 10 pm, until 9 pm Sunday.

DOWNTOWN & FINANCIAL DISTRICT (MAP 4)
Budget
If it's raining, the *Corner Mall Food Court (no phone)*, at Washington and Summer Sts, is convenient for fast-food take-out and crowded, noisy communal seating. Otherwise, look for tastier options at *Downtown Crossing* outdoor lunch carts, especially Herrera's Burrito cart. The pedestrian mall is on Summer St between Washington and Chauncy Sts.

Sasha (☎ 617-482-8822, *55 Bromfield St)*, a small chef-owned eatery with delicious cooked-to-order meals at cafeteria prices, does a brisk take-out business, but you can usually find a table within the unassuming dining room. The shrimp scampi, served over linguini with sautéed vegetables, is a winner. Open for all three meals.

Sam LaGrassa's (☎ 617-357-6861, *44 Province St)* boasts the 'World's No 1 Sandwiches,' and many agree. They're also among the biggest. It's good entertainment to watch businessmen keep overstuffed pastrami sandwiches from spilling onto their starched white shirts. Open for lunch daily except Sunday.

One of the few area joints open on weekends, *Mr Dooley's Boston Tavern* (☎ 617-338-5656, *77 Broad St)*, an Irish-style pub, offers 'real' Irish breakfasts. Look for imported sausage, bacon, black-and-white

pudding, eggs, home fries, homemade brown soda bread, fish and chips and similar grub. Live Irish music rounds out the weekend scene.

Country Life (☎ 617-951-2534, *200 High St)* is worth seeking out for its all-you-can-eat lunch buffet ($7), served 11:30 am to 3 pm weekdays. You'll find lasagna, potpies and soups, but no meat, dairy or refined grains. The decor is pleasant enough and the self-service keeps the prices reasonable. It serves dinner nightly except Monday, and brunch on Sunday.

Sultan's Kitchen (☎ 617-338-7819, *72 Broad St)* is a real find. Line up with the crowds at the fast-moving self-service counter, and take your paper plate upstairs to dine. You'll be rewarded with sizable portions of complex and delicately flavored Turkish dishes. If you can't decide, get the sampler plate ($7.50). Save room for what is perhaps the best rice pudding in the world ($2.50). Too bad it's open only for lunch weekdays (11 am to 5 pm) and Saturday (until 3 pm).

KIM GRANT

Milk St Café

Milk St Café (☎ 617-542-3663, *50 Milk St)* offers large servings of above-average kosher lunch fare ($6 to $8) such as pasta, salads, soups, sandwiches and pastries. Open 7 am to 3 pm weekdays. Its other Post Office Square location (☎ 617-350-7275) is pleasant in summer, when café tables are set out and diners spill into the little park; it's open 7 am to 5 pm weekdays.

Blossoms (☎ 617-423-1911, 99 High St) is a catering operation that doubles as a self-service lunch spot 7 am to 3 pm, Monday through Friday. The creative salads, soups, wraps, and hot and cold sandwiches ($4.50 to $6.50) are a cut above other area options. Blossoms does mostly take-out business, so there are usually plenty of tables.

At *Cosi Sandwich Shop* (☎ 617-292-2674, 133 Federal St), select from 20 fillings such as cranberry roasted turkey, tandoori grilled chicken and roasted red pepper with eggplant feta spread. The hearth-baked flat bread is particularly crusty. 'Cosi One' (one filling) goes for $5.75, 'Cosi Two' for $6.50 and so on; there are always specials with two fillings for the price of one. Open 6 am to 7 pm weekdays. There is another location at 14 Milk St.

At *Jera's Juice Bar* (☎ 617-439-9799, 75–101 Federal St), those without time for a salad can drink the equivalent: The 'Big Dig' contains your daily recommended veggie allotment. It's said that the mango-passion fruit blend is an excellent antidote for a hangover.

Goemon (☎ 617-367-8670, 189 State St) specializes in Japanese snacks (sushi, tempura, dumplings) and noodle soups (soba, udon or ramen). The basement locale, open daily except Sunday for lunch and dinner, has an elegant and soothing ambiance far beyond most restaurants in this price range.

Arrive for an early or late lunch at *Chacarero Chilean Cuisine* (☎ 617-542-0392, 426 Washington St), at the corner of Franklin St, or be prepared to queue up with masses of humanity. They come for hefty take-out grilled chicken, beef or vegetarian sandwiches with guacamole and green beans, in fresh crusty rolls and wrapped in foil, for $4 to $6. Head to a nearby sidewalk bench or to Boston Common with your take-out food.

At lunchtime, *Galleria Italiana* (☎ 617-423-2092, 177 Tremont St) is a self-service Italian pasta and sandwich cafeteria. There are usually five pasta options and three or four meat and vegetarian entrees, which include your choice of soup or salad, for about $5.50 to $8.50. Their bread pudding is

fabulous. For dinner Tuesday through Saturday, the space is transformed into a highly respected trattoria with linens, table service, wine and refined entrees.

Mid-Range

Tatsukichi (☎ 617-720-2468, 189 State St) serves fine traditional Japanese cuisine, especially sushi, in understated elegant surroundings. It's a nice place to take a break from the bustle of Faneuil Hall Marketplace. Open for dinner nightly.

Ben's Café (☎ 617-227-3370, 45 School St), in the Old City Hall within Maison Robert, is one of Boston's best culinary deals. There are two prix fixe menus ($18 and $25) featuring smaller portions of Maison Robert's traditional French fare. Whether on the terrace or in the cozy romantic dining room, you won't remember that you are in the 'bargain basement' of one of Boston's best restaurants. Open for lunch weekdays, dinner nightly.

Top End

Radius (☎ 617-426-1234, 8 High St) answers the burning question, 'How can a restaurant be so hot and so cool at the same time?' Opened in late 1998, it remains the most talked about restaurant in town. Chef/owner Michael Schlow has created a fashionable food-lover's paradise. Although pricey at $85 per person, the six-course tasting brilliantly showcases the kitchen's magnificent range and execution. Exceptional wine pairing elevates the food and drink to even loftier heights (difficult to imagine). You don't have to bust your budget, though: Order roasted organic chicken for $24 or order from the lighter bar menu. Arrive after 7:30 pm to avoid the power suit crowd, and don't miss the elegant restrooms. Open nightly except Sunday.

NORTH END (MAP 5)
Budget

Legendary *Regina Pizzeria* (☎ 617-227-0765, 11½ Thatcher St), with crispy, thin-crust pizza – $12.50 for a large with two toppings – is best consumed with a pitcher of beer (about $9). Part of the fun of this no-

Dessert

The Chocolate Bar at **Café Fleuri** (Map 4; ☎ 617-451-1900, 250 Franklin St), in Le Meridien Boston, is reason enough to visit Boston off-season. Select from 25 mousses, cookies, tarts, gateaux and éclairs at the all-you-can-eat buffet. Chocoholics will assume they've died and gone to heaven. Open 1 to 3 pm Saturday, September through May; $16 adults, $7.75 children under 13.

No trip to the North End would be complete without a sweet from **Mike's Pastry** (Map 5; ☎ 617-742-3050, 300 Hanover St). Muscle your way through the crowds and grab the attention of one of the staff as they scurry to and fro. Rather than opting for an already-filled pastry shell, order a ricotta cannoli ($2), which are filled-to-order in the back room. Open 8 am to 9 pm (until 6 pm Tuesday, until 10 pm Thursday through Saturday).

Dine elsewhere but end up at **Finale Desserterie** (Map 7; 617-423-3184, 1 Columbus Ave). Choose from a long list of tempting treats, from crème brûlée to chocolate soufflé, and enjoy them with a coffee, wine or port. The elegant yet comfortable dining room is set up so that, through mirrors over the pastry chefs' workstation, you can watch their magic. Open 11:30 am to 11 pm or so, from 6 pm Saturday, from 4 pm Sunday.

The Bristol (Map 7; ☎ 617-351-2053, 200 Boylston St), in the Four Seasons Hotel, serves a fabulously decadent Viennese dessert buffet, with live music from 9 pm to midnight Friday and Saturday. Order a single dessert or go whole hog and sample from the buffet ($16). A la carte desserts are available the rest of the week.

LA Burdick Chocolates (Map 11; ☎ 617-491-4340, 52D Brattle St) is not the best place for an intimate conversation since the handful of tiny tables are right on top of each other, but it is one of the best places for tea, coffee and sweets, particularly chocolate sweets. Open 8 am to 11 pm, except 9 am to 9 pm Sunday and Monday.

Carberry's Bakery & Coffee House (Map 12; ☎ 617-576-3530, 74 Prospect St), near Central Square, and in Davis Square (Map 13; ☎ 617-666-2233, 187 Elm St), boasts Scandinavian pastries and a relaxed atmosphere.

In Inman Square, if you look hard enough, **Rosie's Bakery & Dessert Shop** (Map 12; ☎ 617-491-9488, 243 Hampshire St) has one fat-free meringue cookie amid the luscious brownies, tarts and shortbreads. Open 8ish to 8ish.

Tea-Tray in the Sky (Map 13; ☎ 617-492-8327, 1796 Mass Ave) is a charming tea shop/café featuring enticing desserts – cookies, biscotti, tarts, truffles and sophisticated masterpieces that are artfully plated. Pots of tea are brewed to order from among 75 varieties. Open 10 am to 10 pm daily, until 7 pm Sunday.

frills establishment with booths and Formica tables is the waitstaff. Although seemingly brusque and no-nonsense, these gals combine superhuman efficiency with good humor. Open from about 11 am to 11 pm.

Galleria Umberto (☎ 617-227-5709, 289 Hanover St) certainly rivals its pizza pie adversary in quality, but its crust is as thick and

chewy as Regina's is thin and crispy. The 80¢ slices are usually gone by 2:30 pm, at which time the place closes. Open at 11 am daily except Sunday.

Belly up to the self-service counter at *Il Panino Express (☎ 617-720-5720, 266 Hanover St)* for fast food served from 9 am to 11 pm. Pasta, monster-sized calzones and pizza slices fulfill basic cravings for Italian if you don't have the time or inclination for nearby sit-down restaurants.

Mid-Range

The Daily Catch (☎ *617-523-8567, 323 Hanover St)*, also known as the calamari café, is a tiny storefront with four tables, an open kitchen and a line of patrons waiting to get in. Bountiful portions of garlicky, sautéed seafood and linguini cooked al dente are served in the cast-iron skillets in which they were prepared. Get there early, or else. Open 11:30 am to 10 pm.

La Piccola Venezia (☎ *617-523-3888, 263 Hanover St)* provides consistently great value with huge portions of old-fashioned dishes: eggplant parmesan ($12 at dinner, less at lunch), spaghetti and meatballs with red sauce ($11) and more unusual but authentic dishes like tripe and gnocchi. Open 11 am to 9 pm weekdays, 10:30 pm weekends.

Antico Forno (☎ *617-723-6733, 93 Salem St)* is named for its beehive, wood-burning brick oven, the source of all that's warm and wonderful in this North End Neapolitan. It specializes in pizza ($10 to $13); try the 'Vesuvio' (spicy sausage, cherry tomatoes, roasted peppers, mozzarella and ricotta). Southern Italian home cooking ($15 to $18 per entree) and roasted meats aren't slighted either. Open noon to 10 pm.

Massimino's Cucina Italiana (☎ *617-523-5959, 207 Endicott St)* is off the beaten path, thank goodness. For a little effort, you'll be rewarded with a warm welcome, traditional home cooking, reasonable prices and maybe even a table without too much of a wait. Open 11 am to 10 pm, closed Sunday.

Maurizio's (☎ *617-367-1123, 364 Hanover St)* is tiny (all the best North End restaurants seem to be), but the creative Mediterranean preparations are worth the wait and the cramped quarters. Open for lunch Wednesday through Saturday, dinner nightly except Monday.

Pagliuca's (☎ *617-367-1504, 14 Parmenter St)* remains a favorite among the old-fashioned North End establishments. There's nothing fancy here, just dependable, hearty home-style Italian fare like eggplant par-

mesan, chicken cacciatore and veal marsala. Open 11:30 am to 10 pm, until 11 pm on weekends.

Top End

Antico Forno's sibling, *Terramia* (☎ *617-523-3112, 98 Salem St)* is the creation of impresario Mario Nocera, who hand selects every mushroom that enters the kitchen. The seasonal menu transforms old world classics into new world masterpieces, showcasing the essential beauty of vintage balsamic vinegars and rare Italian cheeses. Dishes are pasta- and rice-based ($11 to $18) or centered around seafood and meat ($17 to $31). Open for dinner nightly, noon to 10 pm Sunday.

At *Restaurant Bricco* (☎ *617-248-6800, 241 Hanover St)*, chef Bill Bradley brilliantly fuses northern Italian flavors with those of California, southern France and North Africa. The pastry chef, too, works magic with diverse breads and sweet finales. The handsome dining room is sleek but comfortably Euro-chic, and in good weather, casement windows open onto the street. Entrees are $18 to $26, but you could be very happy ordering lots of antipasti (or tastings, for $4 or $5 each). Open for dinner nightly.

CHARLESTOWN (MAP 5)
Budget

The tiny *Sorelle Bakery Café* (☎ *617-242-2125, 1 Monument Ave)* serves coffees, pastries, salads, sandwiches and cold pasta dishes from 6:30 am to 5 pm on weekdays, from 8 am to 3 pm on Saturday, until 1 pm on Sunday.

Mid-Range

Warren Tavern (☎ *617-241-8142, 2 Pleasant St)*, a circa 1780 neighborhood pub, skillfully chars burgers. The snug, dark quarters are boisterous and congenial, except when the staff is harried and grumpy, that is! Open for lunch and dinner.

At the original *Figs* (☎ *617-242-2229, 67 Main St)*, reward yourself with a pizza after climbing the Bunker Hill Monument and strolling the cobblestone streets. Open for dinner.

Top End

Todd English's *Olives* (☎ 617-242-1999, 10 City Square), with a creative Mediterranean-New American menu prepared in an exposed kitchen, offers spit-roasted meats and savory fish preparations. Entrees are in the $21 to $31 range. There are two drawbacks: It's quite noisy inside and you'll have to wait, unless you arrive very early (at 4:45 pm) or very late. Open nightly except Sunday; no reservations.

WATERFRONT & SEAPORT DISTRICT (MAP 6)
Budget

Within the grandly renovated train terminal, the *South Station Food Court*, on Atlantic Ave at Summer St, offers fast food from burgers to pizza, but hidden among the usual suspects are a few gems. *Rosie's Bakery* (☎ 617-439-4684) satisfies the most demanding sweet tooth and challenges the most determined dieter; try a pecan sticky bun ($2.25) or a savory foccacia ($3). Rosie's is open 7 am to 7 pm weekdays, until 6 pm on Saturday. The *Boston Coffee Exchange* brews flavorful espresso and cappuccino. Open 5 am to 7:30 pm weekdays, 6 am to noon Saturday.

The giant icon *Milk Bottle* (☎ 617-482-3343, 300 Congress St), near the Children's Museum, is both a landmark and a summer lunchtime favorite since 1977. It does a brisk seasonal take-out business in sandwiches and ice cream.

The Blue Diner/Art Zone (☎ 617-695-0087, 150 Kneeland St) has a famously disinterested waitstaff serving traditional American diner fare such as meatloaf, burgers and full breakfasts. The joint's open around-the-clock from 11 am Thursday until 5 am Monday (and for lunch Monday through Wednesday); the bar serves until 4 am. Bleary-eyed types wander in until 4 pm on weekends for the popular 'hangover brunch.'

Café Three Hundred (☎ 617-426-06957, 300 Summer St) nourishes the soul with gallery showings while simultaneously feeding patrons' more temporal bellies. This community gathering place for area artists and

KIM GRANT

Fried heaven

hangers-on is preferred by those who disdain eye candy; it's open 8:30 am to 3:30 pm weekdays.

Mid-Range

Barking Crab (☎ 617-426-2722, 88 Sleeper St), everything a clam shack should be, offers big servings of delicious fried seafood on paper plates at communal picnic tables on the water. The platters ($11 to $15), with fries and coleslaw, are worth every penny.

Intrigue (☎ 617-856-7744, 70 Rowes Wharf), within the Boston Harbor Hotel, is a refined but unpretentious place for a sumptuous breakfast, light meal or dessert and wine. The casually elegant room, complete with harbor view, also serves afternoon tea. Open 7 am to 9 pm, a bit later on weekends.

KIM GRANT

Home of the best New England clam chowder. There. We said it.

Top End

Legal Sea Foods (☎ 617-227-3115, 255 State St) has built a local empire on the motto, 'If it's not fresh, it's not Legal.' The menu is simple: every kind of fish, it seems, broiled, steamed, sautéed, grilled or fried. Freshness and simplicity come at a price, though. Lunch is $10 to $14 (try the bluefish pate and the spicy fish and chips), while dinner runs $15 to $25 per entree. At least servings are generous. The clam chowder ($4 to $5) is justifiably New England's best.

There are also branches near the Theater District (*Map 7;* ☎ *617-426-4444, 26 Park Square*); within the Prudential Center (*Map 8;* ☎ *617-266-6800, 800 Boylston St*); within the Copley Place shopping mall (*Map 8;* ☎ *617-266-7775*); and in Cambridge's Kendall Square (☎ *617-864-3400, 5 Cambridge Center*). All are open from about noon to 10 pm, until 9 pm on Sunday.

THEATER DISTRICT & CHINATOWN (MAP 7)
Budget

Mix Bakery (☎ 617-357-4050, 36 Beach St) features decadent western-style cakes as well as a wide variety of traditional Chinese cookies and sweets. Open 7 am to 7 pm.

Pho Pasteur (☎ *617-482-7467, 682 Washington St*) serves hearty, hot and cheap meals in a bowl. Most people come for pho (pronounced 'fuh'), the sometimes exotic, always fragrant and flavorful noodle soup ($5.50 for extra large). Open from 9 or 10 am to 9 or 10 pm. The Newbury St and Harvard Square locations (see Back Bay and Harvard Square, below) serve the same great food in more elegant surroundings.

At *Hu Tieu Nam Vang* (☎ *617-422-0501, 7 Beach St*), the friendly, helpful staff serves authentic Vietnamese specialties, from pho to vermicelli dishes; they're all delicious. For a great value ($6.50), try a hot pot – a crock of steaming rice, vegetables and meat, seafood or tofu, cooked together in a spicy aromatic sauce. It's enough for two people. There are more than 40 kinds of cold drinks and fresh fruit shakes. Open 9 am to 10 pm.

On the 2nd floor, *Buddha's Delight* (☎ *617-451-2395, 3 Beach St*) thrills vegetarians with noodle soups, tasty tofu dishes and imitation meat dishes such as soybean 'roast pork.' Try a fruit and milk drink for dessert.

PLACES TO EAT

Lunch specials are about $5, dinners are around $10. Open 11 am to 10 pm.

Highlighting food from various regions in China, *Chau Chow* (☎ 617-426-6266, 52 Beach St) has excellent seafood specials, ample portions and renowned ginger and black bean sauces. Try the garlicky sautéed pea pod stems and the crispy, chewy, salted fried squid. The same delicious food is served in newer and bigger digs across the street at *Grand Chau Chow* (☎ 617-292-5166, 45 Beach St). Both are open for lunch and dinner until 2 am; lunch costs about $5 or $6, dinner $8 to $10.

LMNOP (☎ 617-338-4220, 91 Park Plaza) bakes for a posh restaurant next-door, but also sells crusty loaves and delectable baked pastries retail. At lunchtime, there are sandwiches, soups and pasta dishes ($4 to $5.50) for take-out. Open from 7:30 am to 6:45 pm weekdays.

Great for a rainy day when there's not much change in your pocket, *City Place Food Court* (no phone; 10 Park Plaza), within the drab State Transportation Building, has a number of fast-food take-out counters and tables. Most are open for lunch and dinner.

Mid-Range

Penang (☎ 617-451-6373, 685 Washington St) serves Malaysian fare in a festive atmosphere. Test your fortitude with fish heads, pig intestines and chicken feet (some items are listed with the admonition 'Ask your server for advice before you order!!!'). For the less intrepid, there are vegetarian options. Appetizers range from $3.50 to $7; entrees are $8 to $20. Open 11:30 am to 11:30 pm.

A Japanese-Korean late-night hot spot, *Apollo Grill* (☎ 617-423-3888, 84–86 Harrison Ave) features tables with built-in hibachi grills. Tasty appetizers and sushi are a draw, too. Open for lunch weekdays and from 5 pm to 4 am for dinner.

A hip Japanese eatery, *Ginza* (☎ 617-338-2261, 16 Hudson St) serves some of the city's best sushi and maki. If you prefer your fish hot, there's tempura. All this excellence doesn't come cheap; expect to spend $13 to $20 for dinner entrees. Open for lunch; dinner from 4 or 5 pm to 3:30 am (until 1:30 am on Sunday and Monday).

Top End

Lydia Shire's *Biba* (☎ 617-426-7878, 272 Boylston St), one of the original food-chic trendsetters, continues to push the gustatory envelope. The 'food hall' is a boisterous, fashionable scene (and a place to be seen). The menu marries low- and high-brow cuisine, tending toward savory game, and doesn't shy away from liver and kidneys. Even the skate, a rather uninteresting local fish, is 'crisped in goose fat and accompanied by langoustines with truffle puree.' And then there's the lobster pizza…Entrees range from $25 to $39. Open for lunch and dinner.

BACK BAY (MAP 8)
Budget

Terrace Food Court (no phone, 800 Boylston St), a fast-food emporium within the Shops at Prudential Center, offers quick, cheap meals. Most are open for lunch and dinner.

Pho Pasteur (☎ 617-262-8200, 119 Newbury St), a branch of Boston's favorite Vietnamese restaurant (see Theater District & Chinatown, above), is open from 11 am to 10 pm.

Dixie Kitchen (☎ 617-536-3068, 182 Mass Ave) serves home-style Cajun-Creole dishes such as gumbo, catfish, ribs and jumbalaya. Nothing fancy here (and no liquor), just hearty meals at bargain prices.

The storefront eatery *Café Jaffa* (☎ 617-536-0230, 48 Gloucester St) is a great bargain, with large servings and reasonable prices ($3.50 to $10). When was the last time you had authentic Turkish coffee, shwarma or falafel in a place with polished wooden floors and exposed brick? Take out or eat in for lunch and dinner.

If you think 'Boston, books and breakfast' go together, head to *Trident Booksellers & Café* (☎ 617-267-8688, 338 Newbury St). The shelves are filled with New Age titles, while the tables are crowded with down-to-earth salads, soups, sandwiches ($5 to $7), pasta entrees ($8 to $12) and desserts; breakfast is served all day. Vegetarians rejoice over the vegan cashew chili. Open 9 am to midnight.

PLACES TO EAT

Mid-Range

The ever-popular **Kebab-N-Kurry** (☎ 617-536-9835, 30 Mass Ave), a small basement place, boasts consistently good Indian dishes at consistently good prices ($6 lunch, $13 dinner). Open for lunch and dinner (only dinner on Sunday).

Marche Movenpick (☎ 617-578-9700, 800 Boylston St), within the Shops at Prudential Center, is the first American outpost of the European restaurant chain. You choose only your favorites from an assortment of freshly prepared sushi, stir-fry and rotisserie meats at various food stations, and assemble a gourmet meal at cafeteria prices. Open 7:30 am to 2 am.

Slightly hidden down a little alleyway, **Casa Romero** (☎ 617-536-4341, 30 Gloucester St) offers delicious, authentic Mexico City-style cuisine in a lovely courtyard or intimate Talavera-tiled dining room. The enchiladas, verdes or poblanas, are wonderful, as is the *puerco adobado*, roasted pork marinated in sweet oranges and smoked chipotle chile. Open for dinner.

Tapeo (☎ 617-267-4799, 266 Newbury St), a festive Spanish tapas restaurant, has bodega-style dining rooms and, in fine weather, a patio fronting Newbury St (a nonstop parade). It's perfect for sherry-sipping. Open for dinner nightly, lunch on weekends.

Parish Café & Bar (☎ 617-247-4777, 361 Boylston St) is known for creative sandwiches, each designed by a local celebrity chef. Try Rialto chef Jody Adams' prosciutto and buffalo mozzarella with pesto and a touch of basil oil on grilled white bread ($12) – not your average sandwich. Some are accompanied by a salad. Other draws include an outdoor patio, 70 different beers and 20 wines by the glass. Open 11:30 am to 2 am.

Top End

Anago (☎ 617-266-6222, 65 Exeter St), at Boylston St within the Lenox Hotel, serves a

---

Brewpubs

Bostonians take beer seriously. In the past decade a number of 'microbreweries' have sprung up in Boston. What's the difference between a brewery, a bar, a pub and a brewpub? Although there are exceptions, a brewery produces beer for distributors; a bar serves alcoholic drinks, including beer, and snacks; a pub serves simple meals and alcohol, but emphasizes beer; a brewpub serves its own beer brewed on the premises. While all those listed below are recommended for beer and snacks, some serve noteworthy, moderately priced meals.

Within gleaming copper kettles, **Commonwealth Fish & Beer Co** (Map 3; ☎ 617-523-8383, 138 Portland St) produces over 10 kinds of English-style suds served at various temperatures. The menu is heavy on seafood (crispy calamari, grilled fish, chowder), but you can get a BBQ chicken sandwich, too. The basement is comfortably 'clubby' and bands play Thursday through Saturday. The place is packed when the Bruins and Celtics play at the nearby Fleet Center. Food is served until 10 pm; the bar closes at 1 am.

The deservedly popular **Brew Moon** (Map 7; ☎ 617-523-6467, 115 Stuart St, and Map 11; ☎ 499-2739, 50 Church St), with a sophisticated dining room and sleek bar, offers seven seasonal brews and a creative menu from 11 am. Though the Theater District locale is often crowded pre- and post-show, the upside is that the bar serves food until 1 am weekdays, 2 am weekends. Head brewer Darrah Bryans is one of the country's only female master brewers.

The **Back Bay Brewing Co** (Map 8; ☎ 617-424-8300, 755 Boylston St), a sophisticated joint with high ceilings and rich paneling, has more intimate seating on the 2nd floor. The IPA is full bodied, the seasonal brews are fresh and the burgers are good. Open 11 am to 10:30 pm.

(Side tab) **PLACES TO EAT**

Where the pretty people are

Sonsie (☎ 617-351-2500, 327 Newbury St) is perhaps the hippest place to be seen sipping a latte. Europeans descend wearing basic black and dark sunglasses. In warm weather, a wall of French doors is flung open, making the indoor tables seem alfresco. During busy mealtimes, café tables are reserved for diners. Pizza, pasta and other light dishes are available; entrees range from $9 to $29. Although full-fledged dining is pricey, the French and Asian fusion menu is impressive. Open 8 am to 1 am.

hearty blend of Mediterranean and New American cuisine. Entrees such as oven-roasted salmon ($28) and rack of lamb ($35) are creatively prepared and artfully presented in a quiet and sophisticated setting. Appetizers ($10 to $14) are luscious but unduly complicated. At the Sunday jazz brunch ($28 adults, $14 children), order entrees off the menu, and head to the buffet for appetizers and dessert. Open nightly for dinner.

SOUTH END (MAP 9)
Budget
At the *Delux Café* (☎ 617-338-5258, 100 Chandler St) appearances can be both revealing and deceiving. This place looks like a small, dark bar, and it is; but it serves decidedly upscale, globally inspired food in a friendly, funky-kitschy atmosphere. A secret no longer, the place is packed (with more than a few smokers). Open nightly except Sunday.

Brewpubs

Samuel Adams Brewhouse (Map 8; ☎ 617-536-2739, 710 Boylston St), within the Lenox Hotel in Back Bay, capitalizes on Boston's best-known home brew. This tourist haunt is not really a brewpub – the brewery is down the street in Jamaica Plain. Open 11 am to 1:30 am; kitchen closes at midnight.

Boston Beer Works (Map 10; ☎ 617-536-2337, 61 Brookline Ave) has seasonal concoctions brewed in exposed tanks and pipes. About eight different kinds of beer, including Boston Red and Buckeye Oatmeal Stout, are usually available. The appetizers and munchies are pretty good, too. If you don't like sporting crowds, avoid this place after a Sox game. The kitchen serves 11:30 am to 12:45 am; the bar closes at 1:30 am.

Where everybody knows your name...

Subterranean **John Harvard's Brew House** (Map 11; ☎ 617-868-3585, 33 Dunster St), in Harvard Square, smells and feels more like an English pub than the others and has perhaps the best beer among the crowded microbrewery field. You'll find ales and stouts here (plus a sampler rack). Above-average pub grub is available at lunch ($6 to $10) and dinner ($10 to $15), until 11 pm weeknights, 12:30 am weekends.

Cambridge Brewing Co (Map 12; ☎ 617-494-1994, 1 Kendall Square) has reputable seasonal ales, but beyond the burgers, you'd do better eating elsewhere. This is a convenient place to go after a movie, but it's packed on weekends.

PLACES TO EAT

Bertucci's *(☎ 617-247-6161, 43 Stanhope St)* serves Boston's favorite brick-oven pizza, as well as salads and pasta dishes. Open 11 am to 10 pm, until 11 pm on weekends.

A favorite neighborhood joint, ***Anchovies*** *(☎ 617-266-5088, 433 Columbus Ave)* has meatball subs that rule! The rest of the menu features mix-and-match pastas and sauces, as well as pizzas. Open 5 pm to 1:30 am; kitchen closes at 12:45 am.

With a few shared tables and the counter, ***Charlie's Sandwich Shoppe*** *(☎ 617-536-7669, 429 Columbus Ave)*, a classic, has been serving creative omelets ($6 to $8 with a salad), cranberry French toast and other breakfast platters ($3.50 to $5 with meat) since 1927. For lunch, turkey hash with two eggs ($6.25), hot pastrami and homemade pies are gobbled by lawyers in suits and laborers in work boots. Open 6 am to 2:30 pm weekdays, 7:30 am to 1 pm on Saturday.

Bob the Chef *(☎ 617-536-6204, 604 Columbus Ave)* serves Boston's best down-home soul food: We're talking barbecue ribs with a hunk of cornbread, or fried chicken with collard greens or black-eyed peas. Most meals cost about $10; sandwiches are half that. Open 11 am to 10 pm daily except Monday, until midnight Thursday to Saturday. Locals love the Sunday jazz brunch ($15), from 11 am to 3 pm.

Pho Republique *(☎ 617-262-0005, 1415 Washington St)* serves delicious pho chock full of fresh vegetables and herbs in a rich savory broth, as well as crispy spring rolls and beautifully prepared and presented entrees. Open for dinner nightly.

At ***Mike's City Diner*** *(☎ 617-267-9393, 1714 Washington St)*, the service is warm and old-fashioned (in the positive sense). Although the menu may appear to be homespun as well (meatloaf and mashed potatoes and gravy, fried chicken, scrambled eggs and ham, burgers), the preparation is far from retro. Open 6 am to 10 pm (but closed 3 to 5 pm).

Purple Cactus Burrito & Wrap Bar *(☎ 617-338-5675, 312 Shawmut Ave)* is one of the best Tex-Mex-inspired wrap sandwich storefronts springing up around town. Fillings are fresh and the wraps make a tasty

KIM GRANT

Saddened by the impending loss of Fenway Park

meal on the run. Open 11:30 am to 10 pm (from 10 am on weekends).

Tim's Tavern *(☎ 617-437-6898, 329 Columbus Ave)*, another great neighborhood joint serving fabulous food but cloaked as a divey bar, has some of the best (and biggest and cheapest) burgers. Splurge on the fries or onion rings for another buck. Baby back ribs also draw raves. Open 11 am to midnight daily except Sunday.

Mid-Range

Jae's Café & Grill *(☎ 617-421-9405, 520 Columbus Ave)* specializes in Korean food but they have a full pan-Asian menu. Order sushi, satay, pad Thai or vegetarian noodle dishes at this lively spot. Expect to wait for dinner unless you arrive by 6 pm. Lunch specials are $7 or $9, dinner entrees from $14 to $18. Although Jae's has other locations around town, they don't measure up to the original. Open for lunch and dinner.

On the Park *(☎ 617-426-0862, 1 Union Park St)*, a friendly little neighborhood place that feels a bit like it belongs in New York's Greenwich Village, is bright and funky with lots of local art. Cuisine tends toward creative American: marinated pork chops, gingered lamb stew or whole-wheat pasta for

$12 to $16. The weekend brunch ($7 to $10), with mimosas, is particularly popular. Also open for dinner Tuesday through Saturday.

Claremont Café (☎ *617-247-9001, 535 Columbus Ave)*, a tiny romantic place, offers generous portions of South American- and Mediterranean-inspired cuisine. Rice dishes, paella and roast chicken dishes go for $12 to $20. The café draws an artsy cross-section of neighborhood folks, especially for breakfast scones. Open for all three meals Tuesday through Saturday, Sunday brunch from 9 am to 3 pm.

Geoffrey's Café & Bar (☎ *617-266-1122, 578 Tremont St)* dishes up eclectic home cooking with a good-sized serving of South End camp on the side. The menu includes delicious pasta dishes as well as hearty sandwiches and creative variations on meat and potatoes entrees. Open for all three meals.

Franklin Café (☎ *617-350-0010, 278 Shawmut Ave)* is perhaps the South End's most beloved restaurant (and that's saying something in this restaurant-rich neighborhood). Think New American comfort food prepared by a gourmet chef: steamed mussels with Pernod, leeks, garlic and white wine or roasted turkey meatloaf with spiced fig gravy and chive mashed potatoes. The bartender is renowned – have a drink while you wait for a table. Open for dinner.

Top End

Hamersley's Bistro (☎ *617-423-2700, 553 Tremont St)*, consistently at the top of every 'best restaurants' list, serves French/country American cuisine. The seasonal menu might include grilled filet of beef or hot-and-spicy grilled tuna. Roasted chicken with garlic, parsley and lemon ($23) is chef Gordon Hamersley's specialty. (Sunday night is Gordon's night off, though.) This dish is attempted elsewhere, but it's so far unequaled. The ambiance is urban and cool, but not too cool. Open nightly for dinner.

KENMORE SQUARE & FENWAY (MAP 10)
Budget

Bruegger's Bagel Bakery (☎ *617-262-7939, 644 Beacon St)* has a dozen kinds of bagels

and flavors of cream cheese. They'll also slap some deli meat and veggies on a bagel if you want a sandwich. Open from 7 or 8 am to 5 pm.

Baldini's (☎ *617-267-6269, 532 Comm Ave)* is an inexpensive, self-service Italian place with hefty, if uninspired, pizza-by-the-slice ($2.35), calzones ($4) and pasta with meatballs and red sauce ($5.25). Open 11 am to midnight.

International House of Pancakes (☎ *617-859-0458, 500 Comm Ave)*, known as IHOP (pronounced 'eye-hop'), serves breakfast all day. A classic American coffee shop with booths and Formica tables, a la 1953, it's especially popular with neighborhood students after clubbing. Open 22 hours a day (from 6 am to 4 am).

Once the area's favorite Indian dive, *India Quality* (☎ *617-267-4499, 484 Comm Ave)* was transformed into the area's favorite classy restaurant after a fire decimated it. The menu remains the same: dependable, delicious northern Indian cuisine. Open for lunch and dinner (closed 3 to 5 pm weekdays).

The 'other side' in *The Other Side Cosmic Café* (☎ *617-536-9477, 407 Newbury St)* refers to the other side of Mass Ave, which few people crossed before this place opened. The 'cosmic' alludes to its funky, Seattle-inspired style. The 1st floor is done in cast iron, while the 2nd floor is softened by mismatched couches and low ceilings. Vegetarian chili, sandwiches, veggie drinks and strong coffee are the order of the day. Open 10 am to midnight (from noon Sunday).

Bangkok Cuisine (☎ *617-262-5377, 177A Mass Ave)*, Boston's first Thai restaurant, is one of the best. The conventional choices of satay (grilled or broiled for $4) and pad Thai ($4.75 at lunch, $6.50 at dinner) are very good. When the menu says hot, it means it. Open for lunch and dinner (only dinner Sunday).

Thorntons Fenway Grill (☎ *617-421-0104, 100 Peterborough St)*, a boisterous gathering place for hungry sports fans and neighborhood families, features big burgers, hot and cold sandwiches and salads and pub standards such as fish and chips and ribs. Open 9 or 10 am to midnight.

PLACES TO EAT

Lazy Susan Boulangerie (☎ *617-450-9100, 96 Peterborough St*), a lovely spot for breakfast or a light meal of quiche, salad or a sandwich, has several outdoor tables when the weather is fine. When it's not, seating is limited, and the business is mostly take-out. Pastries and baked goods are a specialty. Open from 7 am to 8 pm (8 am to 4 pm Sunday).

El Pelon Taqueria (☎ *617-262-9090, 92 Peterborough St*) serves authentic Mexican, including burritos, chile rellenos, tamales and huge *tortas* (grilled meat on a toasted roll and heaped with black beans, the chef's special limed onions, lettuce and avocado). How do they serve such generous portions of high-quality food when everything is under $5.50? Paper plates and plastic cutlery help. Open 11:30 am to 10 pm.

Buteco (☎ *617-247-9508, 130 Jersey St*) serves bountiful, hearty Brazilian home cooking in a relaxed atmosphere. Though the place is justly known for meat dishes, there are a few chicken, fish and vegetarian ones, too. The weekend dinner special is always *feijoada*, a rich stew of black beans, pork, sausage and dried beef. Open noon to 10 pm weekdays, from 3 pm weekends.

Brown Sugar Café (☎ *617-266-2928, 129 Jersey St*) serves beautifully presented, delectable Thai. Their mango curry is a revelation: tender sliced chicken simmered in a yellow curry with chunks of ripe mango, tomato, red and green pepper, onion and summer squash. Portions are larger when you take out. Open for lunch and dinner.

Audubon Circle (☎ *617-421-1910, 838 Beacon St*), a lively place to just hang out or enjoy a meal, serves some of the best burgers and appetizers you'll find in town. Open 11:30 am to 1 am weekdays, from 4:30 pm on weekends.

Savoy (☎ *617-734-0214, 1003 Beacon St*) is the place for delicious French pastries. Open 7 am to 6:30 pm daily; on Sunday from 8 am until they're sold out, which could be an hour after opening.

Taberna de Haro (☎ *617-277-8272, 999 Beacon St*), an inviting little place serving authentic Spanish tapas and meals, has outdoor seating in warm weather. On a cold blustery evening, order a glass of sherry and enjoy the cozy dining room. Open for dinner nightly except Sunday.

Mid-Range

Betty's Wok & Noodle Diner (☎ *617-424-1950, 250 Huntington Ave*) appeals to students as well as symphony- and theater-goers. Here's the deal: Choose a noodle or rice dish, then add beef or shrimp or chicken, choose your own veggies from the salad bar, then add one of seven sauces like Cuban chipotle citrus or kung pao. The large portions are all thrown in a wok and cooked perfectly – and really quickly! Don't miss the 'cool cucs and weed salad' or the curried rodeo rings. Dishes cost $9 to $14. Open daily for lunch and dinner.

Elephant Walk (☎ *617-247-1500, 900 Beacon St*) is highly regarded for its dual menus of classic French and traditional Cambodian. Many devotees opt for a curry dinner and French dessert. Open for lunch ($7 to $10) and dinner, except no lunch on Sunday. Cambodian dinner entrees cost $10 to $16, French are more like $19 to $25.

Ginza (☎ *617-566-9688, 1002 Beacon St*) may not be as hip as the Chinatown original, but the sushi is as fresh and it has its own following. Open for lunch and dinner (with a hiatus from 2:30 to 5 pm).

Sorento's (☎ *617-424-7070, 86 Peterborough St*) serves brick-oven pizza (from $10 for a large cheese to $17 for the works) and calzones, as well as pasta and seafood dishes prepared to order ($12 to $18). Open for lunch and dinner.

CAMBRIDGE

Head across the Charles to Cambridge's many restaurants, found amid its bustling neighborhoods and tucked away off the beaten track.

Harvard Square Area (Map 11)

Budget You're bound to find something fast, filling and cheap at *The Garage* (no phone, 36 John F Kennedy St), with a dozen places to eat under one roof, including *Pho*

Pasteur (☎ 617-864-4100, 36 Dunster St), another branch of Boston's favorite Vietnamese restaurant (also see Theater District & Chinatown, earlier in this chapter). Open 11 am to 10 or 11 pm.

Bertucci's (☎ 617-864-4748, 21 Brattle St) serves great brick-oven pizza, as well as salads and pasta dishes, from 11 am to 11 pm, until midnight Friday and Saturday.

At *Campo de Fiori (☎ 617-354-3805, 1350 Mass Ave)*, in the Holyoke Center Arcade, the menu revolves around *pane romano*, Roman-style flat bread. The pane, topped with Italian meats, cheeses, vegetables and herbs, makes a quick snack, or can be ordered sandwich-style with fillings. Open 8 am to 8 pm weekdays, 11 am to 6 pm Saturday.

Sabra Grill (☎ 617-868-5777, 20 Eliot St) served fresh and delicious Middle Eastern take-out long before it was trendy. Vegetarians and their contrarians alike will be happy, with spinach pie and Greek salad or chicken shwarma and shish kebab. Open 10 am to 10 pm.

Bartley's Burger Cottage (☎ 617-354-6559, 1246 Mass Ave), the Square's primo burger joint, offers at least 40 different burgers. But if none of those suit your fancy, create your own 7oz, juicy masterpiece topped with guacamole or sprouts. You'll make a veggie burger, too. French fries and onion rings complete the classic American meal. Bartley's is packed with small tables and hungry college students from 11 am to 9 or 10 pm daily, except Sunday. You'll spend about $10 here.

Although service at *Algiers Coffee House (☎ 617-492-1557, 40 Brattle St)* can be glacial, the palatial Middle Eastern decor makes it a comfortable rest spot. Head to the airy 2nd floor and order a falafel sandwich ($7.25), a bowl of lentil soup ($4) or a kebab ($11). The one good thing about the relaxed service is that you won't be rushed to finish your pot of Arabic coffee or mint tea. Open 8 am to midnight.

Hi-Rise Pie Co (☎ 617-492-3003, 56 Brattle St), known for wonderful scones, cookies and crusty loaves, also has light sandwiches and soups. Outdoor tables are popular in warm weather; indoors is cozy. The café and pastry counter are open 8:30 am to 5 pm weekdays, 9 am to 5 pm Saturday. Open Sunday in summer.

Mid-Range *Casablanca (☎ 617-876-0999, 40 Brattle St)* is a classic. The romantic atmosphere, inspired by the film and combined with chef Ana Sortun's flair for modern Mediterranean cuisine, keeps the restaurant high on the tried-and-true list. Grilled sea scallops with basmati, lentil and pistachio pilaf, seared chard and brown butter is but one example of Sortun's magic. Open for lunch and dinner (closed 2:30 to 5:30 pm), bar until 1:45 am.

Bombay Club (☎ 617-661-8100, 57 John F Kennedy St) serves delicious Indian cuisine from all corners of that diverse country in a sleekly elegant dining room removed from the bustling street life. The signature chicken tikka masala ($11) is an excellent choice, as is anything from the tandoor oven. Cheeses and yogurts are made from scratch; the weekend lunch buffet ($9) is a bargain. Open 11:30 am to 11 pm.

Henrietta's Table (☎ 617-864-1200, 1 Bennett St), in the Charles Hotel, features New England regional cuisine highlighting local produce. The creative, 'fresh and honest' preparations, country inn decor and friendly service make it *the* choice for better-than-home cooking. Main dishes average $14, hefty sides about $4. Save an appetite to get your money's worth of the deservedly popular, all-you-can-eat Sunday brunch ($36 per person). Open for all three meals.

Top End Within the Charles Hotel, *Rialto (☎ 617-661-5050, 1 Bennett St)* is a best-of-the-best. You'll pay handsomely for dining in this understated, Euro-chic elegance, but your meal will be romantic and memorable. Chef Jody Adams' Mediterranean-inspired dishes include creamy mussel and saffron stew with leeks or seared beef tenderloin with cognac sauce and shellfish paella. The vegetarian main course is always equally creative. Entrees range from $20 to $33, but you can save some money by dining at the

PLACES TO EAT

bar (off Jody's bar menu). Open for dinner nightly.

East Cambridge (Map 12)

Mid-Range The *Helmand* (☎ *617-492-4646, 143 First St*) serves Afghan cuisine that will satisfy meat-eaters and vegetarians alike. Although the menu features grilled lamb, beef and chicken dishes ($10 to $16), it also has many vegetarian entrees (such as dolma, eggplant stuffed with spinach and sautéed with cauliflower, sweet pepper, corn and

---

Ice Cream

Regardless of weather, Bostonians never lose their appetite for ice cream. Two annual all-you-can-eat festival fund-raisers celebrate the frozen treat. The Scooper Bowl, in Government Center Plaza (three days in early June), benefits the Dana-Farber Cancer Institute's Jimmy Fund for childhood cancer research. The WGBH Ice Cream Funfest, 125 Western Ave, Allston (two days in September), supports the public television station. Tickets cost $10 adults; $5 seniors and children under 10. Otherwise, sample the following faves and make your own funfest.

Steve's (Map 3; ☎ 617-367-0569, Quincy Market, Faneuil Hall Marketplace) won fame for 'smush ins,' chunks of candy or nuts mixed into the flavor of your choice.

Brigham's (Map 4; ☎ 617-482-3524, 109 High St) serves old-fashioned treats such as banana splits and malted milkshakes, known locally as 'frappes' (rhymes with raps). Try the 'Big Dig,' vanilla ice cream with gobs of fudge brownie, caramel swirls and chocolate chunks.

JB Scoops (Map 6; ☎ 617-443-0500, South Station Food Court) dishes out traditional regional flavors such as maple walnut and pumpkin pie.

Vermont's own **Ben & Jerry's** (Map 7; ☎ 617-426-0890, 20 Park Plaza, and Map 8; ☎ 617-536-5456, 174 Newbury St) has ever-changing choices that might include triple caramel chunk and chocolate mint patty.

Wai Wai (Map 7; ☎ 617-338-9833, 26 Oxford St) is Boston's most off-beat choice. Although the tiny basement exudes the aroma of roasting chickens, don't be scared. In addition to quick meals, Wai Wai offers several tropical flavors such as ginger, coconut and banana.

Emack & Bolio's (Map 8; ☎ 617-247-8772, 290 Newbury St) takes pride as an old-timer on the local gourmet scene. Many consider Oreo cookie definitive; nonfat yogurt creations, such as latte espresso chip, are also good.

At **JP Licks** (Map 8; ☎ 617-236-1666, 352 Newbury St, and Map 14; ☎ 617-738-8252, 311 Harvard St), it's a toss-up between white coffee and chocolate turtle.

At **Herrell's** (Map 11; ☎ 617-497-2179, 15 Dunster St, and Map 8; ☎ 617-236-0857, 224 Newbury St), favorites include malted vanilla and chocolate pudding.

Cambridge is lucky to have two branches of **Toscanini's**: near Central Square (Map 12; ☎ 617-491-5877, 899 Main St) and in Harvard Square (Map 11; ☎ 617-354-9350, 1310 Mass Ave). Try the gingersnap molasses or Vienna finger cookie.

In Inman Square, **Christina's Ice Cream** (Map 12; ☎ 617-492-7021, 1255 Cambridge St) has the most eclectic flavors. Scoop up fresh mint, brandy and pecans or lemon basil.

Davis Square's **Denise's Homemade Ice Cream** (Map 13; ☎ 617-628-2764, 4A College Ave) serves sorbet, ice cream and hard and soft yogurt. The flavor of choice is tiramisu.

peas in a spicy tomato and onion sauce), all accompanied by a cool yogurt mint sauce. Open for dinner nightly.

Kendall Square (Map 12)
Budget Known primarily for luscious cakes and tarts, *Rebecca's* (☎ 617-494-6688, 290 Main St) is also a pleasant alternative to nearby fast food. The self-service counter dishes out generous sandwiches, salads, soups and hot entrees. Eat in or take out and sit along the river. Open 7 am to 6 pm weekdays.

Top End At the *Blue Room* (☎ 617-494-9034, One Kendall Square), chef Steve Johnson serves wood-fired, grilled and artfully presented game, beef and fish ($16 to $22). Don't skip dessert. Though it's difficult to forgo the snazzy dining room, there is outdoor patio seating. On Sunday, indulge in one of the city's best jazz brunches. Open for dinner nightly.

Inman Square (Map 12)
Budget The *City Girl Caffè* (☎ 617-864-2809, 204 Hampshire St) is a casual, friendly eatery with thin-crust pizza, panini (Italian sandwiches), calzones, pasta and salads. Or stop by for cappuccino and dessert. Open for lunch and dinner daily except Monday.

Mid-Range Southern regional staples, such as pan-fried catfish, jambalaya and bread pudding with bourbon sauce, are featured at *Magnolias Southern Cuisine* (☎ 617-576-1971, 1193 Cambridge St). The friendly staff and soothing dining room make for a pleasant evening. Open for dinner Tuesday through Saturday.

Lines form early on weekends at *S&S Deli Restaurant* (☎ 617-354-0620, 1334 Cambridge St) for Belgian waffles, pancakes, sandwiches and egg dishes. The place has been a neighborhood family institution since 1919. Open for all three meals.

Lively and colorful, *Ole Mexican Grill* (☎ 617-492-4495, 11 Springfield St) serves tasty, innovative Mexican meals emphasizing meat and seafood hot off the grill. Fresh ingredients are emphasized and the chef, himself a vegetarian, does not treat vegetables like 2nd-class citizens. Entrees range

from $8 to $17. Open for lunch and dinner daily, except no lunch on Monday.

Carnivores make pilgrimages to *Midwest Grill* (☎ 617-354-7536, 1124 Cambridge St), a Brazilian grill house and buffet, open for lunch and dinner.

Daddy O's (☎ 617-354-8371, 134 Hampshire St), a folksy, friendly beatnik-inspired joint, takes down-home food (circa 1950) and infuses it with world flavors and style. The macaroni and cheese, for example, is made with gorgonzola and grilled fennel ($8.50). Save room for a baked-to-order fruit pie ($5.75). Weather permitting, dine in the outdoor garden. Open for Sunday brunch and dinner nightly, except Monday.

Top-End The *East Coast Grille* (☎ 617-491-6568, 1271 Cambridge St) is Boston's hippest and hoppingest seafood bar and grill. The place is boisterous – come to eat, not for quiet conversation. Chef Chris Schlesinger's dynamic menu features eight nightly fresh fish specials ($14 to $28) and the best (and probably priciest) fish and chips. Folks travel miles to belly up to the raw bar. There are always a couple of less expensive BBQ sandwiches for those with less to spend. Open for dinner nightly, plus Sunday brunch.

Central Square (Map 12)
Budget Cool and sleek, *Miracle of Science Bar & Grill* (☎ 617-868-2866, 321 Mass Ave) serves creative burgers, sandwiches, salads and grilled entrees. This popular MIT hangout is open 11:30 am to 1 am.

Moody's Falafel Palace (☎ 617-864-0827, 25 Central Square) has been around since the square's hippie heyday. Moody's can't be beat for a quick bite of tasty wholesome food: tabouli, kebabs and, of course, falafel. Open 11 am to midnight.

Mid-Range Even as its popularity expands, *Green St Grill* (☎ 617-876-1655, 280 Green St) hasn't made any attempts to prettify itself. Dark and smoky, this is a dive by any definition, and it serves seriously spicy Caribbean fare. Monday is especially raucous with live music and a half-price menu. Open 3 pm to 1 am (only from 6 pm to 10 pm for food).

PLACES TO EAT

Baraka Café (☎ 617-868-3951, 80¹/₂ Pearl St), a tiny storefront, serves sublime North African/Mediterranean cuisine. The menu's English descriptions aren't particularly helpful; but be adventurous – you can't go wrong. The *bedenjal mechoui* ($4), an Algerian appetizer of smoked eggplant and roasted peppers, sounds like a typical Middle Eastern dish, but it's worlds apart in flavor and presentation. Open for lunch and dinner (entrees $9 to $16) Tuesday through Saturday, dinner on Sunday.

Mary Chung (☎ 617-864-1991, 464 Mass Ave), a neighborhood institution, is perhaps the most beloved Mandarin-Szechwan place in Cambridge. The wide-ranging menu features about 150 dishes (entrees range from $5 to $10). Open for lunch weekdays, dinner nightly.

At *India Pavilion* (☎ 617-547-7463, 17 Central Square), the dishes are so good and authentic that you'll forget about the simple and tiny dining area. Open for lunch ($4.50 to $6) and dinner ($9 to $12). A $6 lunch buffet, Friday through Sunday, is a bargain.

The *Tandoor House* (☎ 617-661-9001, 569 Mass Ave), with distinctive tandoori and a friendly waitstaff, is open for lunch and dinner. Expect to spend $6 for the lunch buffet and about $9 to $13 for entrees.

Davis Square (Map 13)

Budget Eat real diner food in a real railroad dining car at *Rosebud Diner* (☎ 617-666-6015, 381 Summer St). It's loads of fun since the food surpasses the gimmick. Open 8 am to 12:30 am.

Tiny *Bertucci's* (☎ 617-776-9241, 197 Elm St) is the original of Boston's ubiquitous brick-oven pizza and pasta restaurant.

Picante (☎ 617-628-6394, 217 Elm St) has serviceable Mexican dishes, plus savory home-style tamales (including vegetarian!). Open for lunch and dinner.

Mid-Range Although *Redbones* (☎ 617-628-2200, 55 Chester St) used to be a beloved neighborhood hole-in-the-wall, as Davis Square has become red-hot-hip, Greater Boston learned that Redbones is where you go to chow down on great ribs ($11), collard

greens ($3), corn bread (50¢) and sweet potato pie ($3). Open for lunch (offering a mere four menu choices) and dinner.

Mass Ave to Porter Square (Map 13)

Budget A casual neighborhood eatery popular with college students and locals, *Cambridge Common* (☎ 617-547-1228, 1667 Mass Ave) serves comfort food such as meatloaf, burgers and macaroni and cheese. Open 11:30 am to 1 am (but the kitchen closes at midnight).

Boca Grande (☎ 617-354-7400, 1728 Mass Ave) doesn't serve the best burritos, but for fresh fast food in this part of town, it'll do. Open 11 am to 10 pm.

Mid-Range The *Forest Café* (☎ 617-661-7810, 1682 Mass Ave) is an anomaly: The dark, divey bar with uncomfortable booths specializes in upscale authentic cuisine from Mexico's Yucatan region. Classic pork and seafood dishes dominate the menu, which stretches far beyond the usual nachos, tacos and burritos (entrees range from $9 to $15).

Peking duck is a favorite at *Changsho* (☎ 617-547-6565, 1712 Mass Ave), which serves upscale Chinese meals in an elegant dining room. Open for lunch and dinner.

Christopher's (☎ 617-876-9180, 1920 Mass Ave), known for burgers and microbrews from around the world, also has vegetarian and grain-based dishes. Open for dinner nightly and lunch on weekends.

Top End Chef Paul O'Connell's *Chez Henri* (☎ 617-354-8980, 1 Shepherd St) serves French food with a Cuban accent. The combined draw of delicious down-to-earth food and warm, romantic atmosphere wins raves for this off-the-beaten-track bistro. The bouillabaisse is wonderful, chock full of clams, mussels, lobster claws and monkfish in a fragrant fennel, tomato and saffron broth. The prix fixe three-course menu is a great deal ($30). Open for dinner nightly.

Huron Village (Map 13)

Budget The interior of *Emma's Pizza* (☎ 617-864-8534, 370 Huron Ave) has not changed in 30 years but the pizza sure has. The thin crust pies have innovative flavorful sauces made with fresh oregano, Tuscan rosemary or garlic-infused oil. The cheeses are cow, sheep, goat or dairy-free. Folks from across the river stock their freezers with Emma's. Dine at the counter or do take-out. Open 11:30 am to 8 pm Tuesday through Saturday, from 3 pm Sunday.

Full Moon (☎ 617-354-6699, 344 Huron Ave), with a limited beer and wine list, showcases locally grown produce and dairy products. Open for lunch and dinner.

Hi-Rise Bread Co (☎ 617-876-8766, 208 Concord Ave) packs great picnic sandwiches with its hearty grain breads. The cookies, brownies, scones and granola aren't bad either. Open 8 am to 8 pm weekdays, until 5 pm Saturday, until 3 pm Sunday.

COOLIDGE CORNER & BROOKLINE VILLAGE (MAP 14)

Take the quick T ride into Brookline for an eclectic assortment of cafés and restaurants just outside the Hub. Don't leave without sampling at least one of the kosher eateries that abound.

Coolidge Corner

Budget Loaves of triple chocolate, jalapeño corn and sourdough are baked at **Daily Bread** (☎ 617-277-8810, 1331 Beacon St). Calzones, cookies and spinach pies are also available for take-out. Open 7 am to 8 pm weekdays, until 7 pm Saturday.

Anna's Taqueria (☎ 617-739-7300, 1412 Beacon St) sets the standard to which other Beantown burrito bars aspire. Get in line at the no-frills, cafeteria-style counter and hope someone vacates a table. Open 10 am to 11 pm.

Rod dee (☎ 617-738-4977, 1430 Beacon St), a tiny storefront with a take-out counter and a couple of tables, serves fancy restaurant-quality Thai. If you're on a limited budget or don't have time to sit, this is your place. Open 11:30 am to 11:30 pm.

Greater Boston's original juice bar, **Jera's Juice Bar** (☎ 617-566-9700, 278 Harvard St) serves up your daily allotment of fruit or vegetables in a glass. Open 7 am to 11 pm.

Mid-Range At **Bombay Bistro** (☎ 617-734-2879, 1353 Beacon St), delicious Indian fare is served in an elegant, understated dining room. Though there is nothing terribly exotic on the menu, the friendly staff is happy to explain unfamiliar dishes. Open for lunch, Sunday buffet ($10) and dinner ($8 to $14).

Pandan Leaf (☎ 617-566-9393, 250 Harvard St) is named for an herb used in traditional Malaysian cuisine. With Chinese, Indian, Indonesian and Portuguese influences, Malaysian cooking is one of the original fusion cuisines. For an introduction, try the Portuguese grilled filet, a traditional dish of spiced cod wrapped in banana leaves and chargrilled ($16). Open for lunch and dinner.

Fugakyu (☎ 617-734-1268, 1280 Beacon St) aptly translates to 'house of elegance.' It's a departure for these otherwise homey neighborhood eateries. Sleek and upscale, Fugakyu offers a gorgeous array of the freshest sushi and sashimi, as well as traditional cooked meals, served by an efficient staff. The sushi bar features a water canal; make your order and then watch as the chef prepares it and sails it to you on a little boat (sushi meals cost $16 to $25). Open 11:30 am to 3 pm and 5 pm to 1:30 am.

Zaftigs Eatery (☎ 617-975-0075, 335 Harvard St), is a sit-down deli with hearty comfort food – blintzes ($5), noodle kugel ($3), kosher-style hot dogs ($7) and corned beef and cabbage ($11) – served in a welcoming atmosphere. Breakfast is 8 am to 10 pm.

Brookline Village

Budget A tiny self-service storefront, **Bottega Florentina** (☎ 617-738-5333, 41 Harvard St) offers home-cooked Italian meals to eat in or take out. Open 11 am to 9 pm daily except Sunday.

For a quick wholesome meal at **New England Soup Factory** (☎ 617-739-1899, 2–4 Brookline Place), try the delicious 'triple-strength chicken vegetable' soup; it may be curative. Request a taste before selecting from several hot and cold soups, all accompanied by crusty-chewy sourdough rolls. There are lots of lavish sandwiches, salads and sweets, too. Open 8 am to 9 pm weekdays, 11 am to 5 pm Saturday.

PLACES TO EAT

Mid-Range Scampi and puttanesca sauce are favorites at *Village Fish* (☎ 617-566-3474, 22 Harvard St), specializing in Italian-style, pan-prepared seafood dishes served with pasta. Open for lunch and dinner daily, except no lunch on Sunday.

Texas-sized portions of Texas-style barbecue rule at the *Village Smokehouse* (☎ 617-566-3782, 1 Harvard St). True fans order 'Texas Hawg': beef ribs, brisket, chicken, sausage, and pork baby back ribs ($16). Meals come with corn bread and beans.

Open for lunch and dinner daily, except no lunch on Monday.

Café St Petersburg (☎ 617-277-7100, 236 Washington St) serves authentic Russian food in a charming old-world atmosphere, complete with crystal chandeliers. Caviar is featured, but there's also borscht, steamed sturgeon with potato pancakes and sour cherry blintzes. Top off your evening Russian-style – with a frosty fruit-flavored vodka. Open for lunch and dinner daily, except no dinner on Monday.

Entertainment

Fueled by the vital university scene, the breadth and depth of cultural offerings are impressive. For up-to-the-minute listings of events, entertainment and nightlife, check out the Calendar section of Thursday's *Boston Globe*, Friday's *Boston Herald*, the weekly *Boston Phoenix* or the irreverent magazines *Improper Bostonian* and *Stuff at Night* (free in sidewalk street boxes).

Note: The drinking age for alcoholic beverages is 21, and in most cases you must be 21 to enter a drinking establishment. Some clubs offer '19-plus' nights; check the papers for details. Bars usually close at 1 am, clubs at 2 am. The last Red Line trains pass through Park St station at about 12:30 am, but other lines vary; a good rule is to be at

LEE FOSTER

Quincy Market balancing act

the nearest T station at about midnight. Otherwise, budget for a cab. At press time, the MBTA was considering extending weekend service until 2:30 am; call the MBTA (☎ 617-222-3200).

CAFÉS
Beacon Hill (Map 2)
Across from the State House and popular with Suffolk University students, *Curious Liquids Café* (☎ 617-720-2836, 22B Beacon St) is a two-story, bohemian, London-style coffeehouse. Brightly hued walls and well-worn, mismatched comfy chairs make for a relaxing place to hang out with a good book and a warm cup of something. Since it's self-serve, you won't be rushed. Open 'til 2 am.

North End & Charlestown (Map 5)
Of all the North End cafés, *Caffè Vittoria* (☎ 617-227-7606, 296 Hanover St) has the most old-world charm and serves the best cappuccino. A few of the Italian-speaking patrons have been coming here since it opened in the 1930s. To get the full effect, wait for a table in the original dining room.

Caffè dello Sport (☎ 617-523-5063, 308 Hanover St), nearby, is the primo place for televised sporting events, especially soccer. If you're in Boston during the World Cup, there's no other place.

South End (Map 9)
Kettle Café (☎ 617-236-0777, 288 Columbus St) is a sweet, unassuming place to get a scone and a cup of coffee or tea.

For a generous dishing of camp with coffee on the side, try *Mildred's* (☎ 617-426-0008, 552 Tremont St). Stick to the coffee, pastries and free 'show.'

Francesca's (☎ 617-482-9026, 564 Tremont St) is a lively storefront coffee bar with tables as well as a counter and stools.

Cambridge
Harvard Square's only true sidewalk café, *Au Bon Pain* (Map 11; ☎ 617-497-9797, 1316

Mass Ave) transcends its popular image as a Frenchified fast-food take-out counter. Students, tourists and locals gather here to read, people-watch and chat. An informal, never-ending tournament takes place at the outdoor chess tables.

Café Pamplona *(Map 11; no phone, 12 Bow St)*, located in a cozy unadorned cellar near Harvard Square, is the choice of highbrow intellectuals and those who still enjoy face-to-face conversations and relish the feel of books, pencils and paper. In addition to espresso, they have light snacks such as gazpacho, sandwiches and biscotti. The tiny outdoor terrace is delightful in summer.

The tiny storefront **Loulou's Tealuxe** *(Map 11; ☎ 617-441-0077, Zero Brattle St)*, in Harvard Square, is for lovers of steeped leaves. There are only a few tables, but if you're lucky, you can perch by the window while you sip extra-bergamot Earl Grey and nibble apple coffee cake. Open 8 am to 11 pm or midnight. Look for a new location at the corner of Newbury and Clarendon Sts.

The cozy **Beantowne Coffee House** *(Map 12; ☎ 617-876-4500, 1 Broadway)*, in Kendall Square, is a comfortable place to hang with a cup of joe.

The **1369 Coffee House**, in Central Square *(Map 12; ☎ 617-576-4600, 757 Mass Ave)*, and in Inman Square *(Map 12; ☎ 617-576-1369, 1369 Cambridge St)*, is a bohemian place with folk music, serious coffee, a laudable selection of tea, a limited snack list and a friendly waitstaff who won't rush you.

Furnished with well-worn thrift-shop couches, **Someday Café** *(Map 13; ☎ 617-623-3323, 51 Davis Square)* is a slacker joint with boisterous music and board games, espresso and pastries.

Fuel is leaded and unleaded at **Diesel Café** *(Map 13; ☎ 617-629-8717, 257 Elm St)*, in Davis Square. Smoothies, lots of vegetarian snacks and Toscanini's ice cream are also served in this friendly, vibrant café. There are two pool tables in the back as well as plenty of tables, booths and comfy chairs.

Hollywood Espresso *(Map 13; ☎ 617-497-7766, 1736 Mass Ave)*, between Harvard and Porter Squares and adjacent to Hollywood Video, is surely a tribute to Marcello Mastroianni. Classic Hollywood and foreign

Subway & Street Performers

Boston's streets and T stations have long been a proving ground for talented and enterprising musicians in search of an audience, while aspiring to club gigs and recording contracts. Tracy Chapman, who played in Harvard Square while a Tufts student in the '80s, is the most famous graduate.

Boston's sizable contingent of street performers is active year-round. Most migrate below ground from November to April rather than risk frostbitten fingers and crowds that can't stand still long enough to listen, let alone toss a cold coin. Some choice subway stops to catch solo acoustic performers include: the Red Line (inbound and outbound platforms) at **Park St** (Map 2); the Blue Line platform at **Government Center** (Map 3); the Blue Line (outbound platform) at **State** (Map 4), though the train makes an excruciating, high-pitched squeal as it enters and exits the station; the Red and Orange Lines (inbound and outbound platforms) at **Downtown Crossing** (Map 4); the Red Line (outbound platform) at **South Station** (Map 6); and the Red Line (inbound platform) at **Harvard** (Map 11).

When it's warm enough for rhododendrons to bloom, performers venture forth from the tunnels. Favorite locations to find magicians, clowns and dancers, as well as musical ensembles, concert violinists and folk and rock jammers, include: **Faneuil Hall** (Map 3); the pedestrian mall at **Downtown Crossing** (Map 4), which also has fire-and-brimstone orators and antifur protesters; and the intersection of Brattle and Mt Auburn Sts near **Harvard Square** (Map 11).

videos are shown on a VCR throughout the day. The small café offers light meals, fabulous chocolate cake, every imaginable coffee drink and hand-mixed Italian sodas.

In Coolidge Corner, **Peet's Coffee & Tea** (*Map 14;* ☎ *617-734-4725, 285 Harvard St*) is the first East Coast outpost of the beloved San Francisco Bay Area java emporium. The bright spacious café is just the place to read the paper or chat over a rich dark brew.

BARS & TAVERNS
Beacon Hill (Map 2)
The **Sevens Ale House** (☎ *617-523-9074, 77 Charles St*) is a popular and friendly neighborhood pub crowded from 11:30 am or noon to 1 or 2 am. Sit at the bar or in a booth and order a sandwich and beer ($8).

The **Bull & Finch Pub** (☎ *617-227-9605, 84 Beacon St*) is an authentic English pub (it was dismantled in England, shipped to Boston and reassembled inside this Beacon Hill townhouse, the Hampshire House), but that's not why hundreds of tourists descend on the place daily. The pub served as the inspiration for the TV sitcom *Cheers*. If there ever was a reason to go here, it's long gone.

A favorite of Boston politicos, the **Red Hat** (☎ *617-523-2175, 9 Bowdoin St*) feels more like *Cheers* than its above-mentioned kin.

Government Center & Faneuil Hall (Map 3)
Below the bustling marketplace, the **Oyster Bar at Durgin Park** (☎ *617-227-2038, North Market, Faneuil Hall Marketplace*) remains something of a secret. If you want a few oysters or some clam chowder to go with your beer, venture down the narrow stairway and take a seat.

Always hopping, the **Rack Billiard Club** (☎ *617-725-1051, 20 Clinton St*), on the edge of Faneuil Hall Marketplace, is an upscale pool hall, bar and outdoor café serving above-average pub grub and live music. The young professionals who frequent the place are generally still attired in their business duds. For everyone else, the dress code is strictly enforced. The 22 pool tables cost $12 for a full hour after 4 pm, half-price prior to 4 pm.

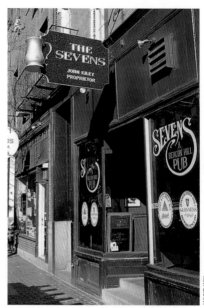

KIM GRANT

Sevens Ale House

Marketplace Café (☎ *617-227-9660, North Market, Faneuil Hall Marketplace*) has an eclectic lineup of live music, from jazzy blues to blue blues to pop. It's free to listen, but you must buy a drink.

The **Black Rose** (☎ *617-742-2286, 160 State St*), on the edge of Faneuil Hall Marketplace, is an Irish-American pub with a boisterous atmosphere, live Irish music and well-poured pints.

The **Irish Embassy** (☎ *617-742-6618, 234 Friend St*), a good place to meet fellow travelers since there is a youth hostel upstairs, is often so loud that you won't be able to hear your new friends' names. There is a $3 to $5 cover Wednesday through Friday, when live bands play rock and roll covers.

Downtown & Financial District (Map 4)
The **Littlest Bar** (☎ *617-523-9766, 47 Province St*) really is. No kidding. There's room at the bar for the bartender, you and maybe three kindred spirits.

ENTERTAINMENT

KIM GRANT

Make friends fast at the Littlest Bar.

North End & Charlestown (Map 5)
The circa 1780 **Warren Tavern** (☎ 617-241-8142, 2 Pleasant St), in Charlestown, is an atmospheric place for a drink.

Back Bay (Map 8)
Cottonwood Café (☎ 617-247-2225, 222 Berkeley St) serves the best margaritas in Boston. They're also in Cambridge, in the Porter Exchange (Map 13; ☎ 617-661-7440, 1815 Mass Ave).

South End (Map 9)
The bar at **Club Café** (☎ 617-536-0966, 209 Columbus Ave) is a convivial gathering place for gay men and lesbians. Straight folks are always welcome, too.

Clery's Bar & Restaurant (☎ 617-262-9874, 113 Dartmouth St) is a nice neighborhood place, though it gets pretty rowdy on weekends. Simple pub grub is served at lunch and dinner.

Kenmore Square & Fenway (Map 10)
Although the three-story **Jillian's Billiard Club** (☎ 617-437-0300, 145 Ipswich St) has 55 billiards tables, people also come to play darts, blackjack, snooker, table tennis and virtual reality games. There are five bars and a full-service menu in this enormous place. Jillian's also sports a dance club.

With a funky industrial atmosphere once aptly described as the 'Jetsons meet the Copacabana,' **Atlas Bar & Grille** (☎ 617-437-0300, 145 Ipswich St) is a fun place to congregate for a beer – before or after serious club-hopping. From Thursday to Saturday, a DJ spins recent Top-40 tunes.

Jake Ivory's (☎ 617-247-1222, 1 Lansdowne St) features dueling rock and roll pianos and, believe it or not, sing-alongs. Open Thursday through Sunday.

With its sleek chrome bar and upholstered seats, **Modern** (☎ 617-536-2100, 36 Lansdowne St) is a sophisticated addition to the Lansdowne St scene. Order a martini and take your place among the glamorous.

At the other end of the spectrum, **Linwood Grill** (☎ 617-247-8099, 81 Kilmarnock St) is a Fenway mainstay – a true neighborhood place to have a beer (make that a Bud!), chow on some barbecue, play darts, pool and pinball and talk sports. They have live music a few nights a week.

Cambridge
For a relaxing beer and game of billiards, **Flat Top Johnny's** (Map 12; ☎ 617-494-9565, 1 Kendall Square) is a good choice. Situated within Cambridge's high-tech mecca, the place is clean and attracts MIT students and young computer professionals.

Welcoming and well adorned with original Celtic artwork, the **Druid** (Map 12; ☎ 617-497-0965, 1357 Cambridge St), in Inman Square, pours a proper pint of Murphy's and boasts no TV. The traditional Sunday Irish jams ('seisiuns') draw a loyal crowd at 5:30 pm.

Plough & Stars (Map 12; ☎ 617-441-3455, 912 Mass Ave), between Central and Harvard Squares, is a friendly Irish bar with the requisite Guinness and Bass on tap, as well as televised English football matches weekends September through May. Rock and rockabilly bands play most weekends for a $3 cover.

In Central Square, the **Phoenix Landing** (Map 12; ☎ 617-576-6260, 512 Mass Ave) is a social Irish pub with space for talkers in front and dancers in back.

The funky pulse of Central Square is still discernible at the **Field** (Map 12; ☎ 617-354-7345, 20 Prospect St), an unpretentious neighborhood bar.

ENTERTAINMENT

With windows that open onto the street, **Temple Bar** *(Map 13;* ☎ *617-547-5055, 1688 Mass Ave)*, between Harvard and Porter Squares, is reminiscent of the Temple Bar area in Dublin's SoHo.

A trendy bar-cum-restaurant in Davis Square, **Joshua Tree** *(Map 13;* ☎ *617-623-9910, 256 Elm St)* has a giant-screen TV for sports action, 32 beers on tap and DJ and live music Thursday through Sunday night. There's a $3 cover for live music.

The **Burren** *(Map 13;* ☎ *617-776-6896, 247 Elm St)*, in Davis Square, a popular and amiable place oozing Irish atmosphere, features traditional Irish music nightly in the front room and various bands (and an open-mic night) in the back. Try to catch the Tar-box Ramblers, a local country and blues band, on Saturday night.

Specializing in rare brews from Belgium to Boston, **Under Bones** *(Map 13;* ☎ *617-628-2200, 55 Chester St)*, in Davis Square, is the amiable basement bar of the Redbones barbecue joint.

Outlying Neighborhoods

South Boston's convivial **Woody's L St Tavern** *(*☎ *617-268-4335, 658A E 8th St)* is the neighborhood hangout featured in the film *Good Will Hunting*.

Matt Murphy's Pub *(Map 14;* ☎ *617-232-0188, 14 Harvard St)*, a traditional Irish pub in Brookline Village, offers not only a warm and welcoming atmosphere, but also great food. There's always live Irish music Thursday and Saturday, ring ahead for Friday.

BREWERY TOURS

Atlantic Coast Brewing Co *(Map 5;* ☎ *617-242-6464, 50 Terminal St, Charlestown)* produces Tremont Ale and offers tours at 4 pm Friday and Saturday.

Mass Bay Brewing Co *(Map 6;* ☎ *617-574-9551, 306 Northern Ave)* also called the Harpoon Brewery, is the largest facility in the state. Free hourlong tours and tastings of their popular Harpoon Ale and India Pale Ale are offered at 1 pm Friday and Saturday.

Boston Beer Co *(*☎ *617-368-5000, 30 Germania St, Jamaica Plain)*, also known as the Samuel Adams brewery and Boston Beer Museum, produces the only local brew that's achieved international fame. Hourlong tours and tastings are at 2 pm Thursday and Friday; noon, 1 and 2 pm on Saturday (in July and August, there's one at 2 pm Wednesday, too). Take the T Orange Line to Stony Brook, and then follow signs for two blocks.

LIVE MUSIC

The **Fleet Boston Pavilion** *(Map 6;* ☎ *617-931-2000, 228-6000, 290 Northern Ave)*, a white sail-like summertime tent with sweeping harbor views, has 5000 seats, unobstructed stage views and decent acoustics. Programming includes nationally known pop, rock and jazz performers, from Aretha Franklin to Barry Manilow to BB King. Shuttle buses run from South Station before and after shows.

Rock

Plenty of nationally known alternative and rock bands got their start in Boston-area clubs; in fact, there are more than 5000 bands registered here.

For more than 25 years, **TT the Bear's** *(Map 12;* ☎ *617-492-0082, 10 Brookline St)*, in Central Square, has been an intimate die-hard rock joint.

The **Middle East** *(Map 12;* ☎ *617-354-8238, 472 Mass Ave)*, in Central Square, usually has three different gigs (from belly dancing to rockabilly to ska) going simultaneously. Cover for local bands is about $7; national acts are a few bucks more. There's always a free jazz show in the 'corner.' The Middle East also serves pretty good (and well-priced) food until midnight or 1 am.

The intimate, basement-level **Lizard Lounge** *(Map 13;* ☎ *617-547-0759, 1667 Mass Ave)*, between Harvard and Porter Squares, features live original music nightly. Casual dress is cool and the cover charge varies.

At the tiny, ultra-casual **Toad** *(Map 13;* ☎ *617-497-4950, 1920 Mass Ave)*, in Porter Square, local bands perform funk, R&B, rock and soul nightly. Amazingly, there's no cover.

One of the city's best and most eclectic venues, **Johnny D's Uptown** *(Map 13;* ☎ *617-776-2004, 17 Holland St)*, in Davis Square,

ENTERTAINMENT

features a different musical style nightly, from blues and Cajun to international and swing. Cover charges vary from $2 to $20. Sunday night blues jams and salsa and Monday night swing are popular; Sunday jazz brunches are mellow.

The *Paradise* (☎ *617-562-8800, 967–969 Comm Ave)*, a small club known for booking groups from all walks of the musical spectrum, has shows throughout the week. Tickets are $8 to $15 depending on the act. From 11:30 pm to 2 am Wednesday, Friday and Saturday, the club becomes M-80 as the dance floor pulses with Euro and Latin house music. Dress to impress. Ride the T Green Line, 'B' branch to Pleasant St, the sixth stop after Kenmore Square.

Jazz

Gritty, smoky and storied, *Wally's Café (Map 9; ☎ 617-424-1408, 427 Mass Ave)* is the last survivor of the jazz clubs that once enlivened this neighborhood. Monday is blues; Tuesday and Wednesday are jazz/funk fusion; Thursday is Latin jazz; Friday and Saturday are traditional; and Sunday sees afternoon jam sessions and evening jazz/funk. There is music 365 days a year, and while there's no cover, there is a one-drink minimum.

The *Berklee Performance Center (Map 10; ☎ 617-266-7455, 747-2261 box office, 136 Mass Ave)* hosts jazz concerts by Berklee College of Music's renowned faculty members and exceptional students for a mere $4 during the school year. The center also hosts big-name performers at big-buck prices.

The *Regattabar (Map 11; ☎ 617-661-5000, 876-7777 tickets, 1 Bennett St)*, on the 3rd floor of the Charles Hotel in Harvard Square, is an upscale yacht-club-sort-of-place that books internationally known groups Tuesday through Saturday. A limited number of general seating tickets go on sale one hour before show time. Ticket prices depend on the fame quotient ($10 to $26).

Ryles (Map 12; ☎ 617-876-9330, 212 Hampshire St), in Inman Square, boasts two floors of local and national recording acts in an intimate dining setting. You'll hear jazz, world music, R&B and blues. Swing lessons

KIM GRANT

The Regattabar brings in top-notch jazz.

are offered on Saturday night ($12). Open from 8 pm nightly except Monday (tickets are between $10 and $25) and for a Sunday jazz brunch (when the music is free).

Scullers Jazz Club (☎ 617-783-0811, 931-2000 tickets, 400 Soldier's Field Rd), in the Doubletree Guest Suites Hotel, is another big-name jazz club, but this one is cozier. There are shows Tuesday through Saturday. Tickets range from $9 to $24, but you can sometimes stay for both sets. You'll have better luck getting tickets to weekday shows.

Blues

The *House of Blues (Map 11; ☎ 617-491-2583, 497-2229 for tickets, 96 Winthrop St)*, in Harvard Square, was opened by 'Blues Brother' Dan Aykroyd in 1992 and has since become a major force on the national blues scene. The music begins at 9 or 10 pm; tickets cost $6 to $25. There's no cover 12:30 to 2:30 pm Friday and 2 to 4 pm Saturday. The all-you-can-eat-and-listen-to Sunday gospel brunch ($26, or $15 for just the food) is a

Dan Aykroyd's House of Blues

The **Nameless Coffeehouse** *(Map 11; ☎ 617-864-1630, 3 Church St)*, in Harvard Square within the First Parish Church (Unitarian Universalist), is a low-key place, run by volunteers, that sponsors acoustic singer-songwriters on most Saturday nights. The suggested donation is $3 to $4. Closed in the summer.

The **Somerville Theatre** *(Map 13; ☎ 617-625-5700, 55 Davis Square)*, a refurbished classic venue, stages concerts.

DANCE CLUBS

The thriving club scene, which has gone upscale in recent years, is fueled by a thriving economy and a constant infusion of thousands of students. Clubs are fairly stable, although the nightly lineup often changes. Check the *Boston Phoenix* or *Improper Bostonian* for up-to-the-minute information. The clubs along Lansdowne St and in Fenway (near Kenmore Square) cater to an international university crowd. Those in the Theater District are favored by young professionals; Man Ray, in Cambridge, defies generalization.

Most clubs reward those who arrive before 11 pm with no waiting in line or lower cover charges. The downside: Early birds may be dancing by themselves. Cover charges vary widely, from free (if you arrive early) to $15, but the average is more like $10 on weekends. Many clubs have dress codes. While you may be admitted in wearing jeans – as long as they're not frayed nor accompanied by a t-shirt, sneakers and a baseball cap – most clubbers are decked-out in their version of their finest. You may feel out of place unless you, too, are wearing something that suggests you've got enough dough to pay your bar tab.

downright religious experience for some. Reservations are required.

Grungy, dark and laid-back, in keeping with the longtime tradition of pre-rehab Central Square, the **Cantab Lounge** *(Map 12; ☎ 617-354-2685, 738 Mass Ave)* remains a well-established bluegrass, blues and oldies venue where students hang with locals and listen to live music nightly.

Folk

Although clubs occasionally book folk acts, two Cambridge places are devoted to folkies.

The venerable **Club Passim** *(Map 11; ☎ 617-492-7679, 47 Palmer St)*, in Harvard Square, is nationally known for supporting the early careers of singer-songwriters Jackson Browne, Tracy Chapman, Nanci Griffith and Patty Larkin. The small club has only 125 seats. Call ahead for the nightly program and show time. Tuesday is open-mic night. Tickets are about $5 to $15. Passim also serves all three meals daily in an alcohol-and smoke-free environment.

Theater District & Chinatown (Map 7)

The decor at the **Big Easy** *(☎ 617-351-7000, 1 Boylston Place)* offers a New Orleans Mardi Gras-style playground. In addition to eclectic cover bands Thursday through Saturday, a DJ spins Latin and international on Tuesday. You can watch from the 2nd-floor balcony if you prefer. 'Proper dress' is

ENTERTAINMENT

Gay & Lesbian Venues

Many straight clubs feature gay and lesbian nights. Since schedules and venues change often, check *Bay Windows* or *In* or talk to the folks at Glad Day Gay Liberation Bookshop (see 'Bookstores' in the Shopping chapter).

Chaps (Map 7; ☎ 617-695-9500, 100 Warrenton St), one of the most popular bars and dance clubs, has something for everyone. Monday it's a quiet piano bar (complimentary pizza is served); Tuesday there's retro disco with a DJ; Wednesday features Latin house music; Thursday starts out quiet as a piano bar then picks up the pace with a rap, hip-hop and new wave mix; Friday is techno and house; Saturday begins quiet and ends with serious dance music; and Sunday tea dances start at 7 pm. Male go-go dancers light up Friday through Sunday.

Drag queen cabaret is the attraction at **Jacques** (Map 7; ☎ 617-426-8902, 79 Broadway St), behind the Radisson Hotel on Stuart St. Shows nightly; cover $4 to $6. **Luxor** (Map 7; ☎ 617-423-6969, 69 Church St) is a more casual men's bar.

A mixed crowd gathers at the bar and restaurant at **Club Café** (Map 9; ☎ 617-536-0966, 209 Columbus Ave). Thursday is girls' night, in the front anyway. Sunday brunch is always packed.

Fritz (Map 9; ☎ 617-482-4428, 26 Chandler St), in the Chandler Inn, is a casual watering hole with a nice atmosphere; it's mostly men, but women certainly aren't turned away.

Dollhouse Theatre (Map 9; ☎ 617-266-8511, 731 Harrison Ave), in the Bates Resource Center, features over-the-top drag theater. The productions, whether 'Medea' or a musical version of 'Charlie's Angels,' are campy, riotous fun. If you can't afford a ticket (around $20) but have 35¢, call their phone line for a delicious hint of the naughty camp you'll be missing. It's enough to make you dig deeper for a few extra bucks.

Avalon (☎ 617-262-2424, 15 Lansdowne St) has blistering house music on Sunday.

Monday is anything but 'Static,' as it's called, when the transgendered community, gays and drag queens converge for **Axis** (☎ 617-262-2437, 13 Lansdowne St). Just about anything goes.

Ramrod (Map 10; ☎ 617-266-2986, 1254 Boylston St) is a traditional leather bar, while downstairs at **Machine** (☎ 617-536-1950), it's a hot, high-tech dance club.

Saturday 'taboo night' is officially for the girls at **Lava Bar** *(Map 10; ☎ 617-267-7707, 575 Comm Ave)*, atop the Howard Johnson Kenmore Square, but it's really quite a mixed (gay, straight, boys, girls) crowd.

Thursday is reserved for the boys at **Man Ray** (Map 12; ☎ 617-864-0400, 21 Brookline St) in Central Square.

required; the crowd is a bit older here. Closed Sunday, Monday and Wednesday.

The aptly named ***Envy*** *(☎ 617-542-3689, 25 Boylston Place)* is the place to see and be seen. Just make sure you get the theme and note the VIP room, to which you will no doubt fail to be invited. A DJ spins Top-40, dance and house music on Friday and Saturday night.

The ***Roxy*** *(☎ 617-338-7699, 279 Tremont St)*, a restored ballroom in the Tremont House, plays Latin on Thursday, Top-40 club classics from the '80s on Friday and techno on Saturday. No jeans, sneakers or t-shirts.

To signal your status as an insider at the super-chic ***Venu*** *(☎ 617-338-8061, 100 Warrenton St)*, pull out your best Armani knock-off and arrive fashionably late (doors don't open until 11:30 pm) for DJ-spun tunes. Men are required to wear jackets on Friday; cover charge is $10 to $15; closed Monday and Wednesday.

The ***Juke Box*** *(☎ 617-542-4077, 275 Tremont St)*, beneath the Tremont House, plays classic rock and roll (from the '50s to the '90s) on one side and disco on the other on Friday and Saturday. Thursday is international; Sunday is Latin.

The plush, Parisian-themed **Aria** (☎ 338-7080, 246 Tremont St), in the basement of the Wilbur Theater, attracts a fashionable crowd and plays the latest house and Top-40 dance tunes Wednesday through Sunday. Reservations and 'proper dress' required.

Kenmore Square & Fenway (Map 10)

Boston's premier dance club, **Avalon** (☎ 617-262-2424, 15 Lansdowne St), received a multimillion-dollar overhaul in 1999 and now sports four lounges, a balcony and up-graded sound, lighting and air-conditioning systems. Some of the world's best DJs fly in to spin international house music on Thursday and Friday. Progressive bands rule early in the evening on Saturday, then a DJ steps back in for dance music.

Next-door, **Axis** (☎ 617-262-2437, 13 Lansdowne St) has two dance floors; Thursday through Saturday, the place has a predominantly punk, subterranean feel with house music.

More formal, **Karma** (☎ 617-421-9595, 9 Lansdowne St) is decorated with Indian tapestries and Tibetan and Nepalese wooden carvings. What would Krishna think of the hip-hop and house beat? Wednesday is gay; Thursday is jazz; Friday and Saturday feature international music. Open Wednesday through Saturday.

The smaller **Bill's Bar** (☎ 617-421-9678, 5½ Lansdowne St) is open nightly and packed with BU students. A house DJ spins alternative music nightly; sometimes Bill's has bands, too. Covers are usually around $7 or $8.

Popular with the Euro glamour set, **Sophia's** (☎ 617-351-7001, 1270 Boylston St), a Latin jazz club, has hardwood floors, exposed brick and a rooftop terrace. In the winter, a tent keeps the roof hot (as if the music didn't). Closed Monday.

The **Lava Bar** (☎ 617-267-7707, 575 Comm Ave), atop the Howard Johnson Kenmore Square, has a lively mixed crowd and a stunning view of the Boston skyline from its floor-to-ceiling windows, which lends the illusion that you have some breathing room. Open Thursday through

Saturday; they usually play soulful house music.

Cambridge (Map 12)

Man Ray (Map 12; ☎ 617-864-0400, 21 Brookline St), in Central Square, is the area's most 'underground' club. Man Ray encourages creative attire; you won't find the Gucci crowd here. Fetish-wear is suggested on Friday; when in doubt wear black rather than flannel. Every night, though, is for exhibitionists; dress to impress, express or distress. Man Ray is open Wednesday through Saturday, with a varied lineup of industrial rock, high-energy dance tunes or campy, classic disco trash and '80s new wave.

CINEMA

Art and foreign film culture is alive and well in Boston and Cambridge. For film buffs, the **Harvard Film Archive & Film Study Library** (Map 11; ☎ 617-495-4700, 24 Quincy St) is reason enough to come to Boston. It screens at least two films per day at the Carpenter Center for the Visual Arts in Harvard Square, and directors and actors are frequently on hand to talk about their work. Tickets are usually a buck less than in a cineplex.

Art Houses

The **Wang Center** (Map 7; ☎ 617-482-9393, 270 Tremont St) occasionally shows vintage films that take full advantage of its massive screen.

The **Brattle St Theatre** (Map 11; ☎ 617-876-6837, 40 Brattle St), in Harvard Square, is a film lover's 'cinema paradiso.' Film noir, independent films and series that celebrate directors or periods are shown regularly in this no-frills 1890 repertory theater. You can often catch a classic double feature for $6. (Toscanini's outstanding ice cream is sold at the concession stand.)

The classiest movie venue in town, the **Kendall Square Cinema** (Map 12; ☎ 617-494-9800, 1 Kendall Square) has nine good-sized screens, comfy seats, neo-Art Deco decor and an espresso machine that can churn out a cup of java every 10 seconds.

Free Outdoor Fun

Shakespeare on the Common (Map 2; ☎ 617-423-7600), at the Parkman Bandstand on Boston Common, is fast becoming a summer tradition. Because of meager funding, they're able to produce only one play for two weeks in early August. Catch 'em if you can.

The summer concert series at **City Hall Plaza** (Map 3; ☎ 617-635-4505) has been going strong for 25 years. At 7:30 pm Wednesday from June through August, the program features oldies and big bands, as well as local musicians and ethnic dance troupes. This is where you'll find the mayor as well as hundreds of seniors, who come from all over Greater Boston to kick up their heels.

During the summer, the city sponsors free concerts at **Copley Square** (Map 8; ☎ 617-635-4505). At lunch on Thursday in June and September, it's classical and at 5:30 pm on Thursday in July and August, it's mellow jazz.

The **Hatch Memorial Shell** (Map 2; ☎ 617-727-9547), on the Charles River Esplanade, hosts rock, jazz and classical performances from late June to mid-September. Check the newspaper for midweek evening shows and midday weekend shows. There are public restrooms and an inexpensive snack bar here. 'Free Friday Flicks' are shown at dusk in July and August. You'll be sitting on the lawn, so bring a blanket and picnic. Most movies are family-oriented.

The **Boston Park Rangers** (see Organized Tours in Getting Around) offer hordes of informative walking tours all year long.

The **Somerville Theatre** (Map 13; ☎ 617-625-5700, 55 Davis Square), another refurbished classic venue, offers second-run films.

The **Coolidge Corner Theatre** (Map 14; ☎ 617-734-2500, 290 Harvard St), in Brookline, is the area's only not-for-profit movie house. Documentaries, foreign films and first-run movies are shown on two screens (one of which is enormous) in this grand Art Deco theater.

International Cinema

The **French Library in Boston** (Map 8; ☎ 617-266-4351, 53 Marlborough St) shows classic and contemporary French films at 8 pm Thursday and Friday. Also see Cultural Centers in Facts for the Visitor.

The **Boston Public Library** (Map 8; ☎ 617-536-5400, 666 Boylston St) screens film festival-quality flicks on Monday night – for free!

The **Museum of Fine Arts, Boston** (Map 10; ☎ 617-369-3306 information, ☎ 617-369-3770 tickets, 465 Huntington Ave), at the West Wing entrance, screens a wide variety of films – silent, avant-garde and local – in the Remis Auditorium.

Cineplexes

With tiny screens, the **Loews Cinema** (Map 8; ☎ 617-266-1300, 100 Huntington Ave), within Copley Place, is recommended only because of its location.

Sony/Loews Cinema Harvard Square (Map 11; ☎ 627-864-4580, 10 Church St) screens first-run Hollywood and some independent and foreign films. Costumes and audience participation are encouraged at the cult classic, *Rocky Horror Picture Show*, shown at midnight Saturday.

IMAX

If you've never encountered IMAX, now's the time. At the Museum of Science, **Mugar Omni Theater** (Map 12; ☎ 617-723-2500, www.mos.org) takes film to another level. Adventure documentaries such as *Sharks!*, *Volcano* and *Everest* are shot with technology designed to make you feel smack in the middle of the action. It's so realistic that it causes motion sickness and scares the wits out of young children. Call for show times and advance ticket purchase. Also see East Cambridge in Things to See & Do.

THEATER
University Companies

Boston University's highly regarded **Huntington Theatre Co** *(Map 10; ☎ 617-266-0800, 264 Huntington Ave)* performs modern and classical plays in the Greek Revival Boston University theater. Rear balcony seats usually are available for $10; tickets go up to $52. Half-price student 'rush' tickets are available two hours prior to curtain for Tuesday through Friday performances.

The prestigious **American Repertory Theater** *(Map 11; ☎ 617-547-8300, 64 Brattle St)*, referred to as the 'A-R-T,' stages new plays and experimental interpretations of classics in Harvard University's Loeb Drama Center. There isn't a bad seat in the small theater; tickets cost $24 to $57. There's another way to get in, too: Every Monday morning the theater sets aside 50 tickets for the following Saturday's (less expensive) matinee. You literally 'pay what you can.' Student 'rush' tickets are sold 30 minutes prior to curtain for $12.

The **Hasty Pudding Theatricals** *(Map 11; ☎ 617-495-5205, 12 Holyoke St)*, in Harvard Square, is home to the Harvard undergraduate dramatic society, founded in 1795 (see 'Hasty Pudding Awards' in America's Walking City).

Smaller Companies

This artist-run center for experimental work, **Mobius** *(Map 6; ☎ 617-542-7416, 354 Congress St)*, on the 5th floor, presents dance, music, film and other art-in-progress almost every weekend. You might catch something like this: A performance artist crawling around the studio on her hands and knees for three days (on and off) picking up grains of rice and placing them into tiny pinch pots. As one bowl fills up she moves to fill another. Could this say something about the way we conduct our lives, she silently posits? Tickets are sometimes free, but usually about $5 to $12.

The two-stage **Charles Playhouse** *(Map 7; 74 Warrenton St)* has presented *Shear Madness* (☎ 617-426-5225), a comical whodunit murder mystery with audience participation, nightly since 1980. It holds the

Buying Tickets

A good place to start if you're not sure what you want to see, **Bostix** (Map 3; ☎ 617-723-5181), south of Faneuil Hall Marketplace, sells half-price tickets to select same-day performances beginning at 11 am; cash only. (You can buy full-price advance tickets here, too.) Another kiosk is located in Copley Square (Map 8; ☎ 617-723-5181). Both are open 10 am to 6 pm Tuesday through Saturday, 11 am to 4 pm on Sunday; the Copley Square kiosk is also open Monday.

Hub Ticket Agency (Map 7; ☎ 617-426-8340) is located in a trailer at the corner of Tremont and Stuart Sts.

Ticketmaster has a cash-only counter at Tower Records (Map 8; ☎ 617-247-5900), 360 Newbury St, in Back Bay.

The **Harvard Box Office** (Map 11; ☎ 617-496-2222, 1350 Mass Ave), in the Holyoke Center Arcade in Harvard Square, sells tickets to Harvard University events and venues.

Out-of-Town Ticket Agency (☎ 617-247-1300, 800-442-1854) has impatient operators, so before dialing, know what you want or suffer.

Copley Square discount ticket booth

record for the world's 'longest-running non-musical play.' The performance, thick with local and insider references, is never the same two nights in a row; that's part of what keeps audiences coming back. Tickets cost $34. *Blue Man Group* (☎ 617-426-6912) occupies the other stage with a mixed-media performance art piece that pokes fun at the arts community. Music and percussion are heavily relied upon, as is the tactic of plucking members from the audience. Tickets are $39 and $49 Wednesday through Sunday.

The long-running *Joey & Maria's Comedy Wedding* at the *Tremont House (Map 7; ☎ 800-733-5639, 275 Tremont St)* spoofs Italian-American nuptials on Friday ($39) and Saturday ($45) at 7:30 pm. The price includes a five-course Italian buffet.

Venues

Theater District & Chinatown (Map 7)

Opulent and enormous, the *Wang Center (☎ 617-482-9393, 270 Tremont St)* hosts the Boston Ballet, extravagant music, dance events and occasional movies. Many seats are so high and far from the stage that they cause nosebleeds. The *Shubert Theatre (☎ 617-482-9393)* hosts the Boston Lyric Opera and smaller ballet productions. The *Colonial Theatre (106 Boylston St)* and *Wilbur Theater (246 Tremont St)* both get pre- and post-Broadway touring companies (☎ 617-426-9366, 931-2787 tickets). Dance Umbrella (see Ballet & Dance, below) performs at the restored Beaux Arts *Emerson Majestic Theatre (☎ 617-824-8000, 219 Tremont St)*.

Colonial Theatre

South End (Map 9) The *Boston Center for the Arts (BCA; ☎ 617-426-7700, 539 Tremont St)* has three distinctive performance spaces (as well as the Mills Gallery, a contemporary art space) perfect for unusual productions. The resident companies, *Speakeasy* and *Theater Offensive*, which produces gay- and lesbian-themed works, guarantee that there's rarely a dull moment at the BCA.

BALLET & DANCE

The highly regarded *Boston Ballet (Map 7; ☎ 617-695-6950 information, ☎ 617-482-9393 tickets)* performs classical and modern works at the Wang Center. Tickets cost $25 to $69, but students can get 'rush' tickets for $12.50 one hour before the performance. The *Nutcracker* is a wildly popular year-end holiday tradition.

Dance Umbrella (Map 7; ☎ 617-482-7570, ☎ 617-824-8000 for tickets), which single-handedly upholds Boston's alternative dance scene, sponsors renowned international touring companies as well as local contemporary dance troupes. The original shows, usually at the Emerson Majestic Theatre, frequently end with a question-and-answer session. Tickets start at about $20 (unless it's a big-name dance company), but again, students can get half-price 'rush' tickets 30 minutes prior to curtain.

CHORAL & CHAMBER MUSIC

The *New England Conservatory of Music (Map 10; ☎ 617-585-1122 concert line, ☎ 617-536-2412 box office, Jordan Hall, 30 Gainsborough St)* hosts free professional and student chamber and orchestral concerts in the acoustically superlative hall. Call for specifics about who's playing when.

Emmanuel Church (Map 8; ☎ 617-536-3356, 15 Newbury St) offers scads of great concerts, many of which carry a moderate fee. Most Sunday services (which begin at 10 am) end with a Bach Cantata. It's best, though, to call their concert line for a detailed listing of who's playing when.

Many churches offer free concerts in reverential surroundings. Check out *Old West Church (Map 3; ☎ 617-227-5088, 131 Cambridge St)*, which offers concerts at 8 pm

BSO & the Boston Pops

The near-perfect acoustics at **Symphony Hall** (Map 10; ☎ 617-266-1492, 266-1200 tickets, 301 Mass Ave) match the ambitious programs of the world-renowned Boston Symphony Orchestra. The BSO, led by music director Seiji Ozawa, performs in Boston from late September to late April. In summer, they take up residence at Tanglewood in the Berkshire Hills of western Massachusetts. If you think classical music is reserved for blue bloods and eggheads, you would have changed your mind after experiencing the free 1998 Boston Common concert, which celebrated the maestro's 25th year with the BSO. Bostonians from all walks of life rose to their feet cheering as Ozawa – while feverish with flu – conducted a rousing Beethoven's Ninth. Ozawa plans to leave the BSO after the 2002 summer season in Tanglewood.

Symphony Hall is also home to the **Boston Pops**. Thanks to its 'Evening at Pops' public television series and an ambitious world touring schedule, the Pops is America's most well-known orchestra. Youthful and exuberant conductor Keith Lockhart leads an upbeat repertoire of Broadway show tunes and popular classical music (hence the name 'Pops') from May to mid-July, and again for most of December.

The Pops' free 4th of July concert at the **Hatch Memorial Shell** (Map 2) is a Boston tradition. Diehards pack a day's worth of provisions and diversions and arrive as early as 4 am to lay their blanket on the lawn and wait.

Maestro Seiji Ozawa

They wait, often in the rain and often in scorching sun, for up to 14 hours for an evening musical program of rousing patriotic marches and Tchaikovsky's *1812 Overture*. The nationally televised spectacle, complete with a choreographed fireworks display, is exhilarating.

The BSO performs on Tuesday and Thursday through Saturday. BSO tickets cost $27 to $80, Pops tickets are slightly less. For BSO same-day discounted 'rush' tickets (one per person; you don't have to be a student), line up at the Cohen box office at 5 pm on Tuesday and Thursday for the 8 pm show, at 9 am Friday for the 2 pm show. Another way to beat the high cost is to catch a sporadic open rehearsal (held from one to four times a month). These $14.50 tickets can be purchased in advance. For the entire week preceding July 4th, the Pops treat their hometown fans to free evening Esplanade concerts.

Tuesday in the summer; *King's Chapel* (Map 4; ☎ 617-227-2155, 58 Tremont St), with year-round concerts at 12:15 pm Tuesday; *Cathedral Church of St Paul* (Map 4; ☎ 617-482-4826, 138 Tremont St), offering classical concerts at 12:15 pm Wednesday, October to May; *Trinity Church* (Map 8; ☎ 617-536-0944, 206 Clarendon St), with organ recitals at 12:15 pm Friday, September through June.

COMEDY CLUBS

The *Comedy Connection* (Map 3; ☎ 617-248-9700, Quincy Market, Faneuil Hall Marketplace), on the 2nd floor above the food court, is one of the city's oldest and biggest comedy venues. Go in the middle of the week when tickets are about $8 to $10, rather than on weekends when tickets range from $12 to $35.

KIM GRANT

When astrology just isn't enough

Improv Asylum (*Map 5;* ☎ *617-263-6887, 216 Hanover St*) showcases some edgy performance art that's a cross between theater and comedy. While the well-regarded troupe remains the same, the material and delivery change with the audience. Tickets are $10 to $15; shows Thursday through Saturday.

Nick's Comedy Stop (*Map 7;* ☎ *617-482-0930, 100 Warrenton St*) features local and national jokesters Thursday through Saturday. Tickets are $10 to $14.

Improv Boston (*Map 12;* ☎ *617-576-1253, 1253 Cambridge St*), at the Back Alley Theater in Inman Square, is a well-respected long-running troupe that makes things up as they go along. Sunday afternoon (2 pm) shows are family-oriented. Friday and Saturday evening shows cost $12.

SPOKEN WORD

The venerable *Ford Hall Forum* (☎ *617-373-5800*), the oldest continuing public lecture series in the country (begun in 1908), sponsors lively and spirited dialogues on issues like campaign finance reform, Kosovo and Y2K and other apocalyptic events in the western world. Speakers have included Martin Luther King, Jr, Maya Angelou, Winston Churchill, Gloria Steinem, Al Gore and MacArthur Genius Award recipient John Bonifaz. Lectures are held in the spring and fall at Old South Meeting House and

Northeastern University; look for details in the Thursday *Boston Globe* Calendar section.

With so many illustrious bookstores and such a literate populace, it's no surprise that publishers send distinguished authors to give readings here. You'll find them at **Barnes & Noble** and **Borders** near Downtown Crossing, **Wordsworth** in Harvard Square, and **Brookline Booksmith** in Coolidge Corner (see 'Bookstores' in the Shopping chapter). **Brattle St Theatre** (see Cinema, earlier in this chapter) often has author readings, too.

The *Grolier Poetry Book Shop* (*Map 11;* ☎ *617-547-4648, 6 Plympton St*), in Harvard Square, sponsors regular readings at the nearby Arthur Sackler Museum. The *Third Rail* (*Map 12;* ☎ *617-354-2685, 738 Mass Ave*), at the Cantab Lounge in Central Square, hosts Wednesday night poetry readings and slams.

PSYCHIC READINGS

You may be surprised that a populace renowned for practicality supports innumerable storefront psychics. Some favorites are: *Tremont Tea Room* (*Map 4;* ☎ *617-338-8100, 48–50 Winter St*), the city's oldest otherworldly establishment; *Mystic Rosa* (*Map 11;* ☎ *617-354-9914, 99 Mt Auburn St*), in Harvard Square; and *Seven Stars* (*Map 12;* ☎ *617-547-1317, 731 Mass Ave*), in Central Square, a New Age bookstore that also specializes in tarot, palm and aura readings.

SPECTATOR SPORTS

Boston is a big sports town, and emotions run high during each sporting season. Be warned that simply asking a local, 'Hey, what do you think of the Sox this season?' could start an impassioned conversation.

Baseball

The Boston Red Sox play in *Fenway Park* (*Map 10;* ☎ *617-267-1700 tickets, 4 Yawkey Way, www.redsox.com*), the nation's oldest ballpark, built in 1912, and certainly one of the most storied (see 'Fenway Park' in Things to See & Do). The season runs from early April to late September or into October if the Sox make it into postseason.

ENTERTAINMENT

Sit with the 'common fan' in outfield bleacher seats for $12 or $14 versus about $18 to $32 for regular seats. Games are at 1:05 pm and 7:05 pm.

Basketball
The Boston Celtics (☎ 617-523-3030 information, ☎ 617-931-2000 tickets, www.celtics .com) play from late October through April at the *Fleet Center (Map 3; 150 Causeway St)*. Tickets start at $10, if you're lucky enough to get one, and go up to $85; the Celtics have won more championships (16 as of 1999) than any other NBA team.

Hockey
The Boston Bruins (☎ 617-624-1900 information, ☎ 617-931-2000 tickets, www.boston-bruins.com) also play in the Fleet Center (see Basketball, above) from mid-October to mid-April. Tickets go for $20 to $75. You can also buy Bruins and Celtics tickets in person at the box office, at the western end of the Fleet Center.

Football
The New England Patriots (☎ 508-543-8200, 800-543-1776, www.patriots.com) play in the uncomfortable *Foxboro Stadium*, on Route 1 in Foxboro, about 50 minutes south of Boston. The season runs from late August to late December, and tickets begin at $26, if you can get one. There are direct trains ($8 roundtrip) and buses ($8 roundtrip) from South Station to and from the stadium; contact the MBTA (☎ 617-222-3200) for exact times.

Soccer
New England Revolution (☎ 877-438-7387) also play in Foxboro Stadium (see Football, above). The season runs from mid-April to early October, and tickets are $10 to $25.

College Teams
Many colleges have teams worth watching, and spirited, loyal fans. In April, look for the annual Bean Pot Tournament, college hockey's local rivalry.

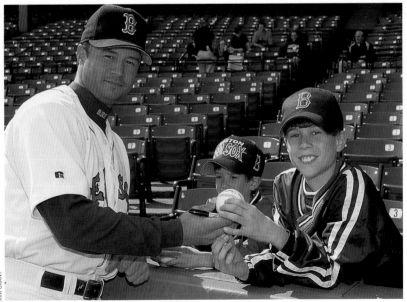

KIM GRANT

The Sox even personally retrieve foul balls from their fans.

Boston University's (Map 10; ☎ 617-353-3838) hockey team plays at *Case Athletic Center* on Babcock St, off Comm Ave. Tickets are $12 adults, $6 children. Take the T Green Line, 'B' branch, to Babcock.

Boston College (☎ 617-552-3000) has a tough hockey team that plays at *Conte Forum*. Tickets are $12 adults, $8 for children. BC football fans are devoted, so tickets are nearly impossible to get. Basketball is also popular. Ride the T Green Line, 'B' branch, to the last stop.

Tickets for Harvard University football at *Harvard Stadium* (Map 11; ☎ 617-495-2211), across the Anderson Bridge south of Harvard Square, usually go for $10, and are generally available unless the match is a famous rivalry with another Ivy League school. The Harvard-Yale match is hosted by Harvard on even-numbered years.

Shopping

Antique delights await you on Charles St.

Shopping in Boston is most interesting when you seek out the offbeat shops and boutiques. Stores are generally open Monday through Saturday from 9 or 10 am until 6 or 7 pm, unless otherwise noted. Most are also open on Sunday from noon to 5 pm.

WHAT TO BUY
Antiques
Antiques in Boston are pricey, but you always can window-shop on Charles and River Sts on Beacon Hill.

Dealers at the Boston Antique Co-op I & II (Map 2; ☎ 617-227-9810, 227-9811), 119 Charles St, specialize in arts and crafts, silver, early 17th- and 18th-century textiles, personal trinkets, pipes, arms and armor.

At the Nostalgia Factory (Map 5; ☎ 617-720-2211), 51 N Margin St, you'll discover authentic Hollywood movie posters, out-of-print magazines and political collectibles.

Minot Hall Antiques Center (Map 9; ☎ 617-236-7800), 1721 Washington St, is home to over 1000 dealers who display pottery, jewelry, silver, collectibles, furniture and decorative items in a 12,000-sq-foot historic building.

The five-story Cambridge Antique Market (Map 12; ☎ 617-868-9655), at 201 McGrath-O'Brien Hwy, has a little something of everything – furniture, glass, clothing, pottery, jewelry.

Art Galleries
While Newbury St has the most expensive and dense concentration (see Newbury St later in this chapter), there are galleries elsewhere that allow you to support local artists

KIM GRANT

without losing your shirt. Poke around in the Leather District (Map 6) bounded by Atlantic Ave and Lincoln, Kneeland and Essex Sts, and on Harrison Ave in the South End (Map 9) for avant-garde galleries.

Fort Point Arts Community Gallery (Map 6; ☎ 617-423-4299), 300 Summer St, is the focal point for Boston's cutting edge arts community. Something interesting is always on display.

The city's oldest cooperative, the Bromfield Art Gallery (Map 9; ☎ 617-451-3605), 560 Harrison Ave, is also one of the more accessible, affordable and reputable galleries.

Kingdom Fine Arts (Map 10; ☎ 617-266-1997), 173 Mass Ave, exhibits work of known and emerging contemporary artists working in various media.

A new gallery in Davis Square, Gallery Bershad (Map 13; ☎ 617-629-9400), 99 Dover St, showcases the work of local and internationally known artists.

Arts & Crafts
The prestigious nonprofit Society of Arts & Crafts, founded in 1897, has a branch downtown (Map 4; ☎ 617-345-0033), at 101 Arch St. Within the small exhibition and retail space are high-quality weaving, leather, ceramics, furniture and other handcrafted items. The original is at 175 Newbury St (see Newbury St Shopping map; ☎ 617-266-1810).

The gift shop at the historic Women's Education & Industrial Union (Map 8; ☎ 617-536-5651), 356 Boylston St, features handcrafted gifts, from quilts and needlepoint to toys, books and stationery.

Painting your own ceramics has become popular. At Pottery Workshop (Map 8; ☎ 617-262-9392), 46 Gloucester St, and Clayroom (Map 9; ☎ 617-859-9779), 603 Tremont St, you select from unadorned plates and cups, play Picasso and return in a few days to pick up your kiln-fired creation.

For Harvard-related gifts without the big 'H' emblazoned all over them, browse through Harvard Collections (Map 11; ☎ 617-496-0700), 1350 Mass Ave. The store has fine reproductions and original works inspired by the immense holdings of the university's museums, from African masks

and carvings to jewelry crafted from ancient coins.

Craftspeople double as sales staff at the Cambridge Artists' Cooperative (Map 11; ☎ 617-868-4434), 59A Church St in Harvard Square, which displays over 200 handcrafted objects ranging from $3 to $1000.

Mobilia Gallery (Map 13; ☎ 617-876-2109), 358 Huron Ave, features whimsical contemporary objects of paper and cloth. Nearby, you'll find decorative and functional pottery, tiles and jewelry, with a wide range of glazing and firing techniques, at the artist-run Fresh Pond Clay Works (Map 13; ☎ 617-492-1907), 368 Huron Ave.

Stone's Throw Gallery (Map 14; ☎ 617-731-3773), 1389 Beacon St in Coolidge Corner, has earthy ceramics and textiles for the home.

KIM GRANT

Boston Souvenirs
Eugene Galleries (Map 2; ☎ 617-227-3062), 76 Charles St, has a remarkable selection of antique Boston prints and maps.

Two shops in historic Faneuil Hall are worth checking. The nonprofit Boston City Store (Map 3; ☎ 617-635-2911), in the basement, sells authentic Boston keepsakes, such as retired street signs ($30) and memorabilia from yesteryear's Boston Marathon. Out of Left Field (Map 3; ☎ 617-722-9401), on the ground floor, specializes in Boston sports mementos.

Boston Globe Store (Map 4; ☎ 617-367-4000), 3 School St, sells memorabilia connected with the city's principal newspaper. Buy selected pages from the day you were born, but don't be disappointed if your arrival on earth didn't make the *Globe*'s front page.

J August (Map 11; ☎ 617-864-6650), 1320 Mass Ave, Harvard Square, sells high-quality Harvard insignia clothing for the relative who asked you to bring home something.

Children

If you'd like to relive your childhood or taste the one you wish you'd had, visit FAO Schwartz (Map 8; ☎ 617-262-5900), 440 Boylston St, an extraordinary 22,000-sq-foot toy emporium.

Two shops in Cambridge's Huron Village (Map 13) cater to children of all ages. One, Henry Bear's Park (☎ 617-547-8424), 361 Huron Ave, has a delightful assortment of unique playthings. Susi's Gallery for Children (☎ 617-876-7874), 348 Huron Ave, has brightly painted furniture, papier-mâché figures and jewelry.

Clothing

Budget & Outlets For jeans, khakis and t-shirts, check out the overstock and irregulars at the Gap Outlet (Map 4; ☎ 617-482-1657), 425 Washington St in the Corner Mall at Downtown Crossing.

The Eddie Bauer Outlet (Map 4; ☎ 617-227-4840), 252 Washington St, offers outdoor wear irregulars for 30% to 70% off.

For the military look, there's the incomparable Mass Army Navy (Map 8; ☎ 617-267-1559), 895 Boylston St.

Shoes Located in a tiny shoebox of a store, Nahas Shoes (Map 2; ☎ 617-723-6176), 65 Charles St, has a solid selection of fashionable and comfortable shoes at reasonable prices.

The emphasis is on casual comfort at Footpaths' two downtown locations: 489 Washington St (Map 4; ☎ 617-338-6008), and (Map 4; ☎ 617-742-7463), 131 State St.

Harvard Square's Jasmine/Sola and Sola Men (Map 11; ☎ 617-354-6043), 37 Brattle St, have funky shoes for both sexes. Caution: Six-inch platforms and cobblestone streets don't mix!

Simons Shoes (Map 14; ☎ 617-277-8980), 282 Harvard St in Coolidge Corner, provides relief for weary feet.

Vintage Boston Costume (Map 7; ☎ 617-482-1632), 69 Kneeland St, where you can pick up fishnet stockings and a feather boa before heading to Fetish Friday at Man Ray (see Dance Clubs in Entertainment), also has plenty of rentals.

In Harvard Square (Map 11), you'll find Second Time Around (☎ 617-491-7185), 8 Eliot St, and Oona's Experienced Clothing (☎ 617-491-2654), 1210 Mass Ave.

In Central Square (Map 12), Great Eastern Trading Co (☎ 617-354-5279), 49 River St, and Justin Tyme (☎ 617-491-1088), 91 River St, offer high-quality goods and costume jewelry.

If your memories of the '60s and '70s have faded like an old pair of jeans, the Garment District (Map 12; ☎ 617-876-5230), 200 Broadway near Kendall Square, with its huge collection of psychedelic clothing, will bring them back with a vengeance.

Downstairs, Dollar-a-Pound Plus (Map 12; ☎ 617-876-5230), a flea market gone berserk, has special merchandise and pricing methods. Piles of mostly nondescript used clothing are dumped on the warehouse floor and folks wade through, looking for their needle in the haystack. Upon checkout, your pile is weighed and you pay 'by the pound' – usually $1.50, but on Friday it's even less. (They gotta get rid of this stuff.) There are also books, records and cassettes and kitchen supplies, all individually priced to move. Hours are irregular; call ahead.

Clothes Encounters (Map 14; ☎ 617-277-3031), 1394 Beacon St near Coolidge Corner, has a fine selection.

Western Wear Helen's Leather (Map 2; ☎ 617-742-2077), 110 Charles St, has gorgeous jackets, and cowboy boots up to size 15! Walker's (Map 7; ☎ 617-423-9050), 122 Boylston St, is Boston's Western wear outpost. The Original Levi's Store (Map 8; ☎ 617-375-9010), which sells only the real thing, is located within the Shops at Prudential Center, 800 Boylston St.

Women's Stylish simplicity and casual comfort reign at these boutiques: Clothware (☎ 617-661-6441), at 52 Brattle St, Jasmine/Sola (☎ 617-354-6043), at 37 Brattle St and Tess (☎ 617-864-8377), at 20 Brattle St, all in Harvard Square (Map 11).

Deborah Mann Atelier (☎ 617-576-0123), 1691 Mass Ave, and Dakini (☎ 617-864-7661), 1704 Mass Ave, are both between Harvard and Porter Squares (Map 13); J Miles (Map 13; ☎ 617-547-9604), 340 Huron Ave, is in Huron Village.

You'll find Leila (Map 14; ☎ 617-738-4448), 1337 Beacon St, in Coolidge Corner.

The place for shoes of unusual sizes

Stop by DeLuca's before a graveyard picnic.

Food & Drink

Organic Vegetables & Health Food Although there are decent fruit and veggies in grocery stores, two Cambridge stores in Central Square (Map 12) stand out. Harvest Co-Op (☎ 617-661-1580), 581 Mass Ave, and Bread & Circus (☎ 617-492-0070), 115 Prospect St, offer great selections of organic produce and lots of healthy prepared foods. There's another Bread & Circus in Boston, just off Mass Ave (Map 10; ☎ 617-375-1010), 15 Westland Ave. Check out the community bulletin boards for neighborhood events.

Gourmet & International Food Two Beacon Hill (Map 2) shops have fancy selections of cheese and deli meats, fresh-baked bread and pastries and fruit and vegetables: Savenor's (☎ 617-723-6328), 160 Charles St, and DeLuca's Market (☎ 617-523-4343), 11 Charles St.

In Harvard Square (Map 11), shop with local gourmands. Sage's Market (☎ 617-876-2211), 60 Church St, has a fine selection of prepared foods, deli meats, fresh produce and wine. Cardullo's (☎ 617-491-8888), 6 Brattle St, carries an impressive assortment of imported treats. Formaggio Kitchen (Map 13; ☎ 617-354-4750), 244 Huron Ave, carries a cornucopia of rare imported and specialty foods. Consult the knowledgeable staff at the cheese counter.

Trader Joe's (Map 14; ☎ 617-278-9997), 1317 Beacon St in Coolidge Corner, imports treats from around the globe, then repackages and sells them under its brand name. Prices are lower than at comparable shops.

For Every Body

Three apothecaries in Harvard Square (Map 11) will appeal to your senses. Harnetts (☎ 617-491-4747), 47 Brattle St, carries a vast array of vitamins, lotions, potions, herbs and aromatic oils – you'll find a visit here therapeutic if not downright curative. Although it stocks standard drugstore cosmetics and personal care products, Colonial Drug (☎ 617-864-2222), 49 Brattle St, is best known as a perfumery. The delightfully quaint establishment produces hundreds of scents. Billings & Stover (☎ 617-547-0502),

Farmers' Markets

Touch the produce and you risk the wrath of pushcart vendors at Haymarket (Map 3). No one else in the city matches their prices on ripe-and-ready fruit and vegetables. Not strictly a farmers' market, the vendors buy wholesale and sell by the pound. They don't take kindly to those buying a peach here, a banana there. The bustling spectacle takes place every Friday and Saturday, with the best bargains on Saturday afternoon.

Most neighborhoods have a seasonal farmers' market from June through October. In addition to just-picked fruit and local vegetables, you might find local goat cheese, crusty loaves of bread and tempting fruit tarts, all fresh, fresh, fresh. Locations include:

Yeahhhh baby

- City Hall Plaza (Map 3) Monday and Wednesday, 11 am to 6 pm, to late November
- Downtown Crossing (Map 4) Washington at Summer Sts, almost daily, 9 am to 5 pm
- Copley Square (Map 8) Tuesday and Friday, 11 am to 6 pm, to late October
- Boston Center for the Arts plaza (Map 9) Monday and Wednesday, 11 am to 6 pm, to mid-October
- Charles Hotel courtyard (Map 11) Sunday, 10 am to 3 pm, to late November
- Central Square (Map 12) parking lot 5 at Bishop Allen Drive Monday, noon to 6 pm, to late November
- Davis Square (Map 13) parking lot at Day and Herbert Sts Wednesday, noon to 6 pm, to late November
- Coolidge Corner (Map 14) parking lot on Webster St Thursday, 1:30 pm to dusk, to late October

41A Brattle St, with an authentic circa 1854 soda fountain, sells old-fashioned cosmetics, salves and balms.

Music

Boston has two music superstores, each with two locations. HMV is at 24 Winter St (Map 4; ☎ 617-357-8444) in Downtown Crossing, and 1 Brattle St (Map 11; ☎ 617-868-9696) in Harvard Square. Tower Records, open until midnight, is in Back Bay (Map 8; 617-247-5900), 360 Newbury St, and Harvard Square (Map 11; 617-876-3377), 95 Mt Auburn St.

With thousands of college students passing through every year, used CD and record stores abound. Favorites include: Looney Tunes (Map 10; ☎ 617-247-2238), 1106 Boylston St; Disc Diggers (Map 13; ☎ 617-776-7560), 401 Highland Ave in Davis Square; and Cheapo Records (Map 12; ☎ 617-354-4455), 645 Mass Ave in Central Square.

Skippy White's Records (Map 12; ☎ 617-491-3345), 538 Mass Ave in Central Square, has the definitive selection of rap, reggae, soul, R&B, funk and gospel.

Sandy's Music (Map 12; ☎ 617-491-2812), 896A Mass Ave near Central Square, specializes in new and used folk and Celtic recordings.

SHOPPING

Bookstores

Boston and Cambridge are a book lover's paradise. The Harvard Square Visitors Information Booth hands out a free brochure of Harvard Square's more than 30 bookstores, and the yellow pages list more than 100. Here are a few worth searching out.

For guidebooks and maps, travel to the **Rand McNally Map & Travel Store** (Map 3; ☎ 617-720-1125), 84 State St.

The **Brattle Book Shop** (Map 4; ☎ 617-542-0210), 9 West St, is a treasure crammed with out-of-print, rare and first-edition books.

Borders (Map 4; ☎ 617-557-7188), 10–24 School St, has more than 200,000 titles and a café for when you tire.

The chain **Barnes & Noble** (Map 4; ☎ 617-426-5502), 395 Washington St, offers 30% off of *New York Times* bestsellers.

The outstanding **Globe Corner Bookstore** has two locations: 500 Boylston St (Map 8; ☎ 617-859-8008) and 49 Palmer St in Cambridge (Map 11; ☎ 617-497-6277) and you can browse many of their titles at www.globecorner.com. Specializing in travel guides and literature from near and far, Globe Corner also carries hundreds of specialty maps, including New England topographical maps.

You could browse away an entire day at the **Avenue Victor Hugo Bookshop** (see Newbury St Shopping map; ☎ 617-266-7746), 339 Newbury St, one of the best used bookstores in Boston.

The popularity of **Spenser's Mystery Books** (see Newbury St Shopping map; ☎ 617-262-0880), 223 Newbury St, is no mystery.

The **Trident Booksellers & Café** (see Newbury St Shopping map; ☎ 617-267-8688), 338 Newbury St, specializes in New Age.

The **Glad Day Gay Liberation Bookshop** (Map 8; ☎ 617-267-3010), 673 Boylston St, is dedicated to gay- and lesbian-related titles. The bulletin board outside the 2nd-floor store is packed with useful community information.

We Think the World of You (Map 9; ☎ 617-574-5000), 540 Tremont St, features gay and lesbian titles, cookbooks and travel.

Lucy Parsons Center (Map 9; ☎ 617-267-6272), 549 Columbus Ave, stocks 'literature of liberation,' including titles on radical environmentalism, radical social thought and anarchy.

The three-story **Barnes & Noble at Boston University** (Map 10; ☎ 617-267-8484), 660 Beacon St, is one of New England's biggest.

Schoenhof's Foreign Books (Map 11; ☎ 617-547-8855), 76A Mt Auburn St near Harvard Square, is nationally known for foreign-language books and dictionaries.

Nearby is one of the most famous poetry bookstores in the US: the **Grolier Poetry Book Shop** (Map 11; ☎ 617-547-4648), at 6 Plympton St.

Starr Book Shop (Map 11; ☎ 617-547-6864), 29 Plympton St, is venerated for its used collection.

The **Harvard Book Store** (Map 11; ☎ 617-661-1515), 1256 Mass Ave, is considered the premiere intellectual bookstore on the Square.

Within a block of each other are the original **Wordsworth** (Map 11; ☎ 617-354-5201), 30 Brattle St, a good general bookstore, and **Curious George Goes to Wordsworth** (☎ 617-498-0062), 1 JFK St, which specializes in children's books.

You don't have to be a student to shop at 'the Coop' (rhymes with snoop). The **Harvard Cooperative Society** (Map 11; ☎ 617-499-2000), 1400 Mass Ave in Harvard Square, carries three floors of books and music and everything emblazoned with the crimson logo.

The **MIT Press Bookstore** (Map 12; ☎ 617-253-5249), 292 Main St in Kendall Square, is the place for science, technology, architecture and political science treatises.

Bookstores

MIT, too, has a **Coop** (Map 12; ☎ 617-499-3200), 3 Cambridge Center in Kendall Square. They carry requisite science and technology tomes, in addition to MIT paraphernalia.

Nearby, **Quantum Books** (Map 12; ☎ 617-494-5042), 4 Cambridge Center, has computer technology, physics, math and engineering books.

In Inman Square, **New Words Women's Bookstore** (Map 12; ☎ 617-876-5310, 800-928-4788), 186 Hampshire St, features women's writing from traditional to radical.

Nearby, **House of Sarah Books** (Map 12; ☎ 617-547-3447), 1309 Cambridge St, has wide aisles for leisurely used book browsing.

Seven Stars (Map 12; ☎ 617-547-1317), 731 Mass Ave in Central Square, specializes in New Age titles (and psychic readings, too!).

In Davis Square, **McIntyre & Moore Booksellers** (Map 13; ☎ 617-629-4840), 255 Elm St, offers friendly environs for used book browsers as well as buyers.

Most texts at **Sasuga Japanese Bookstore** (Map 13; ☎ 617-497-5460), 7 Upland Rd in Porter Square, are in Japanese, but you'll also find English language books on Japanese history, culture and arts, as well as language tapes.

Sleuths should search out **Kate's Mystery Books** (Map 13; 617-491-2660), 2211 Mass Ave, about five blocks north of Porter Square.

Bryn Mawr Bookstore (Map 13; ☎ 617-661-1770), 373 Huron Ave, stocks rare and used books. Browsing the sidewalk display cases is an annual rite of spring.

The **Brookline Booksmith** (Map 14; ☎ 617-566-6660), 279 Harvard St in Coolidge Corner, was voted by *Publishers Weekly* the best independent bookstore in the US in 1998. (Yes, that's right, the US.)

The inviting **Albatross Books** (Map 14; ☎ 617-739-2665), 45 Harvard St in Brookline Village, sells rare and used volumes.

Downtown's Brattle Book Shop

Newspapers & Magazines

In business since the 1930s, the outdoor Copley Square News (Map 8; no phone), on Boylston St at Dartmouth St, sells hundreds of magazines and many foreign-language periodicals.

In Harvard Square, Out of Town News (Map 11; ☎ 617-354-7777) is no ordinary newsstand; in fact, it's a National Historic Landmark. Despite the fact that you can read news on the Internet, this place still sells papers from virtually every major US city, as well as from cities around the world. Open 5 am to 10 pm.

One-of-a-Kind

Check out these shops that defy categorization, carrying interesting stuff not found elsewhere.

Charles St Supply (Map 2; ☎ 617-367-9046), 54 Charles St, has cheap lawn chairs for Esplanade concerts.

Black Ink (Map 2; ☎ 617-723-3883), 101 Charles St, specializes in rubber stamps of antique engravings and trinkets made from recycled detritus.

Windsor Button (Map 4; ☎ 617-482-4969), 35 Temple Place, an institution since 1936, has the most extensive button collection you're likely to encounter. If you've lost a button and despaired of ever finding one to match, try here.

If you've lost your sense of humor, look for it at Jack's Joke Shop (Map 7; ☎ 617-426-9640), 38 Boylston St.

South End kitsch, from Barbies in drag to feather boas, is the raison d'être of Bang (Map 9; ☎ 617-292-9911), 59½ Clarendon St.

Fresh Eggs (Map 9; ☎ 617-247-8150), 58 Clarendon St, features 'everything for your nest.'

MDF (Map 11; ☎ 617-491-2789), 19 Brattle St, Harvard Square, stands for Modern Design Furnishings, and sells small eclectic domestic accessories.

Urban Outfitters (Map 11; ☎ 617-864-0070), 11 JFK St, Harvard Square, specializes in grunge-chic for the home and body.

Who says fun and games aren't educational? Learningsmith (Map 11; ☎ 617-661-

6008), 25 Brattle St in Harvard Square, specializes in mind-stretching gifts.

Sixties kitsch meets '90s retro at Abodeon (Map 13; ☎ 617-497-0137), 1731 Mass Ave between Harvard and Porter Squares. Austin Powers wannabes can find Lucite dining chairs, cocktail shaker sets, mod clothes and old Rat Pack records.

At Nomad (Map 13; ☎ 617-497-6677), 1691 Mass Ave between Harvard and Porter Squares, you'll find brightly painted furniture, glassware, rugs and clothing from around the world and around the corner.

With a nod and a wink, Joie de Vivre (Map 13; ☎ 617-864-8188), 1792 Mass Ave between Harvard and Porter Squares, has lighthearted and hip gifts sure to inspire a smile.

Coromandel (Map 13; ☎ 617-497-6110), 364 Huron Ave, sells distinctive Indian print fabrics, bedclothes, jackets and accessories.

Old Leather & Dried Roses (Map 13; ☎ 617-576-6990), 370½ Huron Ave, specializes in handcrafted leather-bound books, from journals to photo albums.

NV53 (Map 13; ☎ 617-776-0848), 260 Elm St, Davis Square, named after an iconic Danish-designed chair of the '50s, has an intriguing collection of authentic, classic mid-century furniture and knickknacks, most in mint condition.

Equal parts postmodern gallery and store, Pluto (Map 13; ☎ 617-666-2005), 215 Elm St, Davis Square, has description-defying assortments of whimsical housewares and fashion accessories.

Pod (Map 14; ☎ 617-739-3802), 6 Davis Ave in Brookline Village, is a tiny shop with gifts celebrating the art of minimalism.

Outdoor Gear

Although it's dusty and musty, Hilton's Tent City (Map 3; ☎ 617-227-9242), 272 Friend St, boasts four floors of tents (set up to test out) and all the camping and backpacking accessories, equipment and clothing you'll ever need – at the lowest prices around.

Eastern Mountain Sports (EMS; ☎ 617-254-4250), 1041 Comm Ave, is another good source for hiking and camping gear, books and maps. If you can't find it at Hilton's, you'll find it here. Ride the T Green Line, 'B' branch to Babcock.

Pens & Stationery

As a change of pace from chicken scratching on postcards, these shops will inspire you to thoughtful prose or poetry. Look for a wide selection of pens, handmade and specialty stationery, notebooks and cards at Scribe's Delight (Map 3; ☎ 617-523-2572), South Market, Faneuil Hall Marketplace; Bromfield Pen Shop (Map 4; ☎ 617-482-9053), 5 Bromfield St; and Paper Source (Map 13; ☎ 617-497-1077), 1810 Mass Ave near Porter Square.

Thrift Shops

Ritzy neighborhoods have ritzy closets that trickle down to ritzy castoffs, and when proceeds benefit local charitable institutions, everyone's in the mood to give.

Given its tony location, Beacon Hill Thrift Shop (Map 2; ☎ 617-742-2323), 15 Charles St, benefiting the New England Baptist Hospital Nurse Scholarship Fund, is more like an estate sale than a bargain bin. Closed Thursday and Sunday.

Boomerangs (Map 3; ☎ 617-723-2666), 60 Canal St, stocks new department store surplus and private donations, so inventory ranges from the banal (new toasters) to someone's singular version of the ultimate in style (lime-green patent leather go-go boots). It's fun to browse, and all proceeds go to the AIDS Action Committee of Massachusetts.

Who knows what you might find at Transitions (Map 9; ☎ 617-536-8999), 1736 Washington St, a treasure trove of clothing, costume jewelry, furnishings and odds and ends. Profits go to the Pine St Inn, a local homeless shelter.

Planet Aid (Map 13; ☎ 617-776-7703), 250 Elm St in Davis Square, has racks of second-hand clothing and household bric-a-brac; proceeds go to the Institute for International Cooperation & Development.

Morgan Memorial Goodwill has outposts in Davis Square (Map 13; ☎ 617-628-3618), 230 Elm St, and in Central Square (Map 12;

It's a chair, it's a shoe, it's...

868-6330), 520 Mass Ave. Nothing fancy here, just lots of cheap stuff.

The Discovery Shop of the American Cancer Society (Map 14; ☎ 617-277-9499), 300 Washington St in Brookline Village, has a decent selection of gently worn clothing for women of all sizes.

Not cheap, but still a bargain, the friendly Beth Israel Hospital Thrift Shop (Map 14; ☎ 617-566-7016), 25 Harvard St in Brookline Village, has high-quality stuff: clothes, housewares and overstock from Boston boutiques. Proceeds go to special hospital projects. Closed Tuesday and Sunday.

Travel Accessories

For everything from suitcases to passport pouches, try the basic Sherman's (Map 4; ☎ 617-742-4400), at 26 Province St or upscale Willowbee & Kent (Map 8; ☎ 617-437-6700), at 519 Boylston St.

WHERE TO SHOP
Beacon Hill (Map 2)
Lovely Charles St remains Boston's antiques central. In recent years, though, the grande dames have been joined by a number of intriguing shops.

Government Center & Faneuil Hall (Map 3)
Faneuil Hall Marketplace (☎ 617-338-2323), also known as Quincy Market, is perhaps the most popular shopping area. About 14 million people visit annually. The five buildings are filled with 100-plus tourist-oriented shops, pushcart vendors and national chain stores. Be forewarned: The few funky shops are about as easy to find as needles in a haystack. Yes, it's expensive and crowded,

Filene's Basement

The granddaddy of Boston bargain stores, Filene's Basement (Map 4; ☎ 617-542-2011), 426 Washington St, carries overstock and irregular items at everyday low prices. But that's just the beginning. Items are automatically marked down the longer they remain in the store. With a little luck and lots of determination, you could find a $300 designer jacket for $30. In reality, though, the chances of finding something perfect (meaning well-made, undamaged, in your size and in a color other than fire-engine red) are pretty slim.

The annual wedding gown sale is a madhouse. Anxious brides-to-be in bodysuits line up before dawn and stampede in when the doors open. Each then grabs every dress she can put her hands on, regardless of size or style. As mothers and friends guard the stashes, hundreds of women try on dress after dress – in the aisles! Feuds break out over dresses left unattended. Those left standing after the melee usually depart with a designer gown at a fraction of retail.

Even on a normal day, the place looks like a tornado hit it within an hour of opening. Patience and good humor are prerequisites for this unique place; don't miss it.

especially on the weekends, but it can be festive, too. There are lots of fast-food outlets, street performers and outdoor benches to rest your weary feet. Shops are generally open until 9 pm daily, except until 6 pm Sunday.

Downtown & Financial District (Map 4)
Downtown Crossing, an outdoor pedestrian mall, has practical shops geared to everyday needs. There are two flagship department stores, Filene's (☎ 617-357-2100), 426 Washington St, and Macy's (☎ 617-357-3000), 450 Washington St, as well as smaller outlets for clothing, jewelry, shoes, books and electronics. This fun area is enlivened by street musicians, fast-food and souvenir pushcart vendors, a few outdoor cafés and benches for people-watching.

Newbury St
Boston's premier shopping street, Newbury St (www.newbury-st.com) is lined with chic boutiques, cafés and art galleries running the gamut from stodgy to funky. These eight high-rent blocks, second only to New York's Fifth Avenue in price-per-square-foot, are heaven for both Boston's 'old money' elite and international trust-fund students using mom's gold card. For the rest of the world, it's great for strolling, window-shopping and people-watching.

Start at Newbury St and Mass Ave, where you'll find the hipper stores. Walking east, eclectic and internationally inspired craft shops give way to designer boutiques. By the time you reach Berkeley St, you'll question whether or not you're dressed appropriately to even walk down the street, let alone to enter stores. Assume a pose that says, 'Of course you have a Swiss bank account, doesn't everyone?'

Mass Ave to Hereford St Urban Outfitters (☎ 617-236-0088), No 361, stocks the latest in urban-grunge/industrial chic clothing and housewares. A pilgrimage site for music mavens, Tower Records (☎ 617-247-5900), No 360, has the city's largest tune selection. Beadworks (☎ 617-247-7227), No 349,

KIM GRANT

Glitz and glamor are the rule on Newbury St.

has all the components for making your own jewelry. Patagonia (☎ 617-424-1776), No 346, carries the finest outdoor fleecewear. Jasmine (☎ 617-867-4636), No 344, is the first stop for youthful women's clothing. The Avenue Victor Hugo Bookshop is at No 339 and the Trident Booksellers & Café is at No 338 (see 'Bookstores'). Sola (☎ 617-437-8465), No 329, carries stylish women's shoes at affordable prices. Don't ask, don't tell about the throw-away goods at Condom World (☎ 617-267-7233), No 332. Newbury Comics (☎ 617-236-4930), No 332, sells used and new alternative rock CDs and records, as well as comic books. For hip men's clothing and shoes, check out Sola Men (☎ 617-450-9484), No 333.

Hereford to Gloucester Sts Mystery Train II (☎ 617-536-0216), No 304, is another good used CD and record outpost. Shoes at John Fluevog (☎ 617-266-1079), No 302, are more fun to look at than comfortable to walk in. The Israeli gallery Kakadu (☎ 617-437-6666), at No 291, features colorful handcrafted home accessories. Michael Price Gallery (MPG; ☎ 617-437-1596), No 285, showcases art that's about as edgy as Newbury St can handle.

Gloucester to Fairfield Sts In addition to Indian antiques and music, you can get yourself a henna tattoo at India An-

tiques (☎ 617-266-6539), No 279. If you're decorating a Soho loft (or just fantasizing about it), step inside Zoe (☎ 617-375-9135), No 279. Industry (☎ 617-437-0319), No 276, features diverse gifts from pewter-plated steel 'condom caddies' to blown glass. Shambala Tibet (☎ 617-437-0436), No 270, showcases Himalayan jewelry, music, textiles and artifacts. Gargoyles, Grotesques & Chimera (☎ 617-536-2362), No 262, isn't actually a retail shop, but browsing in a dimly lit showroom that feels like the crypt of a medieval cathedral is interesting. Matsu (☎ 617-266-9707), No 259, sells exquisite clothing and gifts inspired by a Japanese Zen aesthetic. Purveyor of gourmet groceries, DeLuca's (☎ 617-262-5990) is at No 239.

Consuming is fun!

NEWBURY ST SHOPPING

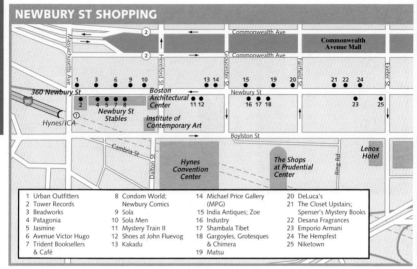

1 Urban Outfitters	8 Condom World;	14 Michael Price Gallery	20 DeLuca's
2 Tower Records	Newbury Comics	(MPG)	21 The Closet Upstairs;
3 Beadworks	9 Sola	15 India Antiques; Zoe	Spenser's Mystery Books
4 Patagonia	10 Sola Men	16 Industry	22 Desana Fragrances
5 Jasmine	11 Mystery Train II	17 Shambala Tibet	23 Emporio Armani
6 Avenue Victor Hugo	12 Shoes at John Fluevog	18 Gargoyles, Grotesques	24 The Hempfest
7 Trident Booksellers	13 Kakadu	& Chimera	25 Niketown
& Café		19 Matsu	

Fairfield to Exeter Sts A bit musty and dingy, the Closet Upstairs (☎ 617-267-5757), No 223, is packed with retro secondhand clothing; Spenser's Mystery Books (see 'Bookstores') is in the same building. Custom-blend your own scent at Desana Fragrances (☎ 617-450-9599), No 211, a perfume bar. The hip-hop outpost of Italian fashion, Emporio Armani (☎ 617-262-7300) is at No 210. The Hempfest (☎ 617-421-9944), No 207, sells products made from hemp, the botanical cousin of marijuana: items to wear, to furnish one's home and even to eat. As much a destination as a store, Niketown (☎ 617-267-3400), No 200, is a palatial footwear emporium dedicated to the proliferation of consumer-oriented American sports culture.

Exeter to Dartmouth Sts A Newbury St institution founded in 1897, the Society of Arts & Crafts (Map 8; ☎ 617-266-1810), No 175, exhibits and sells fine handcrafted weaving, leather, ceramics, jewelry and furniture. Two vintage shops, the Closet (☎ 617-536-1919), No 175, and Second Time Around (☎ 617-247-3504), No 167, are gold mines of barely worn designer clothing. Michalopou-

los Gallery (☎ 617-267-0202), No 166, showcases the painter's singular vision of New England architecture and landscape.

Dartmouth to Clarendon Sts Kelly Barrette Fine Art (☎ 617-266-2475), No 129, features emerging artists and contemporary masters. Check out Loulou's Lost & Found (☎ 617-859-8593), No 121, for an eclectic inventory of retro objects for the home, some from the early 20th century. Shop with the Euro-chic hipsters at riccardi (☎ 617-266-3158), No 116, before hitting the clubs.

Clarendon to Berkeley Sts Located in spacious quarters in the Church of the Covenant, Gallery NAGA (☎ 617-267-9060), No 67, exhibits fine art and crafts by well-known artists as well as up-and-comers. Louis, Boston (☎ 617-262-6100), 234 Berkeley St, caters to discriminating men and women, though not equally; there are three floors of high-end apparel for men, one for women.

Berkeley to Arlington Sts A number of fine galleries congregate at this end of Newbury St. They're worth a look even if

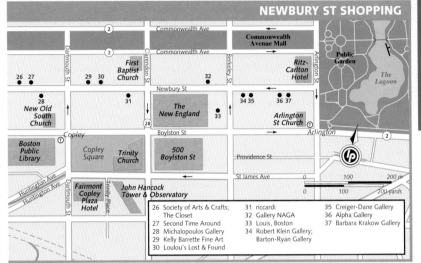

NEWBURY ST SHOPPING

26 Society of Arts & Crafts;
   The Closet
27 Second Time Around
28 Michalopoulos Gallery
29 Kelly Barrette Fine Art
30 Loulou's Lost & Found

31 riccardi
32 Gallery NAGA
33 Louis, Boston
34 Robert Klein Gallery;
   Barton-Ryan Gallery

35 Creiger-Dane Gallery
36 Alpha Gallery
37 Barbara Krakow Gallery

you can't afford to buy. At No 38, 4th floor, check out Robert Klein Gallery (☎ 617-267-7997) for photography, and Barton-Ryan Gallery (☎ 617-867-0662) for contemporary painting and works on paper. Creiger-Dane Gallery (☎ 617-536-8088), No 36, exhibits contemporary abstract painting. Alpha Gallery (☎ 617-536-4465), No 14, 2nd floor, specializes in the work of world-renowned 20th-century American and European painters and sculptors.

Perhaps the most highly respected of the Newbury St galleries, Barbara Krakow Gallery (☎ 617-262-4490), No 10, 5th floor, provides an elegant venue for contemporary artists.

Back Bay (Map 8)

In addition to Newbury St (see above), there are two huge, luxe indoor malls to entice you to part with your cash. Copley Place (☎ 617-369-5000), 100 Huntington Ave, encompasses two hotels, a first-run cineplex, glass walkways, restaurants and dozens of very pricey, elegant shops. The Shops at Prudential Center (☎ 617-267-1002), 800 Boylston St, include about 70 stores and eateries within an atrium-like space. One of the few

urban grocery stores, Star Market, is on the ground level.

Cambridge & Brookline

Harvard Square (Map 11) has 150 shops within a few blocks. Although the area used to boast an avant-garde sensibility and dozens of independent stores, most of the funkier shops have been replaced by national chains. Nevertheless, there's still a bustling street life with plenty of musicians and performance artists.

In East Cambridge (Map 12), the Cambridgeside Galleria (☎ 617-621-8666), 100 Cambridgeside Place just beyond the Science Museum, is a three-story mall with about 100 shops, including the moderately priced department store, Sears.

Kendall Square (Map 12), with its popular movie theater, draws more movie patrons than shoppers, but MIT supports a few technology-related bookstores (see 'Bookstores').

Inman Square (Map 12) has become a magnet for establishments priced-out of their old Central Square digs. Since it's a bit off-the-beaten path, Inman may be able to retain its beatnik charm.

Central Square (Map 12), long considered the edgy-funky heart of Cambridge, is in the midst of a controversial overhaul. The recent opening of Starbucks became the lightening rod for bitter neighborhood protests by those loathe to see Central Square go the way of its gentrified western neighbor. A few unique shops remain, but old-time shopkeepers lament that their future is uncertain.

Somerville's Davis Square (Map 13) is the current happening place to shop, eat and hang out. Over the past five years a number of trendy shops, cafés, restaurants and bars have joined the popular Somerville Theatre and a couple of die-hard neighborhood diners to make Davis Square the place to be.

The bohemian spirit of Harvard Square is making its way up Mass Ave toward Porter Square. Numerous unique boutiques on this stretch of Mass Ave (Map 13) afford a more creative shopping alternative.

Just south of Porter Square, the Porter Exchange (Map 13; no phone), 1815 Mass Ave, contains quick Japanese eateries (including a Japanese bakery at the center of the atrium) and a few clothing, cosmetics and gift shops.

Huron Village (Map 13), west of Harvard Square, has a small collection of eclectic shops. If the weather is fine and you're up for a walk, you'll be treated to a friendly neighborhood shopping experience.

Most stores in Brookline Village and Coolidge Corner (Map 14) are fun, small, unique and individually owned.

Excursions

Part of what makes Boston one of the USA's most livable cities is its easy access to the countryside. To the west, the colonial towns of Lexington and Concord have attractive historic centers. The north shore, including Salem, Marblehead and Gloucester, has rich maritime history.

On the south shore lies Plymouth, where the Pilgrims landed in 1627; today, much of the town is devoted to Pilgrim history. Cape Cod is New England's premier beach playground, accessible by bus and boat, but more convenient by car.

LEXINGTON

Lexington, about 18 miles northwest of Boston, has a colonial village green and plenty of history. On April 18, 1775, Paul Revere, William Dawes and Samuel Prescott set out on their midnight ride from Boston to Lexington and Concord to warn that the British were coming.

Orientation & Information

MA 4 and MA 225 follow Mass Ave from Cambridge through the center of Lexington, passing by Battle Green (formerly known just as Lexington Green).

The Lexington chamber of commerce (☎ 781-862-1450), 1875 Mass Ave, maintains a visitors center opposite Battle Green, next to Buckman Tavern. Exhibits recall the 1775 events. It's open 9 am to 5 pm daily (10 am to 4 pm in winter).

Things to See & Do

The Lexington minuteman statue guards the southeastern end of Battle Green, commemorating the bravery of the militia who met the British here.

The green is tranquil, shaded by tall trees and surrounded by dignified churches and stately houses. Behind the church that towers over the green is Ye Olde Burying Ground, with tombstones dating back to 1690.

Patriot's Day battle reenactment in Lexington

KIM GRANT

Buckman Tavern, colonial and orthopedic

The **Lexington Historical Society** (☎ 781-862-1703), 1332 Mass Ave, maintains three houses open 10 am to 5 pm (1 to 5 pm Sunday) April through October. Admission to each house is $4 adults ($2 children age 6 to 16), or $10 adults for all three houses ($4 children).

Facing the green and built in 1709, **Buckman Tavern** (☎ 781-862-5598), 1 Bedford Rd, where the minutemen spent tense hours anticipating the redcoats' arrival, is now a worthy museum of colonial life.

Munroe Tavern (☎ 781-674-9238), 1332 Mass Ave, built in 1695 about seven blocks southeast of the green, was a British command post and field infirmary, and is now furnished with battle mementos and artifacts from President Washington's 1789 visit.

Built in 1698, **Hancock Clark House** (☎ 781-861-0928), 36 Hancock St, contains furnishings and portraits of leaders of the Hancock and Clark families.

Places to Stay & Eat

Battle Green Inn (☎ 781-862-6100, 800-343-0235, 1720 Mass Ave), a motel in the center of Lexington's business district, has rooms for $95 to $99.

More than a dozen eateries lie within a five-minute walk of Battle Green. *Via Lago Gourmet Foods* (☎ 781-861-6174, 1845 Mass Ave) has pricey sandwiches, soups and salads.

Bertucci's (☎ 781-860-9000, 1777 Mass Ave), right in the center of town, serves pizza, pasta, salad and light meals. For more elaborate Italian fare, go to *Stone Soup Grill & Café* (☎ 781-862-9797, 1709 Mass Ave), at Edison Way, which features steak and innovative cuisine for lunch ($8 to $12) and dinner ($20 to $45).

Lemon Grass Thai Cuisine (☎ 781-862-3530, 1710 Mass Ave) has meal-in-a-bowl soups with noodles for $5 and other delicious Thai dishes for only slightly more. For sushi, try *Dabin* (☎ 781-860-0171, 10 Muzzey St), a half block south of Mass Ave.

Getting There & Away

Take MA 2 west from Boston or Cambridge to exit 54 (Waltham St) or exit 53 (Spring St).

MBTA (☎ 617-222-3200, 800-392-6100, www.mbta.com) bus No 62 (Bedford VA Hospital) and No 76 (Hanscom Field) run from the Alewife Red Line T terminus through Lexington center hourly on weekdays, less frequently on Saturday, with no Sunday service.

The Minuteman Commuter Bikeway runs from the Alewife Red Line stop in Cambridge to Lexington and Bedford, a distance of about 14 miles.

Rent bikes from Bikeway Cycle & Sports Center (☎ 781-861-1199), 3 Bow St, off Mass Ave just west of the Arlington town line.

CONCORD

Colonial Concord, dignified and beautiful, has 19th-century literary history, scenic roads for bicycling and the placid Concord River for canoeing.

On April 19, 1775, direct from Lexington Green, the British were defeated at North Bridge, a battle that Ralph Waldo Emerson called 'the shot heard 'round the world.'

In the 19th century, Concord was home to many literary figures, including essayist, preacher and poet Ralph Waldo Emerson (1803–82); essayist and naturalist Henry David Thoreau (1817–62); short-story writer and novelist Nathaniel Hawthorne (1804–64); and novelist and children's book author Louisa May Alcott (1832–88).

In 1850, resident Ephraim Bull's Concord grape began commercial table grape agriculture in the USA. For years, the Welch's company was headquartered on Main St.

Orientation & Information

Concord (population 17,000) is about 22 miles northwest of Boston along MA 2. The MBTA Commuter Rail train station, Concord Station ('the Depot'), is about a mile west of the town center.

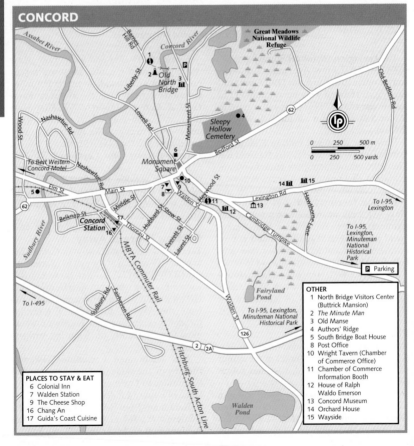

CONCORD

PLACES TO STAY & EAT
6 Colonial Inn
7 Walden Station
9 The Cheese Shop
16 Chang An
17 Guida's Coast Cuisine

OTHER
1 North Bridge Visitors Center (Buttrick Mansion)
2 *The Minute Man*
3 Old Manse
4 Authors' Ridge
5 South Bridge Boat House
8 Post Office
10 Wright Tavern (Chamber of Commerce Office)
11 Chamber of Commerce Information Booth
12 House of Ralph Waldo Emerson
13 Concord Museum
14 Orchard House
15 Wayside

The chamber of commerce information booth (☎ 978-369-3120), Heywood St, is open weekends mid-April through May and daily June through mid-October. When it's not open, head to the chamber's main office in Wright Tavern (see Walking Tour, below). The Concord Post Office (☎ 978-369-3020) is located at 34 Walden St.

The Minuteman National Historical Park (☎ 978-369-6993) is open 9 am to 5 pm mid-May to October, and until 4 pm November to mid-May. The park headquarters and visitors center is off Rte 2A.

Walking Tour

From Monument Square, head southeast on Lexington Rd to **Wright Tavern**, one of the first places British troops searched for rebel arms on April 19, 1775. At the opposite end of the square is the 1716 **Colonial Inn**.

Walk 15 minutes north along Monument St to the **Old Manse** (☎ 978-369-3909), built in 1769 and owned by the Emerson family for 169 years. The museum is filled with Emerson family mementos. (Newly married Hawthorne and his wife lived here from 1842 to 1845.) Guided tours are $5.50 adults, $4 seniors and college students, $3.50 children age 6 to 12, $15 families. It's open 10 am to 5 pm (noon to 5 pm Sunday) mid-April through October; the last tour is at 4:30 pm.

Just north and west is the **Old North Bridge**, site of the first Revolutionary War battle. Across the bridge is Daniel Chester French's statue the **Minute Man**, on the way up the hill to the **Buttrick Mansion**, the park's North Bridge Visitors Center.

Retracing your steps, stop at **Sleepy Hollow Cemetery** (☎ 978-371-6299). Visit **Authors' Ridge**, where lie Emerson, Thoreau and his family, the Alcotts, Hawthorne and his wife and Ephraim Bull.

From Monument Square, head southeast for five minutes to the **House of Ralph Waldo Emerson** (☎ 978-369-2236), 28 Cambridge Turnpike, which contains many original 19th-century furnishings. Emerson hosted his renowned circle of friends here from 1835 until his death in 1882. It's open 10 am to 4:30 pm Thursday to Saturday and 2 to 4:30 pm Sunday mid-April through October.

KIM GRANT

Minuteman National Historical Park

Admission costs $5 adults, $3 children age 7 to 17.

A bit east is the **Concord Museum** (☎ 978-369-9609), 200 Lexington Rd, which contains a lantern hung in Boston's Old North Church as a signal to Revere, Dawes and Prescott; furnishings from Ralph Waldo Emerson's study; and the world's largest collection of Thoreau artifacts. It's open 9 am to 5 pm (noon to 5 pm Sunday) April through December, and 11 am to 4 pm (1 to 4 pm Sunday) January through March. Admission costs $6 adults, $5 seniors, $3 children, $12 families.

Continue east down Lexington Rd to Louisa May Alcott's home, **Orchard House** (☎ 978-369-4118), 399 Lexington Rd. Alcott wrote *Little Women* in 1868 and died here 20 years later. The house and furnishings are open 10 am to 4:30 pm (1 to 4:30 pm Sunday) April through October, and 11 am to 3 pm (10 am to 4:30 pm Saturday, 1 to 4:30 pm Sunday) November through March. You must take a guided tour: $6 adults, $5 seniors, $4 children age 6 to 17, $16 families.

Down the way is the **Wayside** (☎ 978-369-6975), 455 Lexington Rd, where Louisa May Alcott also lived and which she described in *Little Women*. (Nathaniel Hawthorne lived here at one time, too.) The house is open 9:30 am to 5:30 pm mid-April through October, closed Wednesday. Admission is adults $4, children to 17 free.

EXCURSIONS

KIM GRANT

Where transcendence happened, Walden Pond

Walden Pond

Thoreau put the naturalist beliefs of Transcendentalism – that God 'transcended' all things – into practice when he built himself a rustic cabin here, several miles from town. His 1854 memoir of his time there (from 1845–1847), *Walden, or Life in the Woods*, praised nature and disapproved of the stresses of civilized life.

The glacial Walden Pond is about 3 miles south of Monument Square along Walden St (MA 126) south of MA 2. Now a state park with a summer parking fee, there's a swimming beach, facilities and a footpath around the pond. The site of Thoreau's cabin is on the northeast side, marked by a cairn and signs.

Canoeing

The **South Bridge Boat House** (☎ 978-369-9438), 496–502 MA 62, west of Monument Square on the Sudbury River, rents canoes for cruising the Concord, Sudbury and Assabet Rivers from April until the first snowfall. Rates are $9 per hour, $40 per day on weekends, with weekday and student discounts.

Places to Stay & Eat

The *Best Western Concord Motel* (☎ 978-369-6100, 800-528-1234, 740 Elm St), at MA 2 near the Concord Rotary (traffic circle), charges $99 to $114, with light breakfast.

The original 1716 building of the *Colonial Inn* (☎ 978-369-9200, 48 Monument Square) has 15 guest rooms ($55 to $225). The other 32 rooms ($135 to $179) are in the Prescott wing. The inn's dining room, tavern and front porch are a center of town social life.

For a huge sandwich or picnic supplies, visit the *Cheese Shop* (☎ 978-369-5778, 29 Walden St). The tavernlike *Walden Station* (☎ 978-371-2233, 24 Walden St) has sandwiches and moderately priced main courses; dinner prices are slightly higher.

Concord's best restaurant is *Guida's Coast Cuisine* (☎ 978-371-1333, 84 Thoreau St), upstairs in the Concord Station ('the Depot'). A refined, inventive lunch costs about $6 to $12, dinner $16 to $26.

Chang An (☎ 978-369-5288, 10 Concord Crossing) has the best Chinese cuisine in town. Lunch costs $8 to $10, dinner $10 to $18.

Getting There & Away

Driving west on MA 2 from Boston or Cambridge, it's 20-some miles to Concord. From Lexington, follow signs from Battle Green to Concord and Battle Rd, the route taken by the British troops on April 19, 1775.

MBTA Commuter Rail trains (☎ 617-222-3200, 800-392-6100, www.mbta.com) run frequently between Boston's North Station and Concord and West Concord Stations on the Fitchburg/South Acton line. The 40-minute ride costs $3.25, half-price for children age 5 to 11 (under 5 free). In Concord, buy your ticket at Coggins Bakery (☎ 978-371-3040), 68 Thoreau St, northwest of the depot building.

If you biked to Lexington, you can continue on to Concord; see Lexington for details about bicycle rentals.

SALEM

The famous Salem witch trials of 1692 have obscured this beautiful city's true claim to fame: its glorious maritime history.

Orientation & Information

Salem Common, Derby Wharf and Essex St Mall, a pedestrian way through historic Salem, are all walkable. The train station is a five-minute walk from Essex St Mall. The 1.7-mile Heritage Trail connects Salem's major historic sites; follow the red line on the sidewalk.

EXCURSIONS

The chamber of commerce visitors center (☎ 987-744-0004), 32 Derby Square, is open 9 am to 5 pm weekdays, while the National Park Service (NPS) visitors center (☎ 978-740-1650), 2 Liberty St, is open 9 am to 6 pm daily.

The Salem Trolley (☎ 978-744-5469), 8 Central St, with a running commentary, goes by 14 places of interest and departs every half hour or hour, depending on the season. Tickets ($10 for adults, $8 seniors, $5 children age 5 to 12, rates for families) are good all day.

Peabody Essex Museum

America's oldest private museum in continuous operation (☎ 978-745-1876, 800-745-4054), Essex St Mall, houses art, artifacts and curiosities brought back from the Far East by ships out of Salem. It's open 10 am to 5 pm weekdays (9 am to 5 pm weekends) but is closed Monday from November through May. Admission costs $8.50 adults,

$7.50 seniors and college students, $6.50 children age 6 to 18, $20 families.

Witchcraft Sites

The tragic events of 1692 have spawned witch-related attractions, the most authentic of which is the **Witch House** (☎ 978-744-0180), 310½ Essex St. Preliminary examinations of persons accused of witchcraft were held in this magistrate's home. It's open 10 am to 4:30 pm (until 6 pm in July and August); closed December through mid-March. Adults pay $5, seniors $4, children $2.

The **Salem Witch Museum** (☎ 978-744-1692), 19½ Washington Square N, contains dioramas, exhibits and audio-visual shows and has costumed interpretive staff. It's open 10 am to 5 pm (until 7 pm in July and August) and costs $6 adults, $5.50 seniors, $3.75 children age 6 to 14.

The **Witch Dungeon Museum** (☎ 978-741-3570), 16 Lynde St, re-creates a witch trial. It's open 10 am to 5 pm daily April

EXCURSIONS

KIM GRANT

The Witch House

EXCURSIONS

through November. Adults pay $5, seniors $4, children $3.

Salem's best historic house is the **House of the Seven Gables** (☎ 978-744-0991), 54 Turner St, made famous in Nathaniel Hawthorne's novel (1851) that portrays the gloomy Puritan atmosphere of early New England. It's open 10 am to 5 pm daily (noon to 5 pm Sunday, January through March). Adults pay $7, seniors $6, children age 6 to 17 $4.

House lovers should also seek out **Chestnut St**, among the country's most architecturally lovely streets.

The Custom House on Derby Wharf is the centerpiece of the **Salem Maritime National Historic Site** (☎ 978-740-1660), but first go to the Central Wharf Visitors Center, open 9 am to 6 pm in summer, 9 am to 5 pm in winter. Admission to the Custom House, including guided tour, is adults $3, children age 6 to 16 $2, under 6 and seniors free.

Places to Stay & Eat

Winter Island Maritime Park (☎ 978-745-9430, 50 Winter Island Rd) is open May through October for 25 tents ($15) and 30 RVs ($18 with electricity).

The *Clipper Ship Inn* (☎ 978-745-8022, 40 Bridge St/MA 1A) has 60 motel rooms for $78 to $120.

The *Stephen Daniels House* (☎ 978-744-5709, 1 Daniels St) must be Salem's oldest lodging, with parts dating from before the witch trials. Rooms are $85 to $95 single, $115 to $190 double.

Red's Sandwich Shop (☎ 978-745-3527, 15 Central St), in the old London Coffee House building (1698), has (guess what?) sandwiches.

For espresso, lattes, scones and bagels, *Front St Coffeehouse* (☎ 978-740-6697, 20 Front St) is the coolest place. Sandwiches are served 11 am to 4 pm.

Museum Place Mall (2 East India Square) has breakfast and quickie lunch places, including *Thai Place* (☎ 978-741-8008), where a big plate of pad Thai costs $7.

In a Pig's Eye (☎ 978-741-4436, 148 Derby St) has an eclectic menu, including salads, vegetarian dishes and pasta for less than $14.

Monday and Tuesday are Mexican nights, and there's live entertainment most evenings (no dinner on Sunday).

Getting There & Away

MBTA Commuter Rail trains (☎ 617-222-3200, 800-392-6100, www.mbta.com) run frequently from Boston's North Station to Salem. When the station is open, buy tickets before boarding or pay a $2 surcharge.

MBTA bus Nos 450 and 455 from Boston's Haymarket Square (near North Station) take longer than the train and cost no less.

Salem lies 20 miles northeast of Boston, a 35-minute drive if it's not rush hour. From Boston, follow US 1 north across the Mystic River (Tobin) Bridge and bear right onto MA 16 (Revere Beach Parkway) toward Revere Beach, then follow MA 1A (Shore Rd) to Salem. MA 1A becomes Lafayette St in Salem and takes you right to Essex St Mall and the common.

MARBLEHEAD

First settled in 1629, Marblehead's Old Town is a picturesque maritime village with winding streets and brightly painted colonial and early-American houses.

Orientation & Information

Take Pleasant St (MA 114) to the Marblehead Historic District, called Old Town, with its narrow curving streets, many one-way. Parking is a problem in summer, so park inland and explore on foot.

Washington, State and Mugford Sts intersect at Old Town House, the nearest thing Marblehead has to a main square. Heading southeast along Washington and State Sts brings you to the State St Landing, the town's main dock. Marblehead Neck is a wooded island east of the town center. It's

connected to the mainland by the Ocean Ave causeway.

The chamber of commerce information booth (☎ 781-631-2868), on Pleasant St at Essex and Spring Sts, offers a walking tour brochure and map. Off-season, the chamber's office (9 am to 5 pm daily) is in the Masonic Lodge, 62 Pleasant St.

Things to See & Do

Old Town is perfect for strolling, café-sitting, window-shopping, photo-snapping and picnicking. A block west of State St Landing, Crocker Park has excellent harbor views and picnic possibilities. On Marblehead Neck's Ocean Ave is an Audubon Bird Sanctuary (access is on the southwest side via Risley St).

The patriotic painting *The Spirit of '76* (1876) in **Abbott Hall** (☎ 781-631-0000) depicts three Revolutionary War figures – a drummer, a fife player and a flag bearer. It's on view 8 am to 5 pm weekdays, with extended hours from June to October, for free.

The Georgian **Jeremiah Lee Mansion** (☎ 781-631-1069), near Hooper and Washington Sts, houses period furnishings and collections of toys and children's furniture, folk art and nautical and military artifacts. It's open 10 am to 4 pm (1 to 4 pm Sunday) mid-May through October. Adults pay $4, seniors and students $3.50, under 10 free.

Across the street, the historic 1728 **King Hooper Mansion** (☎ 781-631-2608), 8 Hooper St, is home to the Marblehead Arts Association and holds four floors of changing exhibits. Hours are 10 am to 4 pm (1 to 5 pm Sunday). Exhibits are free; the house tour costs $1.

Places to Stay & Eat

Marblehead has two dozen B&Bs; they're small, so reservations are essential. *A Lady Winette Cottage (☎ 781-631-8579, 3 Corinthian Lane)* is a Victorian cottage with two rooms sharing a bath for $85 to $95. *Bishops Bed & Breakfast (☎ 781-631-4954, 10 Harding Lane)*, right on the water, charges $85 to $135 for each of its three rooms. *Harbor Light Inn (☎ 781-631-2186, 58 Washington St)* is Marblehead's 'big' hostelry, with 21 rooms from $125 to $245. Half have fire-

places and five have Jacuzzis. There's a heated pool.

Near State St Landing, the *Landing (☎ 781-631-1878, 81 Front St)* is a full-service restaurant and pub with a long menu and dining inside and out. Lunches cost $10 to $18, dinners are pricier.

Across the parking lot, the inexpensive *Driftwood Café (☎ 781-631-1145, 63 Front St)* is a Marblehead fixture, serving early risers from 5:30 am. It closes at 2 pm after lunch (open until 5 pm weekends in summer).

The *King's Rook (☎ 781-631-9838, 12 State St)* is a café and wine bar good for coffee or rich dessert, or a light meal of pizza, soup and salad or a sandwich. It's open noon to 11:30 pm; closed Monday evening.

Another good place for coffee drinks, pastries or a light meal is *Caffe Appassionato (☎ 781-639-3200, 12 Atlantic Ave)*. It's open 6 am to 9 pm weekdays, from 7 am weekends.

Getting There & Away

From Salem, follow MA 114 southeast for 4 miles to Marblehead, where it becomes Pleasant St.

From Boston, take MBTA bus No 441 or 442 from Boston's Haymarket Square (near North Station) or bus No 448 or 449 from South Station.

CAPE ANN

North of Boston, Cape Ann offers fishing, art galleries and quintessential New England quaintness. The region makes for a relaxing day trip or longer sojourn out of the city.

Gloucester

Incorporated in 1623 by fisherfolk, until the early 1990s Gloucester made its living at fishing. In 1995, when most of the once-rich fishing grounds were closed due to overfishing, up to 20,000 anglers found themselves out of work.

Orientation & Information Washington St runs from Grant Circle (a traffic circle/rotary on MA 128) to St Peter's Square, a brick plaza overlooking the sea. Rogers St,

EXCURSIONS

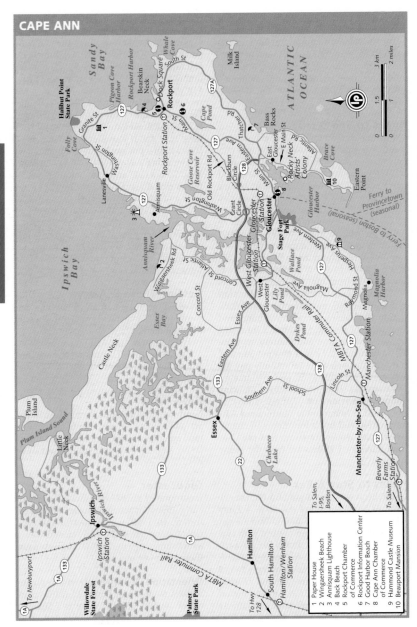

CAPE ANN

Sandy Bay

Halibut Point State Park

Pigeon Cove Harbor

Rockport Harbor

Bearskin Neck

Dock Square

South St

Whale Cove

Milk Island

ATLANTIC OCEAN

3 km
2 miles
1.5
1
0

Granite St

Folly Cove

Washington St

Lanesville

127

Rockport Station

Rockport

Goose Cove Reservoir

Cape Pond

Blackburn Circle

Old Rockport Rd

127

Thatcher Rd

Bass Rocks

Eastern Ave

128

Main St

East Gloucester

Rocky Neck Artists' Colony

Atlantic Rd

Brace Cove

Eastern Point

Ferry to Provincetown (seasonal)

Annisquam

Annisquam River

Wingaersheek Rd

Concord St

Atlantic St

Washington St

Grant Circle

Gloucester Station

Gloucester

Stage Fort Park

Western Ave

Gloucester Harbor

Ipswich Bay

West Gloucester Station

West Gloucester

Lily Pond

Wallace Pond

Magnolia Ave

Dykes Pond

Hesperus Ave

Raymond St

Magnolia

Magnolia Harbor

127

Essex Bay

Castle Neck

Eastern Ave

Essex Ave

School St

Southern Ave

128

Lincoln St

MBTA Commuter Rail

Manchester Station

Plum Island

Plum Island Sound

Little Neck

133

Essex

22

Chebacco Lake

133

Manchester-by-the-Sea

127

Beverly Farms Station

To Salem, I-95, Boston

To Salem

Ipswich River

Ipswich

Ipswich Station

1A

To Newburyport

133

1A

Willowdale State Forest

Hamilton

South Hamilton Station

Hamilton/Wenham Station

MBTA Commuter Rail

Palmer State Park

To Hwy 128

1A

1   Paper House
2   Wingaersheek Beach
3   Annisquam Lighthouse
4   Back Beach
5   Rockport Chamber of Commerce
6   Rockport Information Center
7   Good Harbor Beach
8   Cape Ann Chamber of Commerce
9   Hammond Castle Museum
10   Beauport Mansion

the waterfront road, goes east from the plaza; Main St, the business and shopping thoroughfare, is one block inland. East Gloucester, with the Rocky Neck artists' colony, is on the southeastern side of Gloucester Harbor.

The Cape Ann chamber of commerce (☎ 978-283-1601, 800-321-0133), 33 Commercial St, is just south of St Peter's Square. In summer, a visitors information office is open in Stage Fort Park, on the west side of the Annisquam River. Pick up their fine walking tour map of the Maritime Trail or follow signs posted around town.

Rocky Neck Cape Ann's natural beauty, and in particular the narrow peninsula of Rocky Neck, has attracted artists for at least a century. Follow Main St east and south around the northeastern end of Gloucester Harbor to East Gloucester. Turn onto Rocky Neck Ave, park in the lot on the right and walk five minutes to the galleries and restaurants.

Hammond Castle Museum Dr Hammond collected European art, and today each section of his eccentric castle-home epitomizes a period in European history: Romanesque, medieval, Gothic and Renaissance. Furnishings are sometimes quirky. The museum (☎ 978-283-7673) is open 10 am to 5 pm daily from late May through October, 10 am to 4 pm weekends only from November to late May. The 45-minute guided tour costs $6 adults, $5 seniors and college students, $4 children age 4 to 12.

Beauport Mansion This lavish 'summer cottage' (☎ 978-283-0800), 75 Eastern Point Blvd, East Gloucester, is a wildly eclectic but artistically surprising place. Beauport is open 10 am to 4 pm weekdays from mid-May to mid-October, and also 10 am to 4 pm weekends from mid-September to mid-October. Admission costs $6 adults, $5.50 seniors, $3 children age 6 to 12.

Beaches The best and most popular is **Wingaersheek Beach**, on Ipswich Bay, with a view of the Annisquam lighthouse. Take the

KIM GRANT

Heading home after a particularly cold day

Concord St exit from MA 128 and head north several miles. Admission costs $15 per car on weekends, $10 on weekdays. Another big beach is **Good Harbor Beach**, east of East Gloucester off MA 127A on the way to Rockport. Arrive early on hot days and weekends.

Places to Stay & Eat The *Camp Annisquam Campground* (☎ 978-283-2992, *Stanwood Point, West Gloucester*) has 35 tent and trailer sites for $18 in summer.

Cape Ann Campsite (☎ 978-283-8683, 80 *Atlantic St, Gloucester*) has 300 sites at $17; $20 with hookups.

Follow Eastern Point Ave until it becomes Atlantic Rd to find several sea-view motels. Most of these have rooms from $80 to $190 and most are closed from December through March. There's the *Ocean View Resort & Inn* (☎ 978-283-6200, 800-315-7557, 171 Atlantic Rd); the *Atlantis Motor Inn* (☎ 978-283-0014, 125 Atlantic Rd); and

EXCURSIONS

KIM GRANT

Before cell phones...

the **Bass Rocks Ocean Inn** (☎ 978-283-7600, 800-528-1234, 103 Atlantic Rd).

There are plenty of dining options downtown. Grab pizza ($1.50), picnic supplies and cookies at **Virgilio's Italian Bakery** (☎ 978-283-5295, 29 Main St).

Mike's Pastry & Coffee Shop (☎ 978-283-5333, 37 Main St) has excellent Italian pastries and, in summer, cooling lemon ice.

Captain Carlo's Seafoods (☎ 978-283-6342), with picnic tables on the water on Harbor Loop, is a seafood market offering fresh, inexpensive seafood ($4 to $9, lobster a bit more). The huge fisherman's platter goes for $15.

Blackburn Tavern (☎ 978-282-1919, 2 Main St), at Washington St, is an upscale tavern with sandwiches ($5 to $8), main courses ($9 to $13) and, of course, drinks.

Within Rocky Neck, the **Studio** (☎ 978-283-4123, 51 Rocky Neck Ave) is the epicenter of the local dating scene. It's great for lunch, a light dinner or a drink on the deck

overlooking the harbor. Almost everything is less than $12.

Just down the street, the **Rudder** (☎ 978-283-7967, 73 Rocky Neck Ave) opens at 5:30 pm. Request a table on the seaside deck when making your dinner reservation. The simplest dishes are the best.

Getting There & Away MBTA Commuter Rail trains (☎ 617-222-3200, 800-392-6100, www.mbta.com) run from Boston's North Station to Gloucester (one hour, $3.75).

AC Cruise Line (☎ 617-261-6633), 290 Northern Ave, sails from Boston's Seaport District to Gloucester once daily Tuesday through Sunday from late May to early September. The ferry trip allows for a 2½-hour visit to Gloucester. Roundtrip tickets cost $20 adults, $16 seniors; children 12 and under ride with parents for free.

Rockport

A century ago, Winslow Homer and other acclaimed artists came here to paint fisherfolk who wrested a hard living from the sea. Today, Rockport is supported by tourists who come to watch artists.

Orientation & Information The center of town is Dock Square, at the beginning of Bearskin Neck. Most everything is within a 10-minute walk of it. The railroad station is less than a 15-minute walk west of Dock Square.

Parking is difficult on summer weekends. Park at one of the lots on MA 127 from Gloucester and take the shuttle bus.

The chamber of commerce (☎ 978-546-6575, 888-726-3922), 3 Pier Ave, Rockport, MA 01966, is just off Main St, uphill from Dock Square. It's open 9 am to 5 pm Monday to Saturday (only weekdays in winter). The Rockport Information Center, on MA 127 as you enter Rockport from Gloucester, is open in summer.

Things to See & Do Rockport is a walking town. Start at Dock Square and wander along Bearskin Neck, finally emerging at the breakwater overlooking Rockport Harbor and Sandy Bay. The red fishing shack decorated with colorful buoys is 'Motif No 1.' Artists have been painting and photographing it for so long that it well deserves its tongue-in-cheek name.

Follow Main St west and north from Dock Square to reach Back Beach on Sandy Bay, the nearest beach to the town center.

For excellent views, walk 10 minutes southeast from Dock Square along Mt Pleasant St, then east along Atlantic Ave or Heywood Ave to the public footpath marked 'Way to the Headlands.'

Only a few miles north of Dock Square along MA 127 is **Halibut Point State Park** (☎ 978-546-2997), open daily, with a parking fee of $2. A 10-minute walk brings you to abandoned granite quarries and a granite foreshore perfect for picnicking, sunbathing, reading or painting.

Inland from Pigeon Cove is the **Paper House** (☎ 978-546-2629), 52 Pigeon Hill St, a curiosity that was begun in 1922 and finished 20 years and 100,000 newspapers later. Made of folded, rolled and pasted papers, some walls are 215 layers thick. The furnishings – even a grandfather clock and a piano – are all made of newspapers, too. The house is open 10 am to 5 pm April through October, for a donation.

Places to Stay & Eat Founded in 1906 by the National League of Working Women, *Rockport Lodge* (☎ 978-546-2090, 61 South St) offers beds and two meals to women only for $50 single, $45 per person double or $40 per person triple; without meals it's $35. Linens are provided, but bring your own towels.

Conveniently located, *Lantana House* (☎ 978-546-3535, 800-291-3535, 22 Broadway) has some of the least-expensive rooms: double or twin-bed rooms for $79 to $89.

Sally Webster Inn (☎ 978-546-9251, 877-546-9251, 34 Mt Pleasant St) is a handsome Federal colonial built in 1832, offering rooms with private bath for $80 to $94, while the lovely Greek Revival *Addison Choate Inn* (☎ 978-546-7543, 800-245-7543, 49 Broadway) is among the more charming and historic inns, with a swimming pool. Rooms are $115 to $150.

Bearskin Neck is crowded with ice cream shops, cafés and eateries. You'll pass several places good for a bowl of chowder, fish and chips, or cheap lobster. *Roy Moore Lobster Co* (☎ 978-546-6696) has the cheapest lobster-in-the-rough on the Neck. For more refinement, go upstairs next-door to *Roy Moore's Fish Shack Restaurant* (☎ 978-546-6667), which has fairly low prices given its ocean-view dining. Off to the left on a side street is the *Portside Chowder House* (☎ 978-546-7045), a tiny place specializing in chowders, sandwiches and pies. The most expensive item, except lobster, is only $10. *My Place by the Sea* (☎ 978-546-9667, 68 Bearskin Neck) has panoramic bay views, indoor and outdoor seating and an interesting menu. Lunch (about $8 to $12) is a good value, and the New American dinners ($25 to $40) are very good. *Helmut's Strudel* (☎ 978-546-2824, 49 Bearskin Neck), almost near the outer end, serves strudels, croissants, pastries, cider and coffee.

Remember that Rockport is 'dry,' with no alcohol for sale in stores or restaurants.

Getting There & Away Rockport is the terminus for MBTA Commuter Rail trains (☎ 617-222-3200, 800-392-6100, www.mbta.com) on the Rockport line. The trip from Boston takes about 75 minutes and costs $4 for adults.

If you're driving, MA 127 makes two loops around Cape Ann, both passing through Rockport. From Boston it takes one hour to drive the 40 miles to Rockport; from Gloucester it's 7 miles (about 15 minutes); from Salem it takes about 40 minutes to cover the 23 miles.

Getting Around The Cape Ann Transportation Authority (CATA; ☎ 978-283-7916) operates bus routes around Cape Ann that are both scenic and useful. On Saturday, Sunday and holidays from early June through mid-September, its Saltwater Trolleys make nine runs per day connecting Essex, Gloucester, Rockport and outlying areas. For $4 adults, $2 seniors and children age 5 to 12, you can hop on and off anywhere along the route.

PLYMOUTH
'America's Home Town' is synonymous with the Pilgrims who stepped ashore in 1620, seeking a place to practice their religion without interference from government. Plymouth Rock – a weathered ball of granite – can be seen in a minute, but the symbol is elucidated in nearby museums and exhibits.

Orientation & Information
'The rock' is within walking distance of most museums and restaurants. Main St, the main commercial street, is a block inland.

The town's visitors information center, 'Destination Plymouth' (☎ 508-747-7533), 225 Water St, is open 9 am to 4 pm weekdays year-round. There is also a seasonal information booth at the traffic circle on Water St.

Mayflower II

A Rock & a Ship
If Plymouth Rock, open to view all the time for free, tells little about the Pilgrims, *Mayflower II* (☎ 508-746-1622), a replica of the small ship in which they made the fateful voyage, speaks volumes. With all provisions, animals and seed to establish a colony, 102 people lived on this tiny vessel for 66 days, subsisting on hard, moldy biscuits, rancid butter and brackish water.

Mayflower II is open 9 am to 5 pm daily from April to late November. Admission costs $6.50 adults, $4 children; discounted combination tickets for $19 and $11 include Plimoth Plantation.

Plimoth Plantation
A mile south of Plymouth Rock, Plimoth Plantation (☎ 508-746-1622), MA 3A, is an authentic re-creation of settlements from 1627. Everything in the village – costumes, implements, vocabulary, artistry, recipes and crops – has been painstakingly researched and accurately reproduced. Hobbamock's (Wampanoag) Homesite replicates Native American community life during the same period. Tickets and hours are the same as for the *Mayflower II*.

Historic Houses & Museums
Pilgrim Hall Museum (☎ 508-746-1620), 75 Court St, displays real items the Pilgrims and their Wampanoag neighbors used daily. It's open 9:30 am to 4:30 pm daily; closed in January. Admission costs $5 adults, $4.50 seniors, $3 children.

The **Plymouth National Wax Museum** (☎ 508-746-6468), 16 Carver St, has life-sized wax figures – 180 in 26 scenes – that recount the Pilgrims' progress from England to America. The museum is open 9 am to 5 pm daily (until 7 pm May through October); closed December through February. Admission costs $6 adults, $2.75 children.

The **Richard Sparrow House** (☎ 508-747-1240), 42 Summer St, built in 1640 by an original settler, is the oldest house in Plymouth. It's open 10 am to 5 pm daily (except Wednesday) April through November for $2 adults, $1 children.

KIM GRANT

The 1667 **Howland House** (☎ 508-746-9590), 33 Sandwich St, began as the residence for a family that came over on the *Mayflower*. Tours are given 10 am to 4:30 pm daily from late May to late November; tickets cost $3.50 adults, $3 seniors, $1 children.

The **Mayflower Society Museum** (☎ 508-746-2590), 4 Winslow St, dates from 1754 and shows how wealthy Plymouth became in just over a century. It's open 10 am to 4 pm daily from July to early September (and Friday to Sunday in June and until mid-October).

The Plymouth Antiquarian Society (☎ 508-746-0012) maintains three historic houses. Stop in first at the **Harlow Old Fort House** (1677), 119 Sandwich St, which shows how second-generation Plymouth colonists lived. The houses are open 10 am to 4 pm Thursday to Saturday, early June to mid-October. Tickets are $3 adults, $1 children; combo tickets to all three houses cost $6 adults, $2 children.

Cranberries made it onto the Pilgrims' first Thanksgiving menu and have been a tradition ever since. Learn about the healthful fruit at **Cranberry World** (☎ 508-747-2350), Water St, open 9:30 am to 5 pm daily May through November; free.

Places to Stay & Eat

Myles Standish State Forest (☎ 877-422-6762) is about 6 miles south of Plymouth. Take MA 3 exit 5 or MA 58 to South Carver. Within the 16,000-acre park are 16 miles of bike trails, hiking trails, nine ponds (two with beaches) and 450 campsites. There is camping mid-April to mid-October, but the park is open year-round.

Wompatuck State Park (☎ 781-749-7160, 877-422-6762), off MA 228, Hingham, is 30 miles north of Plymouth. Open late May to early September, the 2900-acre park has 12 miles of paved biking trails, even more mountain biking trails, hiking trails and 250 campsites.

Governor Bradford Inn (☎ 508-746-6200, 800-332-1620, 98 Water St) is convenient and charges $93 to $130 for double rooms; some with sea views. Off-season it's $59 to $79 double.

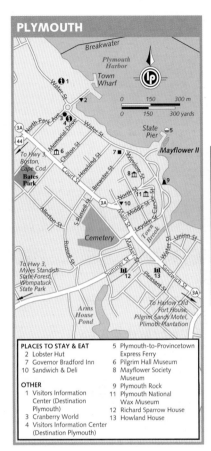

PLYMOUTH

PLACES TO STAY & EAT	5 Plymouth-to-Provincetown
2 Lobster Hut	Express Ferry
7 Governor Bradford Inn	6 Pilgrim Hall Museum
10 Sandwich & Deli	8 Mayflower Society
	Museum
OTHER	9 Plymouth Rock
1 Visitors Information	11 Plymouth National
Center (Destination	Wax Museum
Plymouth)	12 Richard Sparrow House
3 Cranberry World	13 Howland House
4 Visitors Information Center	
(Destination Plymouth)	

The *Pilgrim Sands Motel* (☎ 508-747-0900, 800-729-7263, 150 Warren Ave), just across from Plimoth Plantation, charges $98 to $130 for summertime rooms, $50 to $110 off-season.

Fast-food shops line Water St opposite the *Mayflower II*. For better food at lower prices, walk a block inland to Main St. The *Sandwich & Deli* (☎ 508-746-7773, 65 Main St) has clam chowder, sandwiches and other quick lunches. For a sea view, the *Lobster Hut* (☎ 508-746-2270), at Town Wharf, has indoor and outdoor seating, big plates of

Ah, the peril of losing a contact lens in this Plymouth cranberry bog.

reasonably priced fried clams and tasty fish and chips.

Getting There & Away

Frequent Plymouth & Brockton buses (☎ 508-746-0378, 778-9767, www.p-b.com) connect Boston and Plymouth in a one-hour trip. The P&B terminal is in North Plymouth's Industrial Park off MA 3 at exit 7, about 2 miles from the center of town. Some morning buses stop at the old post office in the middle of town.

Trains depart Boston's South Station (☎ 617-222-3200, 800-392-6100) for Cordage Park, where 'GATRA' buses (☎ 508-222-6106) connect to Plymouth Center. One-way tickets are $3.25.

Plymouth is 40 miles south of Boston via US 3; if it's not rush hour, the drive is less than an hour.

The Plymouth-to-Provincetown Express Ferry (☎ 508-747-2400, 800-242-2469), from State Pier, takes 90 minutes. It departs Plymouth at 10 am and leaves Provincetown at 4:30 pm. From mid-June to early September, service is daily. A roundtrip ticket costs $25 adults, $20 seniors and $16 children under 12; bikes cost an additional $2.

CAPE COD

'The Cape' is arguably New England's favorite summer destination, and it's driven by tourism. Beaches cover much of its 400-mile shoreline, and there's real beauty in the outer Cape's dune-studded landscapes, its tall sea grass and its colonial towns. Although you can see parts of the Cape in a day trip, if you have three or four days, all the better.

Orientation & Information Cape-wide information can be found at the Massachusetts Tourist Information Center (☎ 508-746-1150), in Plymouth at exit 5 off MA 3. The building is open roughly 8:30 am to 4:30 pm daily year-round.

Once on Cape Cod, stop at the Cape Cod chamber of commerce (☎ 508-862-0700, 800-332-2732), just off US 6 at exit 6 in Hyannis.

The Sagamore and Bourne Bridges span the Cape Cod Canal, linking the Cape to the mainland. Use the Sagamore Bridge for points along MA 6A, Hyannis, the Outer Cape and Provincetown.

MA 28, which heads south from the Bourne Bridge to Falmouth, runs along the southern shore past Hyannis and into Chatham, heading north to end in Orleans.

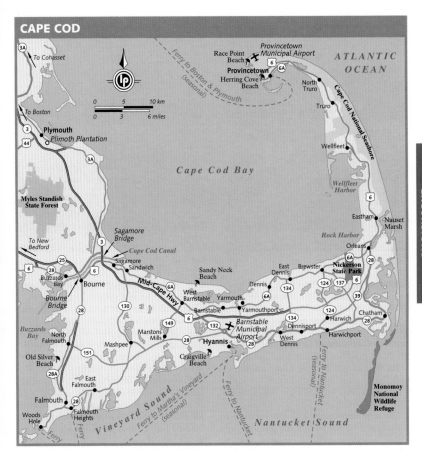

CAPE COD

To Cohasset
To Boston

Plymouth
Plimoth Plantation

Myles Standish
State Forest

To New
Bedford

Sagamore
Bridge

Cape Cod Canal

Sagamore
Sandwich

Buzzards
Bay

Bourne

Bourne
Bridge

Buzzards
Bay

North
Falmouth

Mashpee

Marstons
Mills

Old Silver
Beach

East
Falmouth

Falmouth

Falmouth
Heights

Woods
Hole

Ferry to Boston & Plymouth (seasonal)

Race Point
Beach

Provincetown
Municipal Airport

ATLANTIC
OCEAN

Provincetown

Herring Cove
Beach

North
Truro

Truro

Cape Cod National Seashore

Wellfleet

Cape Cod Bay

Wellfleet
Harbor

Eastham

Nauset
Marsh

Rock Harbor

Orleans

East
Dennis

Brewster

Nickerson
State Park

Sandy Neck
Beach

Dennis

West
Barnstable

Yarmouth

Barnstable

Yarmouthport

Mid-Cape Hwy

Hyannis

Craigville
Beach

Barnstable
Municipal Airport

Dennisport

West
Dennis

Harwich

Harwichport

Chatham

Ferry to Martha's Vineyard (seasonal)

Ferry to Nantucket (seasonal)

Ferry to Nantucket

Vineyard Sound

Nantucket Sound

Monomoy
National
Wildlife
Refuge

Ferry

EXCURSIONS

Between Falmouth and Chatham, MA 28 is congested with strip malls, fast-food joints and motels.

US 6, also called the Mid-Cape Hwy, an inland highway from the canal to Orleans and on to Provincetown, is the only through street. The alternative is MA 6A, a rural and scenic two-lane road between Sandwich and Orleans.

The paved Cape Cod Rail Trail, great for bicycling and in-line skating, follows an abandoned flat railroad bed for 26 miles from Dennis to Wellfleet. Park at Nickerson State Park or the trailhead on Rte 134 in

South Dennis, south of US 6, where you can rent wheels.

Rte 6A

If you have time, you won't regret taking this scenic byway rather than the inland US 6. A historical commission tightly restricts building, keeping the former 'King's Highway' safe from the clutter that plagues MA 28.

Sandwich, founded in 1637, is one of the Cape's most attractive towns. The quaint village center boasts a duck pond and **Dexter Grist Mill** (near Main and River Sts); fine historic houses, including the circa 1675

KIM GRANT

Cape Cod Rail Trail

Hoxie House (☎ 508-888-1173), 18 Water St; the famous **Sandwich Glass Museum** (☎ 508-888-0251), 129 Main St, chronicling the town's glassmaking heyday from 1825 to 1888; and a renowned horticultural park, **Heritage Plantation of Sandwich** (☎ 508-888-3300), with indoor collections of Americana.

Each side of the **Cape Cod Canal** has a well-maintained bike trail. In Sandwich, rent bicycles at Sandwich Cycles (☎ 508-833-2453), 40 MA 6A.

Through **Barnstable**, MA 6A continues as a tranquil, winding route dotted with antique stores, art galleries, craft shops and pricey B&Bs. The **West Parish Meeting House** (☎ 508-362-8624), Rte 149 between US 6 and MA 6A, dates to 1717. Barnstable's best attraction is **Sandy Neck Beach**, off MA 6A, a 6-mile stretch of barrier beach with a 9-mile (roundtrip) trail through dunes and salt marshes. Parking is $10.

In **Yarmouth**, the **Winslow Crocker House** (☎ 508-362-4385), 250 MA 6A, is a lovely Georgian house filled with antiques dating from the 17th century. The **Captain Bangs Hallet House** (☎ 508-362-3021), off MA 6A, was once home to a prosperous sea captain. The historic **Hallet's** (☎ 508-362-3362), 139 MA 6A, began as an apothecary in 1889 and still boasts its original soda fountain. **Grey's Beach** (also known as Bass Hole Beach), off Centre St from MA 6A, has a boardwalk that stretches over a tidal marsh.

Continuing along MA 6A, **Dennis** boasts the **Cape Museum of Fine Arts** (☎ 508-385-4477), MA 6A, representing Cape artists working in a variety of media.

From **Scargo Tower** (take MA 6A to Old Bass River Rd to Scargo Hill Rd), you can see to Provincetown on a clear day. **Chapin Memorial Beach**, off MA 6A, is a long, dune-backed beach. As with all bayside beaches, at low tide you can walk for a mile onto the tidal flats. Parking is $9.

The **Cape Playhouse** (☎ 508-385-3838, 385-3911), 820 MA 6A, is one of the Cape's best summer theaters. Next-door, the **Cape Cinema** (☎ 508-385-2503) shows foreign, art and independent films.

In **Brewster**, stop at the **Cape Cod Museum of Natural History** (☎ 508-896-3867), MA 6A. The museum offers walking trails, plus canoe, kayak and seal-watching trips.

The 2000-acre **Nickerson State Park** boasts eight ponds, trails for bicycling and walking, picnic sites and sandy beaches. You can rent all sorts of boats on Flax Pond within the park. The park is free.

From mid-April to early May, thousands of herring migrate from the ocean to fresh water in order to spawn at the picturesque **Stony Brook Grist Mill & Herring Run**, at Setucket and Stony Brook Rds (both off MA 6A).

Places to Stay With the exception of a couple of campgrounds, MA 6A is lined with former sea captains' houses that have been converted into romantic B&Bs.

Shawme Crowell State Forest (☎ 508-888-0351, 877-422-6762 for reservations), off Rte 130 from MA 6A, Sandwich, has 285 wooded sites on 3000 acres. Open year-round, camping costs $6 to $12.

Nickerson State Park (☎ 508-896-3491, 877-422-6762 for reservations, 3488 MA 6A, Brewster) has the Cape's best campsites. There are 420 wooded sites, some with pond views, that cost $6 to $15. Most sites are rented first-come, first-served. In the summer, don't get your hopes up. Although it's open year-round, there are no toilet facilities or running water in winter.

About 5 miles east of Sandwich, *Spring Garden Motel (☎ 508-888-0710, 800-303-1751, 578 MA 6A)* has nine rooms and two efficiency apartments. Rooms overlook a tranquil salt marsh and rent for $89 to $109 summer, $79 to $99 off-season.

The lovely *Wedgewood Inn (☎ 508-362-5157, 83 MA 6A, Yarmouthport)* has nine spacious rooms filled with antiques, oriental carpets and fireplaces. Rates are $135 to $195 June through October, $105 to $155 off-season.

The *Isaiah Hall B&B Inn (☎ 508-385-9928, 800-736-0160, 152 Whig St)*, off MA 6A, Dennis, offers 11 nice rooms for $96 to $137 in summer, a little lower off-season; closed mid-October to mid-April.

Places to Eat The *Dunbar Tea Shop (☎ 508-833-2485, 1 Water St, Sandwich)* offers a ploughman's lunch, soup, quiche and Scottish shortbread at lunchtime, as well as authentic English tea in the afternoon. It's open daily from late May through October and Thursday through Monday the rest of the year.

Mill Way Fish & Lobster Market (☎ 508-362-2760, Barnstable Harbor) has fish sandwiches and fried seafood from April through October.

Inaho (☎ 508-362-5522, 157 MA 6A, Yarmouthport) offers excellent sushi, traditional bento boxes, tempura and more exotic dishes.

Abbicci (☎ 508-362-3501, 43 MA 6A, Yarmouthport) serves contemporary Italian dishes in a converted 18th-century home. You'll spend $17 to $27 for dinner, half that for lunch.

The *Contrast Bistro & Espresso Bar (☎ 508-385-9100, 605 MA 6A, Dennis)* serves large portions of creative dishes. Desserts are luscious and the coffee's strong.

Hyannis

The commercial and transportation hub of Cape Cod, Hyannis is highly trafficked. The waterfront and Main St area have been rejuvenated, and it's a pleasant place to wait for a bus.

Orientation & Information From US 6, take Rte 132 south (exit 6) to the airport traffic circle/rotary to Barnstable Rd to Main St.

The Hyannis Area chamber of commerce (☎ 508-362-5230, 800-449-6647), 1481 Rte 132, about a mile south of US 6, is generally open 9 am to 5 pm Monday through Saturday year-round. From late May to early September, it's also open on Sunday.

Places to Eat Open morning 'til late at night, the *Prodigal Son (☎ 508-771-1337, 10 Ocean St)*, a laid-back coffeehouse, has a limited but sufficient selection of lunch and dinner plates and a fine selection of microbrews and wine.

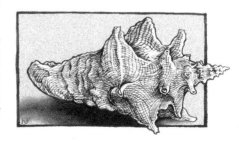

Spiritus (☎ *508-775-2955, 500 Main St*), a popular, funky hangout, serves strong coffee, pizza by the slice and filling sandwiches.

La Petite France (☎ *508-771-4445, 349 Main St*) has onion soup, Mediterranean salads, clam chowder and sandwiches made with baguettes and home-roasted meats.

Getting There & Away The Plymouth & Brockton bus (☎ 508-746-0378, 778-9767, www.p-b.com) connects Boston to Hyannis and points east, to Provincetown. There are about 30 daily buses from Boston to Hyannis ($12 one way) and four daily buses from Hyannis to Provincetown ($9 one way).

Hyannis is one of the few places on Cape Cod where you can rent a car. Hertz (☎ 800-654-3131) and National (☎ 800-227-7368) are at the Barnstable Municipal Airport. U-Save (☎ 508-790-4700) and Trek (☎ 508-771-2459) are two blocks away.

Hyannis is 79 miles (1½ hours) from Boston and 50 miles (1¼ hours) from Provincetown.

Outer Cape

Eastham, Wellfleet and Truro are the most seasonal and quietest towns on the Cape, even in summer. Eastham is perhaps best known for a less than amicable 1620 'encounter' between the Pilgrims and Native Americans. Wellfleet's lure includes its art galleries, fine beaches and famous oysters. Sleepy Truro has good camping and beaches.

Orientation & Information Everything of interest is on or just off US 6, the only highway from Eastham to Provincetown. Beyond North Truro, MA 6A veers off US 6 and is filled with motels as it heads into Provincetown. Wellfleet is best explored by foot or bike. Main and Commercial Sts run more or less parallel to each other in the center of town. Continue west along either road to scenic Chequessett Neck Rd.

The **Cape Cod National Seashore (CCNS)**, which includes the entire eastern shoreline from Chatham to Provincetown, is known for its pristine, seemingly endless beaches, dunes, nature trails, ponds, salt marshes and forests.

At the Salt Pond Visitors Center (☎ 508-255-3421), off US 6 in Eastham, there are excellent exhibits and films about the Cape's geology and history. Check the daily list of ranger- and naturalist-led walks and talks, usually free. The center is open 9 am to 4:30 pm daily (until 5 pm from March through December).

Eastham East of MA 6 atop Fort Hill, the mid-19th-century sea captain's house, the **Edward Penniman House** (☎ 508-255-3421), is slowly being restored by the NPS. Opening times vary; ask at the Salt Pond Visitors Center. Nearby, a lovely 1½-mile (roundtrip) walking trail skirts the marsh and heads inland through a red maple swamp.

A **bike trail** from the Salt Pond Visitors Center to Coast Guard Beach takes you across a salt marsh and through a forest. Rent bikes across from the visitors center at Little Capistrano Bike Shop (☎ 508-255-6515).

Wellfleet Audubon's 1000-acre **Wellfleet Bay Wildlife Sanctuary** (☎ 508-349-2615), west off US 6, boasts walking trails that crisscross tidal creeks, salt marshes and a bay beach.

The 8-mile **Great Island Trail**, off Chequessett Neck Rd in Wellfleet, requires four hours, sunscreen, water and a bit of stamina to walk over soft sand. The lack of human presence more than compensates for the effort.

The **Cape Cod Rail Trail** (see Cape Cod Orientation & Information, earlier in this chapter) ends at LeCount Hollow Rd in Wellfleet, a couple of miles from two good beaches. You can rent bikes at the Idle Times Bike Shop (☎ 508-349-9161) mid-June to mid-September.

Truro The **Highland Light**, also known as Cape Cod Light, east of US 6 in North Truro, replaced the Cape's first lighthouse, built here in 1798. Adjacent is the Cape's oldest public golf course.

Once a summer hotel, the **Highland House Museum** (☎ 508-487-3397), just before the

EXCURSIONS

KIM GRANT

Roam the dunes of the Cape Cod National Seashore.

lighthouse, is now a local museum. It's open 10 am to 4:30 pm daily early June to late September; adults $3.

A 4-mile **bike path** runs from Head of the Meadow Beach in Truro, past the Pilgrim Heights Area, to the end of Highhead Rd.

Beaches In Eastham, **Coast Guard Beach**, east of the visitors center, is backed by tall dune grasses. Facilities include restrooms, showers and changing rooms. Just north, **Nauset Light Beach** is also great. Seasonal passes, valid at any National Seashore beach, are a bargain at $20 and parking permits are transferable.

In Wellfleet, **Marconi Beach**, off US 6, is a narrow ocean beach backed by high dunes; facilities include showers.

In Truro, **Head of the Meadow Beach**, east off US 6, is a wide, dune-backed beach with changing rooms. The bayside **Corn Hill Beach**, off US 6, is lovely for a relaxing walk or for windsurfing. Parking at all beaches is $7.

Places to Stay In Eastham, *Hostelling International, Mid-Cape* (☎ 508-255-2785, 800-909-4776 for reservations in-season, 75 Goody Hallet Drive) is open mid-May to mid-September. The 50 beds in eight cabins cost $14 for members, $17 nonmembers. Reservations are essential in summer. From US 6 and the Orleans traffic circle/rotary, follow Harbor Rd to Bridge Rd to Goody Hallet Drive.

On the rail trail, the *Overlook Inn* (☎ 508-255-1886, US 6), across from the Salt Pond Visitors Center, offers 10 antique-filled rooms and charming common rooms. Rates include full breakfast: $95 to $175 in summer, $95 off-season.

In Wellfleet, *Maurice's Campground* (☎ 508-349-2029, US 6), on the rail trail, reserves a quarter of its 180 sites for tents. They also have cottages and cabins. Open from mid-May to mid-October, tent sites cost $22 for two, cabins $65 for three.

The *Captain's Quarters* (☎ 508-255-5686, 800-327-7769, US 6), a motel with 75 large rooms and a heated pool, offers complimentary bikes. Rates are $97 to $135 in summer, $58 to $89 off-season; closed mid-November through March.

Blue Gateways (☎ *508-349-7530, 252 Main St)* has three homey guest rooms for $90 to $120 late May to September, $70 to $90 off-season.

In Truro, *Hostelling International, Truro* (☎ *508-349-3889, 800-909-4776 for reservations in-season, N Pamet Rd)* is open in summer and costs $14 nightly for members, $17 nonmembers. This former Coast Guard station is just five minutes from the beach.

Open year-round, the *North Truro Camping Area* (☎ *508-487-1847, Highland Rd)* reserves about 100 of its 350 mostly wooded sites for tents; tent sites cost $16 for two.

Places to Eat In Wellfleet, *Beanstock Coffee Roasters* (☎ *508-349-7008, 70 Main St)* dispenses rich espresso and scones from a tiny shop. Hours are irregular.

The *Box Lunch* (☎ *508-349-2178, 50 Briar Lane)* serves deli meats and salads rolled up in pita bread ($4 to $7) year-round.

The *Lighthouse* (☎ *508-349-3681, 317 Main St)*, nothing fancy, just decent food at decent prices and Guinness on tap, is the other place open year-round.

Moby Dick's (☎ *508-349-9795, US 6)*, a self-service place with indoor picnic tables, is the best fried fish joint on the Outer Cape. The clam chowder here is particularly good. Bring your own beer or wine. It's open 11:30 am to 9 pm daily early May to early October.

In Truro, *Jams, Inc* (☎ *508-349-1616)*, off US 6, open late May to early September in 'downtown' Truro, has fancy picnic foods such as rotisserie chicken and salmon pate.

An informal little place, the *Village Café* (☎ 508-487-5800, 4 Highland Rd) offers bagels, sandwiches and soup mid-May through October.

Adrian's (☎ *508-487-4360, US 6, North Truro)*, overlooking the dunes and ocean, offers popular breakfast huevos rancheros and frittatas. An Italian menu with brick-oven pizzas reigns at dinner. It's open nightly mid-May to mid-October and for weekend breakfast in spring and fall, daily in summer.

Entertainment The *Beachcomber* (☎ *508-349-6055, Cahoon Hollow Beach)*, off Ocean View Drive in Wellfleet, is an indoor-outdoor, all-in-one restaurant, bar and nightclub on the beach. Open daily May through September (until 1 am in the summer), it has live music at night and Sunday afternoon concerts and happy hour.

The cozy *Tavern Room* (☎ *508-349-7369, 70 Main St, Wellfleet)* is a fine place to listen to live jazz, folk and Latin music. While you're here you can also nosh on delicious burgers, pizza and upscale but light bistro fare. It's open at 5:30 pm daily May to mid-October.

The *Wellfleet Drive-In* (☎ *508-349-7176, 800-696-3532, US 6)* shows double features at dusk May through September.

Getting There & Away The Plymouth & Brockton bus (☎ 508-746-0378, 778-9767, www.p-b.com) stops at the Eastham Town Hall and the North Eastham village green (both on MA 6); at D&D Market in South Wellfleet (US 6) and the town hall in Wellfleet center (off US 6); and at Jam's in Truro center and Dutra's Market in North Truro (both just off MA 6) on its way from Boston and Hyannis to Provincetown.

Provincetown

Provincetown is the Cape's liveliest resort town and New England's gay mecca. Painters and writers, Portuguese-American anglers and solitude seekers and their families make up this tolerant, year-round community of 3500. The outpost also has long stretches of pristine beach, dramatic sand dunes, contemporary art and one-of-a-kind shops and boutiques. 'P-town,' as it's known to outsiders but never to locals, is jam-packed from late June to early September as its seasonal population swells to 40,000. Because of special events, it's also crowded on weekends through October.

Orientation & Information Commercial St is the town's main drag. About 3 miles long, the one-way street functions as the town's boardwalk. There are plenty of public parking lots. The police station (☎ 508-487-1212) is located at 26 Shank Painter Rd, while the post office (☎ 508-487-0163) is at 211 Commercial St.

The chamber of commerce information booth (☎ 508-487-3424), 305 Commercial St, MacMillan Wharf, is open 9 am to 5 pm daily April through October and 10 am to 4 pm daily (except Wednesday and Sunday) November through December.

The Province Lands Visitors Center (☎ 508-487-1256), at the end of Race Point Rd, is open 9 am to 5 pm daily mid-April through November. It has dozens of scheduled nature-oriented programs.

Flyer's Shuttle (☎ 508-487-0898), 131A Commercial St, ferries sunbathers to remote Long Point mid-May to mid-October; $7 one way, $10 roundtrip.

Art Museums & Galleries Provincetown began attracting artists in the early 1900s and by the 1920s, there was a fashionable art colony. The town remains a vital center of the American arts scene with more than 20 galleries. Pick up a Provincetown Gallery Guide for the current crop.

The **Provincetown Art Association & Museum** (☎ 508-487-1750), 460 Commercial St, one of the country's foremost small museums, was organized in 1914. It's open noon to 5 pm daily (until 8 to 10 pm on Friday and Saturday) late July to early September. Otherwise, hours are limited to noon to 5 pm weekends; admission is $3.

Pilgrim & Pirate Sites The Pilgrims first set foot on American soil in 1620 at Provincetown, at the western end of Commercial St. After failing to find adequate supplies, they forged on to Plymouth. The **Pilgrim Bas-Relief**, behind the Provincetown Town Hall, commemorates the Mayflower Compact, a predecessor to the US Constitution.

The **Pilgrim Monument & Provincetown Museum** (☎ 508-487-1310, 800-247-1620), on High Pole Rd, affords great views, while the museum portrays the Pilgrims' early challenges and the lives of later whaling

captains. It's open 9 am to 5 pm daily April through November, until 7 pm in July and August; nominal admission.

The **Expedition *Whydah*** (☎ *508-487-8899*), 16 MacMillan Wharf, showcases booty from the only pirate ship ever recovered, and it just so happens to be from waters near Marconi Beach (see Beaches, earlier in this chapter). It's open 9 am to 5 pm daily April to September and weekends through January; adults $5, children $3.50.

Beaches Off US 6, **Race Point Beach** has pounding surf and high dunes stretching as far as the eye can see. Parking costs $7 for cars, $2 bicycles. **Herring Cove Beach**, at the end of US 6, has calmer water and more spectacular sunsets. **Long Point Beach** is reached via a water shuttle or a two-hour walk along the stone jetty at the western end of Commercial St.

Activities There are 7 miles of paved **bike trails** within the CCNS. Rent bicycles at Arnold's (☎ 508-487-0844), 329 Commercial

No, no, I've got it.

KIM GRANT

EXCURSIONS

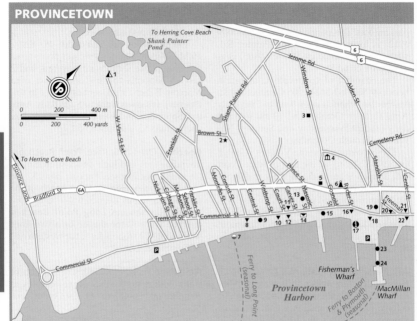

PROVINCETOWN

St, in the center of town, for $3 to $4 per hour, $8 to $12 per half day.

Art's Dune Tours (☎ 508-487-1950), Commercial and Standish Sts, offers hourlong, narrated 4WD dune tours within the CCNS from mid-April to mid-November. Fares are $12 to $15 per person.

Nelson's Riding Stables (☎ 508-487-1112), 43 Race Point Rd, offers one-hour guided horseback rides ($30 per person) traversing dunes and woods from April through October.

Willie Air Tours (☎ 508-487-0240), at the airport on Race Point Rd, offers spectacular 15-minute trips for $25 per person.

The traditional **Schooner *Hindu*** (☎ 508-487-0659) departs from MacMillan Wharf mid-May to mid-October for two-hour bay sails. Adults pay $10 to $15, children $6.

Of the half-dozen companies that offer 3½-hour whale watching trips, the **Dolphin Fleet Whale Watch** (☎ 508-349-1900, 800-826-9300), MacMillan Wharf, is the best,

with onboard naturalists. Tickets cost $18 adults, $15 children, mid-April to October.

Commercial St, lined with creative specialty shops, sells everything from leather implements of torture to artsy t-shirts, from sculpture to handcrafted jewelry. As you wander, don't miss **Marine Specialties** (☎ 508-487-1730), 235 Commercial St, a cavernous store filled with surplus army and navy stuff and random odd items.

Places to Stay The *Coastal Acres Camping Court* (*☎ 508-487-1700, Blueberry Rd*) is open April through October. Tent sites are $23 to $32.

The *Outermost Hostel* (*☎ 508-487-4378, 26/-28 Winslow St*), a privately run hostel, has five cabins housing six bunks ($15 nightly). Common space includes a kitchen and living room; barbecues and picnic tables are handy.

The *Cape Colony Inn* (*☎ 508-487-1755, 280 Bradford St*) has 54 rooms that rent for

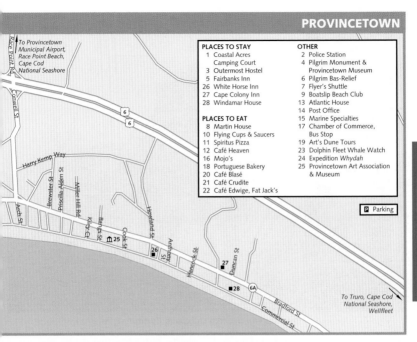

PROVINCETOWN

PLACES TO STAY	OTHER
1 Coastal Acres Camping Court	2 Police Station
3 Outermost Hostel	4 Pilgrim Monument & Provincetown Museum
5 Fairbanks Inn	6 Pilgrim Bas-Relief
26 White Horse Inn	7 Flyer's Shuttle
27 Cape Colony Inn	9 Boatslip Beach Club
28 Windamar House	13 Atlantic House
	14 Post Office
PLACES TO EAT	15 Marine Specialties
8 Martin House	17 Chamber of Commerce, Bus Stop
10 Flying Cups & Saucers	19 Art's Dune Tours
11 Spiritus Pizza	23 Dolphin Fleet Whale Watch
12 Café Heaven	24 Expedition Whydah
16 Mojo's	25 Provincetown Art Association & Museum
18 Portuguese Bakery	
20 Café Blasé	
21 Café Crudite	
22 Café Edwige, Fat Jack's	

P Parking

EXCURSIONS

$85 to $144 double in-season; $67 to $102 off-season; closed November through April.

Provincetown has a hundred delightful small inns and guesthouses. In summer, most of these are booked in advance. If you can't make an advance reservation, arrive early and ask the chamber of commerce for help.

Windamar House (☎ 508-487-0599, 568 Commercial St) has six lovely rooms and two even better apartments. Rooms rent for $70 to $135 in summer; in spring and fall, they drop to $75 to $110; closed January through March.

The *White Horse Inn* (☎ 508-487-1790, 500 Commercial St) rents 12 simple rooms, each decorated with local art, most with shared bath for $70 to $75 double ($40 to $50 single) in summer. Six bungalow-style apartments rent for $125 in summer, with a three-night minimum.

The gracious *Fairbanks Inn* (☎ 508-487-0386, 90 Bradford St), a historic 18th-century hostelry, has been upgraded with fine amenities. The 13 rooms rent for $109 to $225 in summer, $65 to $135 off-season.

Places to Eat Without a doubt, *Spiritus Pizza* (☎ 508-487-2808, 190 Commercial St) is the place to go for a late-night slice; it's open until 2 am. From Memorial Day to Labor Day, their strong coffee and pastries will jump-start you into the next morning.

Flying Cups & Saucers (☎ 508-487-3780, 205–209 Commercial St) makes protein drinks and exotic juice drinks.

Provincetown's favorite snack is a big hunk of hot, sugar-dusted fried dough ($1.50) from the *Portuguese Bakery* (☎ 508-487-1803, 299 Commercial St).

Mojo's (☎ 508-487-3140, Ryder St), at MacMillan Wharf, a classic fried fish shack, is open for lunch mid-May to mid-October, for dinner in summer.

Dark, cozy, moderately priced *Fat Jack's* (☎ 508-487-4822, 335 Commercial St) is a

Provincetown's cluttered and quaint Commercial St

year-round standby for burgers and fish and chips. It's open for lunch and dinner.

The principal activity at *Café Blasé* (☎ 508-487-9465, 328 Commercial St) is dishing people sauntering by. But the crab-meat, Caesar salad with grilled tuna and garden burgers are good, too. Prices are about $7 to $15.

Light and airy but small and crowded, *Café Heaven* (☎ 508-487-9639, 199 Commercial St) is a value-oriented three-meal-a-day place for omelets, cold salads and dinnertime create-your-own-pasta dishes ($12 to $14).

Café Crudite (☎ 508-487-6237, 336 Commercial St) boasts a wide vegetarian menu, a traditional Japanese macrobiotic menu and a veggie burger with upward of 28 ingredients; $6 at lunch, under $10 at dinner.

Café Edwige (☎ 508-487-2008, 333 Commercial St), the most popular breakfast place, offers frittatas, tofu casserole, broiled flounder and fruit pancakes. At night the

eclectic bistro has Thai stir-fry, crab cakes and Asian-style paella for $16 to $23.

The *Martin House* (☎ 508-487-1327, 157 Commercial St), a rustic 18th-century house, is well suited to year-round dining and splurging. An innovative menu ($15 to $28 for main dishes) leaves room for desserts like the caramelized banana and lime tart.

Entertainment Look for posted playbills around town to see what's current.

The *Boatslip Beach Club* (☎ 508-487-1669, 161 Commercial St) is known for its popular afternoon tea dances (3:30 to 6:30 pm). Pool chairs are available to rent.

The waterfront women's bar *Pied Piper* (☎ 508-487-1527, 193A Commercial St) hosts 'post-tea' parties at 6:30 pm.

The *Atlantic House* (the 'A-House'; ☎ 508-487-3821, 4 Masonic Place) features three men's bars: leather, disco and an intimate bar with a fireplace. Some say the A-House is responsible for year-round tourism.

Getting There & Away Cape Air (☎ 508-487-0241, 800-352-0714) provides daily year-round flights from Boston to Provincetown's Municipal Airport, about 4 miles from town and reached via taxi.

From mid-May to mid-October, the Bay State Cruise Co (☎ 617-748-1428), 164 Northern Ave, operates ferries from Boston to Provincetown. The *Provincetown II* takes three hours and costs $18 one way, $30 roundtrip (same day); $16 and $23, respectively, for children age 4 to 12. If you're intent on shaving an hour off that time, it will cost you dearly: tickets aboard the *Provincetown Express* cost $39 one way and $75 roundtrip, regardless of age. The *Provincetown II* operates on weekends mid-May to mid-June and early September to mid-October (daily in summer).

The Plymouth & Brockton bus (☎ 508-746-0378, 778-9767, www.p-b.com), which stops at the chamber of commerce, provides four daily buses (3½ hours; $21 one way) between Provincetown and Boston.

From Boston, it takes about 2½ hours (assuming you don't get bogged down in the traffic exodus) to traverse the 128 miles to Provincetown.

EXCURSIONS

Architectural Glossary

Despite some obvious architectural flaws, many historic buildings still stand in Boston.

Art Deco – Popular in Boston only from about the mid-1920s through the 1930s, this decorative style is marked by ornamentation such as brushed aluminum or etched geometric designs; you'll find examples throughout the Financial District.

Brownstone – These three- or four-story attached row houses were built of reddish-brown sandstone. Back Bay and the South End are loaded with them.

Colonial – This style of simple 17th-century wooden dwelling was based on traditional English architecture. Not many survived a devastating fire in 1676. A well-preserved exception is the North End's Paul Revere House.

Corinthian – The most ornate style of classical Greek architecture is characterized by

a capital adorned with carved acanthus leaves and a slender column incised with flutes – semi-cylindrical grooves that run the length of the shaft.

Doric – This is the oldest and simplest order of classical Greek architecture, marked by austere, fluted columns.

Federal – This postrevolutionary American architecture is distinguished by refined and elegant variations on the Georgian style, with elliptical fanlights and rectangular side-lights around the door. Four-square build-ings with plain and flat facades are often topped with 'widow's walks,' from where a sea captain's wife could see her husband arrive (or not) in the harbor. Bulfinch's First Harrison Gray Otis House is a magnificent example, as is Asher Benjamin's Charles St Meeting House.

Georgian – Named after three reigning British monarchs, this formal 18th-century style is marked by classical-, Renaissance- and baroque-inspired details and stately equilibrium. The majority of Harvard University buildings, with red brick and white cornices, are Georgian; the Old South Meeting House is as well.

Gothic Revival – The Gothic revival, or neo-Gothic movement, took root in the mid-19th century. Builders yearned for the romance of the Middle Ages, and structures from this period are easily identified by their earthen doors, turrets, balconies, pitched roofs, gables, polychromatic bands of brick and pointed arches. William Ralph Emerson (nephew of essayist Ralph Waldo Emerson) is Boston's most fanciful Gothic revivalist and used most of these elements on each of his buildings; note the Boston Art Club.

Granite-style – These solid squat structures were unique to Boston because of the region's abundance of local granite. Many 19th-century city warehouses and commercial buildings are granite-style.

Greek Revival – Based on classical architectural forms, with prime examples looking much like transplanted Aegean temples, Alexander Parris' Faneuil Hall Marketplace (Quincy Market) is a majestic example of Greek Revival architecture.

Ionic – This classical Greek architectural order is exemplified by the Acropolis, with columns topped by scrolled, ram-horned capitals.

Neoclassical – Graceful domes, colonnades and arcades are evident in these updated temple designs, derived from ancient Greek and Roman styles. Charles Bulfinch's state capitol is an example.

Renaissance Revival, Beaux Arts – From the mid-19th century through the early 20th century, Renaissance revival and Beaux Arts architecture paid homage to the grand 15th- and 16th-century homes, churches and palaces of Europe. McKim, Mead & White's Boston Public Library is an inspiring example of Italian Renaissance-inspired architecture, while the Old City Hall evokes Second Empire France.

Romanesque – Usually employing heavy stone work and arches, this romantic, pre-Gothic style is represented by Henry Hobson Richardson's masterpiece Trinity Church.

Skyscraper – Originally coined for buildings about 10 stories high, today they are, quite simply, very tall towers of glass and steel. Boston's two tallest are the 62-story John Hancock Tower and the nearby 50-story Prudential Center.

Triple deckers – These three-story wooden houses were built in the early to mid-1900s by and for the working class. The building's owner lived on one floor and rented the other two floors, with self-contained apartments, to cover the mortgage. This indigenous housing stock is found throughout Dorchester, South Boston and Somerville.

Victorian – Back Bay and the South End are chock full of these eclectic residential edifices, the building of which coincided with the long reign of England's Queen Victoria (1837–1901).

LONELY PLANET

Guides by Region

Lonely Planet is known worldwide for publishing practical, reliable and no-nonsense travel information in our guides and on our Web site. The Lonely Planet list covers just about every accessible part of the world. Currently there are nine series: travel guides, shoestring guides, walking guides, city guides, phrasebooks, audio packs, travel atlases, diving and snorkeling guides and travel literature.

AFRICA Africa – the South • Africa on a shoestring • Arabic (Egyptian) phrasebook • Arabic (Moroccan) phrasebook • Cairo • Cape Town • Central Africa • East Africa • Egypt • Egypt travel atlas • Ethiopian (Amharic) phrasebook • The Gambia & Senegal • Healthy Travel Africa • Kenya • Kenya travel atlas • Malawi, Mozambique & Zambia • Morocco • North Africa • South Africa, Lesotho & Swaziland • South Africa, Lesotho & Swaziland travel atlas • Swahili phrasebook • Trekking in East Africa • Tunisia • West Africa • Zimbabwe, Botswana & Namibia • Zimbabwe, Botswana & Namibia travel atlas
Travel Literature: The Rainbird: A Central African Journey • Songs to an African Sunset: A Zimbabwean Story • Mali Blues: Traveling to an African Beat

AUSTRALIA & THE PACIFIC Australia • Australian phrasebook • Bushwalking in Australia • Bushwalking in Papua New Guinea • Fiji • Fijian phrasebook • Islands of Australia's Great Barrier Reef • Melbourne • Melbourne city map • Micronesia • New Caledonia • New South Wales & the ACT • New Zealand • Northern Territory • Outback Australia • Papua New Guinea • Papua New Guinea (Pidgin) phrasebook • Queensland • Rarotonga & the Cook Islands • Samoa • Solomon Islands • South Australia • South Pacific Languages phrasebook • Sydney • Sydney city map • Tahiti & French Polynesia • Tasmania • Tonga • Tramping in New Zealand • Vanuatu • Victoria • Western Australia
Travel Literature: Islands in the Clouds • Kiwi Tracks • Sean & David's Long Drive

CENTRAL AMERICA & THE CARIBBEAN Bahamas and Turks & Caicos • Bermuda • Central America on a shoestring • Costa Rica • Cuba • Dominican Republic & Haiti • Eastern Caribbean • Guatemala, Belize & Yucatán: La Ruta Maya • Jamaica • Mexico • Mexico City • Panama • Puerto Rico
Travel Literature: Green Dreams: Travels in Central America

EUROPE Amsterdam • Andalucía • Austria • Baltic States phrasebook • Berlin • Berlin city map• Britain • Brussels, Bruges & Antwerp • Central Europe • Central Europe phrasebook • Corsica • Czech & Slovak Republics • Denmark • Dublin • Eastern Europe • Eastern Europe phrasebook • Edinburgh • Estonia, Latvia & Lithuania • Europe • Finland • France • French phrasebook • Germany • German phrasebook • Greece • Greek phrasebook • Hungary • Iceland, Greenland & the Faroe Islands • Ireland • Italian phrasebook • Italy • Lisbon • London • London city map • Mediterranean Europe • Mediterranean Europe phrasebook • Norway • Paris • Paris city map • Poland • Portugal • Portugal travel atlas • Prague • Prague city map • Romania & Moldova • Rome • Russia, Ukraine & Belarus • Russian phrasebook • Scandinavian & Baltic Europe • Scandinavian Europe phrasebook • Scotland • Slovenia • Spain • Spanish phrasebook • St Petersburg • Switzerland • Trekking in Spain • Ukrainian phrasebook • Vienna • Walking in Britain • Walking in Italy • Walking in Switzerland • Western Europe • Western Europe phrasebook
Travel Literature: The Olive Grove: Travels in Greece

INDIAN SUBCONTINENT Bangladesh • Bengali phrasebook • Bhutan • Delhi • Goa • Hindi/Urdu phrasebook • India • India & Bangladesh travel atlas • Indian Himalaya • Karakoram Highway • Mumbai • Nepal • Nepali phrasebook • Pakistan • Rajasthan • South India • Sri Lanka • Sri Lanka phrasebook • Trekking in the Indian Himalaya • Trekking in the Karakoram & Hindukush • Trekking in the Nepal Himalaya
Travel Literature: In Rajasthan • Shopping for Buddhas

LONELY PLANET

Mail Order

Lonely Planet products are distributed worldwide. They are also available by mail order from Lonely Planet, so if you have difficulty finding a title please write to us. North and South American residents should write to 150 Linden St, Oakland, CA 94607, USA; European and African residents should write to 10a Spring Place, London NW5 3BH, UK; and residents of other countries to PO Box 617, Hawthorn, Victoria 3122, Australia.

ISLANDS OF THE INDIAN OCEAN Madagascar & Comoros • Maldives • Mauritius, Réunion & Seychelles

MIDDLE EAST & CENTRAL ASIA Arab Gulf States • Central Asia • Central Asia phrasebook • Hebrew phrasebook • Iran • Israel & the Palestinian Territories • Israel & the Palestinian Territories travel atlas • Istanbul • Jerusalem • Jordan & Syria • Jordan, Syria & Lebanon travel atlas • Lebanon • Middle East on a shoestring • Syria • Turkey • Turkish phrasebook • Turkey travel atlas • Yemen

Travel Literature: The Gates of Damascus • Kingdom of the Film Stars: Journey into Jordan

NORTH AMERICA Alaska • Backpacking in Alaska • Baja California • California & Nevada • Canada • Chicago • Chicago city map • Deep South • Florida • Hawaii • Oahu • Las Vegas • Los Angeles • Miami • New England USA • New Orleans • New York City • New York city map • New York, New Jersey & Pennsylvania • Pacific Northwest USA • Puerto Rico • Rocky Mountain States • San Francisco • San Francisco city map • Seattle • Southwest USA • Texas • USA • USA phrasebook • Vancouver • Washington DC • Virginia & the Capital Region

Travel Literature: Drive Thru America

NORTH-EAST ASIA Beijing • Cantonese phrasebook • China • Hong Kong • Hong Kong city map • Hong Kong, Macau & Guangzhou • Japan • Japanese phrasebook • Japanese audio pack • Korea • Korean phrasebook • Kyoto • Mandarin phrasebook • Mongolia • Mongolian phrasebook • North-East Asia on a shoestring • Seoul • South-West China • Taiwan • Tibet • Tibetan phrasebook • Tokyo

Travel Literature: Lost Japan

SOUTH AMERICA Argentina, Uruguay & Paraguay • Bolivia • Brazil • Brazilian phrasebook • Buenos Aires • Chile & Easter Island • Chile & Easter Island travel atlas • Colombia • Ecuador & the Galapagos Islands • Latin American Spanish phrasebook • Peru • Quechua phrasebook • Rio de Janeiro • Rio de Janeiro city map • South America on a shoestring • Trekking in the Patagonian Andes • Venezuela

Travel Literature: Full Circle: A South American Journey

SOUTH-EAST ASIA Bali & Lombok • Bangkok • Bangkok city map • Burmese phrasebook • Cambodia • Hanoi • Hill Tribes phrasebook • Ho Chi Minh City • Indonesia • Indonesian phrasebook • Indonesian audio pack • Jakarta • Java • Laos • Lao phrasebook • Laos travel atlas • Malay phrasebook • Malaysia, Singapore & Brunei • Myanmar (Burma) • Philippines • Pilipino (Tagalog) phrasebook • Singapore • South-East Asia on a shoestring • South-East Asia phrasebook • Thailand • Thailand's Islands & Beaches • Thailand travel atlas • Thai phrasebook • Thai audio pack • Vietnam • Vietnamese phrasebook • Vietnam travel atlas

ALSO AVAILABLE: Antarctica • Brief Encounters: Stories of Love, Sex & Travel • Chasing Rickshaws • Lonely Planet Unpacked • Not the Only Planet: Travel Stories from Science Fiction • Sacred India • Travel with Children • Traveller's Taless

LONELY PLANET

Phrasebooks

Lonely Planet phrasebooks are packed with essential words and phrases to help travellers communicate with the locals. With color tabs for quick reference, an extensive vocabulary and use of script, these handy pocket-sized language guides cover day-to-day travel situations.

- handy pocket-sized books
- easy to understand Pronunciation chapter
- clear & comprehensive Grammar chapter
- romanization alongside script to allow ease of pronunciation
- script throughout so users can point to phrases for every situation
- full of cultural information and tips for the traveller

'...vital for a real DIY spirit and attitude in language learning'
– Backpacker

'the phrasebooks have good cultural backgrounders and offer solid advice for challenging situations in remote locations'
– San Francisco Examiner

Arabic (Egyptian) • Arabic (Moroccan) • Australian *(Australian English, Aboriginal and Torres Strait languages)* • Baltic States *(Estonian, Latvian, Lithuanian)* • Bengali • Brazilian • Burmese • Cantonese • Central Asia • Central Europe *(Czech, French, German, Hungarian, Italian, Slovak)* • Eastern Europe *(Bulgarian, Czech, Hungarian, Polish, Romanian, Slovak)* • Ethiopian (Amharic) • Fijian • French • German • Greek • Hebrew • Hill Tribes • Hindi/Urdu • Indonesian • Italian • Japanese • Korean • Lao • Latin American Spanish • Malay • Mandarin • Mediterranean Europe *(Albanian, Croatian, Greek, Italian, Macedonian, Maltese, Serbian, Slovene)* • Mongolian • Nepali • Papua New Guinea • Pilipino (Tagalog) • Quechua • Russian • Scandinavian Europe *(Danish, Finnish, Icelandic, Norwegian, Swedish)* • South Pacific Languages • South-East Asia *(Burmese, Indonesian, Khmer, Lao, Malay, Tagalog Pilipino, Thai, Vietnamese)* • Spanish (Castilian) *(also includes Catalan, Galician and Basque)* • Sri Lanka • Swahili • Thai • Tibetan • Turkish • Ukrainian • USA *(US English, Vernacular, Native American languages, Hawaiian)* • Vietnamese • Western Europe *(Basque, Catalan, Dutch, French, German, Greek, Irish)*

Lonely Planet Journeys

J OURNEYS is a unique collection of travel writing – published by the company that understands travel better than anyone else. It is a series for anyone who has ever experienced – or dreamed of – the magical moment when they encountered a strange culture or saw a place for the first time. They are tales to read while you're planning a trip, while you're on the road or while you're in an armchair in front of a fire.

These outstanding titles explore our planet through the eyes of a diverse group of international writers. JOURNEYS books catch the spirit of a place, illuminate a culture, recount a crazy adventure or introduce a fascinating way of life. They always entertain, and always enrich the experience of travel.

FULL CIRCLE
A South American Journey
Luis Sepúlveda (translated by Chris Andrews)

'A journey without a fixed itinerary' with Chilean writer Luis Sepúlveda. Extravagant characters and extraordinary situations are memorably evoked: gauchos organising a tournament of lies, a scheming heiress on the lookout for a husband, a pilot with a corpse on board his plane ... *Full Circle* brings us the distinctive voice of one of South America's most compelling writers.

WINNER 1996 Astrolabe – Etonnants Voyageurs award for the best work of travel literature published in France.

GREEN DREAMS
Travels in Central America
Stephen Benz

On the Amazon, in Costa Rica, Honduras and on the Mayan trail from Guatemala to Mexico, Stephen Benz describes his encounters with water, mud, insects and other wildlife – and not least with the ecotourists themselves. With witty insights into modern travel, *Green Dreams* discusses the paradox of cultural and 'green' tourism.

DRIVE THRU AMERICA
Sean Condon

If you've ever wanted to drive across the USA but couldn't find the time (or afford the gas), *Drive Thru America* is perfect for you. In his search for American myths and realities – along with comfort, cable TV and good, reasonably priced coffee – Sean Condon paints a hilarious road-portrait of the USA.

'entertaining and laugh-out-loud funny'– *Alex Wilber, Travel editor, Amazon.com*

SEAN & DAVID'S LONG DRIVE
Sean Condon

Sean and David are young townies who have rarely strayed beyond city limits. One day, for no good reason, they set out to discover their homeland, and what follows is a wildly entertaining adventure that covers half of Australia.

'a hilariously detailed log of two burned out friends' – *Rolling Stone*

LONELY PLANET

Lonely Planet On-line
www.lonelyplanet.com *or* AOL keyword: lp

W hether you've just begun planning your next trip, or you're chasing down specific info on currency regulations or visa requirements, check out Lonely Planet On-line for up-to-the minute travel information.

As well as mini guides to more than 250 destinations, you'll find maps, photos, travel news, health and visa updates, travel advisories, and discussion of the ecological and political issues you need to be aware of as you travel. You'll also find timely upgrades to popular guidebooks which you can print out and stick in the back of your book.

There's also an on-line travellers' forum where you can share your experience of life on the road, meet travel companions and ask other travellers for their recommendations and advice.

And of course we have a complete and up-to-date list of all Lonely Planet travel products including travel guides, diving and snorkeling guides, phrasebooks, city maps, travel atlases, travel literature and videos, and a simple on-line ordering facility if you can't find the book you want elsewhere.

Lonely Planet Diving & Snorkeling Guides

B eautifully illustrated with full-color photos throughout, Lonely Planet's **Pisces Books** explore the world's best diving and snorkeling areas and prepare divers for what to expect when they get there, both topside and underwater.

Dive sites are described in detail with specifics on depths, visibility, level of difficulty, special conditions, underwater photography tips, and common and unusual marine life present. You'll also find practical logistical information and coverage on topside activities and attractions, sections on diving health and safety, plus listings for diving services, live-aboards, dive resorts and tourist offices.

Lonely Planet Travel Atlases

L onely Planet has long been famous for the number and quality of its guidebook maps. Now we've gone one step further and produced a handy companion series: Lonely Planet travel atlases – maps of a country produced in book form.

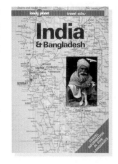

Unlike other maps, which look good but lead travellers astray, our travel atlases have been researched on the road by Lonely Planet's experienced team of writers. All details are carefully checked to ensure the atlas corresponds with the equivalent Lonely Planet guidebook.

- full-color throughout
- maps researched and checked by Lonely Planet authors
- place names correspond with Lonely Planet guidebooks
- no confusing spelling differences
- legend and traveling information in English, French, German, Japanese and Spanish
- size: 230 x 160 mm

Available now: Chile & Easter Island • Egypt • India & Bangladesh • Israel & the Palestinian Territories • Jordan, Syria & Lebanon • Kenya • Laos • Portugal • South Africa, Lesotho & Swaziland • Thailand • Turkey • Vietnam • Zimbabwe, Botswana & Namibia

Lonely Planet TV Series & Videos

L onely Planet travel guides have been brought to life on television screens around the world. Like our guides, the programs are based on the joy of independent travel, and look honestly at some of the most exciting, picturesque and frustrating places in the world. Each show is presented by one of three travellers from Australia, England or the USA and combines an innovative mixture of video, Super-8 film, atmospheric soundscapes and original music.

Videos of each episode – containing additional footage not shown on television – are available from good book and video shops, but the availability of individual videos varies with regional screening schedules.

Video destinations include: Alaska • American Rockies • Australia – The South-East • Baja California & the Copper Canyon • Brazil • Central Asia • Chile & Easter Island • Corsica, Sicily & Sardinia – The Mediterranean Islands • East Africa (Tanzania & Zanzibar) • Ecuador & the Galapagos Islands • Greenland & Iceland • Indonesia • Israel & the Sinai Desert • Jamaica • Japan • La Ruta Maya • Morocco • New York • North India • Pacific Islands (Fiji, Solomon Islands & Vanuatu) • South India • South West China • Turkey • Vietnam • West Africa • Zimbabwe, Botswana • Namibia

The Lonely Planet TV series is produced by: Pilot Productions
The Old Studio
18 Middle Row
London W10 5AT, UK

LONELY PLANET

FREE Lonely Planet Newsletters

We love hearing from you and think you'd like to hear from us.

Planet Talk

Our FREE quarterly printed newsletter is full of tips from travelers and anecdotes from Lonely Planet guidebook authors. Every issue is packed with up-to-date travel news and advice, and includes:

- a postcard from Lonely Planet co-founder Tony Wheeler
- a swag of mail from travellers
- a look at life on the road through the eyes of a Lonely Planet author
- topical health advice
- prizes for the best travel yarn
- news about forthcoming Lonely Planet events
- a complete list of Lonely Planet books and other titles

To join our mailing list, residents of the UK, Europe and Africa can email us at go@lonelyplanet.co.uk; residents of North and South America can email us at info@lonelyplanet.com; the rest of the world can email us at talk2us@lonelyplanet.com.au, or contact any Lonely Planet office.

Comet

Our FREE monthly email newsletter brings you all the latest travel news, features, interviews, competitions, destination ideas, travelers' tips & tales, Q&As, raging debates and related links. Find out what's new on the Lonely Planet Web site and which books are about to hit the shelves.

Subscribe from your desktop: www.lonelyplanet.com/comet

Index

Bold indicates maps.

Boxed Text

Boston Map Section

Public art on the BU Beach

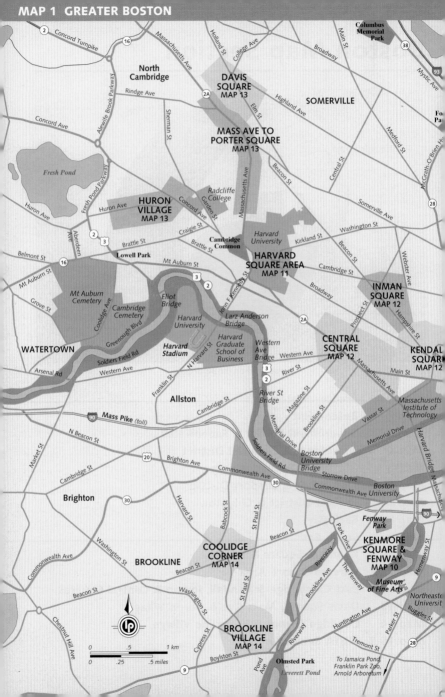

MAP 1 GREATER BOSTON

Concord Turnpike
North Cambridge
Massachusetts Ave
Columbus Memorial Park
Rindge Ave
Holland St
College Ave
Broadway
Main St
Mystic Ave
DAVIS SQUARE
MAP 13
SOMERVILLE
Elm St
Highland Ave
Concord Ave
Sherman St
Medford St
McGrath O'Brien Hi
MASS AVE TO PORTER SQUARE
MAP 13
Fresh Pond
Fresh Pond Parkway
Radcliffe College
Massachusetts Ave
Beacon St
Central St
Somerville Ave
HURON VILLAGE
MAP 13
Concord Ave
Garden St
Aberdeen Ave
Huron Ave
Harvard University
Kirkland St
Washington St
Craigie St
Cambridge Common
Beacon St
Webster Ave
Belmont St
Brattle St
Brattle St
HARVARD SQUARE AREA
MAP 11
Cambridge St
Lowell Park
Mt Auburn St
Cambridge St
INMAN SQUARE
MAP 12
Mt Auburn St
John F Kennedy St
Broadway
Prospect St
Grove St
Mt Auburn Cemetery
Coolidge Ave
Eliot Bridge
Larz Anderson Bridge
2A
Hampshire St
Cambridge Cemetery
Harvard University
CENTRAL SQUARE
MAP 12
KENDAL SQUAR
MAP 12
WATERTOWN
Greenough Blvd
Harvard Stadium
Harvard Graduate School of Business
Western Ave Bridge
Western Ave
River St
Main St
Soldiers Field Rd
N Harvard St
Arsenal Rd
Western Ave
Franklin St
Magazine St
Brookline St
Vassar St
Massachusetts Ave
Massachusetts Institute of Technology
Cambridge St
River St Bridge
Memorial Drive
Harvard Bridge
Mass Pike (toll)
Allston
Memorial Drive
N Beacon St
Market St
Brighton Ave
Boston University Bridge
Storrow Drive
Cambridge St
Commonwealth Ave
Commonwealth Ave
Boston University
Brighton
Harvard St
Babcock St
St Paul St
Fenway Park
Commonwealth Ave
Washington St
Beacon St
Park Drive
KENMORE SQUARE & FENWAY
MAP 10
Hemenway St
BROOKLINE
COOLIDGE CORNER
MAP 14
Beacon St
St Paul St
Riverway
The Fenway
Museum of Fine Arts
Northeaste Universit
Beacon St
Washington St
Brookline Ave
Chestnut Hill Ave
Cypress St
Riverway
Huntington Ave
Parker St
Ruggles St
BROOKLINE VILLAGE
MAP 14
Boylston St
Pond Ave
Olmsted Park
Everett Pond
Tremont St
To Jamaica Pond, Franklin Park Zoo, Arnold Arboretum

0   .5   1 km
0   .25   .5 miles

MAP 2 BEACON HILL

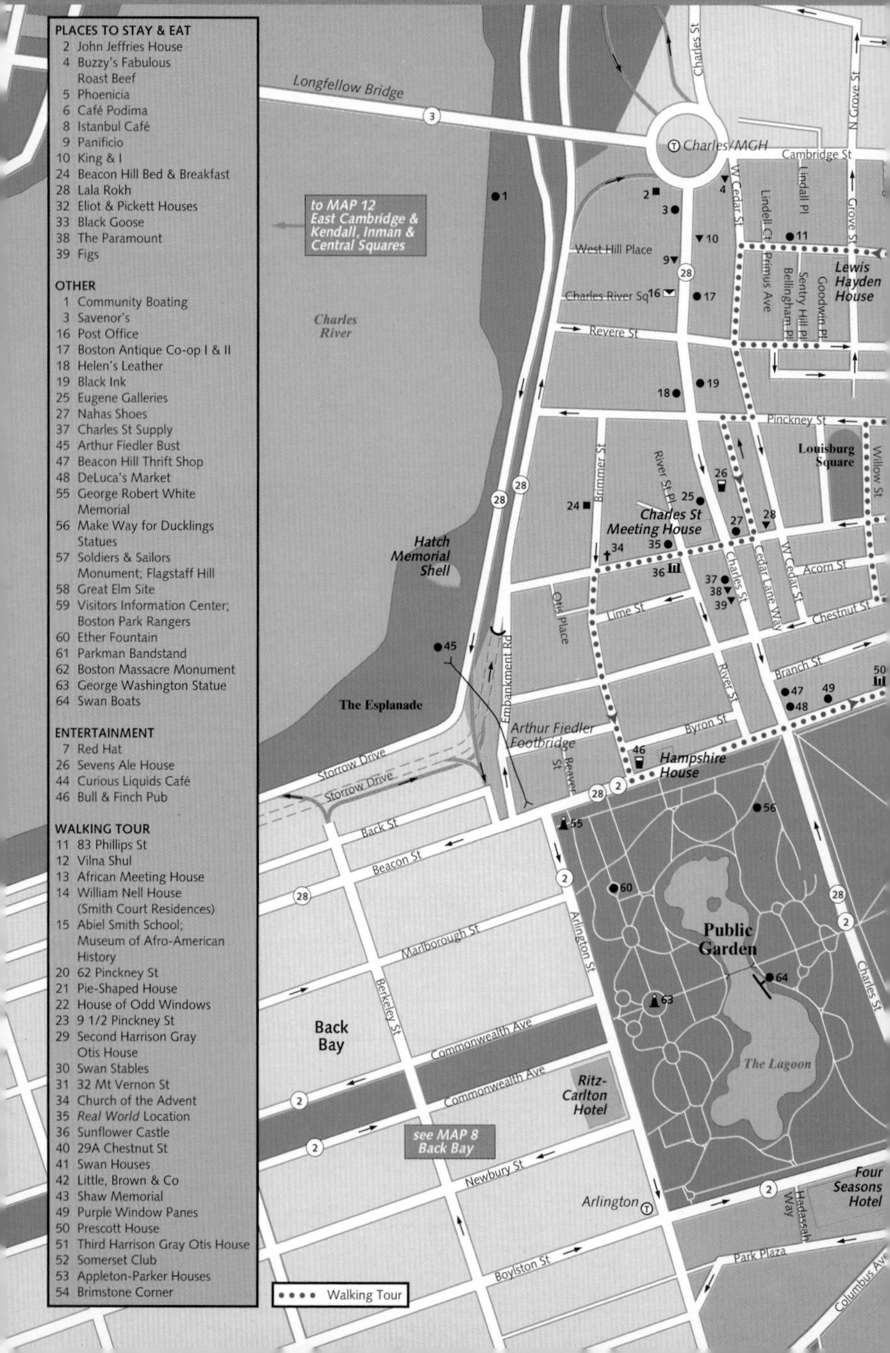
PLACES TO STAY & EAT
2 John Jeffries House
4 Buzzy's Fabulous Roast Beef
5 Phoenicia
6 Café Podima
8 Istanbul Café
9 Panificio
10 King & I
24 Beacon Hill Bed & Breakfast
28 Lala Rokh
32 Eliot & Pickett Houses
33 Black Goose
38 The Paramount
39 Figs
OTHER
1 Community Boating
3 Savenor's
16 Post Office
17 Boston Antique Co-op I & II
18 Helen's Leather
19 Black Ink
25 Eugene Galleries
27 Nahas Shoes
37 Charles St Supply
45 Arthur Fiedler Bust
47 Beacon Hill Thrift Shop
48 DeLuca's Market
55 George Robert White Memorial
56 Make Way for Ducklings Statues
57 Soldiers & Sailors Monument; Flagstaff Hill
58 Great Elm Site
59 Visitors Information Center; Boston Park Rangers
60 Ether Fountain
61 Parkman Bandstand
62 Boston Massacre Monument
63 George Washington Statue
64 Swan Boats
ENTERTAINMENT
7 Red Hat
26 Sevens Ale House
44 Curious Liquids Café
46 Bull & Finch Pub
WALKING TOUR
11 83 Phillips St
12 Vilna Shul
13 African Meeting House
14 William Nell House (Smith Court Residences)
15 Abiel Smith School; Museum of Afro-American History
20 62 Pinckney St
21 Pie-Shaped House
22 House of Odd Windows
23 9 1/2 Pinckney St
29 Second Harrison Gray Otis House
30 Swan Stables
31 32 Mt Vernon St
34 Church of the Advent
35 Real World Location
36 Sunflower Castle
40 29A Chestnut St
41 Swan Houses
42 Little, Brown & Co
43 Shaw Memorial
49 Purple Window Panes
50 Prescott House
51 Third Harrison Gray Otis House
52 Somerset Club
53 Appleton-Parker Houses
54 Brimstone Corner
Walking Tour
Longfellow Bridge
Charles/MGH
Charles St
Cambridge St
N Grove St
to MAP 12 East Cambridge & Kendall, Inman & Central Squares
W Cedar St
Lindell Pl
Lindell Ct
Grove St
West Hill Place
Charles River Sq
Primus Ave
Bellingham Pl
Sentry Hill Pl
Goodwin Pl
Lewis Hayden House
Charles River
Revere St
Pinckney St
Louisburg Square
Willow St
Brimmer St
River St Pl
Charles St Meeting House
Hatch Memorial Shell
Acorn St
Cedar Lane Way
Lime St
Otis Place
Chestnut St
Branch St
Embankment Rd
The Esplanade
River St
Arthur Fiedler Footbridge
Byron St
Beaver St
Hampshire House
Storrow Drive
Back St
Beacon St
Public Garden
Marlborough St
Arlington St
Berkeley St
Back Bay
Commonwealth Ave
Ritz-Carlton Hotel
The Lagoon
see MAP 8 Back Bay
Newbury St
Arlington
Hadassah Way
Four Seasons Hotel
Park Plaza
Boylston St
Columbus Ave

Parkman St
Old West End
N Anderson St
First Harrison Gray Otis House
Old West Church
State Service Center
see MAP 3 Government Center & Faneuil Hall
New Chardon St
Hawkins St
New Sudbury St
JFK Federal Building
Bowdoin
Anderson St
Garden St
Irving St
S Russel St
▼ 5
6
Joy St
Hancock St
Ridgeway Lane
Temple St (Ped Mall)
7 ▼
8 ▼
Bowdoin St
Saltonstall Building
Government Center
Boston City Hall
City Hall Plaza
Phillips St
12
Smith Court
14
15
13
JF McCormick State Office Building
Court House
Center Plaza
Government Center
Cornhill St
hampney Place
Rollins Place
Holmes Alley
Suffolk University
Ashburton Place
Somerset St
Suffolk County Court House
Franklin Ave
Court St
Myrtle St
Derne St
Middleton-Glapion House
23
State
Phillips School
20
21
22
29
Suffolk University
Beacon Hill
Nichols House Museum
Massachusetts State House
Ashburton Park
33 ▼
1 Beacon St
King's Chapel Burying Ground
King's Chapel
School St
Mt Vernon St
30
31
41
40
Appalachian Mountain Club
32
Joy Place
42
44
43
Park St Place
Boston Athenaeum
Old Granary Burying Ground
Tremont Place
Beacon St
Omni Parker House
Province St
see MAP 4 Downtown & Financial District
Milk St
Spruce Place
Walnut St
Beacon St
52
53
51
End
Park St
Park St Church
Start
Bosworth St
Bromfield St
Hamilton Place
Franklin St
Frog Pond
58
59
57
Boston Common
61
62
Tremont St
Winter St (Ped Mall)
Cathedral Church of St Paul
Temple Place
West St
Downtown Crossing
Filene's Department Store
Summer St (Ped Mall)
Arch St
Otis St
Opera House
Harlem Place
Washington St (Ped Mall)
Macy's
Mason St
Avery St
Ave de Lafayette
Chauncy St
Central Burying Ground
Hayward Place
Jonson Ave Ext
0   100   200 m
0   100   200 yards
Millennium Place
Boylston
Charles St S
Boylston Place
Colonial Theatre
Theater District
State Transportation Building
Essex St
Chinatown
see MAP 7 Theater District & Chinatown
Beach St
Chinatown
Oxford St
Ping On St
Edinboro St
93
1
3
see MAP 6 Waterfront & Seaport District
Stuart St

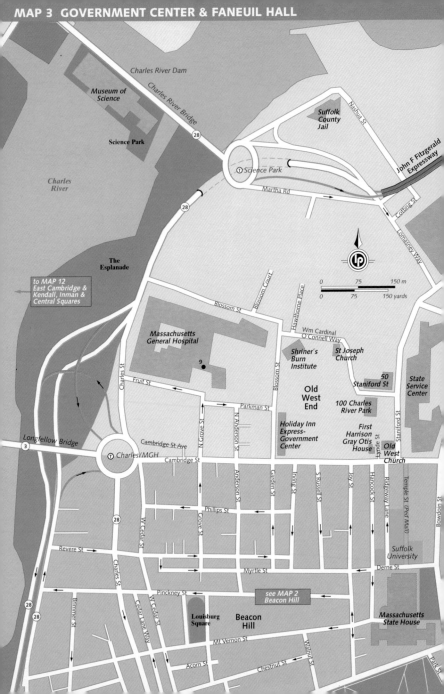

MAP 3 GOVERNMENT CENTER & FANEUIL HALL

Charles River Dam

Museum of Science

Charles River Bridge

Science Park

28

Suffolk County Jail

Nashua St

John F Fitzgerald Expressway

Science Park

Charles River

Martha Rd

Collins St

Tomasney Way

28

The Esplanade

to MAP 12
East Cambridge &
Kendall, Inman &
Central Squares

Blossom St

Blossom Court

Hawthorne Place

0   75   150 m
0   75   150 yards

Wm Cardinal O'Connell Way

Massachusetts General Hospital

Shriner's Burn Institute

St Joseph Church

9

Blossom St

Old West End

50 Staniford St

Staniford St

State Service Center

Charles St

Fruit St

Parkman St

100 Charles River Park

N Grove St

N Anderson St

Holiday Inn Express-Government Center

First Harrison Gray Otis House

Hyde St

Old West Church

Longfellow Bridge

3

Charles/MGH

Cambridge St Ave

Cambridge St

Staniford St

28

Anderson St

Garden St

Irving St

S Russell St

Joy St

Hancock St

Ridgeway Lane

Temple St (Ped Mall)

Bowdoin St

Phillips St

W Cedar St

Grove St

Suffolk University

Revere St

Charles St

Myrtle St

Derne St

Pinckney St

28

W Cedar St

Cedar Lane Way

Louisburg Square

see MAP 2 Beacon Hill

Beacon Hill

Massachusetts State House

28

Brimmer St

Mt Vernon St

Walnut St

Park St

Acorn St

Chestnut St

GOVERNMENT CENTER & FANEUIL HALL   MAP 3

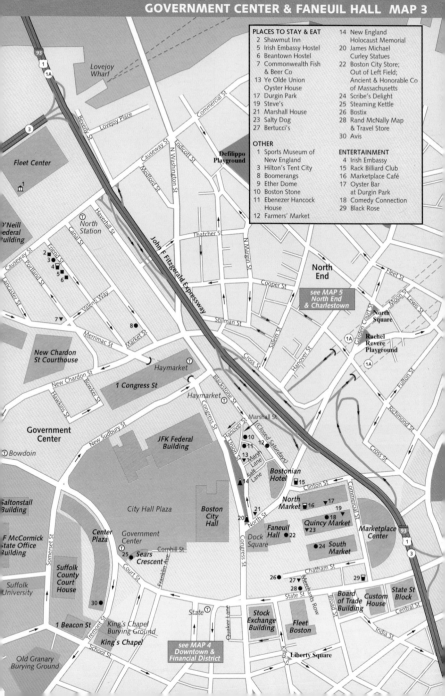

PLACES TO STAY & EAT
2 Shawmut Inn
5 Irish Embassy Hostel
6 Beantown Hostel
7 Commonwealth Fish & Beer Co
13 Ye Olde Union Oyster House
17 Durgin Park
19 Steve's
21 Marshall House
23 Salty Dog
27 Bertucci's

14 New England Holocaust Memorial
20 James Michael Curley Statues
22 Boston City Store; Out of Left Field; Ancient & Honorable Co of Massachusetts
24 Scribe's Delight
25 Steaming Kettle
26 Bostix
28 Rand McNally Map & Travel Store
30 Avis

OTHER
1 Sports Museum of New England
3 Hilton's Tent City
8 Boomerangs
9 Ether Dome
10 Boston Stone
11 Ebenezer Hancock House
12 Farmers' Market

ENTERTAINMENT
4 Irish Embassy
15 Rack Billiard Club
16 Marketplace Café
17 Oyster Bar at Durgin Park
18 Comedy Connection
29 Black Rose

MAP 4 DOWNTOWN & FINANCIAL DISTRICT

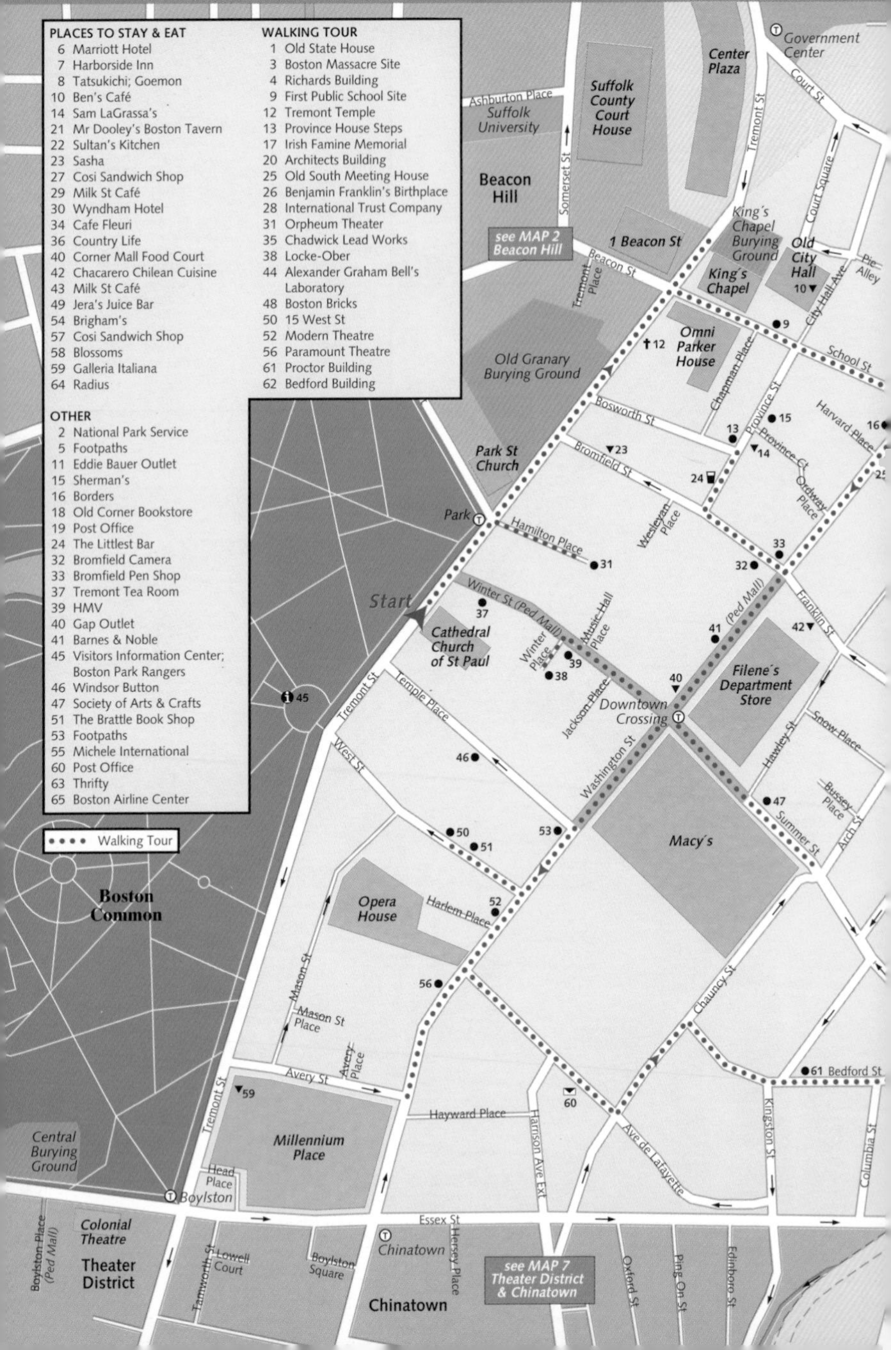

PLACES TO STAY & EAT
6 Marriott Hotel
7 Harborside Inn
8 Tatsukichi; Goemon
10 Ben's Café
14 Sam LaGrassa's
21 Mr Dooley's Boston Tavern
22 Sultan's Kitchen
23 Sasha
27 Cosi Sandwich Shop
29 Milk St Café
30 Wyndham Hotel
34 Cafe Fleuri
36 Country Life
40 Corner Mall Food Court
42 Chacarero Chilean Cuisine
43 Milk St Café
49 Jera's Juice Bar
54 Brigham's
57 Cosi Sandwich Shop
58 Blossoms
59 Galleria Italiana
64 Radius

OTHER
2 National Park Service
5 Footpaths
11 Eddie Bauer Outlet
15 Sherman's
17 Borders
18 Old Corner Bookstore
19 Post Office
24 The Littlest Bar
32 Bromfield Camera
33 Bromfield Pen Shop
37 Tremont Tea Room
39 HMV
40 Gap Outlet
41 Barnes & Noble
45 Visitors Information Center;
   Boston Park Rangers
46 Windsor Button
47 Society of Arts & Crafts
51 The Brattle Book Shop
53 Footpaths
55 Michele International
60 Post Office
63 Thrifty
65 Boston Airline Center

WALKING TOUR
1 Old State House
3 Boston Massacre Site
4 Richards Building
9 First Public School Site
12 Tremont Temple
16 Province House Steps
17 Irish Famine Memorial
20 Architects Building
25 Old South Meeting House
26 Benjamin Franklin's Birthplace
28 International Trust Company
31 Orpheum Theater
35 Chadwick Lead Works
38 Locke-Ober
44 Alexander Graham Bell's
   Laboratory
48 Boston Bricks
50 15 West St
52 Modern Theatre
56 Paramount Theatre
61 Proctor Building
62 Bedford Building

•••• Walking Tour

Government
Center

Center
Plaza

Suffolk
County
Court
House

Ashburton Place
Suffolk
University

Beacon
Hill

see MAP 2
Beacon Hill

1 Beacon St

King's
Chapel
Burying
Ground

King's Chapel

Old
City
Hall 10 ▼

Pie
Alley

Omni
Parker
House   † 12   9

Old Granary
Burying Ground

Bosworth St   13   15

Park St
Church   Bromfield St   ▼23   14
                              24   33
Park ⓣ   Hamilton Place   32

Start   Winter St (Ped Mall)   31
           37   41   42
Cathedral   40
Church   39
of St Paul   38   Filene's
                       Department
              46   Store

Macy's

Boston
Common

        50
        51   53
Opera
House   Harlem Place

          52

          56   61 Bedford
Central
Burying   60
Ground ▼59

        Millennium
        Place

Colonial
Theatre

Theater
District

Chinatown

see MAP 7
Theater District
& Chinatown

Chinatown

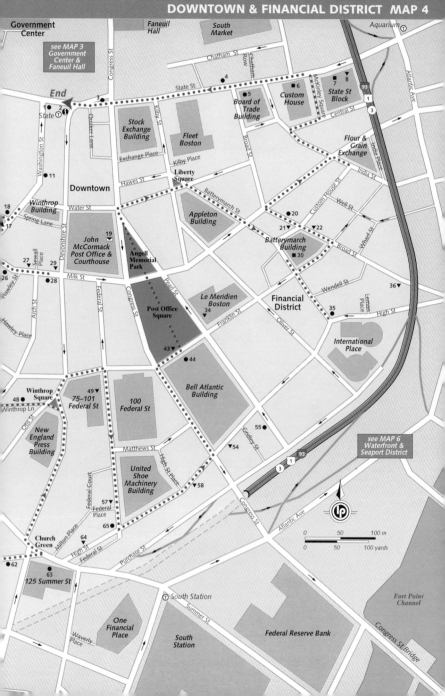

Government Center

Faneuil Hall

South Market

Aquarium T

see MAP 3
Government
Center &
Faneuil Hall

Congress St

Chatham St

Chatham Row

State St

4

End

3

McKinley Square

State St Block

6

7 8

1
2
State T

Quaker Lane

Board of Trade Building

5

Custom House

93
1
3

Atlantic Ave

Stock Exchange Building

Kilby St

Fleet Boston

Central St

11

Exchange Place

Kilby Place

Broad St

Flour & Grain Exchange

Downtown

Hawes St

Liberty Square

India St

India Place

Winthrop Building

Water St

Batterymarch St

Custom House St

Well St

18

17

Spring Lane

Appleton Building

20

21 ▼

22 ▼

Devonshire St

John McCormack Post Office & Courthouse

19 ▼

Angell Memorial Park

Batterymarch Building

30

Broad St

Water St

27

29

Milk St

Pearl St

Wendell St

Lehman Place

36 ▼

26

Sewall Place

28

High St

Hawley St

Arch St

Congress St

Le Meridien Boston

34

Franklin St

Financial District

35

International Place

Hawley Place

Post Office Square

43 ▼

44

Oliver St

Federal St

Bell Atlantic Building

Winthrop Square

49 ▼

48

Winthrop Ln

75–101 Federal St

100 Federal St

55

Otis St

New England Press Building

Matthews St

54 ▼

Gridley St

93
1
3

see MAP 6
Waterfront & Seaport District

Federal Court

United Shoe Machinery Building

High St Place

58 ▼

57 ▼
Federal Place

65

Congress St

Atlantic Ave

Church Green

64

High St

Federal St

Milton Place

Purchase St

0   50   100 m
0   50   100 yards

62

63

125 Summer St

South Station T

Summer St

Fort Point Channel

One Financial Place

Waverly Place

South Station

Federal Reserve Bank

Congress St Bridge

MAP 5 NORTH END & CHARLESTOWN

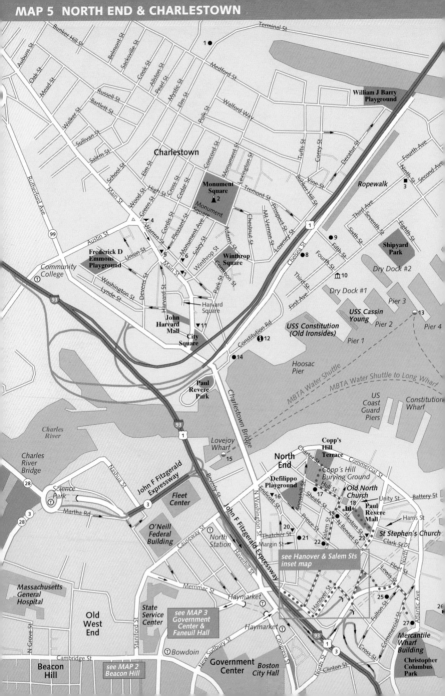

Terminal St

Bunker Hill St
Auburn St
Oak St
Mead St

Richmond St
Sackville St

1

Medford St

Cook St
Allston St
Pearl St
Mystic St

Walford Way

Russell St

Bartlett St

William J Barry
Playground

Walker St

Park St

Sullivan St

Charlestown

Decatur St

Fourth Ave

Salem St

Concord St

Elm St

Tufts St

Vine St

Ropewalk

3

School St

Wood St
High St
Green St
Cordis St
Cedar St

Monument
Square

2

Third Ave

Seventh St

Eighth St

Sixth St

99

Main St

Warren St

Monument
Square

Chestnut St

Tremont St

S Russell St

Prospect St

Bunker Hill St

Mt Vernon St

1

Shipyard
Park

Austin St

4

Dry Dock #2

Frederick D
Emmons
Playground

Cordis St
Pleasant St

Soley St

Adams St

Common St

9

Union St

5

Monument Ave

Winthrop
Square

Lawrence St

8

Community
College

Devens St

Harvard St

Winthrop St

Park St

Crosia Rd

Fourth St

Fifth St

10

Dry Dock #1

Pier 3

Washington St

Lynde St

Harvard
Square

Third St

93

John
Harvard
Mall

USS Cassin
Young

Pier 2

13

11

First Ave

USS Constitution
(Old Ironsides)

Pier 4

City
Square

Constitution Rd

Pier 1

12

14

Hoosac
Pier

Paul
Revere
Park

Charlestown Bridge

MBTA Water Shuttle

MBTA Water Shuttle to Long Wharf

US
Coast
Guard
Piers

Constitution
Wharf

Charles
River

93

1

Lovejoy
Wharf

15

Copp's
Hill
Terrace

Commercial St

Charles
River
Bridge

28

Science
Park

North
End

Copp's
Hill
Burying
Ground

Old North
Church

Battery St

Unity St

3

Martha Rd

Fleet Center

Defilippo
Playground

16

Snowhill St

Hull St

Sheafe St

17

18

Paul
Revere
Mall

Harris St

28

O'Neill
Federal
Building

North
Station

Prince St

Endicott St

N Margin St

19

Salem St

Hanover St

N Bennet St

Clark St

St Stephen's Church

20

21

22

23

John F Fitzgerald Expressway

Thatcher St

Beverly St

N Washington St

Haverhill St

Margin St

see Hanover & Salem Sts
inset map

Massachusetts
General
Hospital

Merrimac St

Haymarket

Lewis St

Fleet St

25

Old
West
End

State
Service
Center

see MAP 3
Government
Center &
Faneuil Hall

Hanover St

Atlantic Ave

27

26

N Grove St

Stanford St

Causeway St

Haymarket

North St

Commercial St

Mercantile
Wharf
Building

Cambridge St

Bowdoin

Government
Center

New Sudbury St

Congress St

93

1

Cross St

Clinton St

Christopher
Columbus
Park

Beacon
Hill

see MAP 2
Beacon Hill

Boston
City Hall

3

NORTH END & CHARLESTOWN MAP 5

PLACES TO STAY & EAT
- 3 Constitution Inn YMCA
- 5 Warren Tavern
- 6 Sorelle Bakery Café
- 7 Figs
- 11 Olives
- 16 Massimino's Cucina Italiana
- 20 Regina Pizzeria
- 23 Maurizio's
- 26 Golden Slipper
- 30 Mike's Pastry
- 32 The Daily Catch
- 33 Terramia
- 38 Pagliuca's
- 39 Il Panino Express
- 41 Galleria Umberto
- 42 Antico Forno
- 47 La Piccola Venezia
- 52 Restaurant Bricco

OTHER
- 1 Atlantic Coast Brewing Co
- 2 Bunker Hill Monument
- 4 Post Office
- 8 Commandant's House
- 9 Telephone Exchange
- 10 USS Constitution Museum
- 12 Charlestown Navy Yard Visitors Center; Bunker Hill Pavilion
- 13 MBTA Water Shuttle; Boston Harbor Cruises; City Water Taxi
- 14 Constitution Cruises
- 15 MBTA Water Shuttle; City Water Taxi
- 21 Nostalgia Factory
- 24 City Water Taxi
- 56 Post Office

ENTERTAINMENT
- 29 Caffé dello Sport
- 31 Caffé Vittoria
- 55 Improv Asylum

WALKING TOUR
- 17 Narrowest House
- 18 Ebenezer Clough House
- 19 N Bennett St School
- 22 Bova Bakery
- 25 McLauthlin Building
- 27 Prince Building
- 28 St Leonard's Church & Peace Garden
- 30 Mike's Pastry
- 34 Polcari's Coffee
- 35 North End Branch Library
- 36 Mariners' House
- 37 Paul Revere House
- 40 Salumeria Toscana
- 42 Pierce-Hichborn House
- 43 J Pace & Son
- 44 Maria's Pastry; A LaFaUci & Sons
- 45 Il Bongustaio
- 48 Salumeria Italiana
- 49 Baker's Alley
- 50 Dairy Fresh Candies
- 51 Modern Pastry
- 53 V Cirace & Son
- 54 Trio's

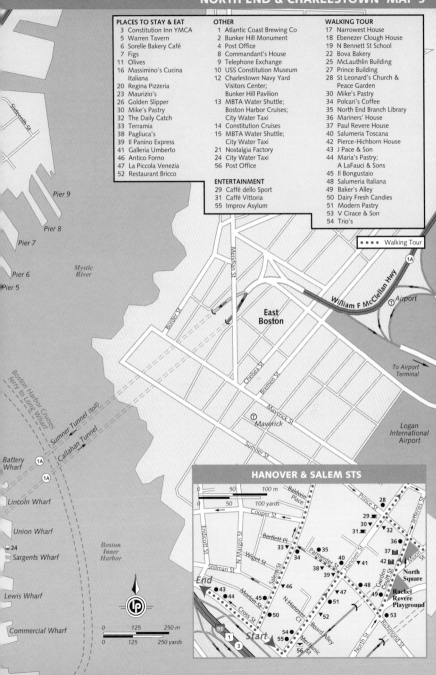

MAP 6 WATERFRONT & SEAPORT DISTRICT

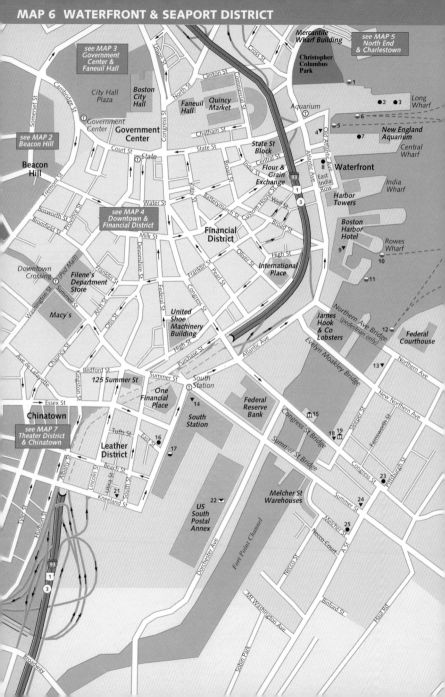

see MAP 3
Government
Center &
Faneuil Hall

Mercantile
Wharf Building

see MAP 5
North End
& Charlestown

Christopher
Columbus
Park

City Hall
Plaza

Boston
City
Hall

Faneuil
Hall

Quincy
Market

Cambridge St

Somerset St

Cross St

North St

Clinton St

Union St

Commercial St

Aquarium

1

Government
Center

Government
Center

Congress St

Chatham St

State St

Long
Wharf

2   3

6

5

New England
Aquarium

7

Central
Wharf

see MAP 2
Beacon Hill

Court St

State

State St

State St
Block

Central St

India St

4

Old Atlantic Ave

Beacon
Hill

Tremont St

Bosworth St

Province St

Bromfield St

Water St

see MAP 4
Downtown &
Financial District

Kirby St

Broad St

Batterymarch St

Custom House St

Flour &
Grain
Exchange

Well St

8

Atlantic Ave

East
India
Row

Waterfront

India
Wharf

Harbor
Towers

Milk St

Devonshire St

Financial
District

Broad St

High St

93

1

3

Downtown
Crossing

Franklin St

Filene's
Department
Store

Arch St

Otis St

Federal St

Franklin St

Pearl St

Oliver St

Congress St

International
Place

Boston
Harbor
Hotel

9

Rowes
Wharf

10

Macy's

Chauncy St

Summer St

Kingston St

Bedford St

United
Shoe
Machinery
Building

High St

Purchase St

11

Ave de Lafayette

Essex St

125 Summer St

Summer St

South
Station

Atlantic Ave

Northern Ave Bridge
(pedestrian only)

James
Hook
& Co
Lobsters

12

Federal
Courthouse

Chinatown

see MAP 7
Theater District
& Chinatown

One
Financial
Place

14

South
Station

Federal
Reserve
Bank

Evelyn Moakley Bridge

Congress St Bridge

13

Northern Ave

New Northern Ave

Leather
District

Tufts St

East St

Beach St

16

17

15

Summer St Bridge

18 19

Sleeper St

Farnsworth St

Congress St

Pittsburgh St

23

Tyler St

Hudson St

Albany St

Lincoln St

Utica St

Kneeland St

21

22

US
South
Postal
Annex

Dorchester Ave

Fort Point Channel

Melcher St
Warehouses

Necco St

Melcher St

Summer St

A St

24

25

Necco Court

93

1

3

Broadway

Mt Washington Ave

Binford St

Haul Rd

Sleeper St

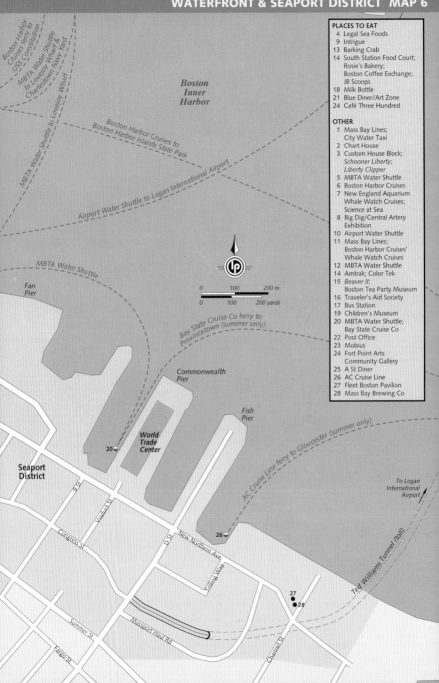

Boston Harbor Cruises ferry to USS Constitution

MBTA Water Shuttle to Lovejoy Wharf & Charlestown Navy Yard

Boston Inner Harbor

MBTA Water Shuttle to Lovejoy Wharf

Boston Harbor Cruises to Boston Harbor Islands State Park

Airport Water Shuttle to Logan International Airport

MBTA Water Shuttle

Fan Pier

Bay State Cruise Co ferry to Provincetown (summer only)

Commonwealth Pier

Fish Pier

World Trade Center

AC Cruise Line ferry to Gloucester (summer only)

Seaport District

To Logan International Airport

B St

Viaduct St

Congress St

D St

New Northern Ave

Tide St

Summer St

Fargo St

Massport Haul Rd

Channel St

Ted Williams Tunnel (toll)

20

26

27
28

PLACES TO EAT
4 Legal Sea Foods
9 Intrigue
13 Barking Crab
14 South Station Food Court;
    Rosie's Bakery;
    Boston Coffee Exchange;
    JB Scoops
18 Milk Bottle
21 Blue Diner/Art Zone
24 Café Three Hundred

OTHER
1 Mass Bay Lines;
   City Water Taxi
2 Chart House
3 Custom House Block;
   Schooner Liberty;
   Liberty Clipper
5 MBTA Water Shuttle
6 Boston Harbor Cruises
7 New England Aquarium
   Whale Watch Cruises;
   Science at Sea
8 Big Dig/Central Artery
   Exhibition
10 Airport Water Shuttle
11 Mass Bay Lines;
    Boston Harbor Cruises'
    Whale Watch Cruises
12 MBTA Water Shuttle
14 Amtrak; Color Tek
15 *Beaver II*;
    Boston Tea Party Museum
16 Traveler's Aid Society
17 Bus Station
19 Children's Museum
20 MBTA Water Shuttle;
    Bay State Cruise Co
22 Post Office
23 Mobius
24 Fort Point Arts
    Community Gallery
25 A St Diner
26 AC Cruise Line
27 Fleet Boston Pavilion
28 Mass Bay Brewing Co

0   100   200 m
0   100   200 yards

MAP 7 THEATER DISTRICT & CHINATOWN

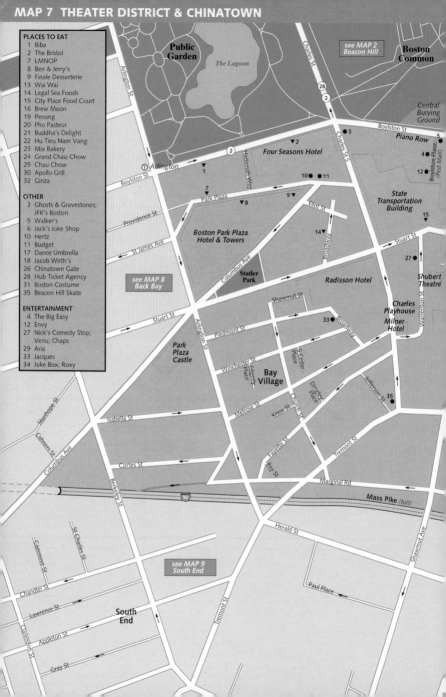

PLACES TO EAT
1 Biba
2 The Bristol
7 LMNOP
8 Ben & Jerry's
9 Finale Desserterie
13 Wai Wai
14 Legal Sea Foods
15 City Place Food Court
16 Brew Moon
19 Penang
20 Pho Pasteur
21 Buddha's Delight
22 Hu Tieu Nam Vang
23 Mix Bakery
24 Grand Chau Chow
25 Chau Chow
30 Apollo Grill
32 Ginza

OTHER
3 Ghosts & Gravestones;
  JFK's Boston
5 Walker's
6 Jack's Joke Shop
10 Hertz
11 Budget
17 Dance Umbrella
18 Jacob Wirth's
26 Chinatown Gate
28 Hub Ticket Agency
31 Boston Costume
35 Beacon Hill Skate

ENTERTAINMENT
4 The Big Easy
12 Envy
27 Nick's Comedy Stop;
  Venu; Chaps
29 Aria
33 Jacques
34 Juke Box; Roxy

Public Garden

The Lagoon

see MAP 2 Beacon Hill

Boston Common

Central Burying Ground

Boylston St

Piano Row

Four Seasons Hotel

Arlington St

Charles St

Charles St S

28
2

State Transportation Building

Boylston St

Arlington St

Providence St

Park Plaza

Hadassah Way

Eliot St

Broadway

St James Ave

Boston Park Plaza Hotel & Towers

Columbus Ave

Statler Park

Radisson Hotel

Stuart St

Shubert Theatre

see MAP 8 Back Bay

Stuart St

Shawmut St

Charles Playhouse
Milner Hotel

Warrenton St

Park Plaza Castle

Arlington St

Piedmont St

Broadway

Winchester St

Bay Village

Melrose St

Knox St

Church St

S Cedar Place

Eckerley Place

Dartmouth Place

Jefferson St

Stanhope St

Cahners Place

Columbus Ave

Isabella St

Cortes St

Fayette St

Bay St

Tremont St

Berkeley St

90

Marginal Rd

Mass Pike (toll)

Shawmut Ave

St Charles St

Cazenove St

Herald St

see MAP 9 South End

Tremont St

Paul Place

Chandler St

Claremont St

Lawrence St

South End

Appleton St

Gray St

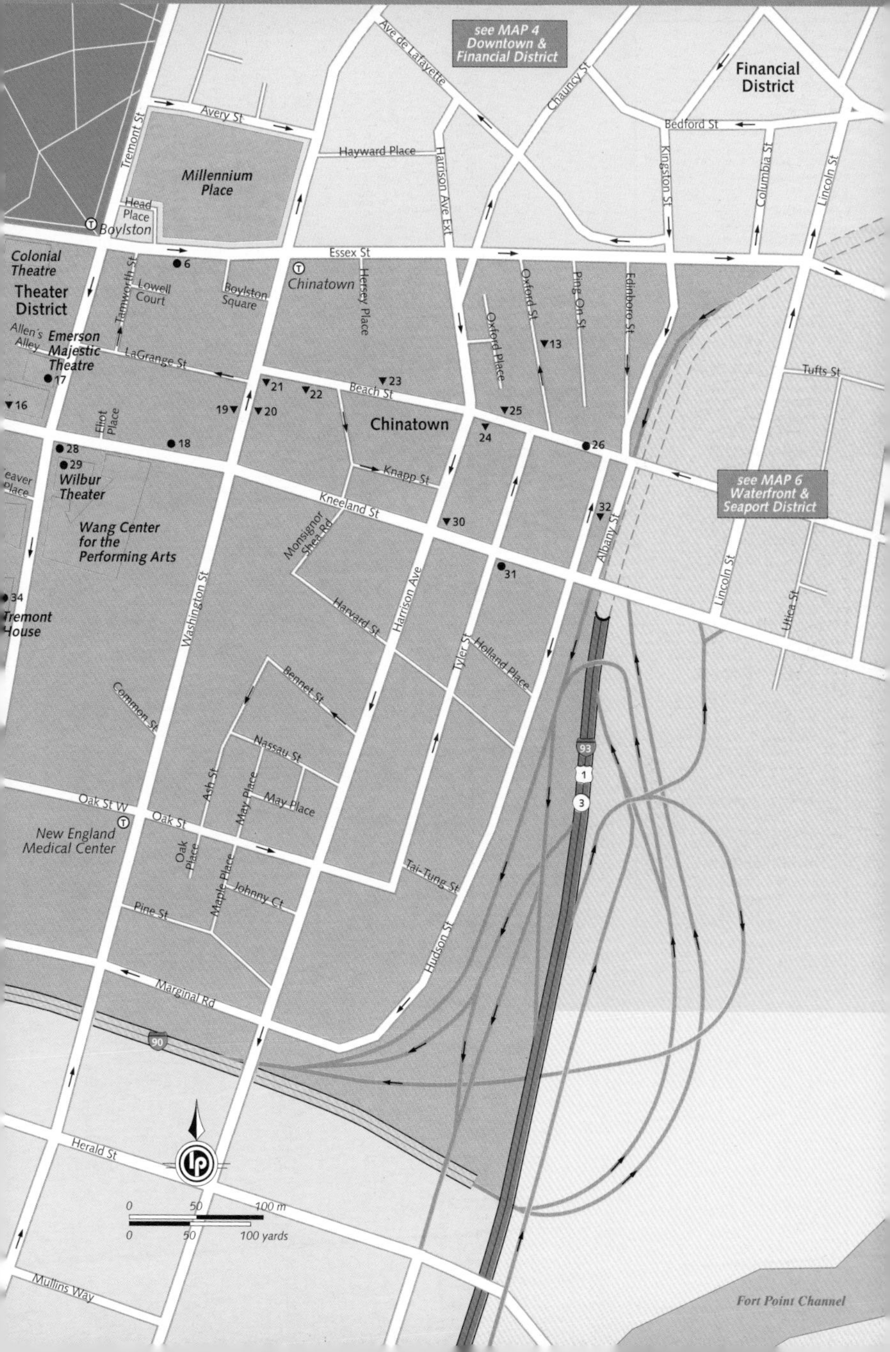

see MAP 4
Downtown &
Financial District

Financial
District

Ave de Lafayette

Chauncy St

Bedford St

Kingston St

Columbia St

Lincoln St

Tremont St

Avery St

Hayward Place

Harrison Ave Ext

Head
Place
Boylston

Essex St

Chinatown

Oxford St

Ping On St

Edinboro St

Colonial
Theatre

Theater
District

Allen's
Alley

Emerson
Majestic
Theatre

●17

▼16

Tamworth St

Lowell
Court

Boylston
Square

LaGrange St

Hersey Place

●6

Oxford Place

Oxford St

▼13

●28
●29

Wilbur
Theater

▼21
▼20

▼19

●18

●22

Beach St

●23

Chinatown

▼25

▼24

●26

Elliot
Place

Knapp St

see MAP 6
Waterfront &
Seaport District

Tufts St

Wang Center
for the
Performing Arts

Kneeland St

Monsignor
Shea Rd

▼30

●31

▲32

Albany St

Lincoln St

Utica St

▼34

Tremont
House

eaver
Place

Washington St

Harvard St

Harrison Ave

Tyler St

Holland Place

Common St

Bennet St

Nassau St

Oak St W

Oak St

New England
Medical Center

Ash St

Oak
Place

May Place

Maple Place

Pine St

Johnny Ct

Tai-Tung St

Hudson St

93
1
3

Marginal Rd

90

Herald St

0   50   100 m
0   50   100 yards

LP

Mullins Way

Fort Point Channel

MAP 8 BACK BAY

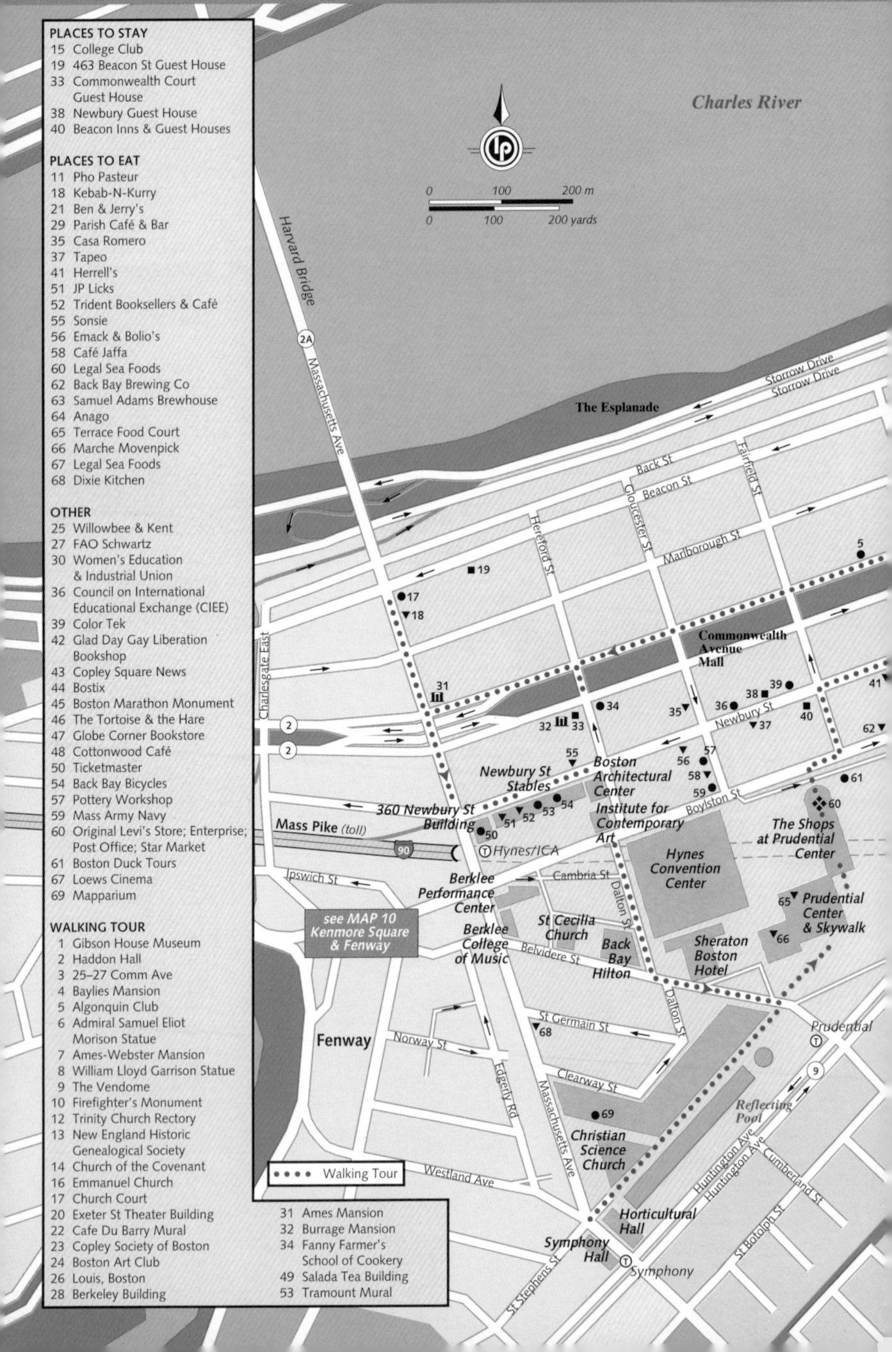

Charles River

0   100   200 m
0   100   200 yards

The Esplanade

Harvard Bridge

Massachusetts Ave

Charlesgate East

Mass Pike (toll)

Storrow Drive
Storrow Drive

Back St
Beacon St
Clarendon St
Dartmouth St
Marlborough St
Hereford St
Gloucester St

Commonwealth
Avenue
Mall

Newbury St

Boylston St

Newbury St
Stables

Boston
Architectural
Center

Institute for
Contemporary
Art

360 Newbury St
Building

Hynes/ICA

Cambria St

Dalton St

Hynes
Convention
Center

The Shops
at Prudential
Center

Prudential
Center &
Skywalk

Berklee
Performance
Center

Berklee
College
of Music

St Cecilia
Church

Belvidere St

Back
Bay
Hilton

Sheraton
Boston
Hotel

Prudential

Ipswich St

see MAP 10
Kenmore Square
& Fenway

Fenway

Norway St

St Germain St

Clearway St

Edgerly Rd

Reflecting
Pool

Westland Ave

Christian
Science
Church

Huntington Ave
Huntington Ave

St Botolph St

•••• Walking Tour

Horticultural
Hall

Symphony
Hall

St Stephens St

Symphony

Hatch
Memorial
Shell

28

The Esplanade

Arthur
Fiedler
Footbridge

Mt Vernon St

Beacon
Hill

Lime St

Charles St

Chestnut St

Branch St

Byron St

Revere St

see MAP 2
Beacon Hill

28 2

Boston
Common

🏛 1

French
Library

28

Clarendon St

First
Lutheran
Church 🏛 3

4
🏛

Start

Public
Garden

28

First &
Second
Church

The
Lagoon

Charles St

Commonwealth
Avenue
Mall

Berkeley St

🏛 15

Ritz-
Carlton
Hotel

16 †

2

Back
Bay

7 🏛

Commonwealth Ave

🏛 8

First
Baptist
Church

2

10

Newbury St

14 †

Arlington
St Church

29 ▼

T
Arlington

East
End

2

Dartmouth St

🏛 6

Commonwealth Ave

9

11 ▼

12 13

26

Boylston St

30

Park Plaza

Boston Park Plaza
Hotel & Towers

New Old
South
Church

22

23 24

The
New England

25

27

28

Providence St

St James Ave

Columbus Ave

Arlington St

Statler
Park

Fairfield St

20

21

Copley
Square

43

47 500
Boylston St

48

Stuart St

Piedmont St

see MAP 7
Theater District
& Chinatown

42

Copley
T

44 45 46

Trinity
Church

Houghton
Mifflin
Building

49

Park
Plaza
Castle

Melrose St

Bay
Village

63

Lenox
Hotel

64 ▼

Boston
Public
Library

Blagden St

John Hancock
Tower &
Observatory

Trinity Pl

Stuart St

Clarendon St

Berkeley St

Isabella St

Fayette St

Copley
Square
Hotel

Fairmont
Copley
Plaza
Hotel

Cortes St

Marginal Rd

Ring Rd

Westin
International
Hotel

Back Bay
T

28

Mass Pike (toll)

Herald St

Marriott
Copley
Place

Copley
Place
▼
67

Dartmouth St

Columbus Ave

Chandler St

Appleton St

Tremont St

E Berkeley St

Dwight St

Garrison St

Yarmouth St

South
End

see MAP 9
South End

Warren Ave

Montgomery St

Milford St

Hanson St

Bond St

Cullen St

Follen St

W Canton St

Holyoke St

28

Braddock Park

Waltham St

Taylor St

Shawmut Ave

Southwest
Corridor
Park

Titus
Sparrow
Park

W Newton St

Columbus
Square

Pembroke St

W Brookline St

W Canton St

Ivanhoe St

Union St

Union
Park

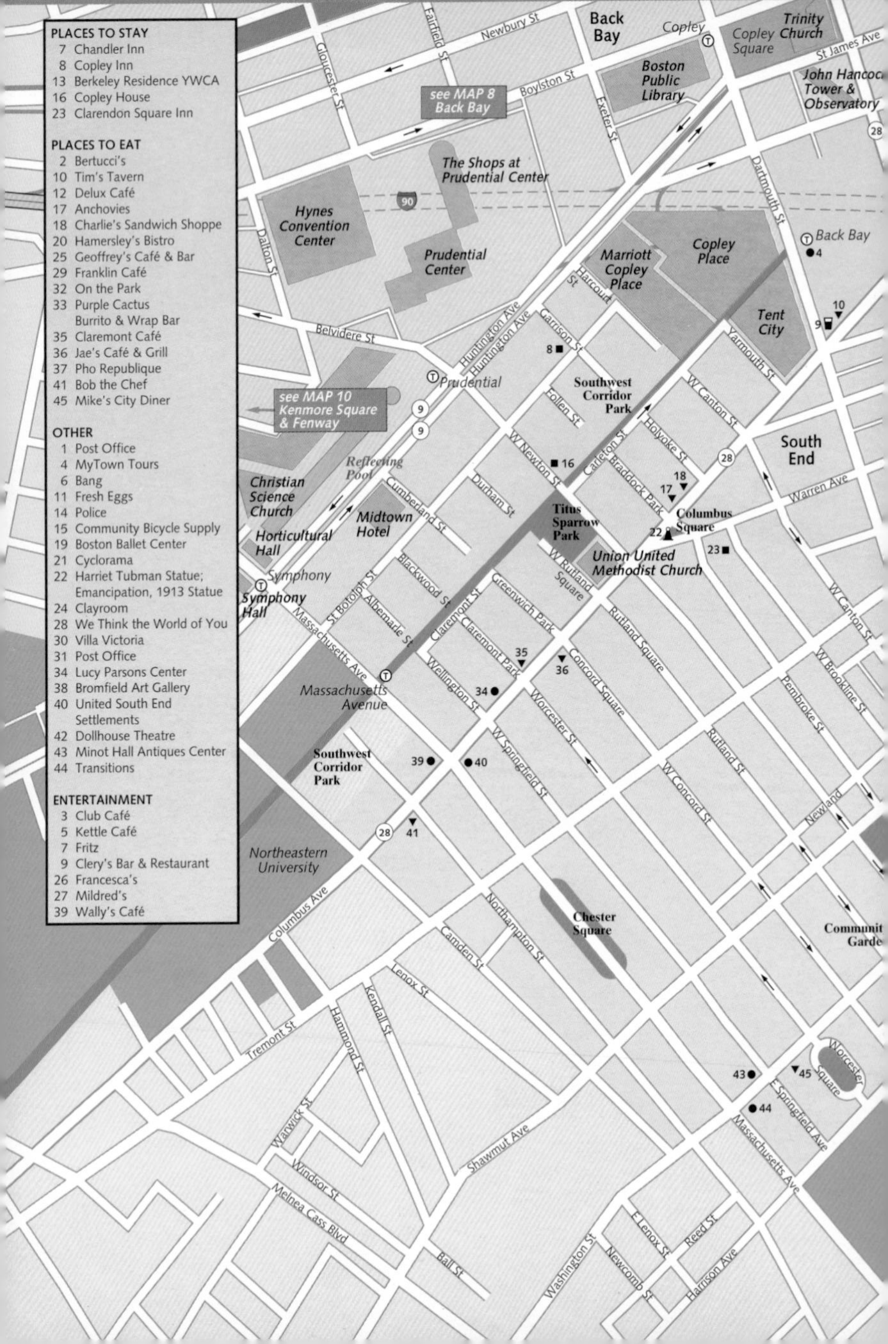

MAP 9 SOUTH END

PLACES TO STAY
7 Chandler Inn
8 Copley Inn
13 Berkeley Residence YWCA
16 Copley House
23 Clarendon Square Inn

PLACES TO EAT
2 Bertucci's
10 Tim's Tavern
12 Delux Café
17 Anchovies
18 Charlie's Sandwich Shoppe
20 Hamersley's Bistro
25 Geoffrey's Café & Bar
29 Franklin Café
32 On the Park
33 Purple Cactus
    Burrito & Wrap Bar
35 Claremont Café
37 Jae's Café & Grill
37 Pho Republique
41 Bob the Chef
45 Mike's City Diner

OTHER
1 Post Office
4 MyTown Tours
6 Bang
11 Fresh Eggs
14 Police
15 Community Bicycle Supply
19 Boston Ballet Center
21 Cyclorama
22 Harriet Tubman Statue;
    Emancipation, 1913 Statue
24 Clayroom
28 We Think the World of You
30 Villa Victoria
31 Post Office
34 Lucy Parsons Center
38 Bromfield Art Gallery
40 United South End
    Settlements
42 Dollhouse Theatre
43 Minot Hall Antiques Center
44 Transitions

ENTERTAINMENT
3 Club Café
5 Kettle Café
7 Fritz
9 Clery's Bar & Restaurant
26 Francesca's
27 Mildred's
39 Wally's Café

Chinatown

see MAP 7
Theater District
& Chinatown

see MAP 6
Waterfront &
Seaport District

Statler
Park

Stuart St

Broadway

Shawmut Ave

Winchester St

Piedmont St

Arlington St

Columbus Ave

Stanhope St

Catherine St

Isabella St

Melrose St

Fayette St

Oak St

Oak St w

Bay
Village

New England
Medical Center

Washington St

Hanson St

Tyler St

Hudson St

Cortes St

93

3

1

St Charles St

Berkeley St

Marginal Rd

Mass Pike   (toll)

90

Cazenove St

Herald St

Chandler St

Paul Place

Lawrence St

Appleton St

Tremont St

Mullins Way

Gray St

Clarendon St

Boston Center
for the Arts

Village
Court

E Berkeley St

Emerald
Court

Waterford
St

Traveler St

Montgomery St

Dwight St

Milford St

Hanson St

William St

Taylor St

Bond St

Shawmut Ave

Union
Park

Upton St

Ivanhoe St

Fay St

Pine
St Inn

Bristol St

Albany St

Fort Point Channel

Broadway

Drapers Lane

Perry St

Thayer St

W Dedham St

Bradford St

W Fourth St

Union Park St

Rollins St

Randolph St

Trehum St

Cathedral
of the
Holy Cross

Blackstone
Square

Washington St

Mystic St

Malden St

Plympton St

Wareham St

Franklin
Square

Harrison Ave

E Dedham St

E Canton St

St George St

Brookline St

Thorn St

Albany St

James St

Newton St

Stoughton St

E Concord St

Boston
Medical
Center

0   100   200 m

0   100   200 yards

93

3

1

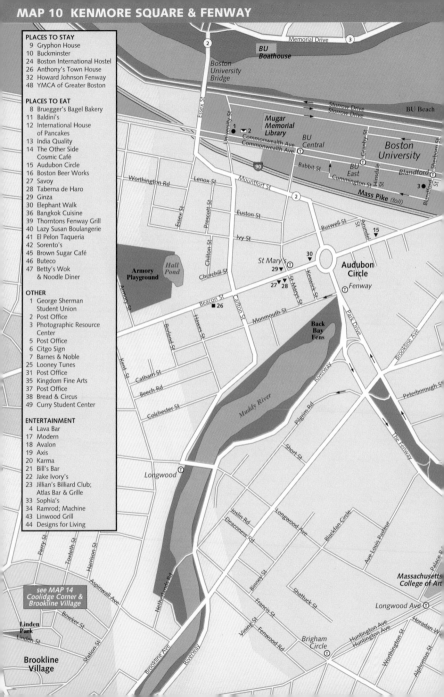

MAP 10 KENMORE SQUARE & FENWAY

see MAP 14
Coolidge Corner &
Brookline Village

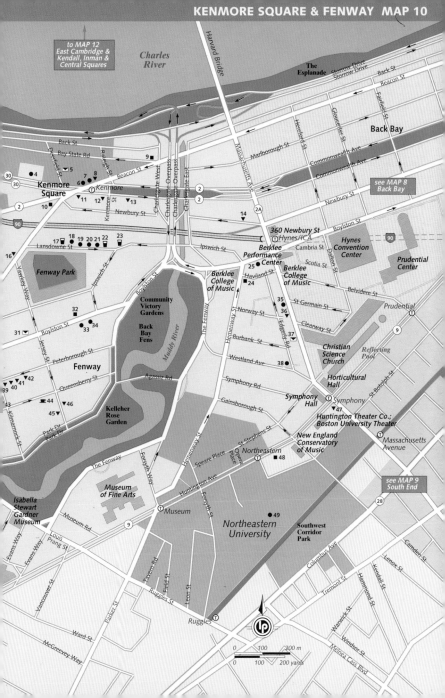

to MAP 12
East Cambridge &
Kendall, Inman &
Central Squares

Charles
River

The
Esplanade

Storrow Drive
Storrow Drive

Back St

Beacon St

Back Bay

Fairfield St

Back St

Bay State Rd

Deerfield St

Raleigh St

9

Marlborough St

Hereford St

Gloucester St

5

Beacon St

Commonwealth Ave

30

30

Kenmore
Square

6

7 8

Kenmore

Charlesgate West

Charlesgate Overpass

Charlesgate East

Massachusetts Ave

Commonwealth Ave

see MAP 8
Back Bay

2

10

11 12 13

Kenmore St

Newbury St

2

2

Newbury St

14

2A

Boylston St

90

90

16

17 18 19 20 21 22 23

Lansdowne St

Ipswich St

360 Newbury St

Hynes/ICA

Berklee
Performance
Center

Cambria St

Dalton St

Hynes
Convention
Center

Prudential
Center

Fenway Park

Ipswich St

Berklee
College
of Music

25

Haviland St

24

Berklee
College
of Music

Scotia St

Belvidere St

Yawkey Way

Boylston St

Community
Victory
Gardens

The Fenway

Muddy River

Norway St

35

36

St Germain St

Edgerly Rd

Clearway St

Prudential

9

32

Back
Bay
Fens

33 34

31

Boylston St

Jersey St

Burbank St

37

Christian
Science
Church

Reflecting
Pool

Peterborough St

WestLand Ave

38

Horticultural
Hall

St Botolph St

Fenway

Queensberry St

Agassiz Rd

Symphony Rd

Symphony
Hall

Symphony

47

39 40 41

42

Gainsborough St

Huntington Theater Co.;
Boston University Theater

43

44

45

46

Kelleher
Rose
Garden

Hemenway St

St Stephens St

New England
Conservatory
of Music

Massachusetts
Avenue

Kilmarnock St

Park Dr

Park Dr

The Fenway

Forsyth Way

Museum
of Fine Arts

Speare Place

Opera Place

Northeastern

48

Isabella
Stewart
Gardner
Museum

Museum Rd

Huntington Ave

Forsyth St

Museum

9

Northeastern
University

49

Southwest
Corridor
Park

Columbus Ave

Camden St

see MAP 9
South End

28

Lenox St

Evans Way

Louis
Prang St

Tavern Rd

Field St

Leon St

Ruggles St

Ruggles

Kendall St

Vancouver St

Parker St

Ward St

McGreevey Way

Windsor St

Warwick St

Tremont St

Hammond St

Melnea Cass Blvd

0   100   200 m

0   100   200 yards

MAP 11 HARVARD SQUARE AREA

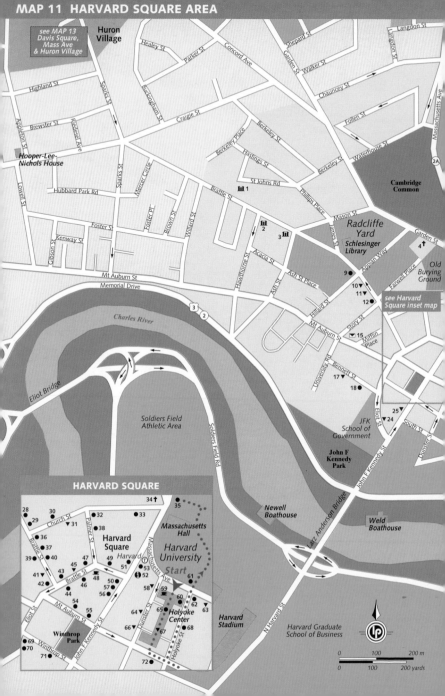

see MAP 13
Davis Square,
Mass Ave
& Huron Village

Huron
Village

Highland St

Appleton St

Brewster St

Lowell St

Hooper-Lee-
Nichols House

Healey St

Parker St

Concord Ave

Shepard St

Garden St

Walker St

Chauncey St

Langdon St

Langdon St

Massachusetts Ave

Sparks St

Reservoir Ave

Sparks St

Buckingham St

Craigie St

Berkeley Place

Berkeley St

Follen St

Waterhouse St

Hubbard Park Rd

Mercer Circle

Foster Pl

Brattle St

Hastings St

St Johns Rd

Phillips Place

Berkeley St

Mason St

2A

Cambridge
Common

Foster St

Brown St

Willard St

lil 1

lil 2

3 lil

James St

Radcliffe
Yard

Schlesinger
Library

Garden St

4 †

Old
Burying
Ground

Kenway St

Gibson St

Mt Auburn St

Memorial Drive

Hawthorne St

Acacia St

Ash St

Ash St place

Hilliard St

Appian Way

9 ●

10 ▼
11 ▼
12 ●

Farwell Place

see Harvard
Square inset map

Charles River

3

2

Story St

Mt Auburn St

Bennett St

15

Mifflin
Place

University Rd

17 ▼

18 ●

25 ▼
24

Eliot St

South St

Dunster St

Eliot Bridge

Soldiers Field
Athletic Area

Soldiers Field Rd

JFK
School of
Government

John F
Kennedy
Park

John F Kennedy St

Newell
Boathouse

Larz Anderson Bridge

Weld
Boathouse

HARVARD SQUARE

28
29

30

Church St

▼ 31

32

33

34 †
35

36

39 ●

37
40

41 ▼

42

Brattle St

43

45

47

48

50

46

44

54

55

Palmer St

38

Harvard
Square

49

Massachusetts Ave

Harvard

51

53

52

Mt Auburn St

Eliot St

John F Kennedy St

57
56

58

64 ▼

66 ▼

Dunster St

Massachusetts Hall

Harvard
University

Start

61

59

60

65

67

62
63

68

Holyoke Center

Holyoke St

72

Harvard
Stadium

N Harvard St

Winthrop
Park

69
70

71

Harvard Graduate
School of Business

0   100   200 m
0   100   200 yards

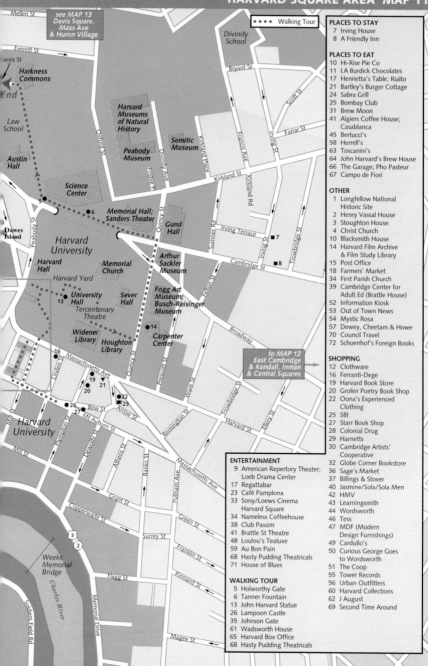

see MAP 13
Davis Square,
Mass Ave
& Huron Village

•••• Walking Tour

to MAP 12
East Cambridge
& Kendall, Inman
& Central Squares

PLACES TO STAY
7 Irving House
8 A Friendly Inn

PLACES TO EAT
10 Hi-Rise Pie Co
11 LA Burdick Chocolates
17 Henrietta's Table; Rialto
21 Bartley's Burger Cottage
24 Sabra Grill
25 Bombay Club
31 Brew Moon
41 Algiers Coffee House;
   Casablanca
45 Bertucci's
58 Herrell's
63 Toscanini's
64 John Harvard's Brew House
66 The Garage; Pho Pasteur
67 Campo de Fiori

OTHER
1 Longfellow National
   Historic Site
2 Henry Vassal House
3 Stoughton House
4 Christ Church
10 Blacksmith House
14 Harvard Film Archive
   & Film Study Library
15 Post Office
18 Farmers' Market
34 First Parish Church
39 Cambridge Center for
   Adult Ed (Brattle House)
52 Information Kiosk
53 Out of Town News
54 Mystic Rosa
55 Dewey, Cheetam & Howe
70 Council Travel
72 Schoenhof's Foreign Books

SHOPPING
12 Clothware
16 Ferranti-Dege
19 Harvard Book Store
20 Grolier Poetry Book Shop
22 Oona's Experienced
   Clothing
25 SBI
27 Starr Book Shop
28 Colonial Drug
29 Harnetts
30 Cambridge Artists'
   Cooperative
32 Globe Corner Bookstore
36 Sage's Market
37 Billings & Stover
40 Jasmine/Sola/Sola Men
42 HMV
43 Learningsmith
44 Wordsworth
46 Tess
47 MDF (Modern
   Design Furnishings)
49 Cardullo's
50 Curious George Goes
   to Wordsworth
51 The Coop
55 Tower Records
56 Urban Outfitters
60 Harvard Collections
62 J August
69 Second Time Around

ENTERTAINMENT
9 American Repertory Theater;
   Loeb Drama Center
17 Regattabar
23 Café Pamplona
33 Sony/Loews Cinema
   Harvard Square
34 Nameless Coffeehouse
35 Club Passim
41 Brattle St Theatre
48 Loulou's Tealuxe
59 Au Bon Pain
68 Hasty Pudding Theatricals
71 House of Blues

WALKING TOUR
5 Holworthy Gate
6 Tanner Fountain
13 John Harvard Statue
26 Lampoon Castle
35 Johnson Gate
61 Wadsworth House
65 Harvard Box Office
68 Hasty Pudding Theatricals

MAP 12 EAST CAMBRIDGE & KENDALL, INMAN & CENTRAL SQUARES

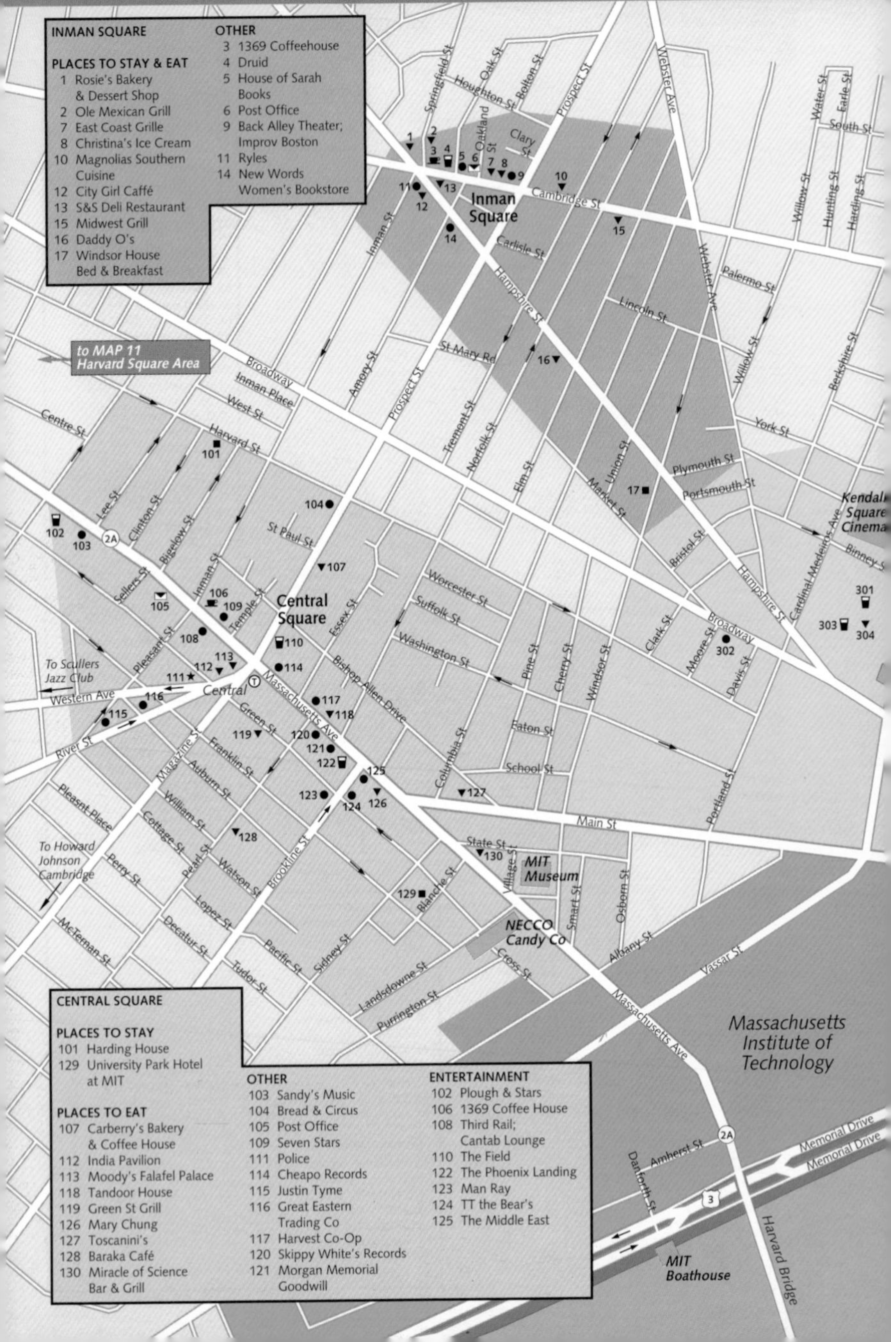

INMAN SQUARE
PLACES TO STAY & EAT
1 Rosie's Bakery & Dessert Shop
2 Ole Mexican Grill
7 East Coast Grille
8 Christina's Ice Cream
10 Magnolias Southern Cuisine
12 City Girl Caffé
13 S&S Deli Restaurant
15 Midwest Grill
16 Daddy O's
17 Windsor House Bed & Breakfast
OTHER
3 1369 Coffeehouse
4 Druid
5 House of Sarah Books
6 Post Office
9 Back Alley Theater; Improv Boston
11 Ryles
14 New Words Women's Bookstore
CENTRAL SQUARE
PLACES TO STAY
101 Harding House
129 University Park Hotel at MIT
PLACES TO EAT
107 Carberry's Bakery & Coffee House
112 India Pavilion
113 Moody's Falafel Palace
118 Tandoor House
119 Green St Grill
126 Mary Chung
127 Toscanini's
128 Baraka Café
130 Miracle of Science Bar & Grill
OTHER
103 Sandy's Music
104 Bread & Circus
105 Post Office
109 Seven Stars
111 Police
114 Cheapo Records
115 Justin Tyme
116 Great Eastern Trading Co
117 Harvest Co-Op
120 Skippy White's Records
121 Morgan Memorial Goodwill
ENTERTAINMENT
102 Plough & Stars
106 1369 Coffee House
108 Third Rail; Cantab Lounge
110 The Field
122 The Phoenix Landing
123 Man Ray
124 TT the Bear's
125 The Middle East
to MAP 11 Harvard Square Area
Inman Square
Central Square
Central
Kendall Square Cinema
MIT Museum
NECCO Candy Co
Massachusetts Institute of Technology
MIT Boathouse
To Scullers Jazz Club
To Howard Johnson Cambridge
Harvard Bridge
Memorial Drive
Massachusetts Ave
Cambridge St
Hampshire St
Broadway
Prospect St
Webster Ave
Main St
Western Ave
River St
Harvard St
Inman St
Bishop Allen Drive

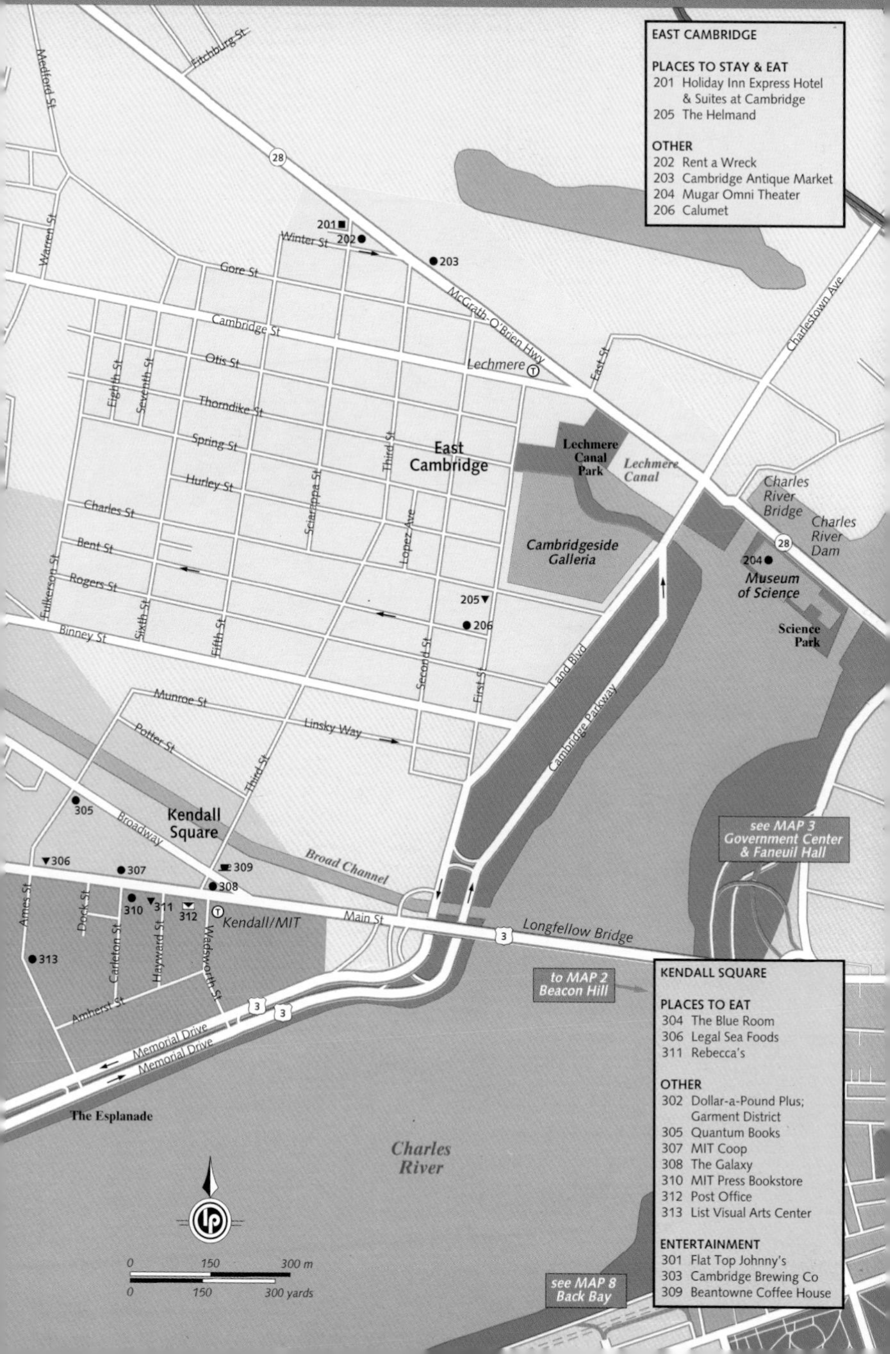

Medford St
Fitchburg St
Warren St
Winter St
201
202
203
Gore St
Cambridge St
McGrath-O'Brien Hwy
Eighth St
Seventh St
Sixth St
Otis St
Thorndike St
Spring St
Hurley St
Charles St
Bent St
Rogers St
Binney St
Fulkerson St
Fifth St
Scamman St
Third St
Lopez Ave
Second St
First St
Lechmere
Lechmere Canal Park
Lechmere Canal
East Cambridge
Cambridgeside Galleria
Charles River Bridge
Charles River Dam
28
204
Museum of Science
Science Park
Charlestown Ave
Erie St
205
206
Land Blvd
Cambridge Parkway
Munroe St
Potter St
Linsky Way
Third St
see MAP 3
Government Center
& Faneuil Hall
305
Broadway
Kendall Square
Broad Channel
306
307
309
308
310
311
312
Kendall/MIT
313
Ames St
Dock St
Hayward St
Carleton St
Wadsworth St
Amherst St
Main St
Longfellow Bridge
3
to MAP 2
Beacon Hill
Memorial Drive
Memorial Drive
The Esplanade
Charles River
see MAP 8
Back Bay

0   150   300 m
0   150   300 yards

MAP 13 DAVIS SQUARE, MASS AVE & HURON VILLAGE

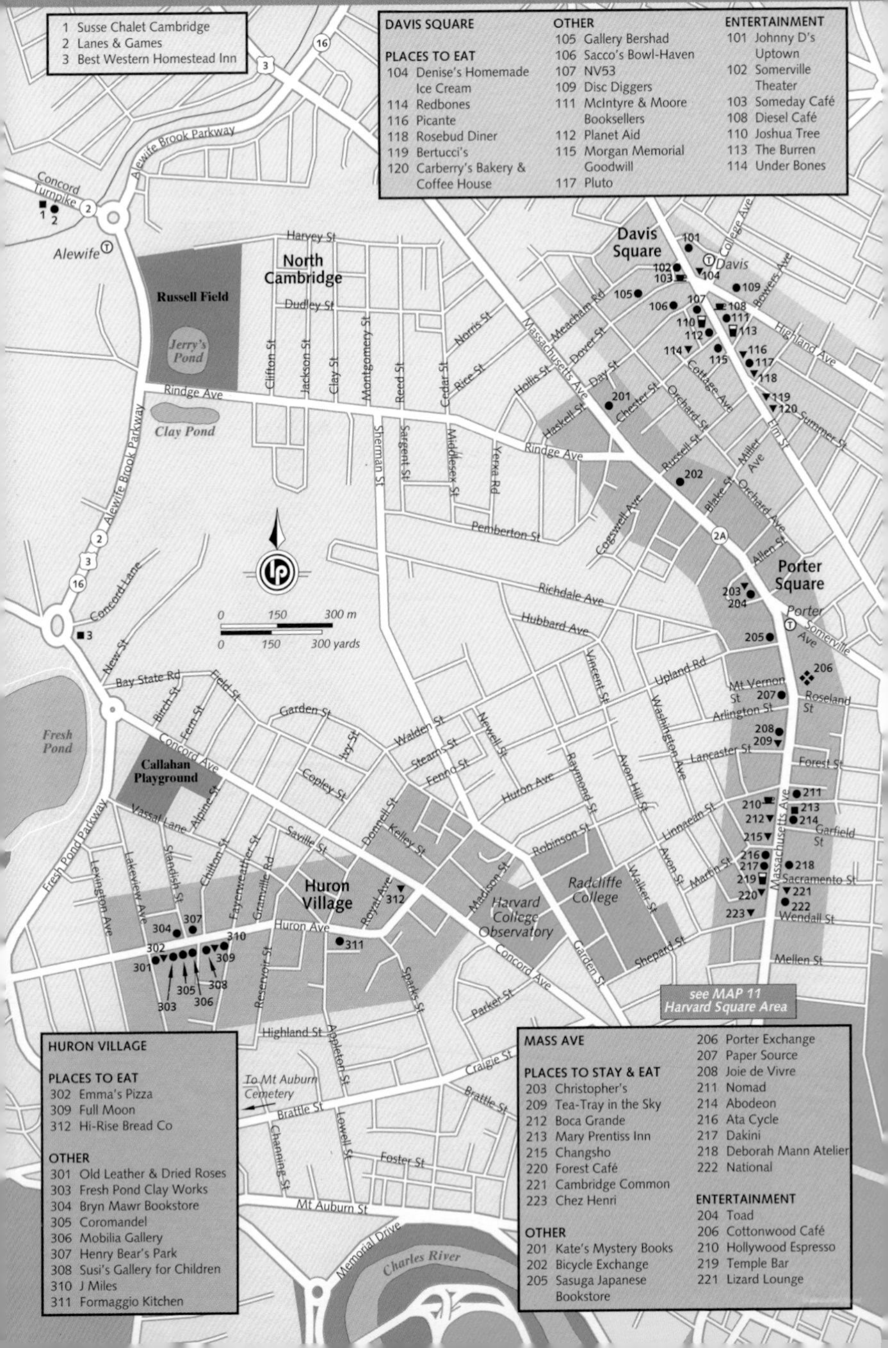

1 Susse Chalet Cambridge
2 Lanes & Games
3 Best Western Homestead Inn

DAVIS SQUARE

PLACES TO EAT
104 Denise's Homemade
    Ice Cream
114 Redbones
116 Picante
118 Rosebud Diner
119 Bertucci's
120 Carberry's Bakery &
    Coffee House

OTHER
105 Gallery Bershad
106 Sacco's Bowl-Haven
107 NV53
109 Disc Diggers
111 McIntyre & Moore
    Booksellers
112 Planet Aid
115 Morgan Memorial
    Goodwill
117 Pluto

ENTERTAINMENT
101 Johnny D's
    Uptown
102 Somerville
    Theater
103 Someday Café
108 Diesel Café
110 Joshua Tree
113 The Burren
114 Under Bones

Map labels

Concord Turnpike
Alewife
North Cambridge
Russell Field
Jerry's Pond
Clay Pond
Fresh Pond
Callahan Playground
Huron Village
Radcliffe College
Harvard College Observatory
Davis Square
Porter Square
Roseland
Mt Vernon
Charles River

Harvey St
Dudley St
Rindge Ave
Richdale Ave
Hubbard Ave
Pemberton St
Bay State Rd
Garden St
Copley St
Highland St
Craigie St
Brattle St
Foster St
Mt Auburn St
Memorial Drive

see MAP 11
Harvard Square Area

Scale

0   150   300 m
0   150   300 yards

HURON VILLAGE

PLACES TO EAT
302 Emma's Pizza
309 Full Moon
312 Hi-Rise Bread Co

OTHER
301 Old Leather & Dried Roses
303 Fresh Pond Clay Works
304 Bryn Mawr Bookstore
305 Coromandel
306 Mobilia Gallery
307 Henry Bear's Park
308 Susi's Gallery for Children
310 J Miles
311 Formaggio Kitchen

To Mt Auburn
Cemetery

MASS AVE

PLACES TO STAY & EAT
203 Christopher's
209 Tea-Tray in the Sky
212 Boca Grande
214 Mary Prentiss Inn
215 Changsho
220 Forest Café
221 Cambridge Common
223 Chez Henri

OTHER
201 Kate's Mystery Books
202 Bicycle Exchange
205 Sasuga Japanese
    Bookstore
206 Porter Exchange
207 Paper Source
208 Joie de Vivre
211 Nomad
214 Abodeon
216 Ata Cycle
217 Dakini
218 Deborah Mann Atelier
222 National

ENTERTAINMENT
204 Toad
206 Cottonwood Café
210 Hollywood Espresso
219 Temple Bar
221 Lizard Lounge

MAP 14 COOLIDGE CORNER & BROOKLINE VILLAGE

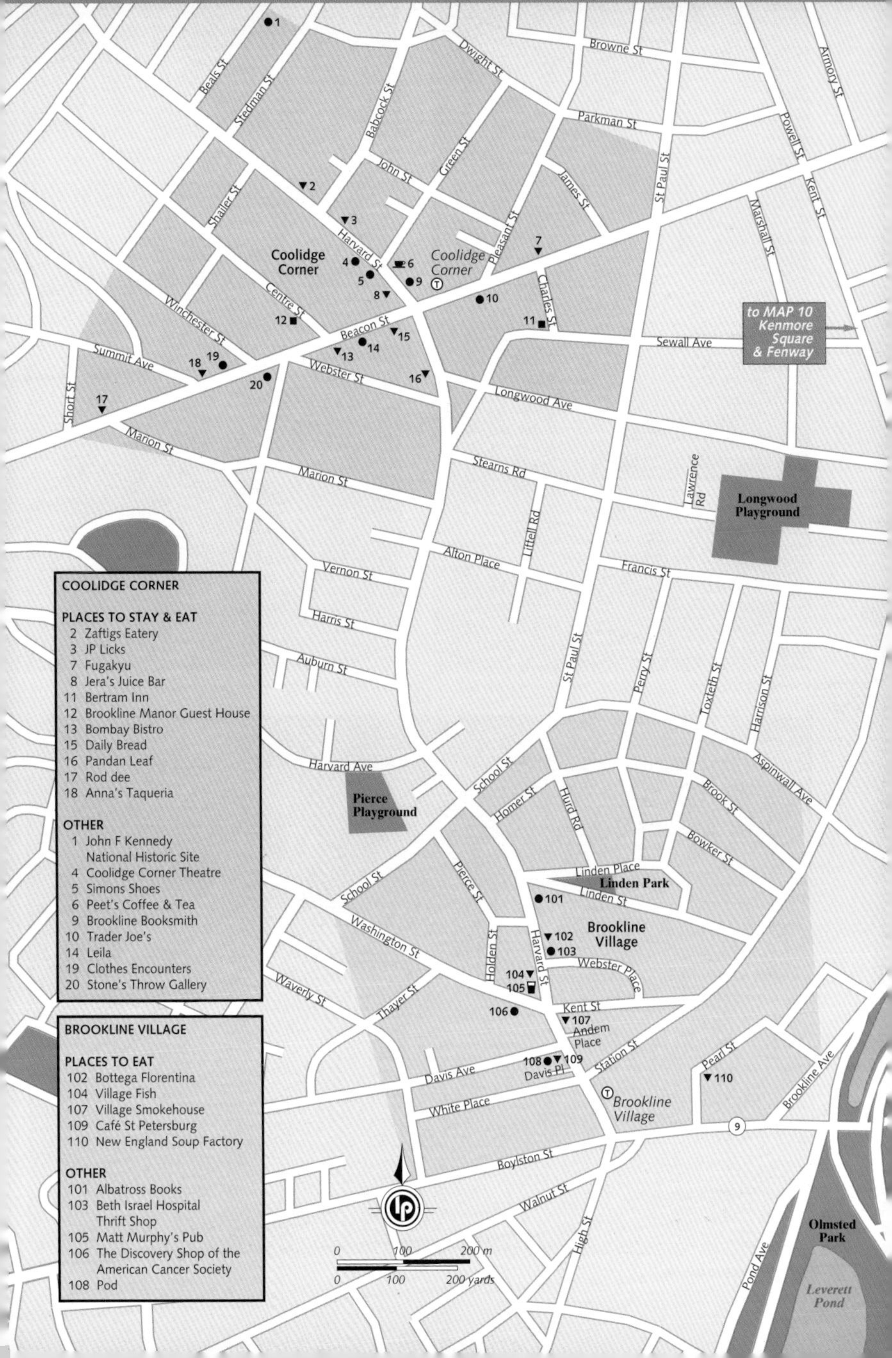

Coolidge Corner

Coolidge Corner

to MAP 10
Kenmore
Square
& Fenway

Longwood
Playground

Pierce
Playground

Linden Park

**Brookline
Village**

Brookline
Village

Olmsted
Park

Leverett
Pond

COOLIDGE CORNER

PLACES TO STAY & EAT
- 2 Zaftigs Eatery
- 3 JP Licks
- 7 Fugakyu
- 8 Jera's Juice Bar
- 11 Bertram Inn
- 12 Brookline Manor Guest House
- 13 Bombay Bistro
- 15 Daily Bread
- 16 Pandan Leaf
- 17 Rod dee
- 18 Anna's Taqueria

OTHER
- 1 John F Kennedy
  National Historic Site
- 4 Coolidge Corner Theatre
- 5 Simons Shoes
- 6 Peet's Coffee & Tea
- 9 Brookline Booksmith
- 10 Trader Joe's
- 14 Leila
- 19 Clothes Encounters
- 20 Stone's Throw Gallery

BROOKLINE VILLAGE

PLACES TO EAT
- 102 Bottega Florentina
- 104 Village Fish
- 107 Village Smokehouse
- 109 Café St Petersburg
- 110 New England Soup Factory

OTHER
- 101 Albatross Books
- 103 Beth Israel Hospital
  Thrift Shop
- 105 Matt Murphy's Pub
- 106 The Discovery Shop of the
  American Cancer Society
- 108 Pod

0   100   200 m
0   100   200 yards

KIM GRANT

Wisteria arbor in the North End's Columbus Park

KIM GRANT

Just one of Back Bay's (formerly) secret gardens

KIM GRANT

Pedal-powered Swan Boats in the Public Garden

MAP 15 MBTA SUBWAY MAP

Massachusetts Bay Transportation Authority Subway Map

To Lowell

Oak Grove

West Medford

Malden Center

Wellington

Sullivan Square

To Reading, Haverhill

To Newburyport, Rockport

Wonderland

Revere Beach

Beachmont

Suffolk Downs

Orient Heights

Wood Island

Davis

Alewife

Porter

Harvard

Central

Kendall/MIT

Lechmere

Science Park

North Station

Community College

Airport

Maverick

Haymarket

Bowdoin

Gov't Center

Aquarium

Charles/MGH

Park St

State/Citizens Bank**

To Fitchburg

Waltham

Belmont Center

Brandeis/Roberts

Waverley

To Fitchburg

Boston College

Cleveland Circle

Riverside

Woodland

Waban

Eliot

Newton Highlands

Newton Centre

Chestnut Hill

Reservoir

Beaconsfield

Brookline Hills

Brookline Village

Longwood

Fenway

Kenmore

Hynes/ICA

Copley

Arlington

Boylston

Downtown Crossing

South Station

Chinatown

NE Medical Ctr

Prudential

Symphony

Northeastern

Brigham Circle

Back Bay

Mass Ave

Ruggles

Roxbury Crossing

Jackson Square

Stony Brook

Green St

Forest Hills

Heath

Broadway

Andrew

JFK/UMass

Savin Hill

Fields Corner

Shawmut

Ashmont

Cedar Grove

Butler

Milton

Central Ave

Valley Rd

Capen St

Mattapan

North Quincy

Wollaston

Quincy Center

Quincy Adams

Uphams Corner

Needham Heights

Needham Center

Needham Junction

West Roxbury

Highland

Bellevue

Roslindale Village

Hyde Park

Fairmount

Readville

Morton St.

To Franklin

Dedham Corp. Center

Islington

Norwood Depot

Endicott

Readville

Route 128

Dedham

To Attleboro, Stoughton, Providence

To Middleborough/Lakeville

Braintree

To Plymouth

To Greenbush

Massachusetts Turnpike

Harvard Ave

Massachusetts Turnpike

LEGEND

Transit lines & stop

Commuter rail & station

Terminal station

Free interchange with other lines

Wheelchair access

Wheelchair access to Red Line only

Parking

* Wheelchair access Oak Grove side only. Southbound riders exit train at NE Medical Center transfer to Oak Grove train. Exit Chinatown on Oak Grove side.

** Blue Line wheelchair access outbound only. Inbound riders transfer to outbound train at Government Center. Exit at State outbound.

KIM GRANT

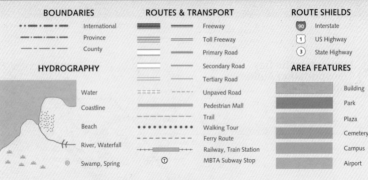

MAP LEGEND

BOUNDARIES

International
Province
County

HYDROGRAPHY

Water
Coastline
Beach
River, Waterfall
Swamp, Spring

ROUTES & TRANSPORT

Freeway
Toll Freeway
Primary Road
Secondary Road
Tertiary Road
Unpaved Road
Pedestrian Mall
Trail
Walking Tour
Ferry Route
Railway, Train Station
MBTA Subway Stop

ROUTE SHIELDS

90 Interstate
1 US Highway
3 State Highway

AREA FEATURES

Building
Park
Plaza
Cemetery
Campus
Airport

NATIONAL CAPITAL
State, Provincial Capital
LARGE CITY
Medium City
Small City
Town, Village
Point of Interest

Place to Stay
Campground
RV Park

Place to Eat
Bar (Place to Drink)
Cafe

MAP SYMBOLS

Airfield
Airport
Archaeological Site, Ruins
Bank
Baseball Diamond
Beach
Border Crossing
Bus Depot, Bus Stop
Cathedral
Cave
Church
Embassy
Ferry
Footbridge
Fish Hatchery
Garden
Gas Station
Hospital, Clinic
Information
Lighthouse
Lookout

Monument
Mosque
Mountain
Museum
Observatory
One-Way Street
Park
Parking
Pass
Picnic Area
Police Station
Pool
Post Office
Shopping Mall
Skiing (Alpine)
Skiing (Nordic)
Stately Home
Synagogue
Trailhead
Winery
Zoo

Note: Not all symbols displayed above appear in this book.

LONELY PLANET OFFICES

Australia
PO Box 617, Hawthorn 3122, Victoria
☎ 03 9819 1877 fax 03 9819 6459
email talk2us@lonelyplanet.com.au

USA
150 Linden Street, Oakland, California 94607
☎ 510 893 8555, TOLL FREE 800 275 8555
fax 510 893 8572
email info@lonelyplanet.com

UK
10A Spring Place, London NW5 3BH
☎ 020 7428 4800 fax020 7428 4828
email go@lonelyplanet.co.uk

France
1 rue du Dahomey, 75011 Paris
☎ 01 55 25 33 00 fax 01 55 25 33 01
www.lonelyplanet.fr

World Wide Web: www.lonelyplanet.com *or* AOL keyword: lp
Lonely Planet Images: lpi@lonelyplanet.com.au